MW00783207

The Fabric of Affect in the
Psychoanalytic Discourse

The Fabric of Affect in the Psychoanalytic Discourse is a seminal work on one of the most neglected topics in psychoanalysis, that of affect.

Originally published in French as *Le Discours vivant*, and considered a classic in the psychoanalytic world, the book is structured into three parts:

- Affect within psychoanalytic literature
- Clinical practice of psychoanalysis: structure and process
- Theoretical study: affect, language and discourse; negative hallucination.

Written in a clear, lucid style, connecting theory to both culture and clinical practice, *The Fabric of Affect in the Psychoanalytic Discourse* will appeal to psychoanalysts and psychotherapists, and also to those involved in cultural studies.

André Green is a psychoanalyst in private practice in Paris.

THE NEW LIBRARY OF PSYCHOANALYSIS

The New Library of Psychoanalysis was launched in 1987 in association with the Institute of Psycho-Analysis, London. Its purpose is to facilitate a greater and more widespread appreciation of what psychoanalysis is really about and to provide a forum for increasing mutual understanding between psychoanalysts and those working in other disciplines such as history, linguistics, literature, medicine, philosophy, psychology and the social sciences. It is intended that the titles selected for publication in the series should deepen and develop psychoanalytic thinking and technique, contribute to psychoanalysis from outside, or contribute to other disciplines from a psychoanalytical perspective.

The Institute, together with the British Psycho-Analytical Society, runs a low-fee psychoanalytic clinic, organizes lectures and scientific events concerned with psychoanalysis, publishes the *International Journal of Psycho-Analysis* (which now incorporates the *International Review of Psycho-Analysis*), and runs the only training course in the UK in psychoanalysis leading to membership of the International Psychoanalytical Association – the body which preserves internationally agreed standards of training, of professional entry, and of professional ethics and practice for psychoanalysis as initiated and developed by Sigmund Freud. Distinguished members of the Institute have included Michael Balint, Wilfred Bion, Ronald Fairbairn, Anna Freud, Ernest Jones, Melanie Klein, John Rickman and Donald Winnicott.

Volumes 1–11 in the series have been prepared under the general editorship of David Tuckett, with Ronald Britton and Eglé Laufer as associate editors. Subsequent volumes are under the general editorship of Elizabeth Bott Spillius, with, from Volume 17, Donald Campbell, Michael Parsons, Rosine Jozef Perelberg and David Taylor as associate editors.

ALSO IN THIS SERIES

NEW LIBRARY OF PSYCHOANALYSIS
37

General Editor: Elizabeth Bott Spillius

The Fabric of Affect in the Psychoanalytic Discourse

ANDRÉ GREEN

Translated by Alan Sheridan

First published as *Le Discours vivant*,
Presses Universitaires de France, 1973

London and New York

First published as *Le Discours vivant* in 1973
by Presses Universitaires de France, Paris

First published in English in 1999
by Routledge
11 New Fetter Lane, London EC4P 4EE

Simultaneously published in USA and Canada
by Routledge
29 West 35th Street, New York, NY 10001

Routledge is an imprint of the Taylor & Francis Group

Typeset in Bembo by M Rules
Printed and bound in Great Britain by
Hartnolls Ltd, Bodmin, Cornwall

British Library Cataloguing in Publication Data
A catalogue record for this book is available from the British Library

Library of Congress Cataloging in Publication Data
Green, André
[Discours vivant. English]
The living discourse : the psychoanalytic conception of affect / André Green.
p. cm. – (New library of psychoanalysis ; 38)
Includes bibliographical references and index.
ISBN 0-415-11525-6 (hbk). – ISBN 0-415-11524–8 (pbk.)
1. Affect (Psychology) 2. Psychoanalysis. I. Title. II. Series
BF175.G7313 1999
152.4–dc21
99–11522
CIP

ISBN 0-415-11525–6 (hbk)
ISBN 0-415-11524–8 (pbk)

If music be the food of love, play on,
Give me excess of it: that surfeiting,
The appetite may sicken, and so die . . .
That strain again! It had a dying fall:
O, it came o'er my ear like the sweet sound
That breathes upon a bank of violets;
Stealing and giving odour . . . Enough! No more!
'Tis not so sweet now as it was before.
O spirit of love, how quick and fresh art thou,
That, notwithstanding thy capacity
Receiveth as the sea, nought enters there,
Of what validity and pitch soe'er,
But falls into abatement and low price,
Even in a minute . . . so full of shapes is fancy
That it alone is high fantastical
        (Shakespeare, *Twelfth Night or What you Will*: I: i, 1–15)

Contents

Preface to the English-language edition

Whenever I am led to express an opinion on the question of affect, I am reminded of the epigraph, which the reader will read below, in which Freud defends the notion that, where certain problems are concerned, it is not so much their obscurity or our ignorance of them that impedes our theorization of them as the difficulty we find in defining the right abstract ideas. Obvious as it may seem, I am not sure that this has always been taken seriously by those who wish to contribute to the theory of affect in psychoanalysis.

In my opinion, this difficulty, which I pointed out in the first version of this work, is still valid today. It is true that Freud's thought varied somewhat on the subject throughout his long work, but between my report to the 1970 Congrés des Psychoanalystes de Langues romanes and the publication of this English edition, the gap between the various views has tended to widen, rather than narrow. By noting, in detail, the different ways of approaching this problem the reader will come to see how far we still are from a united point of view.

The work of various artists and philosophers, as well as our experience in everyday life, suggests that it is very difficult to retain the originality of the affect when it is expressed in language. It is hardly surprising therefore that, when we try to conceptualize it, it is often ideas that do not seem particularly relevant that help us to see the problem more clearly. And if, to remain within the domain of theories (whether or not they are psychoanalytic in origin), we must also take into account the unquestionable part played in them by the body, the whole question becomes more obscure and the margin of interpretation more arbitrary. From ancient times there have been different views as to the primary or secondary nature of this incursion of the body into the psyche and they become clearer here than in any other aspect of psychical life.

Although psychoanalysis has revived the question, there is little unanimity among psychoanalysts: psychoanalysis has simply added other questions to those to be found in philosophy. Since, in France, this question had become once more a subject of controversy, it seemed justified to me to look at the problem in detail.

Since the publication of *Le Discours vivant* in 1973, I have had the opportunity of returning to the question more than once. On the occasion of the 1977 International Congress of Psychoanalysis in Jerusalem, when it was decided that the main theme of the Congress would be the affect, I was asked to write a paper that would prepare the participants for the ensuing discussions. At the end of this paper I developed certain hypotheses that I had put forward earlier.[1] It is possible that the way of approaching the question at that time was felt to be too bound up with the context of French psychoanalysis – since the affair had become an area of dispute between those analysts who owed allegiance to Lacan and the others. Nevertheless, I believe that the propositions that I put forward at that time are still relevant to any discussion of the subject, quite independently of the local context.

My English-language readers might find a few remarks useful. Despite the use of common terms that present no particular semantic ambiguity, it seems to me that the background to the original term *affekt* has different implications in French and English. In France, our analytic circles adopted the equivalent without difficulty, since the noun *affect*, the adjective *affectif* and the verb *affecter* had long been part of everyday vocabulary, even if the meanings given them in our profession were sometimes different – and even when we have given the impression that another term in the language might better render the nuances given it in psychoanalysis. However, it has not been easy to find a substitute. In England, the use of the term 'emotional' seems to have been preferred to 'affective', which often has more neutral resonances. Furthermore, the area covered by this word is less limited than in French usage. When Winnicott writes about emotional development, he certainly seems to refer to the whole of psychical development – apart from the intellectual functions. It should be noted that this extraterritoriality granted the intellect is not without its dangers today in so far as it lends itself to a particular confusion, namely, that psychoanalysis should confine itself to the affect, while the cognitive sciences should define their domain as that of the intellect, which is itself supposed to cover the whole of the psyche – except for the affects.

According to Charles Rycroft, the affect is associated with an idea, whereas emotions are valid independent experiences – a view that I have not found elsewhere. In my opinion, it is hardly justified to simplify the question as do Burness Moore and Fine in their glossary, claiming that the term 'unconscious

1 'Conception of affect'. The article first appeared in 1977 in the *International Journal of Psychoanalysis* and was included in my book *On Private Madness*, London: Hogarth Press, 1986.

affect' is 'an abbreviated reference to a psychic state in which repressed (*uncon-scious*) ideas connected with forbidden wishes threaten to erupt into *consciousness.*' This is an excellent example of the divergences to be found among psychoanalysts concerning 'the right abstract ideas' and one can hardly underestimate their influence. The consequences of these options have all too often been neglected, even concealed. If one claims to be adopting a 'classical' position concerning theory, the least one might expect is a rigorous analysis of the notion. This was an undertaking largely justified by the recognized impor-tance of the affect in clinical psychoanalysis, which nevertheless tolerated the confusion reigning in theory. And if one adopts, as many have, a 'modern' position, in which the old formulations are regarded as superseded, one might expect the innovators to explain how the new ideas are supposed to respond to the questions raised by Freudian theory or explain why these questions should be regarded as irrelevant. This work has not been done either.

If, in certain respects, we may congratulate ourselves that psychoanalytic research has not become bogged down in purely theoretical controversies and has acknowledged the primacy of clinical practice, it is nevertheless regrettable that the 'innovators' have not taken the trouble to situate their contributions in relation to the fundamental debates raised by the examina-tion of the question. Their silence can only be interpreted as an inability to provide a solution. By way of a single example, I might mention the diver-gences concerning the unconscious affect.

Rather than proceed to an account of the literature since my last contri-bution of 1977, which would have required the writing of a new book, I have preferred to adopt a limited solution. In the postscript, the reader will find two items. The first is a contribution to a discussion on the status of representation, in which I defended the idea that the affect might be regarded as a particular kind of representation, rather than as something quite different, as it has traditionally been. The second is a homage to an author who has also taken an interest in the affect, but in a perspective dif-ferent from mine. In it, he provides an account of the work done on the subject in recent years – work that seems to me sometimes worthy of inter-est, sometimes to offer material for discussion, above all because it echoes my own thinking, notwithstanding important disagreements.

The reader will also note my fidelity to the ideas that I have raised from the outset and which still seem to me to be consistent. This does not mean that I regard any subsequent questioning of them to be superfluous, on the contrary. More than ever I believe that real disagreements can only concern fundamentals, that is to say, one's view of the affect, with all the conse-quences that flow from it on the methodological plane. From this point of view, I would affirm once more that the adult patient's experience in the psychoanalytic setting is the principal source of our knowledge and the basis of its elaboration.

Preface to the French edition (1973)

> X (aged 10) – Daddy, what's analysis? What do you do with your patients?
> Y (his brother, aged 11½). – Analysis is . . . analysis. Just like you do logical analysis or grammatical analysis at school, well, Papa does the same thing with his patients.
> X (peremptorily and rather indignantly) – Oh, no! People aren't words!
> (Conversation between a psychoanalyst's sons in the presence of their father)

This book began as a paper. In 1970 I addressed the Congrès des Psychanalystes de Langues romanes in Paris on the subject of the affect. This work took on the dimensions of a book and, in the opinion of many, it was one. And so it is reborn today in that form and, as such, it will bring the subject to a wider public. And yet a report is not a book. What I mean by this is that if the original intention had been to write a book, it would have been written in a different way. So the rather peculiar nature of this text requires a few explanations as to its origin, its aim, its form and the public for which it was intended.

In 1953, Jacques Lacan and a number of his colleagues left the Société psychanalytique de Paris for reasons that I shall not go over here. That same year, Lacan was to deliver a report to the Congrès des Psychanalystes de Langues romanes entitled 'Fonction et champ de la parole et du langage en psychanalyse', now generally referred to as the 'Discours de Rome'.[1]

Lacan's thinking has become increasingly influential. The Colloque de Bonneval on 'L'inconscient', organized by Henri Ey in 1960,[2] was undoubtedly dominated by the Lacanian contribution, direct and indirect, despite the criticism that Lacan later made of the text that was inspired by his thinking.

---

1 This work was first published in 1956 in vol. I of *La Psychanalyse* (Paris: Presses Universitaires de France) and included in Lacan (1966) and in Lacan (1977).
2 *L'Inconscient*, Paris: Desclée de Brouwer, 1966.

However great the attraction exerted on me by Lacan's theory and how-ever eloquent his defence of it, it seemed to me, even then, that the Lacanian project could not be accepted without serious reservations. The starting point, which was declared to be a 'return to Freud' or rather, to be more precise, 'the discovery of Freud by Lacan' (Lacan) eventually led to a destination that seemed more like a Freudian cover for Lacan. Was it Lacan discovering Freud's work or Freud's work, amputated of at least half its substance, that provided Lacan with his passport? The second interpre-tation seemed to me more likely. When I set out in search of that missing half, it soon became evident to me that Lacanian theory was based on an exclusion, a 'forgetting' of the affect. This is apparent on the theoretical level alone, though amply evident in the practical applications that spring from it.

Since that time, I have concerned myself a great deal with this problem. In various works published since 1960, whether or not they were inspired by Lacan's thinking, I have returned again and again to this problem. I am fully aware that I owe a great deal to Lacan, but I also owe a great deal to colleagues who have been more critical of Lacanianism than I have been.

However, the interest of the subject goes well beyond its original context.

Psychoanalysts throughout the world, most of whom have remained out-side this controversy, still deplore the absence of a psychoanalytic theory of the affect, despite the many works devoted to the subject.

This book is an attempt, therefore, to recentre the problem for my French colleagues and, at the same time, to try to present a psychoanalytic theory of the affect in general.

In order to carry out this programme, I have adopted the following method. In the first two chapters, I have drawn up a dossier of the problem. The first chapter is a detailed analytic study of the affect in Freud's work. The second chapter is an account of the principal contributions of the ana-lytic literature after Freud to an understanding of the development of ideas in the psychoanalytic movement. It seemed to me that this chapter was nec-essary if one were to understand the way in which the problem is now posed, more than thirty years since Freud's death.

After an examination of the place of the affect in clinical structures and of the way in which this is revealed in psychoanalytic experience (Chapters 3 and 4), I have devoted the last part of the work to my own theoretical hypotheses (Chapters 5 and 6). I do not believe that I have succeeded in supplying *the* missing psychoanalytical theory of the affect, but I hope that I have contributed towards a possible theory that may lead us to a solution of the problem.

However, I have carried my theoretical hypotheses a little further in a piece that will be found in a Postface. Originally intended as a contribution to the Congress, this text was not so much an introduction as an extension of my thinking, and in it I indulged more in speculation, thus making a sacrifice to what Freud called the 'witch of metapsychology'.

This text is more or less that of 1970. I have made a few small changes with a view to making it more readable. I have added certain new references that have appeared since 1970 that bear directly on the subject.

The question of the affect cannot be confined to debate within the analytic movement. It is up to each discipline to approach it in its own way. While hoping that my work will be of assistance to those in other disciplines, I have tried to keep within my own field: psychoanalysis.

Ladies and gentlemen, – You will not be surprised to hear that I have a number of novelties to report to you about our conception [*Aufassung*] of anxiety and of the basic instincts of mental life; nor will you be surprised to learn that none of these novelties can claim to offer a final solution of these still unsettled problems. I have a particular reason for using the word 'conception' here. These are the most difficult problems that are set to us, but their difficulty does not lie in any insufficiency of observations; what present us with these riddles are actually the commonest and most familiar of phenomena. Nor does the difficulty lie in the recondite nature of the speculations to which they give rise; speculative consideration plays little part in this sphere. But it is truly a matter of conceptions – that is to say, of introducing the right abstract ideas, whose application to the raw material of observation will produce order and clarity in it.

(Freud, Lecture XXXII (1932), S.E., XXII, p. 81)

Introduction

The boundaries of the study

It will be readily admitted that an exhaustive study of the problems posed by the affect in the field of psychoanalytic theory and practice is impossible. It is necessary therefore to define the boundaries within which my work will operate.

From the theoretical point of view, such a study raises two difficulties. The first concerns the place of the affect in Freud's work. Indeed, one cannot assign a particular place to the affect in Freud's work as a whole. Freud did not devote a particular work to the subject. So we have to follow the development of the notion of the affect in the course of his work. The problem of the affect depends on the guidelines operating at the various stages in the development of the theory: the first and second topographies, the various forms taken by the theory of the drives, etc. Sometimes theoretical changes entail a change in the status of the affect, sometimes an appreciation of its functional value will explain a change in theory. For example, the notion of anxiety or repressed libido led to a revaluation of the theory of repression when Freud maintained that repression is released because of anxiety.

The second difficulty will be encountered with the changes brought to Freudian theory by Freud's successors. Changes to the theoretical framework made by Hartmann, Melanie Klein, Winnicott, Bouvet or Lacan imply a different conception of the affect. It may also be said that a different apprehension of the problem of the affect will bring about changes in the theoretical framework in which it is situated. The problem of the affect is in a dialectical relationship with theory, each referring necessarily to the other.

These theoretical difficulties are directly related to practice. Indeed it is more than likely that the theoretical model in which the affect appears derives, in Freud's case, from a psychoanalytic practice that is strictly focused on the field of the neuroses – more particularly the classical neuroses, the

1

transference neuropsychoses. Freud's contributions to the psychoses or to other clinical aspects go no further than general suggestions, though they are no less valuable for that. But, since Freud, psychoanalytic practice has, as we know, extended considerably: character neuroses, psychosomatic structures, borderline states have become part of post-Freudian psychoanalysis and confront the psychoanalyst with affects that were ignored by Freud. It is likely that Freud was concerned first of all to ensure that it would be possible for him to advance, if not with certainty, it least in a steady manner – hence the voluntary limitation of theory.

We are confronted here with the following problem: either to treat affects that are not observable in the treatment of the classical neuroses by the Freudian model, feeling that this model is inadequate, or altering the theoretical framework of psychoanalysis in the light of knowledge deriving from these new clinical aspects by creating a new theoretical model that may be no longer suited to the classical neuroses and might run the risk of shifting the whole of psychoanalytic theory and practice in a different direction. This is what has happened in the development of psychoanalytic thinking. The examination of Freudian and post-Freudian psychoanalytic theories will necessarily be critical: critical of Freud by his successors and critical of Freud's successors by the interpretation of his thought.

These reflections allow me to explain more clearly the central position that will guide me. Psychoanalytic theory and practice compel us to include in the category of the affect many different states that belong to the pleasure–displeasure range. One may well wonder whether a unitary conception can take account of them. In other words, if any single conception is suited to give us the theoretical keys to anxiety (in its various aspects), pain, mourning, questions that Freud came back to again and again – not to mention depersonalization, the affects that sustain the fear of annihilation and aphanisis, which bring us to the boundary of what it is possible to say about the affect.

Most modern authors agree that what we generally encounter in psychoanalytic practice are complex affects, merged affects or, to use Freud's own term, constructions of affects. It is beyond the limits of this study to deal in detail with each affect construction. Given all the considerations that seem to make any attempt at clarification so difficult, I shall have to accept the limitations of my theoretical investigation. In other words, I shall try to locate the most general problems concerning the affect, leaving to one side the detailed examination of this or that particular affect – even if signalling the structural indications relative to the various categories of affects. The wealth and diversity of the emotional life would no doubt be impoverished as a result; my only hope is that a little more clarity will emerge to guide our understanding of specific phenomena in the psychoanalytic field.

It is important that one thing should be made clear here. Emotional life may be studied, and it has been, from very different points of view, from the observation of animals to philosophical speculation. We no doubt have a great deal to learn from ethological observation, from experimental physiology, from ethnology and structural anthropology, from child psychology or psychosociology; philosophers have allowed their thoughts to ramble over this mass of scientific information. I must refrain from doing so, however. Having had to confine my study to the most general problems of the affect, I cannot sacrifice the field of my experience in favour of results obtained from outside my field of reference.

Indeed it should be remembered that modern epistemology has shown that the specificity of the object of knowledge is strictly dependent on the way in which this object is 'carved up' by the discipline confronting it. The 'carving up' of the affect, the object of my study, is closely bound up with the conditions in which it appears to us: the experience of the transference in analysis. This accounts, it must be said, for a certain ambiguity in psychoanalytic works on the affect. Although most of them take as their point of departure the affect in the transference, the construction of a theory of the affect seldom avoids the temptation to include in it data that have come from outside psychoanalytic experience. This is no doubt inevitable. The reconstructive approach of psychoanalysis involves not only the construction of the analysand's past, but the more general construction of the 'psychical personality', to use Freud's words. Psychoanalytic theory, therefore, strives not only to define the structure of affects that have not been revealed by the transference, but also to formulate hypotheses concerning the affects that remain outside the scope of sight, and psychoanalytic experience, whether these are relegated to an unattainable past or whether they belong to levels of the psyche that are difficult to approach. Clearly, any study of the affect presents a challenge. The world of the affect is communicable to us insofar as thing-presentations and word-presentations form an intelligible psychical complex with it. But the general feeling is that the affect sometimes emerges in a state of nature, as it were, without any representation being associated with it. Affective communication is part of the most general analytical experience. But here we are moving into uncertain territory. 'Empathy', so necessary to the analyst, may soon become easy prey to the affects projected by the analyst on to his patient, beyond what is expressible, intelligible and representable, and may take a mystical turn in which scientific truth may well be lost.

The question almost undermines in advance any approach by knowledge. Can one speak of the affect? Does not what one says about it concern the periphery of the phenomenon, mere ripples at the furthest remove from the centre, which remains unknown to us? The same question may be posed in relation to the unconscious. To allow oneself to be fascinated by this enigma, however weighty it may be, would imply a renunciation of psychoanalysis.

Terminology and semantics

Lalande's philosophical vocabulary does not include the term *affect*, but only *affecter* (to affect), *affectif* (emotional), *affection*, *affectivité*. It emerges from these various definitions that they all relate to the sphere of *feeling*. The 'affects', whether they are produced from outside or from within, belong to that contrasted domain of the states and of pleasure or pain, which form, in a way, the psychical matrices. In opposition to the category of the affect is that of representation, rather as feeling is in opposition to the intellect. (However, the subject of '*affective memory*', 'the reliving through simple memories of feelings felt in the past', is surrounded by controversy.) If one recognizes that the affect may have an external cause, one has to admit that there exists an inner tendency towards this or that affective development. In any case, the affective gamut presupposes a scale of states that are more or less violent, more or less critical, more or less accompanied by physiological manifestations.

These few remarks show that we find the same problems in the philosophical vocabulary as in psychoanalysis:

- the affect–representation opposition;
- the primitive affects: pleasure-pain;[1]
- affect as memory;
- the genesis of affect by the combination of an external effect and an internal movement;
- the interdependence of violent affects and physical organization.

In the entry '*Sensibilité*', Lalande remarks on the extreme equivocation of the meanings of the word.

The French language designates by a homonym, *sens* both *sensibilité* (feeling) and *signification* (meaning). This common root extends in two directions: the first affective, the second intellectual. The first is connoted by the dimension of feeling, the second by the dimension of representation. It seems clear that the first sphere belongs to operations that are more or less distinct, more or less immediate, more or less primal, and that the second belongs to operations that are more differentiated, mediatized and secondary. However, it might be abusively schematic to regard the intellectual sphere alone as capable of differentiation and that the affective sphere is doomed to 'primitiveness'. Secondariness relates as much to the affective

---

1 It seems to me however that it would be better to use two dyads: that of the extremes *jouissance*–pain and that of pleasure–unpleasure. The chain would then be: *jouissance*–pleasure–unpleasure–pain.

sphere as to the intellectual, which is what the psychoanalytic literature designates by the terms primary affects and secondary or complex affects. Without going into the links between the first and second, and the ways in which one may pass from the one to the other, the coexistence of both, a reflection of the coexistence of primary and secondary processes, goes side by side with the corresponding 'intellectual' modes of work, which also coexist in the psychical apparatus.

Lalande's *Vocabulaire* provides no definite clarification in the entries quoted, but it is instructive as to the categories of thought that determined Freud's conceptual horizon. If Freud's work upset these categories to some extent, it remained necessarily dependent upon them. It may be said, therefore, that despite its revolutionary contribution, his work remains within western metaphysics. Without being able to claim in any way that we have emerged from it, one may understand the most recent post-Freudian psychoanalytic contributions as an attempt, not a deliberate one, but one obeying a spontaneous necessity, to burst out of the limitations of that framework. So, taking this remark as a guideline, we should stop and think when we see certain authors abandoning this distinction between representation and affect, the intelligible and the emotional, meaning and feeling.

In French, '*affect*' is a specifically psychoanalytic term. It appears neither in Littré, nor in Robert.[2] Its importation into French is due to Freud, who sometimes uses *Affekt*, sometimes *Empfindung*, sometimes *Gefühl*. *Affekt* has always been translated into French by *affect*, *Empfindung* by *sensation* and *Gefühl* by *sentiment*. But the various meanings overlap and translation poses embarrassing problems, as Strachey notes in his introduction to the Standard Edition.[3] Thus, in English, *Empfindung* is sometimes translated as 'feeling', sometimes as 'emotion'. Similarly, *Gefühl* cannot always be validly translated as 'feeling' and may require the term 'emotion'. In 'Obsessions and Phobias', an article written in French in 1895, Freud translates *Affekt* by *état émotif*, a term from the psychiatric vocabulary of the time. Similarly, we later find works in the English-language literature that refer to 'emotions' rather than to 'affects'. Such authors often discuss the terminology to be used and the distinctions to be made.

In this area, where subtlety is of the utmost importance, it is vital to

---

2 Except in the Petit Robert, where it is dated as 1951. Definition: état affectif élementaire. This omission is rectified in the Supplément, which appeared in 1970 and which gives the German origin: Affekt.

3 *The Complete Psychological Works of Sigmund Freud* (known as the *Standard Edition*, abbreviated to *S.E.*). London: Hogarth Press and the Institute of Psycho-Analysis. *S.E.*, I, p. xxiii.

specify the use one is making of terms. When dealing with the emotional life, the French psychological tradition usually distinguished, in the absence of the term *affect*, between *émotion*, an acute, transitory state, *sentiment*, a more attenuated, more durable state, and *passion*, which is violent, profound and lasting. Although *émotion* seems to have preserved a stable meaning, as has *sentiment*, the word *passion*, on the other hand, had a more general, generic meaning, since *passions* cover all the phenomena of emotional life. It was used in this way in the seventeenth century and even right up to the nineteenth.

But although *affect* does not appear in the great dictionaries, *affectif* refers, if one sets aside the obsolete meaning (which indicates *affection*), to feeling, pleasure, pain, emotion (Robert). On the other hand, the verb *affecter* condenses an interesting variety of meanings. In one sense, deriving from Old French, it is simply to apply to a particular use. In a second sense, *affecter* means (from a Latin origin that requires our attention): to try to reach, to strive to do something, or to feign. More generally, it means: to tend to take on this or that form. One might note already the plastic dimension of the affect and the part played in it by deception, display, artifice (in both senses of the word: cunning and the absence of the natural). In a third sense, rather contrary to the first, it means performing an action, causing an impression on the organism. Whereas the previous meaning presupposes a tendency to take on a role in order to act out a feeling, this meaning implies an active mode, involving the alteration, the transformation of a state (usually to perform some harmful act) that affects feelings.

To consider only these ordinary dictionary definitions, it is striking to note that the affect (apart from the first meaning, which does not concern the emotions) always seems to have pejorative associations. This first incursion into the domain of the verb, which supports the noun, confronts us with a desire envisaged from the point of view of deception, dissimulation, insincerity or intimidation. The neutral meanings – to move, to impress, to touch – are in the minority. Even in the dictionary, the affect does not have a good press, the development of the language reflecting the development of culture.

I have described the questions of vocabulary that make the translation of the German terms *Affekt*, *Empfindung* and *Gefühl* so difficult. These difficulties are redoubled in the vocabulary of psychoanalysis. The affect is bound up with the notion of a quantity of 'instinctual impulse' in the term *Affektbetrag*, 'quota of affect'. This term designates the strictly economic aspect of the phenomenon, whereas the affect refers to subjective quality. This relation between subjective quality and quantity of instinctive energy (quality and quantity) has often led to a confusion between the quota of affect and cathectic energy. Moreover, in an article written in French, 'Quelques considérations pour une étude comparative des paralysies motrices organiques et hystériques' (1893), Freud translates *Affektbetrag* by '*valeur affective*'. By a relaxation of psychoanalytic language, one speaks indifferently of an activity being 'laden with affect' or 'cathected'. In their *Language of Psycho-Analysis*, Laplanche and Pontalis give the following definition of 'cathectic energy': 'Substratum of energy postulated as the quantitative factor in the working of the psychical apparatus',[4] without further commentary. Thus cathectic energy relates to a quantity of energy in play in an operation, whereas a quota of affect refers only to the quantitative aspect of energy bound up with the qualitative subjective aspect, which 'qualifies' the affect, as it were. So, although every affect refers to the quantitative aspect of cathectic energy corresponding to it, every quantity of energy is not necessarily related to an affect.

Another term that creates problems in semantic discussion is that of *Triebregung* (*motion pulsionelle* in French; instinctual impulse in English). This is a thorny point that divides Freud's interpreters and translators. For some (Marthe Robert), the difference between *Trieb* (*pulsion*; instinct or drive) and *Triebregung* is negligible. In German the two terms are synonymous and it is neither necessary nor legitimate to use a different term in translation. For others (Laplanche and Pontalis), while agreeing that the difference between the two terms is slight and that Freud often uses them interchangeably, a distinction is necessary. They propose to translate *Triebregung* by *motion pulsionelle*[5] by which they denote the drive in its dynamic aspect. In this way, they use the term appropriated for instinct in action (*pulsion en acte*), the drive acting under the effect of internal stimulation, determined at the biological level. I would add that *motion pulsionelle* would not be unconnected to *énergie d'investissement* (cathected energy). It would represent the dynamic counterpart of what is cathected energy at the economic level. But this is to be understood in a more limited sense, since it does not concern the quantitative, energic aspect of all the operations of the psychical apparatus, but only those attached to the drive. Laplanche and Pontalis, while noting that the term *motion* is related to *motif, mobile, motivation*, all of which entail the notion of movement,[6] reject the translation '*émoi pulsionnel*', on the grounds that it is too linked to affect.

However, I should stress the relationship between *motion, émotion* and *émoi*.[7] With Freud, the notion of affect has always been bound up with that

4 See Laplanche and Pontalis (1973), p. 62.
5 See Laplanche and Pontalis (1973), p. 222.
6 Which also seems to have been the intention of Strachey, who, troubled as to how to render *Triebregung*, finally decided on 'instinctual impulse'.
7 Although Littré proposes contrary etymologies: 'Emoi viendrait de *es* et de l'ancien haut-allemand *magan* être fort', that is, to lose all strength, whereas *émotion* derives directly from *mouvoir* (to move).

of discharge, that is to say, with a process in action and movement. It may be said, therefore, that movement is a general qualification of the instinct, of which the affect indicates a particular direction (the movement towards the interior of the body).

On the subject of instincts with inhibited aim, Freud speaks of feelings of tenderness, friendship, etc. Similarly, on the subject of the Oedipus complex, he speaks of a 'tender object choice directed towards the mother' and of a 'tender, feminine attitude towards the father'. It is clear that he is referring here to what in French we call *sentiments* (feelings) – which should not be confused with states of pleasure (and displeasure), which are prototypes of the affect. The same remark applies to pain and mourning, states that are undeniably affective processes, but ones that are quite different from the anxiety affects in psychoanalytic theory, as Freud makes clear in 'Inhibitions, symptoms and anxiety'.

To make matters clearer I shall use 'affect' as a categorical term grouping together the qualifying subjective aspects of the emotional life in the broad sense, including all the nuances that German (Empfindung, Gefühl) or French (*émotion, sentiment, passion*, etc.) bring to this category. *Affect, therefore, should be understood essentially as a metapsychological term rather than a descriptive one.* For, it should be insisted upon, the psychoanalytic conception of the affect is different from any other approach to the phenomena theorized under this term, whether neurobiological, psychological, sociological or philosophical. Used in the descriptive sense, the term affect may be replaced by another, more adequate one, one closer to the reality that it designates. But all these variants bring us back to the category of the affect.

Questions of method

The quotation from Freud that I placed at the beginning of this work shows that the solution of the difficulties encountered in any examination of the problem of the affect largely depends on the conceptions that are intended to order the data collected by the analyst. A direct reference to psychoanalytic practice, without prejudice, without preconception, might well have been desirable. But I know that such a wish is illusory. Psychoanalytic knowledge rests on Freud's theory, which, by the same token, led to the practice and theory of psychoanalysis. A permanent critical work was undertaken by Freud himself, his disciples and successors in an attempt to circumscribe the facts more accurately and to introduce changes, which, I admit, were inevitable in the light of knowledge acquired through practice. Conversely, new facts were intelligible only thanks to theoretical changes.

My approach will be *historical and structural*, from a *critical* point of view. By this I mean that the critical attitude will bear on the diachronic history of the notion in the work of Freud and his successors, and on a synchronic view of the present field of psychoanalytic practice and theory. But this critical method remains within the framework of a critique internal to psychoanalysis, which with full knowledge of the facts, must pose its own questions and supply its own answers.

Part I
Affect in the psychoanalytic literature

1

Affect in Freud's work

In this analytic chapter, I shall trace the development of Freud's ideas on affect. Several stages may be distinguished:

- from *Studies on Hysteria* (1893–95) to *The Interpretation of Dreams* (1900);
- from *The Interpretation of Dreams* to the *Papers on Metapsychology* (1915);
- from the *Papers on Metapsychology* to the article 'Fetishism' (1927), the subject being taken up again in the article 'The splitting of the ego in the process of defence' (1939).

After 1927, there are few important references to affect.[1]

The most important text on affect after the second topography is *Inhibitions, Symptoms and Anxiety*. I felt that it was logical to group together Freud's various views on anxiety from 1894 to 1932, by separating them from the other texts.

Evolution of the conception of affect

I From the discovery of psychoanalysis to 'The Interpretation of Dreams'

1 *Studies on Hysteria* (1893–95)

The history of affect, like that of psychoanalysis itself, is closely bound up with hysteria. But, before the appearance of the 'Preliminary Communication', Freud, in the entry on hysteria for the *Encyclopédie de*

---

1 Except in articles in which Freud is giving an account of the history of psychoanalysis and its discoveries.

Villaret of 1892, introduced the notion of *modifications in the distribution of the quantities of excitation* in the nervous system. What we are dealing with here is more cathectic energy than the quota of affect as such, but the second is included in the first, as the following quotation shows:

> Alongside of the physical symptoms of hysteria, a number of psychical disturbances are to be observed, in which at some future time the changes characteristic of hysteria will no doubt be found but the analysis of which has hitherto scarcely been begun. These are changes in the passage and in the association of ideas, inhibitions of the activity of the will, magnification and suppression of feelings, etc. – which may be summarized as *changes in the normal distribution over the nervous system of the stable amounts of excitation.*[2]

Freud attaches more value to this hypothesis than to the description of the hysterical temperament that is lacking in many patients. Against a characterlogical conception, he opts for an economic one: that of a surplus of excitation in the nervous system, which 'manifests itself, now as an inhibitor, now as an irritant, and is displaced within the nervous system with great freedom'.

It is the fate of this quantity of excitation to play an important role in the conception of the strangulated affect, as described in the *Studies on Hysteria*. Even in 1893,[3] in the article 'Some points for a comparative study of organic and hysterical motor paralyses', Freud introduced the term quota of affect[4] to indicate the interdependence between an associative content and its affective correlative. 'Every event, every psychical impression is provided with a certain quota of affect (*Affektbetrag*) of which the ego divests itself either by means of a motor reaction or by associative psychical activity'.[5]

The pathogenic mechanism – by which the abreaction of accretions of stimuli is prevented – already appears in this text. For what operates in the

---

2 *S.E.*, I, p. 49.
3 In the same year, Freud published 'A case of successful treatment by hypnotism', in which he is already confronting the question of the affect from the point of view of the waiting affect.
4 This article was written in 1888 and published only in 1893. It should be noted that the German term *Affektbetrag* was translated by him (the article was written in French) as '*valeur affective*'. The word *valeur* (value) must be taken here not only in the sense of the overall term '*valeur affective*', but in its proper sense, *valeur* expressing both a quantitative and qualitative notion. It is therefore, in a sense, more complete than 'quota of affect', which renders only the quantitative sense. See on this matter the entry 'Quota of affect' in Laplanche and Pontalis (1973). It is quite possible that the term '*valeur affective*' was due to Breuer's influence: Strachey remarks that Breuer probably wrote *Affektwert* (literally, '*valeur affective*'), rather than *Affektbetrag*.
5 *S.E.*, I, pp. 171–2.

normal psychical state, the tendency to maintain the sum of constant excitation by the most appropriate means, displaying it associatively or by discharging (abreacting) it,[6] is not possible in hysteria. Paradoxically, however, Freud states in this same text, which was a sketch for the 'Preliminary Communication', that the affect may be the object of a splitting: at the time of the affect, however small and unpathogenic it may be, an impression may later become traumatic. There is the germ of the conception of symbolization here.

In the 'Preliminary Communication' (1893), Breuer and Freud fully worked out the conception of the strangulated affect. This is directly bound up with traumatic theory. With a traumatic event, the memory of which cannot be wiped out in certain cases, it is important to know 'whether there has been an energic reaction to the event that provokes an affect',[7] through which any abreaction of affects – 'from tears to acts of revenge' – could have occurred. In cases where abreaction does not occur, the affect remains attached to the memory, as a result of its not being wiped out. So the pathogenic representations have not undergone the normal wear caused by abreaction or reproduction, with impeded circulation of associations. However, through psychotherapy, an equivalent of abreaction by act may occur, thanks to the language that allows its abreaction. Language relates memory and event associatively, just as it relates the strangulated affects to representations. We must follow Freud attentively here. In this context, a verbalization is not simply an intellectual operation. 'Language serves as a substitute for action; by its help, an affect can be "abreacted" almost as effectively'.[8]

Language not only allows the load to be unblocked and experienced, it is in itself act and abreaction by words. The procedure used enables the affect to be *poured out verbally*; furthermore, it transforms this affective load and leads the pathogenic representation to be modified by means of association, by drawing it into normal consciousness.[9] Freud's words 'the hysteric suffers from memories' have attained a certain celebrity, but insufficient stress has been laid on the role played in them by affect, through which they are linked to memory and the success of treatment. For, to be cured, it is not enough to remember; we are well aware of this today, but Freud shows that he already knew it in his 'Preliminary Communication'.

For we found, to our great surprise at first, that *each individual hysterical symptom immediately and permanently disappeared when we had succeeded in*

---

6 A conception that Freud defended well before the 'Project'. See also 'Sketches for the "Preliminary Communication"' of 1893' (1892), *S.E.*, I, p. 153.

7 *S.E.*, II, p. 8.

8 Ibid.

9 *S.E.*, II, p. 15.

bringing clearly to light the memory of the event by which it was provoked and in arousing its accompanying affect, and when the patient had described that event in the greatest possible detail and had put the affect into words. Recollection without affect almost invariably produces no result.[10]

It is pointless to try to decide whether the affect or the representation is more in evidence. Each depends upon the other:

Running parallel to the sensation of a hysterical 'aura' in the throat, when that feeling appeared after an insult, was the thought 'I shall have to swallow this'. She had a whole quantity of sensations and ideas running parallel with each other. Sometimes the sensation would call up the idea to explain it, sometimes the idea would create the sensation by means of symbolization, and not infrequently it had to be left an open question which of the true elements had been at the primary one.[11]

So, if the psychotherapy of hysteria shows that the two elements are mutually dependent, this suggests that they must both be present in the treatment adopted.

Thus trauma, the memory of it and the pathogenic representations deriving from it, the non-abreacted affect and the verbalization, accompanied by emotion, form an indissociable network. In these circumstances, one cannot give greater importance to memories or pathogenic representations than to the affect, since the reappearance of the affect is the precondition for the method's success. Similarly, language cannot be shifted to the side of the representations, for it is itself a form of abreaction, equivalent to the act.

As we know, Breuer and Freud quarrelled on the question of the hypnoid state.[12] Following P.J. Moebius, Breuer believes that the hypnoid state is an auto-hypnoid state, self-induced, under the influence of daydreams and the appearance of an affect. A certain void of the consciousness occurs during

10 *S.E.*, II, p. 6. Freud repeats the same statement in the first of the *Five Lectures on Psycho-Analysis* (1909). See *S.E.*, XI, p. 18: 'On the other hand, it was found that no result was produced by the recollection of a scene in the doctor's presence if for some reason the recollection took place without any generation of affect. Thus it was what happened to these affects, which might be regarded as displaceable magnitudes, that was the decisive factor both for the onset of illness and for recovery'. It should be noted that the notion of the transference is added here. The notion of defence is closely bound up with the affect. In the chapter 'The psychotherapy of hysteria', in *Studies on Hysteria*, published in 1895, the defence is used in the struggle against the appearance of 'affects of shame, of self-reproach and of psychical pain' (*S.E.*, II, p. 269).
11 *S.E.*, II, p. 180.
12 On this question, see Laplanche and Pontalis (1973), p. 192.

which a representation appears without any resistance. This hypnoid state cuts off a group of representations, which soon link up with other groups of representations formed during other hypnoid states, and, by stopping the circulation of associations, constitutes a splitting off, a *Spaltung*, from the rest of the psyche. For Breuer, this hypnoid state is the precondition of hysteria.[13] In his *Studies on Hysteria*, Freud did support this idea, but he later abandoned it as superfluous. What he retained of it is the idea of a particular psychical group isolated from the rest of psychical life, which he came to see as the kernel of the unconscious. If, today, Breuer's opinion seems unacceptable, we must nevertheless recognize that his conception prefigured what Freud was to discover only some years later: the role of phantasy and its connection[14] with the affect, since together they trigger off the hypnoid state. Thus, with the abandoning of the trauma theory, a solution involving exchange is revealed, though without any need to eliminate the conception of the strangulated affect, for the phantasy may itself activate the contents of the unconscious – when it is not itself the result of it – and thus increase the load of affect, which it tries to bind by its constitution.

Between the 'Preliminary Communication' (1893) and the publication of *Studies on Hysteria* (1895), Freud published in January 1894 'The neuro-psychoses of defence'. In that article he explains in greater detail than before the notion of quota of affect.

> I refer to the concept that in mental functions something is to be distinguished – a quota of affect or sum of excitation – which possesses all the characteristics of a quantity (though we have no means of measuring it), which is capable of increase, diminution, displacement and discharge, and which is spread over the memory-traces of ideas somewhat as an electric charge is spread over the surface of a body.[15]

Freud distinguishes between:

---

13 One may note in this respect the relation between the conceptions of Breuer and Henri Ey, for whom the existence of an earlier dissolution is the explanatory condition of the emergence of the unconscious.

14 I shall say nothing here about the discussion concerning the triggering off of the hypnoid state under the influence alone of daydreaming or emotion. Freud gives an interesting comparison of Breuer's conception of the 'void of consciousness' accompanying the hypnoid state and his own conception of hysterical 'absences' in a passage in the *Five Lectures on Psycho-Analysis* concerning the period of his collaboration with Breuer in 1989 (see *S.E.*, XI, pp. 12–13). It is clear that for Freud this absence is the product of desire and not its condition. See also on the term *absence* the note of August 1938 (*S.E.*, XXIII, p. 300).

15 *S.E.*, III, p. 60. See also Laplanche and Pontalis (1973), entry on 'Quota of affect', p. 374.

1   quantity measurable *de jure* if not *de facto*;
2   the variation of this quantity;
3   the movement bound up with this quantity;
4   the discharge.

In the same year, in a letter to Fliess (of 21 May 1894), this conception is complemented by the idea of the affect being different according to the clinical entities: 'I know three mechanisms: transformation of affect (conversion hysteria), displacement of affect (obsessions) and exchange of affect (anxiety neurosis and melancholia)'.[16]

Thus the earlier conceptions are now joined for the first time by the idea of *transformation* in the broad sense; a transformation that is still the privilege of hysteria, but is also at work in other neuropsychoses; a transformation in which the affect wins out over representations and which does not necessarily lead to conversion.

Furthermore, in that year, Freud's clinical explorations were very advanced. Draft E (undated, but written about June 1894), which deals with the origin of anxiety, and the article 'On the grounds for detaching a particular syndrome from neurasthenia under the description "anxiety neurosis"' show that the idea of transformation between the various forms of energy – physical, sexual and psychical – dominates his thinking at this time. I shall not develop this point any further at the moment, but I shall return to it later when dealing with the question of anxiety.

Indeed it seems to me that if Freud, from the outset, was so sensitive to this notion of moving quantity, which was to dominate the whole of the 'Project for a scientific psychology', it is not only because of his 'physicalist' prejudices. I might almost suppose that the notion of moving quantity derives from his observation of the transformations in the discourse of his first patients.

This notion of transformation is found again in the part of the *Studies on Hysteria* written in 1895, especially on the subject of conversion, of course. When the affect has had to be discharged by a reflex that is not simply 'not normal', but actually 'abnormal', it is from this abnormal reflex that the

---

16 *S.E.*, I, p. 188. See also Laplanche and Pontalis (1973), entry on 'Affect', p. 13. In what follows in the correspondence with Fliess one will find a return of this theme of the transformation of affects. Thus in Draft H of 24 January 1895 on 'Paranoia', he draws up a comparative table for hysteria, obsessional neurosis, hallucinatory confusion, paranoia and hallucinatory psychosis, distinguished according to the categories of affect, content of idea, hallucination and of the achievement defence (*S.E.*, I, pp. 211–12). A year later, in Draft K on 'The neuroses of defence' of 1 January 1896, he describes them as pathological deviations from normal affective states, from *conflict* (hysteria), from *self-reproach* (obsessional neurosis), and from *mortification* (paranoia), from *mourning* (acute hallucinatory amentia) (*S.E.*, I, p. 220).

conversion is produced. There is, therefore, a double transformation here: from the normal reflex to the abnormal reflex and from the abnormal reflex into its conversion. But if the affect is so destined to be transformed by conversion, it is because its origin is bound up, according to Freud, with transformation. The affect is itself, in a sense, the product of a 'conversion turned inside out', as the following text shows:

> All these sensations and innervations belong to the field of 'The Expression of the Emotions', which, as Darwin has taught us, consists of actions which originally had a meaning and served a purpose. These may now for the most part have become so much weakened that the expression of them in words seems to us only to be a figurative picture of them, whereas in all probability the description was once meant literally; and hysteria is right in restoring the original meaning of the words in depicting its unusually strong innervations. Indeed, it is perhaps wrong to say that hysteria creates these sensations by symbolization. It may be that it does not take linguistic usage as its model at all, but that both hysteria and linguistic usage alike draw their material from a common source.[17]

Hysterical conversion, therefore, is a return to the sources of the affect. But this is less important than Freud's remark on symbolization. Thus, if what Lacan says is true, namely that the hysteric speaks with her flesh, it seems to me even truer to say that the hysteric enslaves herself to the language of the flesh, drawing from a spring from which they both derive. The discourse of the hysteric would not seem, therefore, to take on the model of language in order to speak; rather, both language and symptom plunge their roots into a common soil.

2 Draft G (1895)

Before examining the 'Project for a scientific psychology', I should like to draw attention to Draft G ('Melancholia'), which dates from 1 January 1895. There are two reasons for this: first, it deals with a subject very close to the problem of the affect; second, it contains a schema that must constitute a theorization – perhaps the most advanced so far – that seems to me to be a turning point.

After tracing two axes, a vertical one, constituting the ego boundary, separating the ego from the outside world, the other a horizontal one, constituting

17 *S.E.*, II, p. 181.

the somatic psychical boundary, separating the soma in its lower half and the psyche in its upper half, Freud puts in place elements and a circuit.

The elements are:

- in the external world, a sexual object;
- in the corresponding quarter, outside the ego and in the soma, a figure named 'sexual object in favourable position';
- in the quarter corresponding to the somatic part of the ego, an end-organ, somatic sexual excitation (S.s.) and a spinal centre;
- in the quarter corresponding to the psychical part of the ego, an assembly of elements named the 'psychical sexual group'.

The circuit is the following process.

Let there be an object (Δ) in the external world. Following a reaction, it penetrates the body of the subject. Freud then names it 'sexual object in favourable position'; following the circuit, penetrating the somatic part of the ego, provokes a sensation. After executing a loop around the end-organ, in which a reflex action is taking place, the circuit continues towards the psychical part of the ego, conducted along voluptuous feelings, which finally cathect the psychical sexual group (Ps.s.). But, from the end-organ, two other parallel pathways are formed: one, which sets out from the end-organ (after passing through the spinal centre) is that of sexual tension and ends in the network of the psychical sexual group; the other, more complex, moves in the direction of the previous ones, links the Ps.s. to the sexual object[18] and to the end-organ, thus contributing to the response of the reflex action at this level, linking its effects at this point to the influences exerted from its relation to the somatic sexual source. Lastly, from the psychical sexual group a pathway is opened towards the object which is that of the specific action intended to take possession of the object and to discharge energy.

This schema concerns female sexuality. However obscure it may be, the important thing is to note the existence of the three sexual pathways.

The first, the so-called *sexual tension* one, is purely organic and sexual. The second bears a certain affective range, *a pathway for conducting voluptuous feelings* (pleasure), and ends in the psychical sexual group. This pathway is psychical and sexual, for it is part of the circuit that encircles the object and bypasses the end-organ, without emerging from it. The third and last pathway is the most interesting. The work of educators leads to an exchange of sexual somatic stimuli for psychical stimuli; this influences the psychical

---

18 This way, on account of the educative inhibition of sexuality, goes ahead of the object to seek energic provisions to stimulate sexual awakening (activity of seduction) or to inhibit it, exercising its role in reflex action. It would seem to move, therefore, in both directions.

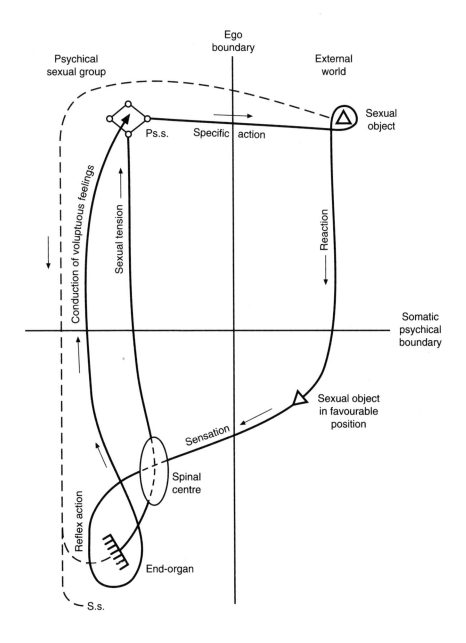

sexual group, but carries their action beyond the sexual object.[19] This pathway, deprived by education of its energic contribution of crude, direct sexuality, solicits in return, on the part of the object (by an attitude of seduction and attraction) the contribution necessary if the discharge of the specific act is to take place. It therefore carries another affective range: disgust for sexuality and, by inhibition of aim, seduction and attraction. Thus the sexual object of the Other functions as an additional source for the extinction of energy by education (repression). Tension is therefore maintained at a low level and the libido is deprived of the necessary force for the subject to carry out the specific act. Nevertheless, this act is carried out by means of the Other. But the object is lost and the whole system is unbalanced as a result, for this loss of the object leads to a loss of libidinal energy.

Freud constructed this schema in order to explain the relationship between frigidity and melancholia, for, by 1895, he was already discovering that 'the affect corresponding to melancholia is that of mourning – that is, longing for something lost. Thus in melancholia it must be a question of a loss – a loss in *instinctual* life'.[20]

The situation of the affect in this schema is complicated, therefore. In a normal state, it is divided between the pathway for conducting voluptuous feelings (pleasure) and the pathway of somatic sexual feelings, modified by education (disgust, defence). In the pathological state, it is the consequence of the loss of object and energy (mourning).

What seems to me to be important here is the distinction between the organic pathways, those that remain organic, those that are psychosexual and those that are transformed by education (repression). The affect belongs to the last two and is psychical and psychosexual in nature.

It seems to me that this heterogeneity of the component parts of the libido and this variation in their destiny have not been given due emphasis in our understanding of the relations between the affect and the bodily, physical sphere. The order of the affect is not that of physical sexual tension, although it spreads over it. Here, once more, the importance of the notion of *anaclisis* (leaking) is found, brought out by Laplanche and Pontalis. But it also depends on the psychical forces that prevent the immediate expression

---

19 I should note here a difference between Strachey's interpretation and my own on this question. Strachey seems to be aware only of the sexual psychical group (Ps.s on the diagram) and unaware of the existence of a psychical group. For me, one must distinguish between the psychical group and the first group, which results from the education and transformation of sexual somatic stimuli into psychical stimuli that change sexuality into disgust. What one has here is the first intuition of repression. I shall leave to one side for the moment the distinction between repression and suppression, and concentrate on the differences between the three ways and the two groups.

20 *S.E.*, I, p. 200.

of the instinct; here the role of defence is encountered again, which has the result of inverting the effect of pleasure into disgust. The affect, therefore, lies between soma and psyche, as between the hammer and the anvil, as it were.

Lastly, this schema seems to me to prefigure the model of the instinct, with its source (somatic, sexual), its object (in the external world), its thrust (here divided into its component parts), its aim (the specific action) and, finally, its circuit.

3 'Project for a scientific psychology' (1895)

The interest of the *Project* for a study of affect goes well beyond the direct references to this notion to be found in it, though these are in themselves very instructive. But for anyone who wishes to take the trouble to penetrate this inextricable undergrowth (and it contains more than one insoluble contradiction), it is well worth the trouble. Nor should one be misled by the argument that Freud opposed its publication. It represents an enormous effort to grapple with theoretical problems and the first appearance, in a single outpouring, of most of the hypotheses that Freud was later to exploit, little by little, over the next twenty years or more: the relationship between quantity and quality, the distinction between free energy and bound energy, the economic hypothesis, the first models of the experience of satisfaction and the experience of pain, the first sketch of the ego and its relationship with the object, the role of symbolization, the definition of the primary process, and the theory of thought and its relationship to language and to consciousness, in which the disturbing role of the affect makes its appearance. The enormous advantage of this work is that it clearly articulates all these fundamental notions of metapsychology. It is undoubtedly a loose articulation, in which there is an element of play on more than one point, but a vitally important articulation.

I shall group under three rubrics the contribution of the 'Project' to the problem of the affect:

A – Affect in the experience of satisfaction, pain and states of desire;
B – The role of the ego in inhibition and the control of affects;
C – The disturbances in thinking caused by affects.

A – The experience of satisfaction, pain and wish states
Before tackling the experiences of satisfaction, pain and wish states, it is important to remember that the notion of quantity and the principle of inertia (the tendency of the psychical apparatus to lower tension to the zero level) are fundamental presuppositions. The aspiration to discharge is primary, the retention of a certain quantity is necessitated by the laws of life.

(a) *Experience of satisfaction* In the experience of satisfaction, the first model of desire, the increase of intense tension caused by need makes necessary an internal modification of this state of affairs. To begin with, there occurs an attempt at internal and external discharge, by emotive manifestations and cries. But this discharge is inoperant, for the situation requires an external modification if an internal modification is to occur: the specific action capable of fulfilling need by satisfaction (brought by the external object). 'In this way this path of discharge acquires a secondary function of the highest importance, that of *communication*, and the initial helplessness of human beings is the *primal source* of all *moral motives*'.[21] One can hardly stress too strongly this primary link between discharge through emotivity and motricity, and the function of communication, from which language springs. Better still, from now on satisfaction will be associated with the image of the object that first aroused it and the moving image of the reflex movement that allowed its discharge. This is a new relationship between the perception of the object and internal discharge (through its trace in the moving image). Moving image and affect are therefore linked. Thus the affect is linked, on the one hand, to the function of communication and therefore to language, and, on the other hand, to bodily experience through the moving image of discharge.

Consequently, in order to prevent the reaction produced by too intense (hallucinatory) an investment of the absent object leading to renewed disappointment, through the impossibility of distinguishing between object hallucinations and object perception, an inhibition from the ego controls this cathexis and provides a criterion of the real presence of the object in perception.

(b) *Experience of pain* Pain is bound up with the breaking through of large quantities of excitation into the psychical apparatus, having penetrated the system of protection, by a solution of continuity produced by eruption. The eruption of this excessive quantity causes a higher level of intensity in the cathexis, a tendency to discharge it in order to eliminate this excessive quantity, and a cathexis of the image of the object that caused the pain, with contact between the last two. It should be added, however, that this erupting external quantity is accompanied by a particular quality. With a new cathexis of the memory-trace of the hostile object, there occurs a similar, but attenuated state.[22] What is then produced is not pain, but

---

21 *S.E.*, I, p. 318.
22 Laplanche and Pontalis (1973), in the entry 'Defence', discuss this experience of pain. It seems to them to contradict the hypothesis of a neuronal apparatus tending to the diminution and the elimination of tensions, that it should repeat pain in the form of the hallucinatory cathexis of the memory-image of the hostile object, which constitutes an increase of the cathexis by arousing the memory of the experience of pain. But one may suppose that the cathexis of the memory-image of the hostile object is revived during a

something like pain (unpleasure), and the cathexis is then discharged (as a result of the facilitation) inside the body. Here Freud introduces a special category of neurones, secreting neurones, the equivalent for internal discharge of the motor neurones for external discharge. Later the traces of the experience of pain entail ever weaker cathexes of the memory-trace of the hostile object, that is to say, playing more and more the role of signals, triggering off ever more important defensive operations.

I have paused here to consider the experience of pain because it refers more explicitly to the model of the affect than does the experience of satisfaction. For, although it is true that satisfaction is accompanied by affect (discharge by emotivity and motility), the traces of the experience of pain make explicit reference to an internal, secretory discharge.[23] Now Freud always maintained, as we shall see later, that the affect was the product of such an internal and secretory discharge. The model of affect is more often invoked for experiences of displeasure, pain and anxiety than for states of pleasure.

(c) *Wish states*   The traces of experiences of pain and satisfaction are affects and wish states. It should not be understood by this that the two co-exist in every experience, but that the wish state is bound up with the experience of satisfaction and the affect with the experience of pain (as traces). Desire and affect both entail a rise in tension, but by means of different mechanisms. In the first, this rise in tension is produced by a summons leading to the hallucinatory cathexis of the object (the future hallucinatory wish fulfilment), whereas in the second the rise in tension is produced by sudden discharge.

Thus, broadly speaking, it may be said that desire is affect insofar as it entails an affective state, in the ordinary sense of the term. But in fact only internal discharge, endogenous and secretory, bound up with the memory-trace

---

too prolonged experience of unsatisfied need, as an awakening of the experience of pain. One may also imagine that given the facilitation set up between this image and the tendency to discharge, such a cathexis plays the role of a signal assisting the provocation of this discharge, the only means of liquidating the excessive accumulated quantity in the absence of any satisfaction after a long period of time. One cannot see how such a quantity could be liquidated. But, although it is true that, on this point, Freud is less explicit and more obscure, one cannot but think that, in a Kleinian theoretical context, this hostile object is a precursor of the bad object. Furthermore, it should be noted that in the following paragraph the state of wish (hallucinated cathexis of the object of satisfaction) involves a rise, on demand, of $Q\eta$ in the psychical system. This rise in quantity does not contradict the hypothesis of the neuronal apparatus insofar as it has the aim of bringing (by similacrum, it is true) a reduction of tension.

23 The endogenous stimuli are assimilated to chemical products, *S.E.*, I, 320.

of the hostile object, merits this name.[24] A dimension of violence is added here in the reaction and bodily participation that confer this specificity upon it. It should also be stressed that the affect is produced during the repetition of the bodily experience of pain. It is this reproductive quality that gives it its properly psychical dimension. Note, furthermore, the stress laid on the closeness of the bonds between the affect and the defence that it mobilizes. This defence is aimed at an ever more advanced sensitivity of the psychical apparatus to the evocation of the affect, *qua* the signal mobilized by the increasingly discrete cathexes of the memory-trace of the hostile object.

B – The role of the ego in inhibition and the masking of affects
The repetition of memory-traces cathected with affect makes them gradually lose their affective quality. Time and repetition play little part in their domination; they tend rather to reinforce them. Whether we are dealing with the hallucinatory cathexis of the wish state or the facilitation of the discharge of unpleasure from the cathexis of the experience of pain, only a binding by the ego can ward it off.

> Here it is plausible to suppose that this capacity for hallucination, as well as the capacity for affect, are indications of the fact that the ego-cathexis has not yet gained any influence on the memory, that the primary lines of discharge and the full or primary process predominate in it.[25]

Two great directions of the activity of the ego are thus traced out: relations to reality (inhibition of the ability to hallucinate in order to allow the distinction between hallucination and perception), and defensive activity (prevention of discharge against unpleasure by the formation of a defence and repression).

C – Disturbances of thought by affects
According to Freud, two conditions are determinant in disturbances of normal psychical processes: sexual discharge must be linked to a memory rather than to an experience and this discharge must take place precociously, prematurely. When there is an accumulation of causes, a production of affect takes place. These ideas are expressed in the *Studies on Hysteria*.

Any production of affect impedes the normal course of thinking by the

---

24 It is probably in order to overcome this disparity that Laplanche and Pontalis propose a thesis that stresses the traumatic character of *any* instinctual manifestation prior to the satisfaction or unsatisfaction that follow it.
25 *S.E.*, I, p. 381. It should be noted that the two circumstances in which the primary process is interrupted for quantitative reasons are the experience of pain (exogenous Q) and affect (endogenous Q, discharged by facilitation) (*S.E.*, I, p. 335).

forgetting of associations, a decline in the capacity for selection and logic, and by the use of abandoned pathways, in particular those that lead to discharge. 'In conclusion, the affective process approximates to the uninhibited primary process.'[26]

Here we have a resumption of the idea of what might be called a propping up of the affect by the idea (or representation): the discharge of an intense affect with the help of the idea that triggers it off. The role of the ego will be to avoid later affective processes and to block old openings to discharge, because discharge disturbs the activity of thought by the intensity of the quantities that it mobilizes. By means of attention, alerting it to signals and enabling it to set up a defence, the ego inhibits the primary process.

Originally, a perceptual cathexis, as inheritor of an experience of pain, released unpleasure; it [the cathexis] was intensified by the $Q\eta$ released, and then proceeded towards discharge along pathways of passage that were in part prefacilitated. After a cathected ego had been formed, 'attention' to fresh perceptual cathexes developed in the manner we know and it [attention] followed with side-cathexes the passage [of quantity] from the perception. By that means the release of unpleasure was quantitatively restricted, and its start was precisely a signal for the ego to set normal defence in action; this guarded against fresh experiences of pain, with their facilitations, developing so easily. Nevertheless, the stronger the release of unpleasure, the harder was the task for the ego, which, with its side-cathexes, can after all provide a counterweight to the $Q\eta$ up to a certain limit, and is thus bound to permit a *primary passage* [of quantity] to occur.

Furthermore, the greater the quantity that is endeavouring to effect a passage, the harder for the ego is the activity of thought, which, as everything goes to show, consists in an experimental displacing of small $Q\eta$s.[27]

Disturbance also occurs whenever, instead of perception, a memory arises. To the many examples of this to be found in the *Studies on Hysteria* may be added the case of Emma, the celebrated *proton pseudos*, who provides an illustration of what went before and who would merit a whole study to herself.

---

26 *S.E.*, I, p. 357. This statement contradicts that of *S.E.*, I, p. 335, in which the affect is regarded as a cause of the interruption of the primary process. No doubt questions of threshold and intensity should be brought in here with a view to reconciling them.

27 *S.E.*, I, p. 358. This passage, which sums up all the statements on the experience of pain, shows the relativity of the functioning of the apparatus given the quantity. Beyond a certain threshold, discharge is unavoidable, going beyond the capacities of the ego. Its consequence is the pathogenic disturbance of thought.

Quantity and quality in the 'Project'   The problem of the affect is so closely bound up with the relations between quantity (quota of affect) and quality (the subjective aspect) that this point should be considered before we leave the 'Project'.

This essay is dominated by an attempt to resolve this opposition, by, as far as possible, bringing the problems of quality back to the vicissitudes of quantity.[28] The avowed aim of the 'Project' is to consider psychical processes as quantitatively determined states of material particles. The consideration of quality is subordinate to this. But what is this mysterious Q?[29] Q exists in two forms. First, it exists in a dynamic state, a flux or current passing from one neurone to another *between* cathexes. Q, therefore, is what distinguishes the activity of repose and is subjected to the general laws of movement. Second, there is a static state, when it loads the neurones with part of itself: this is cathexis.[30] As for the nature of Q, this is not made clear and remains enigmatic, for nowhere does Freud say that it is a psychical energy. It seems more likely that it is an undifferentiated energy cathecting several systems, including the ψ system.

The properties of Q derive from the hypothesis posed by Freud in 1894 in an article, 'The neuro-psychoses of defence'.[31] Faced with quantity, Freud discusses the problem of quality with much less ease.

While writing the 'Project', Freud considered, in addition to the φ system (exogenous and physical quantities) and the ψ system (internal, psychical quantities), a third ω system specifically dealing with quality. It is linked to perception – the ω neurones are excited during perception; the discharge of this excitation gives quality to consciousness. But quality appears only where the Qs have been previously reduced.[32] What we are witnessing here is the transformation of an external quantity into quality (φ into ω). The receptivity acquired by such a system requires complete permeability and an absence of orientation or modification by excitation. The conscious state represents the subjective side of the psychical processes. The clearest proof of the attempt to

28 This position will be maintained later. In 'Instincts and their vicissitudes', one finds the idea that there are qualitative differences between the various drives: 'We are much more likely to find the simpler assumption sufficient – that the instincts are all qualitatively alike and owe the effect to the amount of excitation they carry, or perhaps, in addition, to certain functions of that quantity' (*S.E.*, XIV, p. 123).

29 On this question see Strachey's Appendix C to the 'Project', *S.E.*, I, to which I am indebted in the writing of this passage.

30 It is clear that the different states of Q already suggest later formulations concerning free energy and bound energy, the primary and secondary processes, and that it is closely related to the future economic point of view.

31 *S.E.*, III, p. 60.

32 What we have is a precursor of the protective shield.

reduce quality to quantity may be seen in Freud's affirmation that the tendency to avoid unpleasure tends to be confused with the primary tendency to inertia, which, for him, implies a communication between ω and φ.[33]

The indices of quality only survive in perceptions. What is at stake, then, is to obtain a perception of the passage of $Q\eta$.[34]

> If a discharge were linked to the passage of $Q\eta$ (in addition to the [mere] circulation), then, like every movement, it [the discharge] would furnish information of the movement. After all, indications of quality themselves are only information of discharge (of what kind [we may learn] later perhaps).[35]

This remark about affect is an important one, though I do not intend to expand upon it here. For Freud will insist a great deal, in the definitions that he will later provide, on the sense that a modification gives the impression of an internal movement. This awareness of a movement directed towards the body, which entails a discharge, is accompanied by the specific quality of the affect.[36] Attention is directed, therefore, not solely to the indices of quality belonging to the external properties of the object, but to the perception of the internal process of the passage of a $Q\eta$.

In all this, he does not refer to the ω system. It is impossible to say, therefore, whether it provides this perception of the movement that translates the passage of the Q at the time of the discharge that it brings. But what is certain is that Freud later reduces its role considerably.

As soon as the 'Project' was finished and sent to Fliess, Freud wrote a rectification to his friend that is really a complete reinterpretation of the text. In it he explains that the Ω system, far from transmitting the quality of the perceptions issuing from ψ, conveys neither quantity nor quality, but merely

---

33 It should be remembered that ψ receives both the transformed cathexes of φ and the cathexes of the ways of 'endogenous conduction': perception and representation.

34 In the 'Project', the question of quality is much more confused than that of quantity, which is no small matter. In fact, one must distinguish between: quality linked to external perception; quality linked to representation: hallucinatory cathexis of the object; quality linked to affect; and quality linked to processes, see later. One should also distinguish between *indices of quality* and *awareness* of quality. The first are deceptive factors in that they may lead to a confusion between objects of satisfaction and those similar to them.

35 *S.E.*, I, p. 364.

36 One may remember that in the experience of satisfaction occurs an innervation of the motor image of the movements executed by the body, which assist the awareness of the body. 'The perception may correspond to an object–nucleus + a motor image. While one is perceiving the perception, one copies the movement oneself – that is, one innervates so strongly the motor image of one's own which is aroused towards coinciding [with the perception], that the movement is carried out' (*S.E.*, I, p. 333).

excites; that is to say, shows the way to be followed. This has an important result: since ω does not transmit quality to ψ, the unconscious processes will remain unconscious. They acquire only a 'secondary, artificial consciousness through being linked with processes of discharge and perception (speech-association)'.[37] Thus Freud is trying to free the qualitative aspect of psychical phenomena. Two reasons may be given for this insistence, this obstinacy perhaps. The first is to link his scientific ambition to describe psychical processes with the objectivity of the natural sciences and therefore to reduce the subjective to the strict minimum. The second is to separate psychical activity and conscious activity, the latter necessarily involving the intervention of subjective quality.

It was not until 1924 ('The economic problem of masochism') that Freud questioned the quantitative–qualitative relation of the pleasure–unpleasure principle. Until then, unpleasure was related to tension (that is to say, the increase of a psychical quantity of internal excitation) and pleasure with relaxation. Freud is now forced to admit the relative independence of quantity and quality.

However, distinguishing between the roles of quality and quantity leaves in suspense certain enigmas, such as the phenomenon of the inversion of quality (the transformation of pleasure into unpleasure by repression). And one cannot deny the economic factor in evaluating the return of the repressed, compromise formations, symptoms, etc.

In short, although one cannot properly reduce quality to quantity, one cannot claim their total independence from one another either.

Let us note, however, that quality is almost always linked, for Freud, to a process of discharge through hyper-cathexis or by reaching a threshold that is beyond challenge.

Thus the processes of thought acquired the quality of consciousness through the speech-associations that give it concrete expression and abstract relations through language. Language transforms the processes of thought into perceptions. As for the affect, the consciousness that is attached to it is contemporary with the discharge that it brings to the body. Short of that threshold, the affect may pass unperceived by consciousness.

So we are now at the two extremes of the psychical apparatus in the unconsciousness of thought and the unconsciousness of the body; in the gap between the two, word-presentation and the affect present to consciousness what takes place outside its field; in that gap, as at the heart of the unconscious, is a complex formed by thing-presentation and its quota of affect.

---

37 Letter no. 39, *S.E.*, I, p. 389.

4 *The Interpretation of Dreams* (1899–1900)

It is acknowledged that *The Interpretation of Dreams* is the work in which Freud reveals most clearly the 'epistemological break'[38] in his thinking in relation to his earlier loyalties. He had gone beyond the clinical gropings of his early treatment of the neuropsychoses; he had put an end to the theoretical compromises imposed by his collaboration with Breuer; he was cured of his fascination for Charcot; he had turned his back on his past as a biologist of the school of Brücke, of which the 'Project', addressed to that other biologist, Fliess, is the testament. Freud could now simply be Freud. *The Interpretation of Dreams* sums up and goes beyond the earlier essays and presents itself as the fruit of a coherent, completed theory. I shall now situate the place of the affect in this monumental work.

But there is another interest in comparing affects with dreams: it enables us to see the treatment to which the dream was subjected on that other stage of the unconscious.

A – Affect and representative content in dreams and the neuropsychoses
Freud's statements regarding the unconscious (especially those early ones) have contributed enormously to the defence of structural theory, in the French sense of the term. This theory, based on work concerning the representations, derives from the analysis of the great axes of language. In these theorizations, no mention is made of affects in dreams, which is nevertheless the title of a sub-chapter in the chapter on the dream-work. And yet Freud writes there: 'Dreams insist with greater energy upon their right to be included among our real mental experiences more in respect to their affective than in respect to their ideational content'.[39] On waking, it is impossible to reject the affect of dreams as absurd, as one might be tempted to do with their contents. Dreams allow us to make a strange discrepancy between the representative content and the affective state that would correspond to it in a waking state. An examination of the relations between manifest content and latent content forces us to acknowledge that the affect is right: 'Analysis shows us that the ideational material has undergone displacements and substitutions, whereas the affects have remained unaltered.'[40]

In dreams, as in the neuropsychoses, the representative contents are subject to disguises and distortions. The censorship that is exerted on them comes up against the affects, which are now 'the constituent which is least

---

38 On this matter, see my article 'De l'esquisse à l'Interprétation des rêves: coupure et clôture', *Nouvelle Revue de Psychanalyse*. Paris: Gallimard, 1972, no. 5, pp. 155–80.
39 *S.E.*, V, p. 460.
40 Ibid.

influenced and which alone can give us a pointer as to how we should fill in the missing thoughts'. But although, as we can see, they share certain similarities, they have a few differences from the point of view of the affect. In the neuropsychoses, the 'affects are always appropriate'[41] in the discrepancy that unites them to a content. Unlike the contents, the affect does not mislead. But, unlike in dreams, it may be that, while preserving its quality, the affect may be intensified by 'displacements of neurotic attention'. In dreams, on the other hand, the preservation of quality is accompanied by a diminution, an affective inhibition. This is what the various transformations in the dream show.

B – Dreams under the domination of affects
Before coming to the transformations of affects in dreams, we must consider the cases in which the dreamer is in the grip of an affective state that determines a dream. This affective state may have two origins, psychological or physical. In the first case, it finds its root in the thoughts of the day before, in the second, in a somatic state. In the first case, the representative content of these thoughts will induce the affective state; in the second, the representative content will be induced by the affective state, itself linked to the physical state. Again what we find here is that middle position of the affective state: it is the active product of the psychological cause and the passive reflection of the physical cause. But on the stage of dreams, that double origin loses all specificity and is subordinated to wish-fulfilment. Dreams can borrow their instinctual force only from wishes. Even if the affects are painful, they arouse vigorous wishes that clamour to be fulfilled in dreams.[42]

These considerations bring us to the problem of the nightmare, the affective dream par excellence, the dream laden with anxiety, which overwhelms the problem of dreams,[43] but touches on the psychology of the neuroses. The primacy of wish-fulfilment (and the wish may be a desire for punishment) dominates dreams. In any case, what we are dealing with here are not affects in their crude state, but affects bound up with representative contents with a view to wish-fulfilment and subjected to the dream-work.

---

41 *S.E.*, V, p. 461.
42 This observation hardly conforms with the role of censorship in dreams, which ought rather, faced with such affects, to act in a stronger way on this fulfilment, at least in terms of the disguises that it would impose upon it.
43 Today one tends to make a radical distinction between the dream and the nightmare, which metapsychology and neurophysiology suggest should be seen as a failure of the dream function.

C – *Transformations of affects in dreams*

(a) *Disappearance of affects in dreams*   A representative content may be totally deprived of the affect that corresponds to it in a waking state. An anxious representation is accompanied by indifference.

(b) *The transference of the affect far from its representative to another part of the dream.*

(c) *Impoverishment of the affect of the dream-thoughts in the dream*   When an affect is present in the dream, it is to be found in the dream-thoughts; but the reverse is not true. The dream carries out, therefore, a *reductive* work on the affect. This is the typical case of the *repression of affects* in dreams, which I shall examine later. A comparison might be suggested between this reduction of the affects and the condensation of the dream-thoughts of which a dream is the result. Freud also calls it compression.

(d) *Transformation of an affect into its opposite*   This is a result of the censorship, as if the previous mechanism were insufficient. Forbidden feelings are replaced by their opposite (hostility/friendship). Wish-fulfilment dreams are transformed into punishment (hypocritical) dreams. Freud shows that this transformation cannot but operate in the dream itself, but is to be found ready-made in the thoughts of the day before.

(e) *Strengthening of the affect of the dream in relation to the affect of the dream-thoughts, permitted affects making up for the expression of forbidden affects*   When an affect in the dream seems to correspond to the affect of the dream-thoughts, we should not take it to be simply its expression in the dream. In this case, competition is offered to the dream affect by non-forbidden affects that mask forbidden affects, often in relation to forbidden contents.

This group of transformations – suppression, displacement, subtraction (impoverishment), reversal and strengthening by another affective source – is worth commenting on. There seems to be a contradiction between the hypothesis of the unchanged state of the affect and these transformations. In fact, the affect, says Freud, is unchanged as to its quality, but diminished, inhibited. This statement is valid for certain of the transformations, such as suppression and subtraction, which seem to be the direct consequences of a quantitative reduction. But how is it to be applied to the strengthening of the affect by a second source of the same kind or, again, displacement and transformation into its opposite, which are mechanisms to be seen acting on the representative contents and which have no less an ability to disguise themselves? Strictly speaking, Freud's hypothesis does not stand up to examination. But what we must keep in mind is the aim of all these mechanisms. Although some procedures are used that go beyond mere reduction, reduction itself is not enough. Reducing hostile feelings provides insufficient protection: one may watch what one says, but a gesture or an attitude may betray the concealed feeling; one must therefore shift the affect on to another representative or, better still, imitate its opposite. In any case, the aim is to obtain the *repression of the affect*, which is also what the censorship in the dream is aiming at.

What Freud means is that, despite the presence of mechanisms that act similarly on the representative contents and on the affect, the affects, unlike the representative contents, cannot break up into a small number of elements and form new totalities, entirely distorted in relation to the sequence of dream-thoughts, assembled in an incomprehensible and at first sight unintelligible group. The affect resists such a fragmentation, which is why, generally speaking, it is the element that must not be lost sight of in the analysis of dreams. In order to interpret a dream, we must restore its original strength and restore it to its exact place. This is a conjectural operation, but scarcely more so than the reconstitution of the associative puzzle. The affect is the surest guide. Thus the censorship has two effects: distortion of representative contents and inhibition of affects. *Repression of contents* and *repression of affects* will provide an instructive contrast.

D – *Theory of the repression of affects*

Repression would seem, therefore, to be the special destiny of the affect in the unconscious. Freud defends the idea that the triggering off of the affect is a process directed towards the inside of the body. As such, it is to the body what motor discharges are to the outside world. Since these motor discharges have been suppressed in the course of sleep, a similar paralysis would appear to affect discharges towards the inside of the body, and the affective impulses that would be produced in the course of the dream would themselves be weak.

According to this initial idea, the suppression of affects would seem to be the result, not of the dream-work, but of sleep. But, as always with Freud, this physical hypothesis is corrected because it is too simple. At the strictly psychical level, any dream is a compromise between opposed psychical forces (wish and censorship). Besides, in the unconscious, any thought is bound up with its opposite, since the unconscious knows no contradiction. The suppression of the affects becomes a consequence of the inhibition exerted by opposites upon one another and of the action of the censorship on the impulses. 'The inhibition of affect, accordingly, must be considered as the second consequence of the censorship of dreams, just as dream-distortion is its first consequence'.[44]

It might be thought, then, that an absolute opposition should be made between repression and suppression. Some of Freud's interpreters

44 *S.E.*, V, p. 468.

recommend that this should be so.[45] However, an examination of the texts does not support such a conclusion, since Freud's statements on the subject are insufficiently precise.

Pursuing his theoretical outline of affect, which appears in the chapter on 'The dream-work', Chapter VII, 'The psychology of the dream-processes', formulates it in metapsychological terms. The aim of suppression is to prevent the development of the affective states that originally provoked pleasure, but, as a result of repression, release unpleasure. 'The purpose, and the result too, of suppression is to prevent this release of unpleasure'.[46] Thus the affect is suppressed through its content. This statement may also be compared with another, a little later on: 'The fulfilment of these wishes would no longer generate an affect of pleasure but of unpleasure; and it is precisely this transformation of affect which constitutes the essence of what we term "repression" [i.e. suppression]'.[47]

Thus it is not possible to set suppression and repression in an absolute opposition. In any case, it is through the preconscious that this inhibiting suppression occurs. This inhibiting suppression prevents the representative content of the unconscious from sending impulses that trigger off the secretory motor effect that is accompanied by the production of the affect. However, the reduction of the preconscious (Pcs.) cathexis allows the freed unconscious excitations to trigger off those affects – which is what happens in dreams and accounts for anxiety dreams. It is this, therefore, that motivates the direct suppression of the affects in dreams, since the reduction of the effects of the Pcs. weakens their indirect suppression (through the representative content).

As has been shown, it was difficult to apply repression exclusively to content, since suppression would concern only the affect. Indeed Freud explains this in a note to Chapter VII: 'For instance, I have omitted to state whether I attribute different meanings to the words "suppressed" [*unterdrückt*] and "repressed" [*verdrängt*]. It should have been clear, however, that the latter lays more stress than the former upon the fact of attachment to the unconscious'.[48]

In no way, therefore, can a difference of nature be drawn between the mechanisms, only a difference of degree. All the earlier discussion on the subject is found here. Dream-work mechanisms bearing on the representative contents of repressed wishes may be put to work in the affects of dreams, in order to facilitate their suppression. Suppression cannot be seen as a solely quantitative process, since it has to have recourse to distortions

---

45 See Laplanche and Pontalis (1973), 'Repression'.
46 *S.E.*, V, p. 582.
47 *S.E.*, V, p. 604 (Freud's italics).
48 *S.E.*, V, p. 606.

and disguises in order to achieve affective reduction. Suppression may bear on representative contents (preconscious ones, it is true), but the essence of repression is a *transformation* of affects.

It is as if one had wanted to push some of Freud's hypotheses too far, further than Freud himself did. The idea of the *relative independence* of representative and affect has encouraged the notion of *absolute opposition*, intended to link, in a single strictly structural concept, on the one hand, representative content and unconscious repression, and on the other, affect, suppression, conscious and preconscious. Now although Freud maintains a distinction of destiny (in the neuropsychoses) between representative and affect, the opposition was never as clear as this. This brings us to a discussion that is not yet over and which will continue with an examination of the *Papers on Metapsychology*.

II The stage of the 'Papers on Metapsychology'

1 Between *The Interpretation of Dreams* and the *Papers on Metapsychology* (1900–1915)

Between 1900 and 1915, the question of affect remained in suspense in Freud's work, since he added only points of detail in the various writings of the period. In *Three Essays on the Theory of Sexuality* (1905), Freud makes little reference to it. However, he does stress its role in activating sexuality. All the affective processes, 'including even terrifying ones', have a bearing on sexuality.[49] And the reverse is also true: affect and sexuality summon up and reinforce one another.

Finally, there is a reference to all those negative affects that form psychical dikes against sexuality, such as disgust, which Freud always comes back to as an example of the reversal of the affect into its opposite.[50]

In his analysis of 'Dora' in 1901, he links disgust to sexual excitation, the reversal of the affect occurring between the two: 'The elucidation of the mechanism of this *reversal of affect* is one of the most important and at the same time one of the most difficult problems in the psychology of the neuroses'.[51]

Furthermore, this idea of a reversal may be compared with another feature of the instinctual life: contrasted pairs. Indeed it is in the analyses of 'Little Hans' and the 'Rat Man' that we see the development of an idea that

---

49   *S.E.*, VII, p. 123.
50   *S.E.*, I, p. 271, n. 1.
51   *S.E.*, VII, p. 28.

was to be fully exploited only in the *Papers on Metapsychology*. 'The emotional life of man is in general made up of contraries such as these. Indeed, if it were not so, repressions and neuroses would perhaps never come about'.[52] Thus the mechanism of repression that proceeds to the reversal of the affect presupposes the existence of the double structure of the affect. There would be reversal into its opposite only because the contrasted pair is there at the outset. Of course, it is a question here more of the relations between love and hate or of the sadism–masochism, voyeurism–exhibitionism oppositions. But repression has to depend on one component of a pair in order to repress the other; qualitative transformation is linked to an original qualitative duality, which Freud was to associate with ambivalence.

This ambivalence is revealed in all its breadth in 'The Rat Man', where, Freud notes, his patient's 'opposed feelings may subsist side by side'.[53] This conflictual structure in obsessional neurosis is the object of a precocious separation of opposites and the cancelling out of one by the other.[54] The neurosis shows us, too, the other great mechanism of the affect, the separation of the representative and the affect, and the replacement of a significant representative, congruent with the affect, by an insignificant one. At first sight, it is the affect that seems disproportionate, but Freud reminds us again: it is the affect that is justified and orders the search for an adequate representative. The role of the affect in obsessional neurosis is extremely wide, since the affect recathects the thought that had freed itself from it. The attempt of the cognitive ego and thought to master the affect brings with it secondarily, in obsessional neurosis, a return of the affect. The affect then bears down on the activity of control that has controlled it. The same thing occurs with paranoia, where one observes a return of sexuality on the social bonds through the secondary sexuality of those bonds, after they have been desexualized.

To sum up, it may be said that during this period Freud rediscovers the two great mechanisms that he had observed in the neuropsychoses and in dreams: displacement and reversal into its opposite. The principal novelty introduced is the notion of contrasted pairs and its corollary, ambivalence.

---

52 *S.E.*, X, p. 113.

53 *S.E.*, X, p. 239.

54 The ambivalence is also stressed in the last two of *Five Lectures on Psycho-Analysis*. Freud recalls Schreber's relationship with his God, showing 'the strangest mixture of blasphemous criticism and mutinous insubordination on the one hand and of reverent devotion on the other' (*S.E.*, XII, p. 51). Lastly, the Wolf Man is at the mercy of the same duplicity: the 'pious ceremonial' at bedtime, in which holy pictures are kissed was 'utterly inconsistent, or, on the other hand, quite consistent' with the 'blasphemous thoughts' that accompanied them and which he attributed to the inspiration of the devil (*S.E.*, XVII, pp. 16–17).

Ambivalence may help to throw light on reversal into its opposite. Thus the notion of a reaffectivation of disaffected processes shows the importance of the return of the affect, which concerns not only the material related to the return of the repressed, but also the most complicated psychical processes (cognitive thought, social relations).

2 *Papers on Metapsychology* (1915)

The *Papers on Metapsychology*, especially the articles on 'Repression' and 'The unconscious', is the major source of any discussion of the affect. But it is not the only one and it would be a great mistake to confine the discussion to what is contained in that work, ignoring what preceded it and, more importantly, what followed it.

A – Repression

Affect appears in the *Papers on Metapsychology* only in an article on 'Repression', and not at all in the article 'Instincts and their vicissitudes', any more indeed than does the term representative. It is as if Freud had let it be understood that, before the effect of repression, affect as such could not be individualized at the level of instinctual functioning, where representative and affect are confused. And yet the effect of repression, its essence, says Freud, is certainly a transformation of affect (pleasure into unpleasure) and the effect of the instinct is certainly that of a production of affect. All that can be said is that repression throws particular light on the split between representation and affect, and makes it possible to consider the latter on its own.

Primal repression has a bearing on the psychical representative of the drive, which is 'denied entrance into the unconscious'. This refusal then has a bearing on the affect of unpleasure that would follow. One may conclude from this that repression operates an indirect affective inhibition through the representative.[55] Hence what might be called the paradox of repression. Repression strives to prevent the appearance of unpleasure, but unpleasure is itself the effect of the repression that transformed pleasure into unpleasure. Similarly, the temporary suspension of repression allows the appearance of pleasure, where otherwise there would have been only unpleasure (the witticism).

There is more to the operation as a whole than the repression of the representative. Variations in the quantity of energic cathexis play a crucial role on the repressed offshoots, on their maintenance in a repressed state and on the tolerance shown them by consciousness, to the point of being accepted within it.

---

55 S.E., XIV, p. 148. This is reminiscent of the thesis of the repression of the affects in *The Interpretation of Dreams*.

It is an everyday occurrence that such a derivative remains unrepressed so long as it represents only a small amount of energy, although its content would be calculated to give rise to conflict with what is dominant in consciousness. The quantitative factor proves decisive for this conflict: as soon as the basically obnoxious idea exceeds a certain degree of strength, the conflict becomes a real one, and it is precisely this activation that leads to repression.

What we have, then, is a second mechanism, one of an economic nature; it complements the first, which, it might be said, is of a semantic nature. The two support one another and are equivalent: approach to the unconscious (to its active kernel) and increase of energic cathexis have the same result, just as remoteness from the unconscious or distortion accompany decrease of cathexis. This forces Freud to draw a distinction here.

In our discussion so far we have dealt with the repression of an instinctual representative, and by the latter we have understood an idea or group of ideas which is cathected with a definite quota of psychical energy (libido or interest) coming from an instinct. Clinical observation now obliges us to divide up what we have hitherto regarded as a single entity; for it shows us that besides the idea, some other element representing the instinct has to be taken into account, and that this other element undergoes vicissitudes of repression which may be quite different from those undergone by the idea. For this other element of the psychical representative the term *quota of affect* has been generally adopted. It corresponds to the instinct in so far as the latter has become detached from the idea and finds expression, proportionate to its quantity, in processes which are sensed as affects.[56]

This important quotation is worthy of greater consideration. When Freud declares that he must now break down what he had hitherto regarded as a single entity under the term instinctual representative (which includes the cathected representation or group of representations of a particular quota of psychical energy), one must reinterpret the whole of the earlier text. In my opinion, this modification must go back to the conception of primal repression. One cannot, it seems to me, declare that it is only the psychical representative (ideational representative) of the instinct that is prevented from taking charge in the consciousness, *but the psychical representative, with its particular quota of psychical energy*. This quota is not – it should be said – a negligible quantity, compared with the noble raw material of representation.

56 *S.E.*, XIV, p. 152.

Freud says that it is 'something else which *represents* the instinct', existing therefore at an equally noble level. And although Freud specifies that it is this other element of the psychical representative of the instinct, this is because the psychical representative is then broken up into ideational representative and affect, which ought logically to be called the representative–affect.

The difference in vicissitude between representation and affect shows us that the representative moves away or disappears from consciousness, whereas the vicissitude of the affect is threefold:

1 repression of the drive (and not only of the affect), of which there remains no trace;
2 expression of a qualitatively defined affect;
3 *transposition* of the psychical energies of the *drives* into *affects* and, particularly, into *anxiety*.

It has been concluded from this text that there is a specificity in the action of repression on the representations, the affect being regarded as the object of suppression. A very different picture emerges from what follows:

> The motive and purpose of repression was nothing else than the avoidance of unpleasure. It follows that the vicissitude of the quota of affect belonging to the representative is far more important than the vicissitude of the idea, and this fact is decisive for our assessment of the process of repression. If a repression does not succeed in preventing feelings of unpleasure or anxiety from arising, we may say that it has failed, even though it may have achieved its purpose as far as the ideational portion is concerned.[57]

This shows that not only must that 'other thing' that accompanies representation be considered, but that the success of the operation depends on its vicissitude. For the aim of repression is precisely this total inhibition of the affect of unpleasure. It is as if, as in dreams, beside the indirect pathway of affective inhibition representatives capable of arousing the undesirable affect, another direct pathway were opened up by the action of the repression (whether or not one calls it suppression hardly matters) on the affect. Of course, the question requires a complementary examination of the relations between repressed and unconscious and, consequently, between unconscious and affect. But, as for the action of repression on the affect, an examination of what precedes shows clearly enough that one would

---

57 *S.E.*, XIV, p. 153.

underestimate its importance if one were to make suppression a minor substitute of repression.

B − *The unconscious*

After posing the problem of the multiple meanings of the term unconscious and bringing out the one that best suits the topographical point of view, that is to say, the unconscious as a system,[58] Freud returns to the problem of the affect in the chapter 'Unconscious emotions'. Here we must read Freud with particular attention if we are to follow him in all the nuances of his thinking: 'Are there also unconscious instinctual impulses, emotions and feelings, or is it in this instance meaningless to form combinations of the kind?'[59]

An initial question has to be asked here: why ask such a question? Against the objections of psychologists and philosophers, Freud has just defended at length the legitimacy of the unconscious and dissolved the traditional identification of the psychical with the conscious. He has affirmed the existence of unconscious thoughts, unconscious psychical processes and even an unconscious system, arguing against those who deny it. Is he capable of carrying out a *reductio ad absurdum* of the hypothesis of unconscious affects? Perhaps one must give in to him on this point.

In fact, the question asked entails an amalgam of what could not be unconscious (any more than conscious) and the problematic. Indeed, the conscious–unconscious opposition does not apply to the instinct, a 'crossroads' concept between the somatic and the psychical: 'An instinct can never become an object of consciousness − only the idea that represents the instinct can. Even in the unconscious, moreover, an instinct cannot be represented otherwise than by an idea.'

It is here, usually, that we come to the end of the quotations that claim that the unconscious is above all the place of representations of the instinct. Yet this is very surprising: did not Freud stress sufficiently in the preceding chapter the role of the quantitative factor of affect? Is not affect the privileged mode of representation for the instinct? What follows shows us that this is a carelessness on Freud's part: 'If the instinct did not attach itself to an idea [a representation] or manifest itself as an affective state, we could know nothing about it'.[60]

---

58 In my opinion, this does not justify an interpretation of the unconscious in a strictly structural sense. The whole of Chapter 4, 'Topography and dynamics of repression' never ceases to consider the vicissitudes of energy cathexis. The chapter title becomes paradoxical as a result, since it is precisely at this point that Freud introduces the economic point of view and replaces the topographical hypothesis by the functional (economic) hypothesis.

59 *S.E.*, XIV, p. 177.

60 Ibid.

Thus the instinctual impulse, the instinct, cannot become directly the object of consciousness: representation and affect are necessary mediators that make the instinct conscious. This remark concerning the affect justifies the distinction drawn between it and the instinctual impulse, in view of the possibility of its being unconscious. At first sight, this seems impossible: it is of the essence of a feeling to be perceived, therefore to be known to the consciousness. And yet such expressions as unconscious love, hate, anger, even such a curious expression as 'unconscious consciousness of guilt', spring readily to the psychoanalyst's pen.

Freud then goes on to consider cases in which the affect is not recognized. This occurs when it is detached from the representative that has been linked to it and another representative put in its place. It is the case most frequently encountered in obsessional neurosis. In fact, when one speaks of unconscious affects or feelings, one thinks above all of the vicissitude of the quantitative factor of the instinctual impulse. And Freud reminds us here of the three vicissitudes of this factor (the affect remains, transformation into anxiety, suppression). The case of suppression compels us to return to the matter again. I repeat: the relations between repression and suppression are ambiguous. Freud declares at the beginning of the article that the essence of repression is not to annihilate a representation that represents the instinct, but to prevent it from becoming conscious. Freud now declares: 'We know, too, that to suppress the development of affect is the true aim of repression and that its work is incomplete if this aim is not achieved'.[61]

Thus repression spares the existence of the representation, providing it remains unconscious (absent, latent, made unrecognizable by distortions and associations, etc.); on the other hand, it aims at suppressing the quantitative factor, the energic cathexis that must, as far as possible, be annihilated. In the economic sense, it is the affect that must be made unconscious; in the topographical, systematic sense, it is representation that must be. The means by which repression operates on the affect is suppression, although repression increases the unconscious character (in the topographical sense). Thus suppression appears as one of the methods at the disposal of repression to maintain what must be distanced from consciousness. The suppressed affect is made unconscious; suppression is *the specific aim* of repression: 'In every instance where repression has succeeded in inhibiting the development of affects, we term those affects (which we restore when we undo the work of repression) "unconscious" '.[62]

The difference of treatment that I indicated between representation and

61 *S.E.*, XIV, p. 178.
62 Ibid.

affect is extended by their different state in the unconscious (Ucs.): the representation remains as a complete formation in the Ucs., whereas the suppressed affect survives only as a basic element, with no possibility of development. Strictly speaking, 'there are no unconscious affects as there are unconscious ideas'.[63] This does not mean that there are no unconscious affects, *but that the unconscious does not appear in the same way for affect and representation* – though Freud does admit that there may exist formations of affects in the Ucs. Is this a difference of nature or degree? It depends how one looks at it. If one wishes to stress the possibility of a structuring, which is considerable for the representation, limited for the affect, one speaks of a difference of nature. If one is concerned with the aim of the unconscious, one sees only a difference of degree between the rudimentary character of the affect in the unconscious and the repressed representations that fail to be recognized. We are brought back here to the problems of *The Interpretation of Dreams*. Freud goes on to give the reason for all these differences:

> The whole difference arises from the fact that ideas are cathexes – basically of memory-traces – whilst affects and emotions correspond to processes of discharge, the final manifestations of which are perceived as feelings. In the present state of our knowledge of affects and emotions we cannot express this difference more clearly.[64]

Thus representations and affect are linked to different systems: the representations to the memory system (the trace) – retention, modification of the cathexis, concatenation, absence, virtuality, etc. – the affect to the system of quality – discharge, exhaustion in non-preservation, resistance to distortion and association, the refusal or inability to be connected, presence, manifestation, etc. But the opposition cannot be pushed too far or too absolutely: for does not the cathexis of the trace involve a discharge (not only in the 'Project', but also in *The Interpretation of Dreams*) and is not the affect given by Freud (before and after the *Papers on Metapsychology*) as the product of a certain physical memory? The truth is, the problem remains almost in its entirety, insofar as any quantitative factor is concerned: in the affect, the quantitative factor is uncontrollable, demanding discharge, recalcitrant and resistant to treatment, whereas in the memory trace it is reducible, manipulable, capable of making links and combining with other factors. Once more we find the opposition between a process that brings into play a combinatory and a force that resists it and finds expression by discharge into the immediate environment, when it is not being stifled by suppression.

63 Ibid.
64 Ibid.

It seems to me, however, that Freud is fully justified in postulating that when the affect is maintained in the unconscious it is reduced to the state of a rudiment. When the 'Rat Man' leapt up, in Freud's consulting room, at the mention of torturing rats, Freud could see, depicted on his patient's face, the horror of a pleasure 'unknown to him'. Can it really be said that the affect in the unconscious existed as a mere rudiment, when we see it develop with such force? Did not the 'Rat Man' feel this pleasure consciously, while trying to remain ignorant of it? Would any intervention by Freud in such pleasure have had any other effect than furious denial? It seems curious to me that Freud did not consider here the problem, perhaps the most obscure but also the most revealing one, of the relations between affect and unconscious: the transformation of the affect into its opposite. Of course, with the transformation into anxiety, he implicitly refers to it. But Freud says nothing about it. For one cannot explain this transformation simply by a substitution of representation; one must take into account that the affect's change of sign is the condition for the maintenance of the affect in an unconscious state.

If repression has succeeded in inhibiting the transposition of the instinctual impulse into affect, it follows that its action is exerted on admission to consciousness, the development of the affect and access to movement. As far as the last two activities are concerned, it may be said that repression is opposed to the development of movement, as much towards the outside world as towards the body.[65] As I have pointed out, the affect is opposed to the system of representation and of memory (memory traces). I would now add that it is also opposed to the system of the act. But whereas control of the conscious (Cs.) over movement is firmly established, its control over affectivity is much more vulnerable. *Cs. and Ucs. dispute the primacy of affectivity.* The admission of the affect to consciousness must usually be subordinate to its link to a representative that takes the place of the representative to which it was originally assigned. But a direct transmission is possible when the affect is transformed into anxiety. We shall return later to the case of anxiety. I would just observe that Freud is compelled to accept an extreme case: that of a quota of affective energy erupting from the unconscious into the consciousness. In this case the original affect, the one that gave rise to the transformation into anxiety, was certainly unconscious.

---

65 On this matter, let us remember Freud's definition of affectivity: 'Affectivity manifests itself essentially in that motor (secretory and vaso-motor) discharge resulting in an [internal] alteration of the subject's own body, without reference to the external world; motility, in actions designed to reflect changes in the external world' (*S.E.*, XIV, p. 179, n. 1).

Here the chapter on 'Unconscious emotions' comes to an end. But Freud has not finished with the problem, either in this text or elsewhere. During the next few chapters the closeness of the links between representations and affect is stressed. The representation is largely dependent on quantitative variations of cathexis in the formation of the symptom: withdrawal of pre-conscious cathexis, preservation of unconscious cathexis or substitution of an unconscious cathexis for a preconscious one, transformation of affect into anxiety by separation from preconscious cathexis and direct expression of the unconscious, the role of counter-cathexis in the substitute formation, variations of instinctual excitation from within by strengthening movement, etc. Similarly, the definition of the particular properties of the *Ucs.* system confirms this indissoluble unity: 'The nucleus of the *Ucs.* consists of instinctual representatives which seek to discharge their cathexis; that is to say, it consists of wishful impulses'.[66]

III *From* The Ego and the Id *to the end of Freud's work*

1 *The Ego and the Id* (1923)

The problems left in suspense in 1915 are taken up again in 1923 with chapter II of *The Ego and the Id*. Freud's thinking sets off with a statement concerning the existence of an unrepressed unconscious, which cannot be made conscious simply by activating it. But what does 'to make conscious' mean? Consciousness is a property of the psychical apparatus or, to be more precise, of its external surface, which is the first to be influenced by the outside world. From its internal surface, the psychical apparatus also receives internal impressions. Thus the perceptions received from outside (senses) or from the inside (feelings, emotions) are conscious from the outset. Perception (external or internal) and consciousness are linked.

From the 'Project', and from, in any case, *The Interpretation of Dreams*,[67] Freud maintained that the processes of thought are acts of cathexis that operate according to modalities very far removed from the perceptions. They are deprived of consciousness and therefore of quality. The processes of thought are displacements of small quantities of mental energy that are

---

66 *S.E.*, XIV, p. 186.
67 Which does not date, as has been wrongly asserted, from the second topography. As early as the *Papers on Metapsychology*, Freud had an intuition of where it would lead. At the head of the article 'The unconscious', he wrote: 'Everything that it is repressed must remain unconscious; but let us state at the very outset that the repressed does not cover everything that is unconscious', *S.E.*, XIV, p. 166. It is not legitimate, therefore, to date the repressed and the unconscious from the same time, even in 1915.

produced when this mental energy moves towards action. There is a fundamental difference, however, between an unconscious idea and a preconscious one. The Ucs. is based on a raw material that remains unknown to us, whereas the Pcs. is connected to the word-presentations. Now word-presentations derive from sense perception (as do thing-presentations). Word-presentations are memory traces, traces that may become conscious again, for only something that has once been conscious can become conscious again. Language has conferred on the processes of thought consciousness (and particularly consciousness of relationships), quality and at the same time the possibility, by reducing the state of trace, of memory. As a result 'anything arising from within (apart from feelings) that seeks to become conscious must try to transform itself into external perceptions: this becomes possible by means of memory-traces'.[68]

We may now answer the question 'What does it mean to become conscious?' by substituting another: 'What does it mean to become preconscious?' It is to connect thing-presentations with word-presentations, by providing intermediary links between them through the work of analysis. This does not apply to feelings. For what seems to have been solved in the case of external perceptions does not apply to the internal perceptions.

> Internal perceptions yield sensations of processes arising in the most diverse and certainly also in the deepest strata of the mental apparatus. Very little is known about these sensations and feelings; those belonging to the pleasure–unpleasure series may still be regarded as the best examples of them. They are more primordial, more elementary, than perceptions arising externally and they can come about even when consciousness is clouded. I have elsewhere expressed my views about their greater economic significance and the metapsychological reasons for this. These sensations are multilocular, like external perceptions; they may come from different places simultaneously and may thus have different or even opposite qualities.
>
> Sensations of a pleasurable nature have not anything inherently impelling about them, whereas unpleasurable ones have it in the highest degree. The latter impel towards change, towards discharge, and that is why we interpret unpleasure as implying a heightening and pleasure a lowering of energic cathexis. Let us call what becomes conscious as pleasure and unpleasure a quantitative and qualitative 'something'[69] in the course of mental events; the question then is whether this 'something' can

---

68 *S.E.*, XIX, p. 20.
69 *Andere* in the original German, which is not unrelated to 'other'.

become conscious in the place where it is, or whether it must first be transmitted to the system Pcpt.[70]

This mysterious 'something' acts as a repressed impulse, which may exercise a force for propulsion without the ego being in a position to note the compulsion. It becomes conscious only in the case of resistance, followed by a lifting of this resistance. At first sight, then, transmission to the Pcs. system does seem necessary. But

> if the way forward is barred, they do not come into being as sensations, although the 'something' that corresponds to them in the course of excitation is the same as if they did. We then come to speak, in a condensed and not entirely correct manner, of 'unconscious feelings', keeping up an analogy with unconscious ideas which is not altogether justifiable. Actually the difference is that, whereas with Ucs. *ideas* connecting links must be created before they can be brought into the Cs., with *feelings,* which are themselves transmitted directly, this does not occur. In other words: the distinction between Cs. and Pcs. has no meaning where feelings are concerned; the Pcs. here drops out – and feelings are either conscious or unconscious. Even when they are attached to word-presentations, their becoming conscious is not due to that circumstance, but they become so directly.[71]

It follows from these quotations that:

- the inappropriateness of the term unconscious, as far as the affect is concerned, derives from the analogy with unconscious ideas, whose status in the unconscious is not the same, through the connections that they establish with word-presentations;
- one may perfectly well speak of unconscious affects, since they are so by a modality that is proper to them;
- the links between the unconscious and language are valid above all for unconscious ideas, but that the affect seems to short-circuit these relationships;
- the affect mediated by language, when this is the case, entails a relationship with it, which cannot be assimilated to the relationship between the unconscious idea and language, which is the condition of its becoming conscious. The verbalized affect is not linked to language as is the idea. Similarly, the value of the verbalization cannot be identical in both cases.

70 *S.E.,* XIX, pp. 21–3.
71 *S.E.,* XIX, pp. 22–3.

A new problem in the general discussion of the affect must now be confronted: that of the relations between affect and language, which was subjacent to the problematic of the relations between representations and affects.

This development in Freud's thinking seems to be another step forward in the consideration of affect, a development concomitant with the substitution of the second topography for the first and the replacement of the unconscious by the id.[72] There is no reference here to the rudimentary character of affect in the unconscious and Freud's thought seems to be moving in the direction of stressing the non-representative aspect of the unconscious.

Freud's new examination of the question is a considerable advance. The step forward made here is dependent on the abandonment of the unconscious as a system. As long as Freud linked the problem of the affect to the unconscious as a system, he was concerned above all with the question of unconscious ideas (representations, contents). Of course, the old unconscious idea could not be envisaged without its energic connotations, its cathexis tending to discharge. Forced to deprive these ideas of all quality, since they were unconscious, Freud, while abandoning quality, had at the same time to show reticence regarding the existence of unconscious affects.

What is found, in the second chapter of *The Ego and the Id*, is that there are different ways of being unconscious. The dissociation between repressed and unconscious (cases of unconscious resistance) also leads to a distinction, within the repressed part of the unconscious, between the various unconscious states and, consequently, various ways of acceding to consciousness. In fact, the unconscious state and accession to consciousness depend essentially on the unconscious raw material in question. Unconscious representations reach consciousness through their connection with word-presentations. The hyper-cathexis of the memory trace gives back to representation something of the its original perceptual status.

Quite different are the internal perceptions: these, says Freud, are 'more primary, more elementary' than the external perceptions. An acute or lucid consciousness is not necessary for them to be felt. These perceptions are manifested as a conductive force, without the ego being able to note their action. They will reach consciousness by short-circuiting the preconscious. Their link with language, when it exists, is at most contingent.

Thus, to exist in the unconscious state and to become conscious – that is to say, to pass through the perceptual system – are different for content and affect. The first must pass through language, the second may well be able to short-circuit language.

Affect may allow itself to be expressed by language, but it is essentially

72   Although, on the other hand, a fraction of the ego and superego is also unconscious.

outside it. What characterizes it is precisely that direct pathway that links unconscious to conscious. It might well be thought, without distorting the facts, that Freud sees in affects (especially those linked to pleasure– unpleasure states) the most archaic part of man: the one that language may accompany,[73] but which follows its own way independently of it.

This is the moment to point out a possible misunderstanding. Freud is not setting up an opposition between intellect and passions, which would rob his approach of any originality, but showing how affect is not apprehended outside a structure (the two topographies), a conflict (opposition of contrary affects), an economy (quantitative relationships and transformation), how above all the affective states are subjected to a principle: the pleasure–unpleasure principle, linked to the primary processes, just as the reality principle is linked to the secondary processes.

The Ego and the Id approaches the problem of affect in a different way. I should now like to speak of the place occupied by the affect in the Oedipus complex and its dissolution.

The Oedipal stage is marked by a distribution of affects between the persons forming the Oedipal triangle: feelings of tenderness for the parent of the opposite sex to that of the subject and hostility to the parent of the same sex. Freud adds to this division of the positive Oedipus complex that of the negative Oedipus complex, which co-exists with the first and in which the affects are inverted. Thus a network, a structure, is formed, each person being affected by feelings of tenderness and hostility. In each individual, remaining vestiges belonging to one or other of the two ends of the chain remain in the unconscious state, the rest having succumbed to repression. The affective bipolarity never ceases therefore to operate, despite their 'affectation' from one of the two terms that form it to one of the parents. Hence the rule of analysing all the aspects of the Oedipal network, in its positive and negative aspects. The Oedipus complex is presented, therefore, as a structure in which one may locate behind the formations of affects a complete set. Each affect calls up its complement towards the same parental imago as it does towards the other. The young boy's tenderness towards his mother is accompanied by hostility to his father and conjointly arouses hostility to the mother when she shows tenderness for the father. It can easily be understood that the subject is lost in these cross exchanges of affects. There is no solution to the tragedy of the Oedipus complex, outside identification with the parent of the same sex, which entails the abandonment of the affective feelings towards him and their replacement by that other type of link that is identification. The threat of castration (inevitable whatever form the Oedipus complex takes, positive or negative, that the subject has adopted) drives the subject towards the solution dictated by the superego.

73 And no doubt structure to some extent. But to what extent?

49

The transformation of object–libido into narcissistic libido that accompanies identification is also the essential motive force of sublimation. But this triumph of the superego, more apparent than real, demands a very high price: the destruction of the Oedipus complex.

In this case, one can no longer say that the complex is repressed: it is dissolved, destroyed, buried. In other words, what will succumb, often for ever, are the original cathexes of the Oedipus complex. The task of analysis will be to disinter the feelings of tenderness or hostility, but usually the feelings of sexual, passionate love or murderous hate will remain buried forever.[74] It is now easier to understand why Freud insists in his earlier works on the fact that the ultimate aim of repression is affective neutralization. Analytic treatment has little effect when the experience of the transference allows only a theoretical construction of the subject's Oedipus complex, without the analyst being loved or hated with the original affective intensity. The opposite is also true: an exclusively affective transference will forbid any intellectual elaboration, without which there can be no awareness of the situation.

The Oedipus complex, like the transference, can be understood only as the totality of the conjunctive and disjunctive effects of the force and meaning that structure the subject in his relationship to his parents and to their substitutes.

In *The Ego and the Id*, Freud reminds us that the ego was above all the representative of the outside world, of reality, while the superego, on the contrary, was the representative of the internal world of the id. Hence the difficulty of speaking of the relations between affect and the superego, without repeating what has already been said of the relations between affect and the id. Clinical analysis clearly shows how the affects of the superego are like those of the id: the attacks of the superego, assailing the ego by surprise, destroying its defences, imperiously demanding satisfaction by punishment, with the same intensity and the same brutality as the instinctual demands that come from the id. Does not Freud speak sadly of a pure culture of the death instincts in the field of the superego? Moreover, in 'The economic problem of masochism', Freud observes that masochism resexualizes morality, which implies that through moral masochism the links that bind id and superego are rediscovered. To declare that the superego is right and to satisfy it by the same wish is to kill two birds with one stone.

It should not be thought, however, that the action of the superego is only ever felt in disapproval, in punishment. The celebrated 'unconscious feeling of guilt', which Freud preferred to replace by the 'need for punishment', raised all the questions concerning the unconscious affect. Freud goes much further, since the anxiety of the superego is attributed to the superego's loss of love and suicide appears as the desperate act caused by 'the abandonment

---

74 Sometimes one will manage to revive one of the terms of the dyad fully, but never both at once.

of the protective powers of destiny', which we would now call, in more modern language, 'the categorical turning away from God' (Hölderlin).

On what does the 'alliance' between ego and superego rest, that is to say, to what conditions must the ego subscribe in order to benefit from the love of the superego? The demand of the superego is the negation of the demand of the id, that is, renunciation of the demand for instinctual satisfaction. This is the price that has to be paid for the protection demanded.

This satisfaction accorded to the superego leads to a desexualization of the cathexes and to the replacement of the object-cathexes by identifications. The consequence of these transformations is the idealization of the wish-object and the idealization of the subject himself. In this case, one may speak of the transformation of the affects, under the influence of the superego, into object-relations, into narcissistic affects. The triumph of the instincts, the renunciation of sexual pleasure or emancipation from dependence on the object lead to a return of the cathexes on to the ego, which loves itself with all the love that it denies the object and takes pleasure in itself to infinity – megalomania.

This object-disaffection, this narcissistic affectation that I have just described in its most extreme form, in its alienation, exists *in potentia* in every subject.

The renunciation begins very early in the object-relation: renunciation of the aspiration to fusion with the object, in order to save the narcissistic integrity of subject and object outside the fulfilment of their separation; renunciation of the habit of regarding the mother at all times as an extension of the ego, in order to satisfy the pleasure–unpleasure principle; renunciation of complete sexual pleasure by the unimpeded exercise of the erotic and destructive instincts, which solicit the intervention of mechanisms internal to the instinct (aim-inhibition) and external to them (repression), leading to inversion of the affect (pleasure into unpleasure); renunciation of the free disposal of one's own body (the pleasure given by the penis, the sense of the faeces being clean, the total incorporation of the breast must be abandoned); and renunciation of the fulfilment of Oedipal wishes (incest and parricide), etc.

All these renunciations are imposed by external reality and by an internal censorship that has sometimes been seen as an expression of the precursors of the superego. It would seem that one must admit with the notion of a quasi-original conflict that whatever opposes the expression of the affects, when linked with a type of instinct, assumes a prohibiting significance, even though this effect may be due only to an opposition of antagonistic drives. The expulsion of the bad, that idealizing alienation, does not resist experience for long.[75] Henceforth, the outside must be internalized and

---

75 See my article 'Projection', *On Private Madness*, London: Hogarth Press, 1986.

excluded at the same time by the operation of repression. Hatred for the object may seem like a precursor of the superego forbidding its love. Love for the object may appear a first precursor of the superego forbidding hatred. The profound original complicity between id and superego is now clear, since the opposition between antagonistic instincts prefigures later attempts to neutralize the instincts of the id in order to satisfy a special agency, whose every order, by finger, eye or voice, will have to be obeyed if love is to be returned. Confronted by the powerlessness of the ego and the infernal powers of the id, the superego will appear cruel and blood-thirsty, but also sublime and heavenly. Thus the superego is an agency that plays a double game. Its action may as easily satisfy the drives of the id as annihilate them, by taking refuge in idealizing narcissistic omnipotence, having succeeded in a teratological neutralization. We find here once more the effects of a reduction in tension to the zero level, which would be attained not by total discharge, but by total suppression, leading to the carrying out of the tasks deriving from the Nirvana principle.

The general discussion of the relations between affect and unconscious come to an end with *The Ego and the Id*. We should consider, however, a group of works all written after the appearance of the second topography, in which Freud returns to the problem of quality and to the role of splitting in the affect, while dealing with other questions. I do not think that I am distorting Freud's thinking when I declare that, in his last works, the affect takes on a relief that reminds us of its place in his earliest work, eclipsed for a while by the first topography – or at least by an intellectualist interpretation given to it in order to relegate the affect to second-rank status.

2 'The economic problem of masochism' (1924)

A few years after *Beyond the Pleasure Principle*, Freud introduced a decisive reshaping of the theory of affects. At this point, he dissociated the states of pleasure and unpleasure from the economic factors of relaxation and tension, 'although at first sight they have a great deal to do with this factor'.

But, in the end, the old dream of a total reduction of quality to quantity had to be abandoned. The qualitative factor is a mystery: the explanations that Freud proposed, without getting very far with them, are certainly poor: rhythm, temporal sequences of modifications, the rise and fall of stimuli fall far short of restoring the subjective reality of the affects.

Insofar as the Nirvana principle and the pleasure principle must be distinguished, as Freud recommends, it might be thought that it would be the task of the first to reduce the purely quantitative to the zero level, while the task of the second would be the qualitative avoidance of unpleasure and the search for pleasure. Thus the Nirvana principle would be at the service of the death instinct, whereas the pleasure principle would be at the service of the libido. But insofar as Freud maintains that the pleasure principle is the heir of the Nirvana principle, the latter having been subjected to a mutation in living creatures, the pleasure principle must now comprise both the old Nirvana principle and the new pleasure principle. This explains why the pleasure principle is unable to achieve absolute, complete discharge without placing itself entirely at the service of the death instinct, but must be content with the lowest possible level, which, in a sense, is matched by the quality of pleasure. The search for any increase of pleasure is admissible for the psychical apparatus only within certain limits of intensity and time.

The reality principle, whose essential function is detour, difference,[76] will alter the pleasure principle by its capacity to tolerate the greatest tensions without becoming disorganized and authorizing only infinitesimal discharges for the exploration of the outside world and the functioning of thought. It should be noted here that this inhibition on discharge and this energic fragmentation must be freed in a similar way from the principal reference to pleasure and, changing aim, must try to establish the conditions of possibility for objects, independently of their pleasing or displeasing value.

Thus the affect is always in an intermediary position. It is caught between its annihilation (reduction to zero) through discharge and its necessary supersession (inhibition on the discharge, emancipation of the pleasant or unpleasant quality necessary to the functioning of thought). The affect is between the two deaths, before and beyond life, between biological death and psychical death, which is the work of thought. Caught in the pleasure–unpleasure duality, the survival of the affect is always solicited by its opposite and double, threat or hope, depending on the case. So its reality appears very fragile, very evanescent, very threatened. However, the rule under which it is held by these two deaths periodically breaks down. There is then an overwhelming upsurge – and it is usually difficult to determine whether this is caused by the forces of life or by forces of destruction.

3 'Negation' (1925)

The affect is scarcely mentioned in this crucially important article, but an attentive reading reveals that it occupies a more important place in it than might be thought. What negation teaches us in the experience of psychoanalysis is that, thanks to it, the repressed may attain consciousness, or at least

76 Already installed in the gap between Nirvana and pleasure, but revealed to itself by the postponement of the reality principle to discharge.

its ideational content. The work of analysis may even be brought to a conclusion by negation itself, by leading the analysand to full intellectual acceptance of the repressed; yet this does not mean that the process of repression comes to an end. What is lacking in it, then, if not the apparently accepted affect attached to the idea? It is as if the analysand were behaving in the analysis like the fetishist with regard to castration.

The work of thought, says Freud, frees itself from the restrictions of repression with the help of the symbol of negation. All that is needed is a change of sign from plus to minus for the repressed, lost content to be recovered.[77] By this change of sign, the subject is delivered from the affect. The obsessional neurotic, a positive goldsmith in such matters, even accepts the reinstatement of the original sign; he will agree to the replacement of the minus by the plus, but the affect will remain absent. A comparison is suggested here with the hysteric. In the case of the hysteric, as we know, the repressed affect resurfaces in an inverted form. Desire is turned into disgust, pleasure into unpleasure. Thus the equivalent of negation in the intellectual processes is to be found in the inversion of the affects. However, an appreciable difference separates the two registers. The emancipation from the restrictions of repression is accomplished at the price of a simple negation and accepts the repressed idea into the conscious for the intellectual processes, whereas unpleasure necessitates a counter-cathexis that expends more energy. Furthermore, the activity of thought thus finds itself impeded by the thrust of the repressed affect.

Thus the relations between the repressed (idea and affect) and the conscious may be understood in terms of their various vicissitudes:

1   the repressed (idea plus affect) remains entirely repressed;
2   the repressed (idea) attains consciousness in the form of negation;
3   the repressed (idea) attains consciousness in the form of intellectual acceptance;
4   the repressed (affect) attains consciousness in a direct or inverted form.

Cases 2 and 3 do not lift the repression.

5   the repressed (idea) attains consciousness with the affect: the repression is lifted.

Isn't Freud returning here to his early observations in *Studies on Hysteria*, in which he declares that the verbalized memory without affect has no

---

77 'No, it wasn't my mother', says the dreamer, wondering who the person in his dream could be.

effect on the morbid process? Thus, only the ideo-affective complex reconstituted by memory or interpretation may lift the repression. But we must
insist on the fact that it is a partial lifting involving by reaction a strengthening of the counter-cathexes. A total lifting of repression is impossible, as
a result of the original repression, which is in any case the most powerful
motive for sublimation. The work of analysis is to construct a network of
partial (or secondary) repressions capable of providing the hypothesis of the
primary repression, which, when communicated to the analysand, produces an ideo-affective complex in relation with it.

The work of the intellectual processes involves an emancipation from the
affect, at the price of negation, but, as far as psychical reality is concerned,
any analysis based on the combinatory of ideas, even if it recognizes the play
of the negations, may culminate in a theory of the analysand's unconscious
that is perfectly possible and even true, without any lifting of the repression.
The referent of the analysis can, therefore, only be the affect – or, more
specifically, the affect of unpleasure, which alone is indicative of the
repressed. That is why treatment experienced in a mutually happy relationship cannot claim to involve an analysis of the unconscious, but only a
process of affective orthopaedia. It is only when the analysis of what, for
Freud, stems from the judgement of attribution according to the good–bad
dichotomy is sufficiently advanced that the reintegration of the expelled, the
'spit out', the repressed will make possible a complete view of the psychical
reality, which will then enable the subject to operate according to the
subjective–objective dichotomy. As far as psychoanalytic theories are concerned, it would be interesting to evaluate them not only in terms of their
logical coherence, since their objectivity is not verifiable, but on the plane
of their affective effect: namely, what affect of pleasure do they give, what
affect of unpleasure do they spare the subject?

4 'Fetishism' (1927)

Analysing the structure of fetishism, Freud drew a distinction that was to
throw light on the relations between the different varieties of repression and
on the material on which they act.

For a long time, it was thought that only representations were *repressed*,
whereas the affect was only *suppressed*. The difference between these two
terms was difficult to grasp. Let us say simply that suppression was an inhibition of the expression of the affect, whereas repression went hand in hand
with the effacement of the representation and its survival in the form of
memory trace. With the analysis of fetishism, Freud, by one of those rever-
sals that one sometimes finds in his work, was to maintain that repression
was the mechanism that targeted the affect: 'If we wanted to differentiate

more sharply between the vicissitude of the *idea* as distinct from that of the *affect*, and reserve the word "Verdrängung" [repression] for the affect, then the correct German word for the vicissitude of the idea would be "*Verleügnung*" [disavowal]'.[78]

This may be regarded as the last word on the relations between affect and repression. Not only is the affect repressed, but repression operates specifically on the affect, whereas the representation falls under disavowal.

The affect that accompanies the view of the mother's genital organs must submit to repression. The perception of the lack of a penis is a cause of anxiety insofar as the phantasy of castration is thus authenticated. By means of this authentification, the act of castration is evoked. That is to say, the threat bearing on physical integrity at its most sensitive point: the loss of the penis 'signifies enjoyment (*jouissance*)'. Thus, on the one hand, in external reality and the outside world, two orders of facts – *perception* and *the act* – are linked. On the other hand, in internal (psychical) reality and the inner world, representation and affect are the object of an encounter sealed by the phantasy. Henceforth, the defence aims at splitting them: repression of the affect, disavowal of the representation. To this splitting of affect from representation will correspond the splitting between external and internal reality – allowing the co-existence of two equally accepted versions. Yes, castration exists – women have lost the penis – and there is nothing I can do about it. No, castration does not exist: in place of the missing penis, any object contiguous to the female sex or any other object that suggests a similarity with the penis will take its place; the fetish is and is not the sex that it represents. The affect is subjected to the same splitting; the representation of a castrated sex arouses intense anxiety and horror in the unconscious; the perception of the female sex leaves the subject indifferent, unaltered by a fact that he has always known: men and women are anatomically different.

The situation of the affect is becoming clearer: it may be aroused either by external perception (evocation of a danger coming from an action in the real world), or by representation (evocation of a phantasy constructed in the psyche). Similarly, any lack of satisfaction caused by the object increases internal tension and provokes either the representation of the missing object, or an attempt at a hallucinatory wish-fulfilment (hallucinated satisfaction). Here again, the arousing role played by lack should be noted. The effect of the affect will be concomitant with increasing tension and discharge. Discharge will be directed primarily towards the body (physiological reactions) and secondarily towards the external world (movements of motor agitation).

Thus the affect is at the crossroads of various orders of givens that accompany its appearance, its development and its disappearance.

78 *S.E.*, XXI, p. 153.

At its appearance preside:

- in the external world: the perception that evokes the act;
- in the internal world: the wish and the representation of the object or of satisfaction.

To its development, correspond:

- in the external world: the movement of motor agitation, appeal to the object;
- in the internal world: phantasy, the visceral body.

At the disappearance that follows the exhaustion of discharge and satisfaction:

- in the external world: motor repose followed by the experience of satisfaction and the avoidance of perceptual conditions that evoke the inherent danger of the act;
- in the internal world: the quality of pleasure, followed by the silence of representation and affect.

This schema takes into account only a favourable outcome. In the opposite case:

- in the external world: the agitation will lead to exhaustion and a fall into torpor or abandonment to external danger;
- in the internal world: to the experience of catastrophe, despair and powerlessness, leading to abandonment to internal danger – abandonment, says Freud, by the powers of destiny.

Between these two extreme situations may operate, within certain limits, defence mechanisms that are more or less solid, more or less costly, more or less effective, from the external and internal counter-cathexis, in its most radical forms, bearing on external and internal reality, to the subtlest mechanisms, with their partial, temporary, reversible effects, offering a whole gamut of possible symbolization, warding off the consequences of economic disturbance. I shall return to these in due course.

5 'Splitting of the ego in the process of defence' (1939)

Freud's metapsychological construction of 1927 was taken up, as we know, twelve years later, in this final article. Two things strike one about his return to the subject: first, he is unsure whether this discovery is old and banal or new and original, and, second, he wonders what application it will have to psychosis.

Freud's self-questioning as to the value of his discovery is no mere rhetorical trick. The question that he is asking himself might be put in the following way: 'Am I making a decisive advance here, or am I merely repeating what I have already said elsewhere?' It was a question that left this article unfinished and unpublished during Freud's lifetime. The question is soundly based and it is true in its contradiction, just as the splitting of the ego is true. For, indeed, Freud merely repeats what he had said at the beginning of his letters to Fliess (Draft K): he always knew this. But, on the other hand, he had never formulated it in this particular way – 'he never thought to'.

This article seems to me to be the last word on affect, though the term is not mentioned in it. What Freud shows us is the irreducible splitting that affects the ego. This agency is the essential agency of conflict: on the one hand, its role is to recognize the demands of reality and to obey them by a renunciation of instinct, while, on the other hand, its functions must give satisfaction to the pleasure–unpleasure principle, that is to say, the avoidance of unpleasure (reminder of the sanctions that follow in cases of an obstinate search for pleasure) and to find a means that makes possible the pursuit of pleasure by an experience of satisfaction. We now have a better understanding of the structural heterogeneity of the ego.

The principal functions of the ego might be stated thus:

- the maintenance of self-preservation;
- the recognition of external reality;
- the mechanisms of defence, whose many roles are:
  - the disavowal of painful reality;
  - the struggle against dangerous instinctual demands;
  - the search for compromises between the effects of the other two new agencies and reality;
- narcissistic cathexis;
- identification;
- desexualization;
- the link between free energy and control of the affects.

This multiplicity of tasks explains in part the contradictions that may be observed in the various conceptions of the ego. Some stress its adaptive role, others its defensive work, others again its transactional functions, while, on the contrary, some stress its susceptibility being captured by the imaginary (phantasy) and the snare (*leurre*); finally, it has been seen as the essential agency of the fate of the drives, which is sublimation by identification and desexualization.

What demonstrates the validity of this last work by Freud is the co-existence, within the ego, of contradictory functions. That is to say, at the level of this agency, however potent the reality test and the reality principle may be, the pleasure–unpleasure principle is still powerful enough to disavow the reality test and to construct a more or less extensive neo-reality: from the fetish as penis substitute to delusion as offspring of the unconscious, which steps in to block up the hole left by repressed reality.

This brings us to Freud's second concern: the application of his discovery to the field of psychosis. My interpretation leads me to think that Freud implicitly opposes two problematics: the first, that of the fetishist, who defends himself against castration-anxiety with the fetish; the second, that of the delusional subject, who defends himself against fragmentation-anxiety with the neo-reality of delusion. In the second case one is tempted to say that it is the ego that castrates itself in order not to be fragmented. The splitting may therefore bear on the difference of the sexes, or on the narcissistic identity. Repression may go from radical rejection (foreclosure) to negation (denial).

We must go further than Freud does in his conclusion. The problematic of fetishism is a paradigm that we see illustrated throughout psychoanalysis. Its extension to psychosis does not cover all its applications – far from it. Since Winnicott, we know that the closest links unite the structure of the transitional object and the fetish. Furthermore, in a large number of clinical structures, including 'normality', fetishism and perversion have been opposed to more extensive fetishistic behaviour. Indeed the fetish is found again in areas far removed from psychoanalysis.[79] Although one may observe the constitution of the fetish object with particular clarity in certain individuals, it seems to me to sustain the very constitution of the psychical object. This can only mean that the psychical object is never detached from its original link and from its essential function: it is taken as part of the mother's body (part-object) and destined for pleasure.

The renunciation of the enjoyment of the mother's body (either directly, or indirectly by masturbation) is pronounced, under pain of castration in the Name of the Father (Lacan). The position of the subject confronting this decree issued by the Other is to recognize this law at the same time as it discovers a way of getting round it. The mother's body comes back through the affect. The affect, always double, recalls in its duality the satisfaction sought in the form of pleasure and its prohibition in the form of unpleasure.

Evolution of the conception of anxiety (1893–1932)

Although I promised not to go into detail concerning any particular affect, but to deal only with the most general problems of the affect, I shall make

---

79 See 'Objets du fétichisme', in *Nouvelle Revue de Psychanalyse*, 2. Paris: Gallimard, 1970.

an exception for anxiety, since, through this example, one may follow the development of Freud's thought on affect.

One may distinguish three essential periods in Freud's conceptualization of anxiety:

1   1893–95: around the anxiety neurosis and its relations with sexual life.
2   1909–17: relations between anxiety and repressed libido.
3   1926–32: relations between anxiety and the psychical apparatus.

I shall now provide a brief outline of them.

I First period: the anxiety neurosis (1893–95)

This first group of works may be limited to the Drafts sent to Fliess (B,[80] E,[81] F, J), and the first works on the phobias.[82] But it is above all the article on anxiety neurosis and his reply to the criticisms that it raised that contain the essence of Freud's position at this time (1895).[83]

The main idea at this early stage is that the source of anxiety must be sought not in the psychical, but in the physical sphere. The production of anxiety depends on a mechanism that entails *quantitative and qualitative transformations*. Originally, one finds an accumulation of physical sexual tension. When this physical sexual tension goes beyond a certain threshold, it may be transformed into affect by psychical elaboration. At this time, Freud distinguishes between different elements in the sexual life: the physical element, the psychosexual element and, no doubt (but this is open to controversy), a psychical element. In normal sexuality, when physical sexual tension reaches a certain threshold, it 'takes psychical advantage of it', that is to say, makes contact with certain ideational contents that implement the specific action that allows discharge by satisfaction. The model of this kind of reaction is described in Draft G on melancholia, which may be regarded as a precursor of the model of the drive. Physical sexual tension, therefore, has a capacity to arouse the psychical libido, which then brings it to the indispensable experience of satisfaction.

This arrangement may undergo certain disturbances (by inadequate development or decline in the psychosexual life, by excessive *defence* or by 'alienation' between physical and psychical sexuality); in this case, sexual

80   *S.E.*, I, p. 182.
81   *S.E.*, I, p. 190.
82   *S.E.*, III, p. 81.
83   *S.E.*, III, p. 90.

tension is transformed into anxiety. The mechanism at work here is not, therefore, made up solely of a quantitative accumulation of tension, as is usually said to be the case, but a qualitative change also takes place: instead of being transformed into (or resting on) psychosexual tension, physical sexual tension is transformed into anxiety. The mechanism, therefore, has a symmetrical, inverted relation to that of hysterical conversion. The anxiety neurosis is the somatic counterpart of hysteria.

If, in conversion, one sees a leap from the psychical sexual to the somatic, in anxiety neurosis this leap appears to be from the sexual physical to the somatic. The differences, however, are important: the leap to the somatic in the case of hysteria preserves the ability to symbolize the psychical sexual; hysterical conversion continues to belong to the symbolic. The leap from the physical sexual to the somatic brought about by anxiety has no links with symbolization. In this instance, therefore, one may speak of *a disqualifying economic and symbolic disturbance.*

The main cause of the formation of anxiety lies, according to Freud, in the fact that *a sexual affect cannot be formed; physical tension cannot be linked psychically.* Anxiety appears as a substitute for the *missing representation*, a somatic substitute, as the phenomenology and symptomatology of anxiety show. For the physical manifestations of anxiety cannot be contingent; they dominate the picture. What takes place here is an inversion of the relations that normally exist in coitus. Whereas in coitus the principal path of discharge is psychosexual and the secondary path somatic (dyspnoea, cardiac acceleration, etc.), in anxiety *the secondary path of discharge becomes the principal one.*[84] The article on anxiety neurosis of 1895, a masterpiece of clinical observation, stresses the difference between anxiety neurosis and phobia. Anxiety neurosis does not spring from a repressed idea; it does not belong, for Freud, to psychological analysis; although certain ideational contents may be encountered there, they are secondary additions, alien borrowings from the content of anxiety. The substitution of one idea for another is primary in phobia, secondary in anxiety neurosis. It is clear that all the mechanisms tending to quantitative accumulation make the situation worse: predisposing factors, accumulations, reinforcements, combine together. But the essential disturbance lies in the impossibility for somatic excitation to be *psychically worked out.* Somatic excitation is redirected towards other paths than the psychical one. The symptoms of anxiety neurosis are substitutes for the specific action (coitus) that ought normally to follow sexual excitation.

These radical declarations are somewhat tempered in Freud by the possibility of mixed neuroses, but the essence of the thesis remains: that of a

---

84 We should note here the inversion of the model of the 'Project' on the use of the way of discharge to the purposes of communication.

distinction in nature between anxiety neurosis, actual neurosis, on the one side, and the psychoneuroses, transference neuroses of the psychosexual libido, on the other.

It is clear that Freud's first theses on anxiety cannot be maintained as they are. But it would be wrong to think that Freud gave them up entirely. Echoes of them can be found in the later stages of his work: particularly in the persistence of the thesis of the impossibility of a psychical working out of energic tension, that is to say, in the last analysis, of its link with representative contents. In any case, that first theory of anxiety cannot fail to remind us today of the psychosomatic conceptions of the modern French school. Of course, it is no longer a question of anxiety here, but the decline of physical sexual tension or its redirection towards ways of somatic (internal) discharge is at the forefront of our modern ideas on psychosomatic structures.

II Second period: anxiety and repressed libido (1909–17)

The earliest theories of anxiety concern the relationship between anxiety and the body. The second period concerns the link between anxiety and repressed libido, as is apparent in 'Little Hans' ('Analysis of a phobia in a five-year-old boy', 1909), the article '"Wild" psychoanalysis' (1910), the *Papers on Metapsychology* (1915), the twenty-fifth of the *Introductory Lectures on Psychoanalysis* (1917) and the 'Wolf Man' ('From the history of an infantile neurosis', 1918. The stress shifts here to the dominance of the psychical conflict, to the relations between affect and the ideational representative of the drive. Freud's attention is directed to the vicissitudes and transformation of affects.

As Freud progresses in the study of infantile sexuality and the neuroses, he becomes aware of the importance of anxiety in its relations with repression. Although anxiety responds to a repressed libidinal aspiration, it is not this aspiration itself; the repression is the cause of its transformation into anxiety. Now repression is inseparable from a situation of danger. That is why it is important to deepen our understanding of the nature and origin of the danger in order to grasp its consequences. The mechanistic hypothesis of anxiety neurosis proves to be inadequate. Freud makes great play with the discovery of the danger of castration. The nosographical distinction that led to the separation of the anxiety that is manifested in anxiety neurosis and anxiety as it appears in phobia is pursued here with a new opposition: *anxiety confronting a real danger and neurotic anxiety*.

Anxiety before a real danger is dependent on the impulses of self-preservation; it is the consequence of the interpretation of the signs of danger threatening the individual's physical integrity. Neurotic anxiety is quite different: apparently nothing justifies it from the point of view of self-preservation. The threat comes from elsewhere.

Any sign of danger induces a state of alert: arousal of the senses and motor tension mobilize the ability to respond to this danger by combat or flight, depending on the circumstances. Reactions to danger are useful and necessary, because they prepare the subject for a response. But anxiety has no use, since it has a disorganizing effect, disturbing the behaviour necessary to confront danger. Anxiety, then, has the opposite effect to the one sought: preparation for a response before the threat of danger. Absence of preparation is harmful: the traumatic neuroses, which testify to the surprise that overcomes the subject and takes him unawares, show this. Unpreparedness for danger encourages the splitting of the ego and the quantity of uncontrollable excitation. Man defends himself against fear by anxiety.

Pathological anxiety takes essentially two forms: *floating anxiety*, ready to attach itself to any representation, as in the anxious waiting of anxiety neurosis, and *a limited anxiety linked to danger*. This opposition may be summarized by saying that, in the first case, danger is everywhere, security nowhere, while, in the second, the danger is localized, security everywhere else. This comparison enables us to return to two states of anxiety: the anxiety in which any attempt to avoid it is pointless because of the ego's cathexis by the affect, and the anxiety controlled to some extent by the avoidance of the anxiety-inducing situations, the defence mechanism put into operation by the ego.

Freud, therefore, maintains the opposition of the first period. Floating anxiety is still interpreted as an inhibition on discharge. This may be attributed either to an avatar of the drive's vicissitudes (inadequacy of displacement mechanisms, aim–inhibition, desexualization, in short, sublimation), or to an increase of acquired quantitative factors (puberty, menopause). In floating anxiety, therefore, one finds once more the lack of psychical working out postulated in 1895 and the aggravating role of quantitative factors. The conclusion remains the same: the hindrance of the libido gives rise to processes that are all of a solely somatic nature.

In the neuropsychoses, it is quite different: the symptoms (hysteria, phobia, obsession) are produced in order to prevent the appearance of anxiety. The avoidance of unpleasure may be effective in conversion, moderately effective in the phobias and ineffective in obsessional neurosis. But in each case the relation to symbolization is preserved. The hysteric continues to symbolize through his body, the phobic and obsessional symbolize through other psychical productions.

There is an opposition of two different mechanisms:

• inhibition on discharge involving a deflection towards the body (a physical discharge), without real psychical working out, but able to cover itself with a 'plated' psychical superstructure. Here repression is not really in play; it is only an ineffective challenge, and without symbolic production, physical or psychical;

- inhibition on discharge entailing a transformation by an operation that combines the vicissitudes of the drives and the ego's defence mechanisms. The result of the work of repression culminates in symbolic productions, physical or psychical. Here repression is fully at work producing anticathexes and withdrawal of cathexis. The recent repressed is subjected to the attraction of the pre-existing repressed. A splitting may then occur between the affect and the ideational representative of the drive. The dismantling of the groups of representations may lead to redistribution and permutations. As for the affect, it may undergo various quantitative transformations (suppression) or qualitative transformations, of which anxiety is the principal expression. Freud will add that *this transformation of the affective state constitutes by far the most important one brought about by the process of repression.* However, throughout his work, Freud always maintained that the significance of the affect was linked to the function of memory. The affect evokes the repetition of an important, significant event. Where is this event to be found? Before Rank, Freud propounded the hypothesis of primal anxiety, the one accompanying birth. But can the traumatic experience of birth be called anxiety? Observation of children suggests that anxiety in the strict sense appears later (anxiety before strangers, before new situations, before unknown objects), as Spitz shows fully (anxiety of the eighth month). In any case, anxiety appears when the presence of the mother and the security she gives are lacking.

In the final analysis, Freud concludes that the child's anxiety has almost nothing in common with anxiety before real danger. On the other hand, it is very close to the neurotic anxiety of adults. Like the latter, it springs from unused – I would say unaffected – libido. The lack of an object on which the libido may be cathected is replaced by another, external object or by a situation.

The progress achieved during this first period in the theory of anxiety was considerable. The opposition between the two forms of anxiety is given more satisfactory metapsychological explanations. If little is added to the conception of anxiety as it appears in actual neuroses, there is progress as far as the conception of anxiety in the psychoneuroses is concerned. A number of points remain to be elucidated as far as the nature of the danger to be feared is concerned, which is not the same at the various stages of development. Besides it may be said that the theory of anxiety remains, even here, more economic than symbolic. Anxiety appears here as a consequence and not, as Freud was later to maintain, as a cause of repression. The articulation between the two forms of anxiety is still to come.

Before leaving this second period of the theory of anxiety, we should note the interest that Freud takes in certain affects linked to anxiety, such as the minor forms of depersonalization, the déjà-vu, the Wolf Man's 'veil', the uncanny. The need to differentiate between anxiety, fear and terror is matched by a more radical differentiation between anxiety and mourning ('Mourning and melancholia').

III Third period: anxiety and the psychical apparatus (1926–32)

Many analysts see *Inhibitions, Symptoms and Anxiety* as the masterpiece of Freud's thought in clinical psychoanalysis. I see it as Freud's final touch to the theory of the affect. Many earlier observations are repeated in it, but I shall be concerned above all with the new ideas on the affect that the work introduces. Freud lays down the broad outlines in Lecture XXXII. Pasche's report 'Anxiety and the theory of the instincts' that opened the 1953 Congrès des Langues romanes provides a good summary: 'It is no use denying the fact, though it is not pleasant to recall it, that I have on many occasions asserted that in repression the instinctual representative is distorted, displaced, and so on, while the libido belonging to the instinctual impulse is transformed into anxiety'.[85]

This self-criticism indicates the change, but, as we shall see, it is only relative.

All psychoanalysts know that, from 1926, Freud altered his earlier positions. At this date, he stated the following propositions:

1   *Anxiety resides in the ego. Only the ego can experience anxiety* The source of this anxiety may be found in the external world (anxiety before a real danger), in the id (neurotic anxiety), or in the superego (anxiety of conscience).
2   *It is not repression that produces anxiety, but anxiety that produces repression* The internal threat (libidinal or aggressive aspiration) triggers off anxiety (danger of castration, for example), which causes repression (renunciation of the object of desire and its aim). Anxiety, therefore, has *an anticipatory role* when one is faced by a threat (loss of the mother or sight of her sex).
3   *Anxiety is a reminder from the ego, in terms of a new instinctual demand, of an old situation of danger* Hence the need to suppress, repress, extinguish the instinctual demand. The ego anticipates the satisfaction demanded and regarded as dangerous (it withdraws its cathexis from the representation and frees unpleasure).
4   *The signal of unpleasure (anxiety) arouses, on the part of the ego, a passive or*

---

85 *S.E.*, XX, p. 109. We should note that Freud uses affect and libido synonymously here.

active reaction   In the first place, the anxiety develops and invades the subject. In the second, anticathexes are set up (formation of a symptom or character trait). The activization of the ego's defence mechanisms is intended to *bind* psychically what has been repressed.

5   *The energy of the instinctual demand may undergo various vicissitudes* Indeed, either the instinctual demand, uncontrolled by the ego's defences, maintains its thrust despite the defences and continues without let to exert pressure, or it succumbs and may be destroyed (example of the dissolution of the Oedipus complex). In certain cases, suppression sets in (as in obsessional neurosis), as a consequence of the conflict and as a mode of defence.

6   *In its relations of conjunction and disjunction with the id, the ego is, on the one hand, dependent on the id but, on the other hand, proves less powerless than it seems, since it is capable of implementing repression by triggering off the alarm signal.*   It is therefore as untrue to claim that the ego is sovereign, as does academic psychology, as to maintain that it is totally powerless, as certain opposed theses of a philosophical bent maintain.

7   *Neurotic anxiety is caused by the appearance in the psyche of a state of great tension felt as unpleasure, freedom from which by discharge is impossible*   A reunification of the various aspects of anxiety is attempted here – castration anxiety derives from the threatened loss of the part-object, the penis, which would have the effect of making any reunion with the mother impossible; the anxiety of the object loss derives from the threatened loss of the total object. Castration anxiety entails abandoning enjoyment of the penis in order to preserve narcissistic integrity (sacrifice of the function in order to preserve the organ). Object-loss anxiety entails abandoning the wish to preserve the object (sacrifice of autonomy in order to preserve the mother).

8   *Libidinal development entails that the danger incurred is not the same at different stages of development*   The danger of psychical abandonment coincides with the awakening of the ego, the danger of losing the object (or the object's love) with infantile dependence, the danger of castration with the phallic phase, and fear of the superego with the latency period. But this genetic sequence does not relativize castration because of deferred structurings. The genetic point of view does not prevail over the structural point of view by virtue of the 'colossal narcissistic cathexis of the penis'. The object of the anxiety is always linked, however, to a traumatic (internal) factor that it is impossible to overcome in accordance with the norms of the pleasure–unpleasure principle. The affect of anxiety remains linked therefore to the impossibility of eliminating a tension. The quantitative dimension remains unavoidable: the affect is the result of a quantity of excitation *that cannot be bound or discharged.*

9   *Anxiety is dependent on the dual mechanism of primal repression and deferred action*   Secondary repressions are triggered off in accordance with reminders of an old situation of danger. The primal repression is dependent on too many large libidinal demands, whose disorganized tension the infant cannot bear. In the first case, therefore, the anxiety may be an alarm signal; in the second, the expression of a traumatic situation.

10 *Both aspects of anxiety, alarm signal and expression of a traumatic situation, correspond to the role played by the agencies*   In the case of automatic-traumatic anxiety, it is supposed that the anxiety is due to a direct manifestation of the id, invading and swamping the ego's defensive possibilities, inducing a state of panic, powerlessness and despair. In the case of anxiety as alarm signal, the anxiety is a manifestation of the ego, which uses it to order the implementation of defensive operations against the drives emanating from the id or their representatives. In the first case, the ego can only submit to the anxiety and, since its possibilities of response are paralysed, any psychical working out is expressed through a complete failure of the defences. In the second case, the ego's defence mechanisms, however imperfect, reveal a symbolic activity functioning without major damage, in a way similar to thought.

I say symbolic activity and not, as has become the practice in the psychoanalytic (principally Anglo-American) literature, activity of signalization. Suffice it to say that I prefer to use the term symbol rather than signal, because, as we have seen, there is no one-to-one relation between anxiety and the danger feared; because of its various cross-checkings, anxiety refers to a polysemy of the dangerous situation, the dangers feared referring back to one another and forming together a symbolic network.

However, the opposition between automatic anxiety and signal of anxiety must be articulated in such a way as to make the transition from one to the other understandable. For Freud, the mainspring is external perception.

When the infant has found out by experience that the external, perceptible object can put an end to the dangerous situation which is reminiscent of birth, the content of the danger it fears is displaced from the economic situation on to the condition which determined that situation, viz., the loss of object. It is the absence of the mother that is now the danger; and as soon as that danger arises the infant gives the signal of anxiety, before the dreaded economic situation has set in. This change constitutes a first great step forward in the provision made by the infant for its self-preservation, and at the same time represents a transition from the automatic and involuntary fresh appearance of anxiety to the intentional reproduction of anxiety a signal of danger.[86]

Freud emphasises therefore the importance of the *perceptual* function in its anticipatory function, as opposed to the situation in which the child can only register after the event the absence of the mother by its effect: disorganizing excessive libidinal tension. This 'externalization', which forces the child to find outside himself the signs that announce a state of danger from within is in itself a sign that testifies to a transference of activity from the id to the ego. It is a transference of economic activity towards a symbolic activity that is completed in language. Freud's insistence on the role of loss of the mother as a determining condition of anxiety leads him, in the appendices to the work, to the most penetrating remarks on the relations between anxiety and waiting, between anxiety, pain and mourning.

Hilflosigkeit, that psychical distress felt by the child, is the most fearsome, the most feared anxiety, the one whose return must be anticipated at all costs. The anticipatory function develops only under the effect of this spur. For it is not only the lack of support that induces anxiety, but the disorganizing character of libidinal tensions for which no satisfaction is possible outside the mother. The threat here bears on one of the first matrices of the ego's organization, whose precarious constructions find it difficult to resist a libidinal inundation, in so far as the erotic tension bound up with lack of satisfaction is combined with aggressive tension deriving from frustration.

In this respect, the links between anxiety, pain and object-mourning must be made clear. Freud maintains that pain is the proper reaction to the loss of the object, whereas anxiety is the reaction to the danger that this loss entails, and consequently a displacement, the reaction to the danger of the loss itself. Thus the loss of the object produces pain by the irruption of an uncontrollable quantity into the ego, which provokes a feeling of helplessness (*Hilflosigkeit*). To avoid pain and helplessness, the signal of anxiety anticipates the catastrophe and orders the ego to set up defensive operations capable of controlling the disorganizing threat. For the characteristic of the signal of anxiety is to appear in a series, a chain made up of representations of the drive and of the danger incurred, preconscious representations derived from the unconscious representation maintained by the original repression.

What do we learn from this whole development concerning affect? From 1895, it pursues with remarkable coherence the question of the relation of the affect to the unconscious. The affect may originate directly in the id and pass directly into the ego by breaking in like a force that smashes the pro-

---

86 *S.E.*, XX, pp. 137–8.

tective shield, and it is an automatic anxiety, uncontrolled, unreduced, unbound by the ego, equivalent to psychical pain. In this case, the preconscious and the verbal memory traces are short-circuited; speech is reduced to silence. Here the id speaks its own language: that of the unverbalizable affect, and the ego is under an attack that induces a sense of helplessness (*Hilflosigkeit*). Elsewhere, the affect activates certain reactions of the ego, which may filter the instinctual energies from the id and allow only a modest quantity of them to enter the ego. In this case, it is the alarm signal of anxiety; the affect, passing through the preconscious, arrives at the ego with its corresponding representations and memory traces. Here the ego, as locus of anxiety, is also a locus of work on the affect. The *linking* may then try, by employing all the resources of defensive activity, to confront, with the help of representations and language, the signification of the danger feared, relived in the transference experience. By tracing the course of the representations, the analysand may relive and rethink the meaning of the anxiety through an act of awareness. Such an act of awareness is an act *on the part of the consciousness* operating by partial insights, throughout the transference experience, taking possession of fragments of the id hitherto cut off from the ego. The role of the ego may seem overestimated here. And yet Freud says on this matter:

> The ego is an organization. It is based on the maintenance of free intercourse and of the possibility of reciprocal influence between all its parts. Its desexualized energy still shows traces of its origin in its impulsion to bind together and unify, and this necessity to synthesize grows stronger in proportion as the strength of the ego increases.[87]

So everything depends on the organization of the ego confronting the disorganizing power of the id. But on a more fundamental plane, everything depends on Eros, on the strength of linking that may, at the level of the id, allow the unifying tendency of the life-drives to prevail over the disorganizing tendency of the destructive drives. Conversely, the organization of the ego depends on its differentiation from the id, that is, on their relative separation; this separation depends on factors of disjunction, which are one of the aspects of the destructive drives.

Again what is found here is the importance of the economic factor. Too marked a tendency to conjunction dissolves the separation between the agencies and threatens the ego with total fusion with the id. Too marked a tendency to disjunction totally splits the ego from the id and does not allow

87 *S.E.*, XX, p. 98.

any appropriation of fragments of the id by the ego. Where the id was the ego can no longer be.

However tempting it may be to give primacy to the affect in all these processes, its necessary link with representation must be stressed. It is by introducing adequate but repressed representations that the work of the affect will be possible, in other words, that the progression of the analytic process will be effective. In the same way, it is by mastery of the most disorganizing affects that the most alienating fixations may be overcome and allow the development of the libido and of the ego to continue.

Given these points, it may be imagined that analysability depends strictly on the structural relations between the id and the ego in the various pathological organizations. Again I am struck by the importance of a psychoanalytic nosography, and of a differential clinical practice of the transferences observable in psychoanalytic experience that allows the structural distinctions between transference neuroses – well established in psychoanalysis – and structures that have tempted analysis since Freud: character neuroses, borderline states, depressive states, psychosomatic illnesses, perversions, etc., whose problems have been thoroughly debated in contemporary psychoanalytic literature.[88]

Conclusion

What conclusion is to be drawn from this partial balance-sheet of works dealing directly or indirectly with the affect?

According to psychoanalysis, the affect may be understood only through the theoretical model of the drive. The drive, though unknowable, is its reference. The affect is one of the two elements of the psychical representations of the drive. It denotes the element of energy in this representation, endowed with a quantity and quality, linked to the ideational representative, but capable of being dissociated in the unconscious. The affect is a moving quantity, accompanied by a subjective tonality. It is through discharge that it becomes conscious, or through resistance to the increasing tension that characterizes it, followed by the lifting of resistance. This discharge is oriented inwards, largely towards the body. Coming from the body, it returns to the body.

The link that binds it to representation is that of a reciprocal appeal: the

---

88 Since Freud, contemporary psychoanalytic literature has attempted a unification of the theory of anxiety. L. Rangell brings together the various hypotheses that have been proposed to this end in the article: 'A further attempt to resolve the problem of anxiety', *Journal of the American Psychoanalytic Association*, 16, 1968, pp. 371–404.

representation arouses the affect, the mobilized affect is in search of a representation. On both sides other relations are joined to them; on the side of representation, through the perception that warns of danger or carries an erotic or comforting message; on the side of the affect by the act, the counterpart in the external world of the movement of discharge attempting to modify the prevailing conditions. The affect-representation complex develops each of its terms in opposite directions: the representation is deployed in various directions, from phantasy to language, while the affect stretches from its crudest to its most subtle forms. These various vicissitudes depend on the work on the affect, carried out under the control of the ego. Apart from the well-known defence mechanisms, special mention should be made of the suppressions, an extreme form of repression, as the ultimate task of repression. But, better still, is the linking activity carried out by libidinal energy, which ensures the binding of a floating affective energy.

If a simplified genetic view allows us to conceive of libidinal development in terms of an increasing affective maturity characterized by mastery of the affects, this view contrasts not only with the notion of timelessness, peculiar to the unconscious, but also with the structural situation of the affects, namely, their submission to the sovereignty of the pleasure–unpleasure principle. Their pre-eminent place in the primary processes increased even more after the unconscious ceased to play in Freud's work the role of a system and was replaced by the id, in which are stressed, far more than in the first topography, the economic point of view and the role of the drive's tendency to discharge.

Although the unconscious status of repressed representations was always perceived by Freud more clearly than that of affects, it does not follow that affects are necessarily conscious. A thorough examination of the question suggests the existence of id affects, the result of a crude, violent transformation of the discharged libido that breaks into the ego, before working out has been able to operate at this level, and of ego affects, affects on which the organizations of the ego (binding, control, desexualization, etc.) have been able to play. In the first case, the affect is manifested essentially by an *economic affect*, in the second by an *affect of symbolization* (signal-affect). Thus, on the one hand, one may say that the signification of the affects is inseparable from the labour power that they represent and of the work carried out on that power itself from an economic point of view and, on the other hand, that the symbolic function that they give rise to is compatible only within an organization characterized by the combination of quantities of energies reduced and bound by a stable, constant level of cathexis.

The situation may be summed up by saying that *the ego is caught between 'too much' anxiety and 'too little' anxiety*. The opposition between economic and symbolic may be turned round: *the economy is symbolic, the symbolic is economy*.

The essential difficulty of a psychoanalytic theory of the affect is to sub-stitute surreptitiously a phenomenological for a metapsychological point of view. This difficulty increases if one claims to be taking into account all the qualitative nuances and all the quantitative degrees of the affective life. The strict demands of theory require that the stages of an argument be clearly marked and maintained against all the temptations of diversion. This locus of the affect cannot be anywhere other than in the sexual, aggressive affect. This is the price that has to be paid if psychoanalytic theory is to preserve its specificity, while insisting on the organizing role of these affects for the unconscious and the structural differentiation of the agencies. It is by setting out from this knot that the threads that constitute it will be able to lead to ways that leave from it or that lead to it. It may be that, because it has not always recognized this conceptual imperative, the post-Freudian literature has tended to dissolve this specificity by situating the affective life in the context of a genetic theory of personality in which the Freudian heritage seems to have got bogged down.

2
An overall view of the psychoanalytic literature since Freud

When one considers the work of the psychoanalysts of the first generation, one cannot but be struck by the solitary character of Freud's reflection on the affect. We seek in vain in the writings of Ferenczi or Abraham, to mention only the most important, for some reflection of Freud's preoccupations with, for example, the status of affect and of representation in relation to the unconscious. In Ferenczi, one can already observe an extensive use of the notion of affect, which contemporary psychoanalytic practice has confirmed. What has happened to the affect in modern psychoanalytic literature?

In this overview of psychoanalytic work since Freud, devoted to affect, I shall deal with the most substantial, that associated with such names as Brierley, Rapaport, Jacobson, Schur and, lastly, those associated with the school of Melanie Klein, in which Bion occupies an eminent place. All these names belong to the Anglo-American movement. Although French-speaking authors give an important place to affect in their work, few of them have taken the trouble to name it explicitly. In this respect, Bouvet and Mallet are exceptions, as is, in a quite opposite way, Lacan.

I Analytic bibliography of the principal English-language works on the affect

Apart from Freud, most of the authors take an article by Ernest Jones, 'Fear, guilt and hate' (1929) as the starting-point of their work on affect. The essential idea of this work seems to be inspired by Melanie Klein's views on primary affects.[1] In his study of these three affects – fear, guilt and hate –

---

1 Although Melanie Klein more or less directly influenced a number of authors that I am about to comment on, one does not find in her writings a specific conception of affect.

Jones shows that a defensive function may be detected in the mobilization of one affect against another; thus fear conceals guilt, just as hate may serve as a screen against it or, again, hate conceals fear. Jones's originality consists in showing that things do not stop there. More profoundly, the affect that serves as a defence against a more unconscious affect is to be found *under* the unconscious affect. Thus fear in turn is to be found under the guilt for which it will serve as a defence, just as hate will be found *under* guilt or fear. In short, the conscious affect is in communication with *the most unconscious* affect of the same type as itself, these two affects being mediated by another unconscious affect, but not the most unconscious one. However, the conscious affect and the most unconscious affect are not connected in the same context. Superficial fear and the most deeply buried fear are different. The first is a rationalized anxiety, the second an archaic anxiety, evoking major dangers of a traumatic nature. What we have here are the two sides of anxiety: signal or trauma. The *Urangst* is responsible for the primitive mechanism that Jones describes as *aphanisis*:

> It means total annihilation of the capacity for sexual gratification, direct or indirect, a matter on which we shall again have to lay emphasis when we come to consider the primary traumatic situation. In the second place it is intended to represent an intellectual description on our part of *a state of affairs that originally has no ideational counterpart whatever in the child's mind, consciously or unconsciously* (my italics).[2]

This concept of *aphanisis* shows us another aspect of the primary affect and of the defensive reaction that it entails: *a massive blockage, without ideational context, with annihilation of the affects of pleasure*.[3] *Aphanisis* is one of the possible responses when confronted by the *Urangst*, the other being an attempt to deal with internal excitations by discharge, which culminates in the extinction of the excitation.

After Jones, Edward Glover (1939) and Marjorie Brierley (1937–49) continued to study the primary affects – their articles share a profound unity of thought, still marked here by implicit reference to Melanie Klein.

---

2 Jones (1929), pp. 391–2.
3 After Jones, Fenichel (1941) stressed the massive blockage of affects in a work in which he examines the relations between the ego and affects. Comparing affect and trauma, he analyses the various defensive procedures adopted by the ego to attain control of affects. One may compare Fenichel's position with that of Laplanche and Pontalis, who stress the traumatic value for the ego of instinctual excitation. This conception shifts the emphasis from trauma as external event, towards trauma as the effect of an instinctual mobilization. The trauma that comes from the outside would then play this role of provoking instinctual excitation, an intrusion of adult sexuality into infantile sexuality.

A common inspiration leads the authors to question the importance, in their view exaggerated, accorded to the ideational and representative element of the drive. They both challenge Freud's definition of affect, which takes into consideration only the discharge aspect and proposes to distinguish between *tension-affects* and *discharge-affects*. Glover insists on the fact that we are usually dealing with combined affects (Freud calls these constructions or formations of affects). The ambivalence is clearly apparent. Furthermore, it emphasizes the fact that it is very difficult to distinguish between affective experience and physical sensation. In order to understand Glover's position (his influence was to be considerable), perhaps something should be said about his notion of the ego's *nuclei*, which derive from primitive physical sensations. Only gradual development will make possible the fusion of these *nuclei* – and of the experiences associated with them – and thus give rise to the feeling of the ego's unity, which Federn had already emphasized so strongly. We should also take into account the influence on this theory of Karl Abraham, whose pupil Glover was.

However, the overload of primitive sado-masochistic energies thwarts this development. The *affects of shattering, explosion, disintegration*, which can be observed in psychoanalytic practice in the most varied states are evidence of this. The variety of contexts in which they may appear (Oedipal as well as pre-Oedipal structures) leads Glover to conclude that 'psychic feeling of disruption is thus a typical and very early tension affect, which in course of development may become fixed in different forms ("canalized" by association with phantasy systems) according to the experiences and unconscious ideations of different developmental periods'.[4] That is to say, in the appreciation of the unconscious, the representative element connotes an affective experience that is revelatory of the functioning of the drives, the phantasy system 'dressing up' the affect in intelligible, but perhaps misleading clothing.

Brierley's contribution (1937–49) complements Glover's hypotheses and outlines the change in perspectives since Freud. In the Freudian metapsychology, there is a conflict between ideas and affective charges. After Freud, one speaks of *object cathexis rather than of affective charges of ideas*. However, this does not always cast light on the relations between drives and affects. The affect must be regarded as the most direct 'drive derivative'. Insofar as the affects may be regarded as affects either of tension or of discharge – a reflection of an afferent or efferent position on the instinctual curve – it would be better to place them at the summit of that curve. Indeed the affect, as Fenichel maintains, may be due either to a sudden excess of internal stimuli or to the effect of an accumulation of undischarged tensions that are

4 Glover (1939), p. 305.

discharged under the influence of a minimal stimulus. These quantitative considerations are little help, however, with the qualitative aspect. Each motion has its own quality and threshold. The fate of the affects is to be subjected to the control, the 'training' of the ego (Fenichel); they are therefore bound up with the evolution of the ego and with the powers that the ego acquires by its gradual unification. The affective experiences are not separable from the relations that are established between the ego and objects. Indeed it should be remembered that the role of primary identification intervenes before the differentiation between ego and object: cathexis precedes differentiation and cognitive discrimination. This formulation recalls the one that Lebovici proposes: the object is cathected before being perceived. Brierley says: 'The child must sense the breast, for instance, before it begins to perceive (i.e. recognize) it, and it must feel its sucking sensations before it recognizes its own mouth'.[5] Thus knowledge and self-cathexis, as well as knowledge and cathexis of the object go hand in hand. The constitution of the primary affects is therefore bound up with their *object-carriers*. The mechanisms of introjection and projection are essentially methods of controlling phantasized emotions as concrete modes of relations with objects. Hence the importance of the contrast between good and bad objects.

Freud linked the birth of the object to its absence, that is to say to the experience of unsatisfaction. The object is known in hate. He attributed a fundamental role to this affect in establishing the reality principle. Brierley adds that such an experience is also the matrix of 'a constant focus for "bad object" formation'.[6] Following Melanie Klein and Rivière on this point, she links the formation of the I with that of the total object. But one should be under no illusion as to the power of integration, which is never acquired definitively. *No one completes the integration of their ego.*

This plunge into the primary affects leads Marjorie Brierley to speak, if we may be allowed this neologism, of pre-affects: that is to say, of affective inclinations, dispositions to live out certain affects; tendencies in short. Certain affects are inaccessible to consciousness, for the precursors of primary affects have never been conscious and are thus isolated at the heart of the unconscious. One can see how this theorization tends to rob the unconscious of its semantic value as 'locus of representations' and to stress an affectivity lacking any representative counterpart, which, for her, is what is at stake in the transference. 'Affect language is older than speech'. With the affect, we are dealing not only with archaic objects, but with the primitive system of the ego: 'not only with impulse-object tensions but with inter- and

5 Brierley (1937–49), p. 262.
6 Ibid., p. 263.

intra–ego tensions'.[7] The interpretation of the affects in the transference allows the reintegration of the primitive partial ego into the principal ego.

Brierley's position cannot be better summed up than by citing the qualities that she regards as necessary in psychoanalytic practice: *the combination of intelligent insight and affective understanding.* This lofty requirement might discourage more than one individual to take up psychoanalysis.

This first phase of works on the affect coming from the English school show the influence of the work of Melanie Klein. It is not important that Melanie Klein and her followers wrote very little about the affect. Nor does it matter that, in her work, the affect as such disappears behind the phantasy. What is important here is the change of direction made in the conception of the unconscious and the revaluation of the relation between representation affect. This orientation was to be continued by authors who moved away from the Kleinian influence, such as Winnicott, who envisaged primary emotional development (1945) according to similar parameters. It was no doubt Winnicott who brought out the role of the maternal environment in the most striking way.[8] In any case, knowing it and experiencing it would make relations with the being of the analysand accessible (Masud Khan 1969). An ever greater place was to be accorded communication with the patient's inner experience. This attitude entailed particular attention to interpretation. Primary imagination (prior to the secondary imagination of symbolization) would be the essential requirement of the analyst, and would enable him or her to relate to the being of the analysand.

In modern psychoanalytic theory and practice, no author has thrown more light on the role of affect than Winnicott. The approach of his thought combines very happily an ability to observe the particular with the intuitions of the creative imagination. His work aims to restore primary affective states – which, in his view, occur much earlier than anything described by Melanie Klein – constituted by alternations of states of disintegration and partial integration of the 'self'. Winnicott's originality is to have shown that a concept like 'the baby' does not exist and that it is necessary to include the mother in the indissoluble couple that they form. *That is to say, no discourse on the affect can be sustained that does not take account of the mother's affects,* her tolerance of the child's regressive needs, even of a state of informal chaos, the necessary condition for the establishment of a kernel of vital affective continuity. Winnicott's work belongs to the English psychoanalytic tradition, but carries to the maximum that supersession of the representation–affect opposition in order to confront the affective basis of the sense of existence.

---

7 Ibid., p. 265.
8 As in the works of Michael Balint.

The influence of Melanie Klein on the work of the English school was to be counterbalanced by theoretical tendencies from North America, associated in particular with the name of Heinz Hartmann. Like Melanie Klein, Hartmann wrote very little about affect, yet his conceptions were to dominate the contributions of American psychoanalysts on the subject.[9]

It is no doubt difficult for an analyst outside the movement of ideas in North America to appreciate the contribution made to them by Rapaport and Hartmann. Nevertheless Rapaport's article, 'On the psychoanalytic theory of affects' (1953), may be regarded as typical of the Hartmannian view on the matter. Like most of the authors, Rapaport shows how difficult it is to define precisely the sphere of affect, which, in the psychoanalytic field, embraces states and forms between which it is difficult to find a unity. The difficulty in theorizing the problem of affect in psychoanalysis stems from the fact that we have to reconcile Freud's different approaches to the concept, which, depending on the shifting metapsychological contexts in which it occurs, is variously linked to a theory of catharsis, conflict or signal.

According to the first conception, affect, libido and cathexis are equivalents. According to the second, the affect, produced by the operation of a safety valve, is in opposition to representation. Whereas representation persists in the form of a memory trace, the affect exists only *in potentia*. In this context, the innate aptitude to conflict implies innate thresholds of discharge, of which tolerance to frustration is a reflection. For Rapaport, the transition to the third conception of affect, that of affect as signal of the ego, represents an opening up to a 'structural-adaptive' point of view and implies that the stress is to be placed on the genetic point of view. This interpretation of Freud's thought leads Rapaport to propose his own conception.

Originally affects 'use inborn channels and thresholds of discharge' before the id–ego differentiation. Apart from a discharge function, they have a socio-communitive role that is expressed according to hereditary predispositions. At the stage at which the sovereignty of the pleasure principle is established, the affect functions as a safety-valve when there are tensions

9 Of course, it is not my intention to suggest that *all* the North American works are of Hartmannian inspiration, any more than I believe that Hartmann's influence is confined to North America. Many authors in the United States are only distantly related to the Hartmannian current and make no more than passing references to it. Furthermore, although Hartmann's thought has had little impact in France, it has penetrated certain circles in British psychoanalysis (see later the work of Sandler and Joffe). Recent criticisms (Apfelbaum, Eissler), 'evaluations' of Hartmann's thought (Holt), a certain distance taken with regard to the major themes of that thought (Schafer) are so many hints of a change in direction.

caused by the absence of the object. But a complete discharge is impossible. In fact, the affect survives when it reaches a threshold beyond which the innate ways are able to support the tension. The discharge merely brings the said ways back to a tolerable quantity of tension. The mobility of the cathexes of free energy takes account of 'massive affect-storms'. The effect of the internalizations and of the contributions of reality leads to an increase in the tolerance threshold and makes it possible to postpone the discharge. This modification of the thresholds gives rise to 'a hierarchy of motivations ranging from drives to interests and preferences'.[10] This transition, which corresponds to the development of the secondary processes, is achieved through the activity of linking; the experimental action of thought and memory on the hallucinatory activity.

The predominance of the idea over the affect in the representation of the drive tends to give an ever larger place to the idea of 'thought representing reality'. The control of the affects is achieved with their neutralization. The affective loads are subjected to anticathexes. However, the old structures persist beyond anticathexes and are likely to reappear during affective storms and in the primary processes. But the neutralization has culminated in the production of signal-affects that gradually become 'signals of signals'. 'Regressions in the service of the ego' (Kris) may, according to Rapaport, explain certain affective states. Normality would not consist in affective neutralization alone, but also in variability and affective modulation, whereas the pathological states will be characterized by the rigidity, intensity and sheer massiveness of the productions of affect.

At each level, however, one detects a conflict between the various levels (the dynamic point of view), between neutralization and discharge (the economic point of view). Lastly, the various agencies act in a synergic or antagonistic way, from a point of view that takes reality into account (the structural or adaptive point of view).

This article, whose influence on American psychoanalytic thought is considerable (few authors risk not quoting it), shows the way followed since Freud. Never has Freud's thought been more secularized. Freud was content with the dynamic, economic and topographical points of view. The topographical has become structural, and as if something were lacking in the Freudian metapsychology, the genetic and adaptive point of view will complete it. In fact, the last two theoretical axes have devoured the others, as we shall see later.

Jacobson (1953) is the author of what may rightly be regarded as the most interesting article on the subject in the psychoanalytic literature. She develops her own thinking while arguing the opinions expressed notably by

10   D. Rapaport (1953), p. 194.

Glover, Brierley and Rapaport. She proposes the following classification of the affects:

1 *Simple and compound affects arising from intrasystemic tensions*:
   (a) affects that represent instinctual drives proper; i.e. that arise directly from tensions in the id (e.g. sexual excitement, rage);
   (b) affects that develop directly from tensions in the ego (e.g. fear of reality and physical pain, as well as components of the more enduring feelings and feeling attitudes, such as object love and hate, or thing interests);
2 *Simple and compound affects induced by intersystemic tensions*:
   (a) affects induced by tensions between the ego and the id (e.g. fear of the id, components of disgust, shame and pity);
   (b) affects induced by tensions between ego and superego (e.g. guilt feelings, components of depression).[11]

Jacobson proposes an interesting solution to the question as to whether the affect should be regarded as a phenomenon of tension or as a phenomenon of discharge. In her view, the two aspects are inseparable:

Viewed from the socioeconomical standpoint, an external or internal stimulus leads to rises of tension resulting in a psychic release and discharge process; this process finds expression in motor phenomena as well as in sensations and feelings perceived by the outer and inner surface of consciousness.[12]

From this point of view, the affects are conceived as 'responses' or 'reactions' to stimuli. The affect derives from the coupling of phenomena of tension and phenomena of discharge. Tension increasing at one point may develop while it is already decreasing at another point through partial discharge. Cathexis and anticathexis co-exist. In pleasure, discharge may begin when tension is still increasing. The psychical situation calls for change. The pleasure of tension may induce a need for greater excitement, maximum pleasure for reduction, and the pleasure of reduction nostalgia for a pleasure of tension.

These remarks weaken the conception of the affect as a result of non-discharge (Rapaport); the affect is just as much the result of instinctual cathexis.

It is not difficult to imagine the effect that this new formulation of the

11 E. Jacobson (1953), p. 46.
12 Ibid., p. 50.

affect had on the most fundamental data of theory. Thus the pleasure principle no longer has the aim of reducing tensions.

> The pleasure principle and, later on, its modification, the reality princi-
> ple, would only direct the course of the biological swings around a middle
> axis of tensions; i.e., the modes of the discharge processes. Pleasure qual-
> ities would be attached to the swings of the tension pendulum to either
> side, as long as the corresponding psychophysiological discharge processes
> can select certain preferred pathways and as the changes of tension can
> take a definite course – depending, so it seems, on certain still unknown
> proportions between the amounts of excitation and the speed and rhythm
> of discharge.[13]

The metapsychological conclusions to be drawn from these formulations
profoundly alter the Freudian conception: 'The essential biological laws that
govern psychic life are the function of a control and gratification of the
psychic drives, the function of adaptation and the function of self-
preservation'.[14]

Homeostasis is, in the final analysis, the centre of a psychical–biological
homology. The pleasure principle is itself subjected to a higher, homeostatic principle. This reference to biology leads to the reformulation of the
conception of aggressivity. Aggressivity is in direct relation to frustration.
Tolerance of tension is envisaged only in relation to the control of frustration. In short, it is the genetic point of view that accounts for the success or
failure of affective maturity, that is to say, the success of adaptation to the
reality principle, by reducing the affect to its function as signal.

These two contributions from the North American school lay down the
new theoretical axes of psychoanalysis:

- introduction of the structural and genetic points of view;
- reference to the adaptive aim from a psychobiological perspective in the
  study of the stimulus-response dyad;
- study of phenomena from the point of view of the gratification–frustration
  dyad, linking the libido to the first and aggressivity to the second;
- maturative scale tending to the establishment of the function of signalization to the aims of adaptation;
- distinction between the ego and the self (and the id, for Max Schur), the
  ego providing autonomous apparatuses with a view to adaptation.

13 Ibid., p. 58.
14 Ibid.

The gulf between the psychoanalysis deriving from Hartmann's conceptions and that deriving from Melanie Klein's grows wider. The Freudian heritage will be divided between these two new patrimonies.

Since 1953, a large number of works on the affect have appeared that followed the directions laid down by Hartmann and Rapaport.

Some of these are purely theoretical, others more oriented towards clinical practice, a small number based on the observation of affects in treatment.

1 Theoretical works

In an analysis of Freud's works from 1888 to 1898, that is, from the first ten years of his work, Stewart (1967) sets out to show that the essential purpose of the anxiety affect – its function as signal, awakening the ego, in the interests of adaptation – was envisaged by Freud from the outset. In short, from the beginning, well before *Inhibitions, Symptoms and Anxiety*, Freud seems to have maintained the signal hypothesis. The affect, therefore, is a message, bearing information, inscribed in the regulatory processes of the psychical apparatus as a whole.

The North American authors are divided in their metapsychological writings, on the relations between the economic point of view and the point of view that might be called signaletic. Many of them tried to abandon all economic perspectives and stress exclusively the function of signalization, conceived in the context of stimulus–response relations.

Among the authors who maintained the economic conception is Borje-Löfgren (1964), who proposes a purely energic conception of affect. Psychical excitation will be understood according to the data of nervous excitation (the study of energic potentials, transference of charges of potentials raised to the least high potentials, wave of negativity, isolation of pools of energy, etc.). Here affect is the pure product of energy exchanges, without any reference to quality other than as a result of operations of drainage between the ego and the id. Later, this author was to extend his views and rally to the thesis of affect as mimetic expression with communicative value (1968), attempting a difficult harmonization with his earlier opinions.

We owe to Louis Kaywin (1960) an essay of *epigenetic* inspiration. Freud's energic reference is rejected, for, according to Kaywin, energy cannot be studied outside *the structuro-energic functions and processes of reaction-patterns*. These reaction-patterns are stratified in *hierarchies of structuro-functional units*. Thus Kaywin takes us from *chemico-energic* units to *genetic* units, then to *embryological* units, to end finally with *psycho-biological and psychoanalytic* units.

According to Kaywin, it is not legitimate to refer to an energic point of view in psychoanalysis in that it is unnecessary to differentiate between psychical and biological energy, the latter being the only one whose existence is accepted. From this point of view, affects are representations of internal and external signals that undergo structuralizations and become representations of the self. The affect is a sense of self, positive or negative, whose function is to represent psychical activities. '*These tonal perceptions relative to (associated with) the self* (more correctly, parts of the self) *may be described as affects.*'

It is not without some anxiety that one comes to the end of Kaywin's article, where, referring to Rapaport, he makes the following propositions:

1. The concepts of drive, drive fusion, specific drives (sex, aggression, life and death instincts, etc.) are of a lesser generality, and may well change or be replaced as the theory changes.
2. The concepts of cathexis, binding, and neutralization . . . it is uncertain whether they will survive in their present form.
3. The concepts of id, ego, superego [are not] indispensable.
4. The classic conception of libido development . . . may well undergo radical change, as it becomes one aspect of the integral process of epigenesis.[15]

This extremist position, from a psychobiological point of view, gave rise to less radical contributions. One might mention the work of Burgess E. Moore (1968), which connects the physiologically dischargeable affect to cerebral structures (the limbic system). The unconscious status of the primary affects is due, according to this view, to their physiological nature.

Only the differentiation between self and non-self would allow the affect to be attached to ideation and therefore to be turned into a psychical production. We should remember that Max Schur, in his work on the id, defends the idea of a physiological continuum and postulates a continuity between need, drive and desire. Jacobson has also argued the hypothesis of a psychophysiological self.

It is in the genetic study of development that many authors seek the key to the problem.

The Rochester group, around Engel, best known for his studies of the child Monica, has examined the problem of *the primary affects of unpleasure in the child* (1962). This author studies the transition from the biological field to the psychological field, stressing the value of affect as a mode of archaic communication. Engel divides affect into two broad categories. The first

---

15   L. Kaywin (1964), pp. 639 and 651.

belongs to biology and includes the affects of instinctual discharge. These are prior to the constitution of the ego. They possess a feeble value as signal, their whole effect being concentrated in discharge. The division into pleasure–unpleasure does not operate here; only libidinal or aggressive expression may emerge through them, a fusion between these two types being possible. These affects are responses to psychodynamic situations that cannot be acted out.

The advent of the ego (ninth month) marks the passage to the psychobiological field. The affects then take on a value as signal scanning. Their information may be decoded in the registers of pleasure or unpleasure. At this stage, the reality test functions and the ego is subjected to the reality principle. The function of discharge moves into the second plane.

In order to support his hypothesis, Engel uses the distinction proposed by Freud between automatic and signal anxiety. However, automatic anxiety induces two types of response. One belongs to the *active model* (tears, movement expressing an appeal for gratification), whereas the other belongs to a *passive model* (reaction of astonishment of a self-preserving kind).

Thus two broad types of affect may be contrasted. *Anxiety* mobilizes a warning system signalling a danger for the ego and evoking a threat to the self, in the context of a relationship that allows a distinction between self and object. Anxiety then appears as an effort to guarantee the satisfaction of needs in regressive mode; this anxiety is accompanied by an activation of the primitive, neuro-endocrinal and psychical systems.

The other broad type of affect is the reaction to loss of the object: *depression withdrawal.* This massive regression marks the defeat of the ego, the failure of the mechanisms described by Melanie Klein – denial, introjection, and projection. The only solution is a return to the stage of *pre-object indifferentiation*, which is expressed by a collapse into comatose sleep. At a less profound level, we see the appearance of affects of *helplessness* and *despair.* This hibernating regression is a sort of self-preserving withdrawal, tending to the minimum reduction of energic expenditure, at once self-abandonment and waiting for external help. In the most desperate cases there may even be psychical and somatic disorganizations leading to death.

Following Engel, Schmale (1964) proposed a genetic classification of the affects laid out in two broad stages; first of non-distinction between self and object and, later, their differentiation. The epigenetic point of view is still the determining factor of metapsychology. However, it may well be asked whether these studies might better find their place in psychobiology or genetic psychology, rather than in psychoanalysis.

As we have seen, theorizations of affect have depended more and more clearly on relations between self and object. Leo Spiegel (1966) set out to study affects from this point of view, that is to say, by considering the relations between affect and narcissism. His work was to be centred not so much on anxiety as on pain considered in terms of metapsychological concepts, always oriented by a genetic perspective.

For Spiegel, narcissism represents the quantity of cathexis of the self-presentation, insofar as it may be opposed to cathexis of the object presentation, in each individual. Narcissism does not denote the cathexis of the total person in object relations and cannot be confined to the subject of the said relationship. One may speak of the connection of the narcissism of both sides in object relations.

The self is a psychical entity within the psychical apparatus. It is distinct from the presentations of the self, which are vectors of individual memory traces with their cathexes. The self is the result of the pooling of these affects to form a single overall cathexis. *The self is the constant average cathexis of all the presentations of the self.* According to Spiegel, therefore, one may suppose the existence of a barrier (similar to that of the protective shield) between self-presentation and object presentation, which prevents the breaking in of elements from one field to the other.

This model is used to explain the origin and nature of many affects. The same quantity of energy passing through the elements of this model may produce qualitative varieties of affects. For example, desire may be understood as the hyper-cathexis of self-presentation, whereas nostalgia relates to the hyper-cathexis of object presentation. It should be made clear that, according to Spiegel, there is desire only insofar as there is a subjective consciousness (a desiring I = self), which is not the case when there is excitation without intervention of the subject (but only of an isolated presentation of the self = self-presentation). Anxiety is defined as a response to the temporary loss of the external object that provides satisfaction, whereas pain is a response to the prolonged or definitive loss of the permanent external object (different from the object that provides satisfaction). In nostalgia, the maintenance of the cathexis of the absent object intervenes despite satisfaction (provided by another object). If the absence of the object is prolonged, the cathexis of the permanent object is oriented in accordance with the ways of least resistance towards the id, towards the object–self barrier. The lowering of the cathexes of the self leads to a thrust of the id that breaks the self–object barrier and produces the affect of psychical pain against which the ego strives to struggle.

To a lesser degree, the affects of humiliation and shame testify to narcissistic wounding. Spiegel defends the hypothesis of a primary ideal ego, the agency that matches the child's ability to make the mother appear (an ability that lies at the origin of a feeling of power and triumph), whose failure entails negative affects (above all helplessness and defeat). This matrix-agency of the later ego ideal will serve as a buffer to the effects of the object on the ego.

Psychical pain is due therefore to the absence of an external influence from the permanent, external object. The internalization of this affect entails the constant presentation of the object in the self. The fact that protection can be obtained only through the intervention of the Other entails a humiliating dependence on the Other. Since the absence of the Other is inevitable, the agency of the precocious ego ideal tends therefore to diminish the effects of this lack of object by a narcissistic provision.

Although Spiegel provides a useful description of the relations between self and object, one cannot help but feel that a shift of emphasis is placed *on real experience* to the detriment of phantasied reality, as illustrated in the work of the Kleinian authors.

To end this consideration of the metapsychological constructions, mention should be made of the work of Sandler and Joffe (1967),[16] which overtly claims allegiance to 'the psychoanalytic psychology of adaptation'. These authors propose a model in which the influence of Hartmann is evident. They conceive of the neuroses as pathogenic adaptations to the secondary effects of an event, reality or particular experience belonging to the external world. Recalling certain of Freud's hypotheses, they see the affect as the result of a traumatic experience (the thesis of *Studies on Hysteria*), as indicator (Hartmann) of an instinctual quantity and as response to a stimulus. As such, the affect becomes a mediator of adaptation. Adopting the position of Max Schur, who regards the pleasure principle as a homeostatic principle of constancy, regulating mental functioning and instinctual balance, Sandler and Joffe dissociate the principle of pleasure–unpleasure from the affective experiences of pleasure and unpleasure.

Since the regulatory and adaptive aim has been assigned to this principle, psychical functioning proceeds through successive positive integrations. These integrations are accompanied by psychical and physical feelings. Sandler and Joffe then propose to introduce into metapsychology a *principle of safety*. Its aim is the constitution of a *central affective state*. 'The maintenance of this *central affective state* is perhaps the most powerful motive for ego development'.[17] This hypothesis leads one to envisage the functioning of the ego as a maintenance at all costs of a feeling of well-being aimed at eliminating all conscious or unconscious disharmony with this ideal. Its ultimate aim is the reduction of that gap between the ideal self deriving from a harmonious psychobiological function and the actual self. Individuation consists in a gradual development in which reality-adapted ideals replace infantile ideals. The article ends with the declaration that psychoanalytic psychology

---

16 I have dealt with this work here on account of its closeness to the thinking of the North American school.
17 Joffe and Sandler (1968), p. 449.

is the psychology of adaptation to changes in the affective states and that 'any particular aspect of the theory of adaptation (e.g. adaptation to the demands of the drives, or to the external environment) can be encompassed within the framework of the wider model'.[18]

This final metapsychological reference testifies to the importance of Hartmann's thought in British psychoanalytic thought.

Throughout the analysis of these works of theoretical inspiration, one finds Hartmann's thesis of the affects as 'indicators', which has led most of the authors to subscribe to the notion of the cognitive value of the affect. Max Schur thought fit to recall it in 1969.[19] The analysis of the Freudian writings leads him to conclude that 'the affects and their vicissitudes are linked with a cognitive process, influenced by perceptions and memories'. All the affects have both an aspect as response and a cognitive aspect. Freud's last conception of the signal of anxiety, which comes into play when faced with a dangerous situation, displays this view, for *the concept of signal is a cognitive concept.*

Perhaps I should make it clear that although I do subscribe to the notion of the cognitive function of the affect, I cannot view it in the same way. What the American authors repeat over and over again is that *the signal of affect has an adaptive value.*[20] The link between signal and thing is implicit in their work. In my opinion, it is heuristically much more fruitful to link the affect to the process of symbolization and to the other types of *signifiers* present in the psychoanalytic process. This difference is, in my opinion, an important one.

18 Ibid., p. 453.
19 In this work, Max Schur also discusses the Freudian thesis of the *Papers on Metapsychology* that challenges the possibility that the affect could be unconscious. The debate seems to be continuing on this matter, if an article by Pulver (1971) is anything to go by. There Pulver enumerates a number of positions on the question to be found in works that, while not dealing directly with it, are obviously concerned with a subject on which psychoanalysts are divided. Thus Eisler, G.S. Klein, Knapp, Schafer, and Joffe and Sandler admit the possibility of unconscious affects, whereas Blau, Moore and Fine, and Siegal remain faithful to the position expressed by Freud in the *Papers on Metapsychology*. Fenichel takes up position between the two. It is regrettable that Pulver does not take into consideration a passage in *The Ego and the Id* that marks a decisive step forward towards a solution of the problem. The distinction between unconscious affect and potential affect does not seem very enlightening and ought to be included in a broader framework.
20 Modell (1971) thinks that the data on the study of the affect provided by collective psychology has been unduly neglected. In his opinion, the adaptational intentions of the affect are no longer of use to anyone: they are at the service of the group's adaptational needs. For him, the notion of group is an extremely broad one, since it includes any situation involving two partners: the mother–child relation, the analytic situation, etc. In this context, the affect would have a communicative, adaptational value, while taking into account the real elements of the situation. Modell recalls the interesting observation made by Charles Rycroft, for whom the essence of the affect is its perception by others and the fact that the affect has the capacity to arouse on the part of the object who perceives it identical or complementary affective responses.

2 Clinical works

However artificial the distinction that I have adopted between the theoretical works and others may be, it enables the isolation of certain authors who have been less influenced by Hartmann.

Blau (1955) has focused discussion on the affect around the opposition between the actual neuroses and the transference neuroses, as in Freud's various theories concerning anxiety. In an attempt to make a synthesis of the different aspects of affect (physiological and psychological), he recalls Freud's hypotheses on the anxiety neurosis. In the affective states related to it, what is at work is essentially a process of a physiological nature; the psychological reactions associated with it are, in every sense of the term, secondary. With the neuroses and psychoses, it is 'the false ideational roads' that gave rise to the productions of the neuroses and psychoses. What we find here is an idea dear to psychosomaticians of the Paris school concerning the paucity of mentalizations in the psychosomatic affections. However, Blau recalls that the actual neuroses are originally transference neuroses and psychoses. He concludes from this that the anxiety neuroses may either give rise to neuropsychoses in which the unconscious conflict is of an ideational nature, the affective disturbances deriving from them, or to the functional (or affective) psychoses, these being related to the somatic element of the anxiety neurosis, the ideational aspect having, in their clinical picture, to be relegated to a secondary rank.

The discussion that has opened up here concerns the relations between affect and representation. An echo of this is to be found in Novey (1959 and 1961), who is concerned with the relations between primary and secondary affects. Although Novey takes up most of the themes that have occurred in the discussion of affect (unconscious-affect, memory-affect, cognitive affect, etc.), he is notable for his unusual view of the problems of *the psychical representation of objects*. 'It is, in fact, difficult to say whether one had better speak of an internal representation of an object as a constellation of ideas with an affective colouring or as an affective experience which is only secondarily perceived as having ideational content'[21] The second solution seems to him to be more dynamic. Whereas the secondary defences involve the participation of language, the primary defences (introjection–projection) exclude it. The affects dominate these processes of incorporation. Certain affects play an *organizing* role in the orientation towards and the reactions to the object. This role is to be found in the organization of the character, what Weinshel (1968) was to develop in his study of moods. Clinical practice shows that, whereas in the neuroses the

---

21 Novey (1959), p. 23.

distinction between idea and affect is present, in the borderline states, such a distinction does not apply. Novey speaks of non-representative empty spaces.

Following Novey, Schafer (1964) confronts the problem of affect in a way not often to be found among the English-speaking authors. His work is notable for its non-genetic orientation. He subjects the study of affect to the examination of eight parameters:

A – *Existence* The expression of affects is no proof of their authenticity, nor, on the other hand, is absence of expression any proof of their dissimulation, any more than their hyper-expressivity necessarily proves their artificiality. Thus any phenomenological approach to affects is inadequate.

B – *Formation* Formation rather than development, which lends itself to ambiguity. The interpretation of the defences reveals new affects that are difficult to define. The formation of precise affects seems to depend on a work of isolation, of fragmentation, as well as on a work of representation and synthesis. The affect is interdependent on a configuration that supports its manifestations.

C – *Strength* The optimum force for the expression of the affect is not the maximum force. The signal affect is certainly the result of an evolved elaboration. However, affective reduction cannot be interpreted as a sign of maturity. Openness to the affect is a better one.

D – *Stimuli* Their origin is neither internal nor external. Affects are sometimes derived from objects, sometimes oriented towards them or in reaction against them.

E – *Complexity and paradox* Analysis reconstructs the affective aggregates, given a more or less secondary autonomy. However, one cannot lose sight of the fact that a certain psychologism reduces the affect to a mere pseudo-reality. Affective authenticity involves complexity, ambiguity, and not the simplicity required by an idealizing approach.

F – *Location* Affects must be located in relation to *time* (substitution of one affect by another), in relation to *level* (affective stratification), in relation to *persons* (role of the borrowing of one affect belonging to a person with whom one identifies) and in relation to *corporal zones* (attribution of affects from one zone to another). The reference to the body is a starting point, not an end.

G – *Communication* The affect is a relation between a message and a response. It may be used in the manipulation of other people (interpsychical communication) or in relation to oneself (intra- and inter-psychical communication). Empathy is not solely oriented towards others; it also applies to oneself, by a process of exchange between the affect and consciousness.

H – *History*　This is the ontogenetic aspect – one that hardly needs to be stressed.

Bertram Lewin (1963) made an important contribution to the theoretical problems posed by affect. Our mental habits lead us to seek 'pure' intellectual and affective categories. Yet primitive (or primary) subjective experiences are by nature experiences in which what later development will allow us to distinguish as intellectual and affective are mixed up in an indissociable whole. We 'decondense' the primitive subjective experience that comes to us in that massive, undifferentiated form. Freudian metapsychology has perhaps remained prisoner to a psychological atomism that strives at all costs to distinguish between the destiny of an affect and the destiny of a representation. However, Lewin remains attached to the thesis of affect as conscious subjective formation. Psychoanalytic practice provides examples of pure affects in 'blank dreams' without representative connotations in which only the affect is present. But, according to Lewin, such dreams, which belong to manifest content, are highly elaborate products, the ego's defence mechanisms (split, denial, isolation, etc.), playing an important role in their production, as also does regression of course. In fact, the affects are always composite formations, compromises – like symptoms – between the emanations of the id and the activities of the ego. Thus we may observe certain 'screen-affects' that are similar to screen-memories. There is therefore a structuring of the affects, in the direction either of differentiation (affective–intellectual) or of affective elaboration (constructions of affects), in which the ego intervenes in a major way.

3 Works centred on the experience of treatment

Peto (1967) has brought together the various kinds of *affect control* on the basis of psychoanalytic experience. He distinguishes between two situations: that in which the analysand is able to break with an affect in its earliest stages and that in which he allows himself to sink into the affect and becomes drowned by it. These two situations encountered in treatment reveal two different structures. When the subject is able to break the affective wave, it is not that he rejects it, but that he changes representation and theme. In this case, the affect is linked, in a superficial, functional way, with a circumscribed, isolated, very limited representation. However, this work, which uses other means, may end up in a mood that blocks the progress of representations: this leads to the second possibility. Peto interprets the first situation as a movement of states from the ego to the id. On the other hand, an affective wave may be controlled by being fragmented into limited representations: this indicates work proceeding from the id to the ego. What we find here is the signal affect as affect of the ego, which proceeds through work on other representations, and the affect as instinctual derivative of the id. In the first instance, tension, according to the terminology of Hartmann and Jacobson, is intrasystemic; in the second, it is intersystemic.

Faced with the first affective mobilizations, the appearance of affective nuances, subdued affects, is linked to the displacement of representations towards new (regressive or more adapted) groups of images. For Peto, these various affective nuances are linked to a *central agency*, which maintains control over the affective symbolization and the emergent units in the psychical process. In short, the anticipatory function of the ego continues to act on these bearers of affects in such a way as not to allow itself to be overwhelmed by tension and tries, by fragmenting it, to divert that tension on to contiguous representations.

But if this capacity of the ego is overwhelmed, the subject is invaded by a sudden upsurge of archaic affects, or by a mood that imbues all the psychical processes. Defensive reactions indicate the possibility of responses by the operating, functional parts of the ego. When the split between the ego and the other agencies loses its efficacity, the ego becomes incapable of carrying out its functions of self-observation and this may lead, in certain cases, to an obscuring of consciousness by the affect. Violent affective reactions, outbursts of anger, in depression or depersonalizion, empty the ego in the first case or lead to a shattering of it in the second. In either case, the outcome represents a defeat of the ego.

Despite the reference to Hartmann's metapsychology, this work has the merit of placing the problem of the affect in the chain of associative productions. The phenomenology of the affect is less important than its appearance in a psychical thought process. This process operates in certain cases possessing symbolic efficacity, whereas in others the affect shatters this process and becomes dispersed. We shall see later the usefulness of this way of seeing things.

Valenstein (1961) considers the affect above all in terms of an emotional reliving, of insight achieved during treatment. He describes a defence mechanism, *affectualization*, that consists in the production during treatment of an excess of affect whose essential aim is to forbid any insight. The dramatic affective turbulence constitutes a smokescreen preventing insight and paralysing intellectual awareness. This is close to Bouvet's description of transference resistance and also to Freud in his article 'Observations on transference-love'. However, we should not be too hasty in concluding that affective abreaction in treatment is entirely negative. A series of sterile abreactions, paralysing for the analytic work, may in the long term make the ego, freed of its affective excess, sensitive to an interpretation that was rejected during earlier storms. As we know, consideration of the affective nature of the psychoanalytic process led Ferenczi and Rank to advocate an active technique to encourage a positive atmosphere likely to bring to the surface affects that are unconscious because they have never been conscious. Alexander has praised the advantages of corrective emotional experience and Nacht became the defender of a technique of similar inspiration. However, many regard these changes as *acting-out* on the part of the analyst. With great subtlety, Valenstein shows that the problem cannot be considered without reference to structures. Although certain structures require the analyst to depart from his benevolent neutrality in order to encourage a positive transference, without which no progress in the transference neurosis can occur, the classical neuroses still require the classical technique.

In fact, the kernel of a structured unconscious is constituted by the ideo-affective complex. The *cognitive* aspect is doubled by a *conative*[22] aspect. Thus, if one wishes to bring out knowledge through the affect, it is more justified to refer knowledge to conation, in order to avoid sliding towards an intellectualist interpretation of the affect, of which many an example can be found in the North American literature.

Valenstein's conclusion reminds us, through the phenomena of treatment, of the impossibility of solving the problems of the affect without reference to the analytic processes and without the help of rigorous theory.

At the beginning of this chapter, I stressed the importance of the works of Melanie Klein and her school. Here, again, I am faced with a paradoxical situation. For, although it is true that Kleinian authors have contributed much to our knowledge of affect, very few of them have confronted the problem from a theoretical angle.

Bion, in his complex, well argued oeuvre, high in ambition and open in outlook, confronted the problem in a series of works. I shall confine my attention to his book *Elements of Psychoanalysis* (1963), in which he makes some valuable observations. It would be impossible to provide a detailed exposition of it here, for to do so would entail an examination of the entire theoretical framework of which it is a part.[23] Suffice it to say that Bion proposes a double-entry grid in which a vertical sequence represents the

---

22 Conation is to be found neither in Littré nor in Robert. Lalande makes it the synonym of *effort* or *tendance*. Whereas effort is applied to action, tendency applies to the passions. 'Conation presents rather the idea of effort as a fact that may be given either a voluntarist or an intellectualist interpretation – perhaps as a result of its link with *conatus*, used by Spinoza, *Ethics*, III, proposition 7.' Spinoza writes: 'The effort by which each thing strives to persevere in its being is nothing outside the actual essence of that thing.' We can see that Lalande seems to eliminate the affective sense from conation. Webster gives the sense to which Valenstein refers: the biological force that may make its appearance in the consciousness as volition of desire or in behaviour as a tendency to action.

23 Luzès gave a general exposé of the question to the 1968 Congrès des Langues romanes, Lisbon.

historico-genetic dimension and a horizontal sequence the synchronic thought processes. From this point of view, the emotions as well as the precursors of emotion are considered. Premonition is to affect what pre-conception is to conception in the intellectual sense. By preconception, we must understand not preconceived judgement, but a matrix of conception, an innate unconscious disposition, based on waiting for and expecting a fulfilment involving the participation of an object. Bion compares this theorization of the concept of empty thoughts with Kant. Thus a correspondence is set up between ideational categorization and emotional categorization. Far from defending the idea that categorization distinguishes in a very clear way between idea and emotion, Bion, on the contrary, shows the equivalence of the two registers by shifting the stress towards the emotional register.

> I shall represent this shift of emphasis by using the term 'feeling' instead of the term 'thinking'. This substitution is based on the common usage, in analytic practice, of phrases such as 'I feel I had a dream last night,' or, 'I feel you hate me,' or 'I feel that I am going to have a breakdown.' Such locutions imply an emotional experience and are therefore more appropriate to my purpose than the more austere implication of 'I think . . .' Communications introduced by terms such as 'I feel . . .' are often methods of expressing emotions or premonitions. It is in their function as expressions of emotion that I wish to consider these phenomena.[24]

Bion concludes, therefore, that there is an equivalence between 'I think' and 'I feel' and applies the term 'thought' to emotion as well as to thought itself. Indeed Bion's theory of thought certainly looks like *a structural theory of the affects*, filling the gap between intellect and affect. However, this does not entail a 'confusionism' in which empathic intuition would forbid any work of analytic deconstruction. The separation of registers between intellect and affects may be useful *in the analysis of the elements of psychical activity*.

> The analyst must decide whether the idea that is expressed is intended to be an instrument whereby feelings are communicated or whether the feelings are secondary to the idea. Many subtle expressions of feeling can be missed if the ideas by which they are expressed are regarded, wrongly, to be the main burden of the communication.[25]

24 Bion (1963), p. 95.
25 Ibid., p. 96.

At the level of the most elementary units of psychical activity – what Bion calls 'elements' – one defines a structure in which 'thoughts' and 'things' are equivalent. But where one observes such an equivalence (as in psychotics), one also finds an equivalence between phantasy and 'facts'. Bion is led therefore to interpret phantasy as the affective counterpart of thoughts at this level. 'These phantasies that are indistinguishable from facts must be considered as the emotional counterpart of β-element "thoughts" that are indistinguishable from "things"'.[26]

From my analysis of psychoanalytic works on the affect in the English-speaking literature, from Jones to Max Schur, have emerged two broad currents of thought stemming from two of Freud's contemporaries: Melanie Klein and Hartmann. In the course of that analysis it has also become clear that my own preference is for the Kleinian tendency rather than the Hartmannian. There is nothing dogmatic, however, about this preference: I am happy to include in that tendency, despite the radical splits that have occurred within it, many authors who broke with Melanie Klein after being strongly influenced by her. One of my most surprising discoveries was the extent to which the North American literature possesses features – abstraction and intellectualization, for example – that it shares with the work of the French analysts. This disembodiment of psychoanalytic theory assumes different forms, of course, from those current in France. North American psychoanalytic theory is directed towards psychology – has not psychoanalysis been referred to as psychoanalytic psychology? – in which Piaget is very much in the forefront. This psychology is resolutely genetic. At this point, I should like to remove any possible misunderstanding. Although my reticence with regard to genetic psychoanalysis may have become evident in these pages, it is not because I tend in any way to diminish the infantile origins of the unconscious. However, it is one thing to formulate a theory of diachrony in psychoanalysis, but quite another to drown the specificity of psychoanalytic thought in a theory of the development of personality. Whatever criticism might be levelled at Kleinian authors concerning the correspondence between the facts that they describe and the place of those facts in the calendar of chronology, this 'incredible' version of development strikes me as more credible than that of the authors who have more or less followed Hartmann.

These remarks directly concern the problem of the affect, since the historical dimension is pre-eminently associated with it.

It now remains to me to say something about the situation of the problem in France. One should bear in mind that, despite the excellent

26 Ibid., p. 97.

information available in the 'Latin' countries concerning the work of English-speaking analysts – the reverse is not the case – few authors associate themselves with the thought either of Hartmann or Melanie Klein.

II Theoretical positions on affect in France

We should be under no illusion about the scarcity of works devoted to affect in the French psychoanalytic literature. There is a constant implicit reference to the affect to be found there, whether in theoretical, clinical or technical discussions.[27]

Mallet from a theoretical and Bouvet from a clinical point of view have directly confronted the problem.

Mallet (1969), like Pasche in his report on *L'angoisse et la théorie des instincts* (1953), has made a particularly careful study of the relations between affect and representation.

> Whereas representation is directed at the aim to be achieved and the (substitutable) object of desire, affect allows the ego to experience through the states that it feels and in relation to the body. Thus affect and ego are indissolubly linked. Affects may be accepted or rejected by the ego, hence the broad categories: affects related to appetites, put it into play by the drive accepted by the ego and inhibiting affects, whose type is the anxiety triggered off by anticipation of satisfaction refused by the ego.[28]

It is the intervention of the ego in the announcement of an instinctual demand that, from the latency period, 'decides' on the acceptance or rejection of the impulse. The link between ego and affect explains how identification plays a major role in affect. Affect is then felt when the subject is targeted by the desire of the object or when it takes the place of the object, experiencing the satisfaction that it attributes to it. Diachronic latency of the ego, or identificatory, synchronic effect, in either case, the attitude of the ego towards affects is always more or less imbued with suspicion towards an unleashing that runs the risk of compromising the organization of the ego or of triggering off the rigour of superego or object, a reminder of primal affective experiences.

---

27 Apart from Pasche's 'L'angoisse et la théorie des instincts' and 'La dépression', these include, of course, 'Les états dépressifs' by Nacht and Racamier, Fain's 'Le processus psychanalytique', the essays by Neyraut and Geahchan on nostalgia, and those of David on love. J. Gillibert's works, which go well beyond the problem of the affect, allude implicitly to it.
28 Mallet (1969), p. 169.

Although it is true that affect is first of all information for the ego, the primary discharge function serving as a support to the secondary function of communication with the object, affect its endowed with a power of information for others. The advent of spoken language makes a considerable affective economy possible, but affect does not accommodate itself to restrictions imposed by the preconscious. Where speech aims at disguising desire, affect denies speech and approaches the ego directly. Hence the struggle against the masking of the id's desires by controlling the expression of affects, their signifying function. However, escape from control is the rule for affect, whereas action may be inhibited successfully. The arrival of affect is interdependent, therefore, with a regression of the ego. The tightening of control on affect dissociates the crudest instinctual expressions and rests on the contingent of drives with inhibited aim that express no more than tender feelings in place of more immediately sensual instinctual expressions. The defensive work of the ego bears extensively on the aim, the object (representation at least) and affect. Let us consider the dissolution of the Oedipus complex. At most the ego may evoke the repressed representation, freely, thanks to a new cathexis, but not the affect. The repressed may be accepted intellectually, but not affectively. Everything depends on whether the cathexis used here is that of desexualized energy, in which case it entails only knowledge, or sexualized energy, in which case the ego 'catches fire'. This blazing up of the ego brings the ego back to its origins. In any state involving appetite, 'the ego's mode of being is that of the *subjective* body in the exercise of its internal movements'. A differential clinical analysis of the affects – horror, pity, sexual shyness, disgust, shame, anger – must be related to their inhibited partial drives.

Affects of an aggressive type demand particular attention: when they are linked to pure, destructive tendencies, they escape anxiety (which affects only the fused erotic and destructive drives).

Sometimes the self-destructive tendencies remain the only possible defences against the expression of the aggressive drives. Mallet recalls that Freud, in *Civilization and its Discontents*, attributes the sense of guilt to the destructive drives alone. The repression of the aggressive drive can occur only when it is sufficiently libidinized. We must also distinguish between aggressivity as appetite and aggressivity as reaction (to frustration). Although the appetite-affects are situated in the ego, they originate in the id, whereas the reaction-affects are situated and originate in the ego. Hence the amputation of the ego that their rejection involves, with the possibility of permanent intracorporal modifications, by narcissistic attack. There is, therefore, a difference between the sense of guilt, the consequence of a prejudice against the object through the expression of appetite-affects, in which, because of transgression, the subject 'feels bad', and the sanction set in train by the reaction-aggressivity consequent on frustration, in which guilt does not intervene; self-punishment then assumes the form of retaliation, on account of the narcissistic origin of the affect.

The conclusion of Mallet's work returns to its premises: compared with imaginary dangers, the real dangers represented by the outside world 'signify nothing at first for the ego and very little later when the adult has accepted the notion'. Fear is an affect much more tolerable than anxiety, moral pain or mourning.

It is in his studies on the transference that Bouvet (1954–9) refers directly to affect. He contrasts the transference of affects and emotions with the transference of defences. The relationship at a distance enables the patient not to become conscious of the transference of affects and emotions. However, the repetitive structure of the transference of affects and emotions forces the patient to become aware of the role of the imagos in the transference. Nevertheless, although the transference of defences forms an obstacle to the transference of affects and emotions, the latter may itself be used for defensive ends. Following Lagache, Bouvet describes transference resistance as being very close to the defence by 'affectualization' described by Valenstein (1961).[29] The transference is marked by a series of stormy emotional abreactions, devoid of awareness, in which the affect vanishes in a puff of smoke after being discharged, the acting out completing the affective collapse. The defence that he describes as being kaleidoscopic may be interpreted in the same way. Nevertheless, what is striking here is the mobility and lability of the affective cathexes, which make the material unintelligible on account of its incessant affective and intellectual variability.

'Any transference that is a living experience is, to some extent, very different to remembering and, when it attains a certain intensity, becomes a source of resistances.' This is reminiscent of certain of the observations of

---

29 What is being described by Bouvet (resistance by transference and experiencing too much) and Valenstein (defence by affectualization) seems to belong to the same category as what David (1972) calls 'affective perversion'. By this term, he denotes an 'isolated' mode of satisfaction, in which the subject gets more enjoyment from the provocation of his affects through the phantasy activity that he 'stages', than from the instinctual satisfaction accompanying wish–fulfilment. The affective discharge replaces sexual discharge. Satisfaction is derived from 'the ingenious and refined self-affectation of sensibility, which has come to occupy almost the whole stage and to be substituted as sexual aim (at least as the principal aim) for the normal physiological and psychical aim of the genital function' ('La perversion affective', in *La sexualité perverse*, Paris: Payot, 1972, p. 202). Should we see this as a perversion? David himself seems to hesitate, placing this structure rather between neurosis (in particular, hysterical neurosis) and perversion. His rich description seems to me to be related to what I have described as moral narcissism. However, this is to be is distinguished from it, despite the elements that they share.

Freud, who had originally understood the transference to be an obstacle to psychoanalytic treatment.

By contrasting transference resistance and resistance to transference, the first being manifested by 'feeling too much' or 'experiencing too much' and the second by 'understanding too much', Bouvet returns, as does many an author, to the opposition between hysterico–phobic structures and obsessional structures. Resistance of a hysterico–phobic type subjugates the ego's capacity for self-observation by a sort of hypnotic fascination before the dramatic character of what is being played out in the psyche, in which phantastic scenarios are not only enacted, but also acted out. This has the other consequence of allowing the exercise of the ego's defensive activity only in the implementation, once the affective storm has been liquidated, of a massive repression whose function is to bury in oblivion everything that has appeared as a result of the emotional explosion. We know how much hysterico–phobics find it hard to abandon their fixation on parental objects. This is what the transference resistance aims at maintaining, when the patient has not taken flight, breaking off the analytic relationship. Transference resistance does not necessarily mean positive transference. Of course, excessive positive transference is intended to mask the subjacent negative transference. But the transference resistance may also be expressed in the form of negative transference, all the arguments to denigrate the analyst in his *actual* person being put at the service of misrepresentation.

However, this opposition between two broad types of resistance in analysis intersects with another distinction: that between genital structures and pregenital structures. Their description is familiar. I will simply point out that the fundamental characteristic of the pregenital structures described by Bouvet amounts to the structure of the affects of the object relation (massiveness, unsubtle expression, stormy externalization, absolute demand, projective infiltration, etc.). It is manifested when an approach is made, whether a drawing closer or a rejection.

Bouvet's conception, which has left a mark on the work of French psychoanalysts, is a conception above all of economic inspiration, with all the advantages and inconveniences of such a focus. It continues to inspire psychoanalysts who describe their practical experience of treatments attempted outside the classical rules. It is a conception based on clinical practice rather than on any concern for theoretical elegance.

We know with what 'affective charge' Bouvet's works have been attacked by Lacan and his pupils.[30] The polemic that has arisen between psychoanalysts

---

30 I am referring to Leclaire's criticism – in the Name of the Father – of Bouvet's article 'La cure type' in *L'évolution psychiatrique*.

must not be used as an excuse for rejecting any examination of Lacan's concepts in so far as they concern our subject.

Lacan's work is exemplary in this regard, not only because affect has no place in it, but also because it is explicitly excluded from it. 'In the Freudian field . . . affect is unsuited to play the role of the protopathic subject, since it is a service that has no holder.'[31] This peremptory declaration is arguable, for although it is true that the Freudian field takes no account of the 'protopathic subject', this judgement becomes more and more questionable as we approach Freud's last formulations, which dethrone the unconscious in favour of the id. Moreover, the most valuable acquisitions of post-Freudian psychoanalytic thought throw light, if not on the protopathic subject, at least on the place of affect in psychical activity. How indeed are we to reconcile this affirmation with the subject's relation to *jouissance* and even with the concept of the drive, of which Lacan says: 'The concept of drive, in which he is designated by an organic, oral, anal, etc., mapping that satisfies the requirement being all the farther away from speaking the more he speaks'.[32] How can one deny the role of the affective in instinctual speech?

These quotations are taken from the last period in Lacan's work, when the formalization of language overrode any other consideration. In 1953, however, Lacan wrote:

> Speech is in fact a gift of language, and language is not immaterial. It is a subtle body, but body it is. Words are trapped in all the corporeal images that captivate the subject; they may make the hysteric 'pregnant', be identified with the object of *penis-neid*, represent the flood of urine of urethral ambition, or the retained faeces of avaricious *jouissance* . . . In this way speech may become an imaginary, or even real object in the subject and, as such, swallow up in more than one respect the function of language. We shall then place speech inside the parentheses of the resistance that it manifests.[33]

Thus speech may reveal the fall of language. Indeed, whatever is attached to the body, to the imaginary or to the real makes it descend from the symbolic status in which it resides. Going even further back in Lacan's work, one finds these sentences on the image, particularly severe on associationism:

> This extraordinary phenomenon, whose problems stretch from mental phenomenology to biology and whose action echoes from the conditions

31 Lacan (1977), p. 297.
32 Ibid., p. 314.
33 Ibid., p. 87–8.

of the mind to organic determinisms of a perhaps unsuspected depth, seems to me, in associationism, to be reduced to its function of illusion.[34]

The critique continues with a denunciation of the absurdity of associationism that resides in 'the intellectualist impoverishment that it imposes on the image'. The text of 1936 was written just before 'The mirror stage', in which the words 'jubilant assumption' can only refer to affect. This retrogressive reading of Lacan's work shows how he gradually acquired an aversion for affect, even to the point of banning it from his theory.

Those who have had the misfortune to remind him of this have been subjected to his sarcasm.[35] Despite repeated attempts, Lacan's accommodation between the first phase of his oeuvre, centred on the imaginary, and the second, centred on the symbolic, is questionable. The growing formalization of the Lacanian system seems to me to bear the mark of this unsurmounted difficulty. For indeed this accommodation would have involved a *de facto* reference to the affect.

It is not possible, within the confines of this book, to examine in detail Lacan's conception of the signifier, in the context of his theoretical system.[36] I should be prepared to accept what is essential in it – the relation between

34 Lacan (1966), p. 77.
35 '"Logomachia!" goes the strophe on one side. "What are you doing with the preverbal, gesture and mime, tone, the tune of a song, mood and af-fective con-tact?"' To which others no less animated give the antistrophe: "Everything is language: language when my heart beats faster when I'm in a funk, and if my patient flinches at the throbbing of an aeroplane at its zenith it is a way of *saying* how she remembers the last bomb attack." Yes, eagle of thought, and when the plane's shape cuts out your likeness in the night-piercing brush of the searchlight, it is the sky's answer' (Lacan 1977, pp. 124–5). Lacan's performance certainly wins over his audience's affect, but it eliminates the question. See also Lacan (1966), p. 462: 'And to denote this immediacy of the transcendent we were spared none of the metaphors of compact: affect, experience, attitude, discharge, need, love, latent aggressivity, the armour of character and the bolt of defence, abracadabra and hey presto!, recognition of which was now no longer accessible except to I know not what, of which the click of the tongue is the last probation and which introduces into teaching a new requirement: that of the inarticulate.' Yet it was one of Lacan's pupils who has made a career out of certain unarticulated sounds.
36 I undertook to do this at the 1960 Colloque de Bonneval, where, with Stein, Lebovici and Diatkine, I took up the discussion of Lacan's position through the work of Laplanche (whose own position has evolved since) and Leclaire. The Bonneval discussion has been revived recently (see *L'Inconscient*, no. 4), with contributions from Pasche, de M'Uzan and David. I then pursued the discussion in 1965 and 1966 at the seminars of Jacques Lacan, whose teaching I followed from 1960 to 1967. (See 'L'objet de Lacan, sa logique et la théorie freudienne', *Cahiers pour l'analyse*, no. 3.) This experience enabled me not only to enter Lacan's thought more profoundly and to benefit from it, but also to become aware of its limitations with regard to psychoanalytic practice.

the subject and the signifier – providing it were made clear how the originality of what may be subsumed under the term signifier in psychoanalysis
cannot be identified in any way with the signifier of linguistics. That is to
say, what specifies the signifier in psychoanalysis is its non-homogeneous
structure. The heterogeneity of the signifier is such that Freud invites us to
distinguish, to go no further, between thing-presentations and word-
presentations. Although the effects of the symbolic extend as far as
thing-presentation, the raw material of thing-presentation, which intervenes in symbolic structuring, is not alien to it: thing-presentations are not
stitched together as are word-presentations. But that is not all; a structural
conception of the affect leads to the affect being regarded – when it is
clearly differentiated from representation and appears in an isolated state – as
a variety of signifier, and not of signal, as certain American authors have
maintained. At other levels, I would willingly adopt the concept of *trace*,
which is valid not only for memory traces, but also for the potentialities of
affects. Similarly, if we are to complete the list of signifiers operating in the
psychoanalytic field, one should, in my opinion, link to this series the
bodily states and the act. Reference to language implies a homogeneous
body, extending from phonemes to sentences. If language is much more
than language, one can infer from language only to speak of language.
Language is the domain of the linguist, whether he or she is a phonologist
or a logico-mathematician.[37] The domain of the psychoanalyst is no doubt
structured by linguistic effects, but not only by them; the effects of the body
and those of the Law account for the fundamental heterogeneity of what
Freud called the psychical personality, constituted by the three agencies
destined to co-exist, while remaining irreconcilable to one another. I shall
return to this later.

The process of the linkage of language and that of the primary process
differ profoundly by the very fact that they use different raw materials. It is
arguable whether we can identify linkage and language.

If the unconscious has a language, it can only be that of an ideal geo-
metrical place, the focus of various expressions of those registers designated
as heterogeneous by their raw materials, which make the signifier of the signifiers a principle that is not identical with itself. The discourse of the
unconscious, which is not language, is a polyphony, its writing a polygraphy
layered over several stages dominating the gamut of frequencies from the
deepest to the highest. The tessitura of language is too narrow to contain

---

37 And, of course, it is true that Lacan is right to observe that there is no metalanguage. The
   problem is rather to ask oneself, a question ignored by Lacan, of what language would
   be the meta and, if this were not the case, how language might cover the totality of the
   field that Lacan assigns to it.

those various registers in itself. Language is situated between cry and silence. Psychoanalytic experience covers a range in which transformations of substance may take us from the birth cry to the silence of the grave. If speaking is situated in that area between the two, analysis lies both before and beyond it, even if the vehicle of the relations uniting analyst and analysand is the speech by which everything is supposed to happen. But every analyst, unless he falls into the phantasy of omnipotence, knows that, although speech is his best ally, speech has its limits. We have only to think of those whom we refuse as patients and those with whom all our efforts come to nothing. Speech is powerless to prevent holocausts. Not that a structure of speech is not detectable in them; but what matters is the extent of its power, which poses that of its limits and the field that it cannot but leave outside itself; not that this situation throws us into that outside (neither prior to, nor beyond) language, in the outer darkness in which Lacan would like to confine us.

Psychoanalytic formalization is wishful thinking, the product of a certain psychoanalytic ideology. Although we may rightly denounce the ideology that hides behind the myth of adaptation, we may also seek out the ideology that hides behind linguistic formalization. The topology of psychoanalysis (or its algebrization) belong to the phantasy of an absolute transparency of the unconscious, which would bring psychoanalytic work close to eidetic reduction.[38]

And so this long study of affect through the psychoanalytic literature comes to an end. The analysis of the conception of affect in Freud's work has shown the solitary character of his preoccupations with the unconscious status of affect, his ambiguities and hesitations, in any case his embarrassment at arriving at a satisfactory solution of the problem, when one compares the

---

38 The fact that Lacan maintains the irreducibility of desire does not really change anything. It is not the reductive character of psychoanalysis that I am rejecting, on the contrary. It is that the symbolic structure in the Lacanian sense approaches the drive through language, if only in the form of the 'treasury of signifiers', as 'essential' and exclusive model. And although it is true that the character of any reduction is to remain incomplete, what is open to question here is that structural relationship with essence (algorithms as 'index of an absolute signification', Lacan (1977), p. 314). For it is less important to note that Lacan does not refer explicitly to the essence than to stress what, in fact, becomes of language in his theory. Lacan's taking up of a theme from Spinoza – desire is the essence of Man – is only meaningful when articulated on the desire of the Other (Lacan 1977, p. 311). Now the unconscious is the discourse of the Other and the unconscious is structured like a language. The inference that I am supposing here between Other and language comes from the fact that Lacan marks them with the same sign. That language reveals its fault in demand does not in any way alter the fact that the Lacanian system sees it, in my opinion, as an essence.

way in which the problem of affect in relation to representation is treated.

After Freud, what is striking is the tendency to wish to go beyond the impasse in which psychoanalysts have felt trapped by the affect–representation dichotomy. Beyond the influence of Melanie Klein at the heart of the English school, the empirical tradition of that school has succeeded, in its reformulations of Freud's work, in giving its descriptions a living, open character, perhaps more concerned with clinical truth than with theoretical rigour (some would say rigidity). In the United States, the theoretical development has been guided very largely by a concern to integrate psychoanalytic theory in a wider whole – psychobiology or psychology – in which the originality of psychoanalysis often seems to be dissolved. Perhaps that is the result of interdisciplinary communication, as opposed to British insularity – not only geographical, but also psychoanalytic. However, despite the excesses of a not always discriminating approach, from the genetic point of view (always tending to psychobiology and psychology) the cognitive function of affect is well emphasized in these works, as also is the double value of affect: sometimes a disorganizing flux, sometimes a message. But other formulations seem to be necessary.

The situation in France has been dominated by the controversy around Lacan's theories, which has no doubt distorted the examination of the problem of affect. Before returning to our theoretical discussion, it is necessary to leave the texts, examine the clinical structures and learn what can be taught by treatment.

Part II
Clinical practice in psychoanalysis: structures and processes

3

Affect in clinical structures

In the title of this chapter I speak advisedly of clinical structures. I shall not be dealing here, therefore, with affect in clinical practice, but rather of the place of the affect in various structures. For affect, as it presents itself in the psychical organization of this or that individual, is what is identified most readily with what is most irreducibly particular, most singularly individual about that individual. My approach could have taken the form either of a monograph in which an individual's affective organization would be studied, but which would produce no general conclusions, or of an attempt to systematize the psychoanalytic field as a whole, considered from the point of view of affect. Since it seemed to me that I should try to elucidate a general problematic, without ignoring the dangers of a superficial examination of the question, I have chosen the second solution.

The principle of my study will be to define the situation of affect in the four great clinical forms that I have referred to as the four cardinal points of the compass. Indeed hysteria and obsessional neurosis structure my examination of the psychoanalytic field of the neuroses, rather as manic-depressive psychosis and schizophrenia structure the field of the psychoses. Reference to these nosographical entities is, for many, open to question. I should make it clear however that I refer to them not as 'illnesses' in the psychiatric sense of the term, but as forms of organization in which certain structural models are revealed with particular coherence. Those models, which Freud and Melanie Klein always used, constitute in a sense shapings of the Oedipal structure. They are defined not by their frequency, but by the significant character of the work of the psychical apparatus culminating in their fulfilment. They enable us to understand the atypical or incomplete structures, much more frequent than typical ones, by referring the second to the first. Hence the usefulness of this investigation.

Thus the various vicissitudes of affects according to the structures will be understood in a comparatively reciprocal structural spirit.

As for the clinical configurations situated outside those four sub-groups, I shall deal with them more summarily.

I Affect in neurotic structures

In this category I shall consider only the transference psychoneuroses. Indeed, by remaining within Freudian psychoanalytic clinical practice, I assume that the so-called actual neuroses are to be distinguished not only from the so-called transference neuroses by the actuality of the conflict, or by the effects of libidinal stasis, but above all by the non-elaboration of psychical energy.

In an earlier work,[1] I proposed two structural models for obsessional neurosis and hysteria. I shall refer to them here only insofar as they bear upon the affect.

1 Hysteria: conversion and condensation

In hysteria . . . the incompatible idea is rendered innocuous by its *sum of excitation* being *transformed into something somatic.* For this I should like to propose the name of *conversion.*[2]

Conversion is the kernel of hysteria. However, by that short sentence, Freud, unusually, explains nothing, elucidates nothing, is content to state and to name conversion. The leap into the somatic is shrouded in mystery and the somatic 'compliance' inferred in *Dora* has scarcely any more explanatory value than 'refuge in illness' or 'the sleep-inducing virtue' of opium. What is posited hypothetically, by a hypothesis that assumes its heuristic value only in the differential dialectic that opposes it to the anxiety neurosis, is this transformation of the sum of excitation into something somatic. This is a change of the state and nature of psychical libido into somatic libido, though different from the somatic energy to be found in anxiety neurosis. Of course, this mutation continues to operate in the register of the symbolizable. Conversion is not a de-differentiated somatization. The language changes tools, but it continues to sustain a discourse. The hysteric 'speaks with his flesh' as Lacan puts it. As such he is very different from the anxiety neurotic or psychosomatic subject. I shall postpone until later a

---

1 'Névrose obsessionelle et hystérie, leurs relations chez Freud et depuis', *R.F.P.*, vol. XXVIII, 1964, pp. 679–716.
2 *S.E.*, III, p. 49.

necessarily brief study of the psychosomatic illnesses. I should now like to relate conversion with other elements of the hysterical structure.

Among these, one might note:

- *the inversion of affect*: the replacement of desire by disgust, with a particular intensity of the affect, which has thus changed sign;
- *the signification of the hysterical symptoms as embodied phantasies*. The hysteric, says Freud, *acts out* many of his memories and phantasies instead of remembering them in treatment. This tendency to discharge accentuates the affective tonality of the hysterical structure;
- the phantasies reveal the prevalence of the mechanisms of condensation.[3]

Condensation is present in it by the assumption of antagonistic roles in the phenomena of multiple identification, of 'mimed' representations. The phantasies themselves may be condensed into an overall phantasy, insofar as it induces a symptom in order to introduce the indispensable compromise between desire and defence. But condensation is not only condensation of the signifiers present at the level of the phantasy, indeed of several phantasies; it is not only the condensation of roles in the hysterical attack miming coitus; it is also the condensation of affects that drives to discharge in the form of an enactment that becomes an acting out. Condensation achieves an increase in energic density.

Acting out is well understood as one of the privileged vicissitudes of the hysteric's desire. Its demonstrative value is not the only one that may be detected; the value of discharge of the condensation of affects and the value of affective summation on accumulation must also be taken into account.

One may now wonder whether a narrower link does not unite condensation and conversion. Condensation of signifiers, plus condensation of affects (anticathected and inverted) equals conversion. If conversion becomes necessary, it is because its role is to wipe out the effects of tension increased by condensation. For condensation is not only a quantitative effect. It is also a qualitative variation, one that tends to a hardening of the unconscious kernel, which as such must be transformed if it is not to be reduced.

Following Charcot, Freud was struck by the hysteric's 'belle indifférence'. Once the *substitutive formation* is created, the affective tension drops. This represents a success for repression, since all the intolerable excess of the psychical conflict has changed nature and site. Having passed into the somatic, the hysteric finds peace once more.

---

3   *S.E.*, IX, p. 229.

It is not the case, far from it, that indifference always accompanies the symptom. Anxiety may co-exist with the symptom. But it is no longer anxiety linked to conflict, rather anxiety linked to the symptom. The aim of the symptom is to anticipate anxiety, as Freud was to discover later. When anxiety subsists, in spite of the symptom, it is either because the neurotic structure is overwhelmed, or because the anxiety attached to the symptom has not been wiped out by it.

In any case, all the authors recognize in the hysteric the importance of repression that confers on amnesia its character as obstacle to remembering memories in treatment. One can understand how conversion collaborates with repression – that it is both its effect and its ally. But conversion is this extreme recourse to the amputation of desire and of psychical life at the expense of the somatic only because condensation creates a state of threat, as if the forces of psychical conflict were concentrated within it.

It is not essential to my thesis to say much more about conversion hysteria in the typology of the hysterical or hysterico-phobic characteristics according to Fenichel, Federn or Bouvet. Lability of the cathexes, superficial eroticization of defences against desire, flight before conflict, these characteristics may generally be found among hysterics. But the links that exist between conversion hysteria (with symptoms) and the asymptomatic hysteric character structures should be made clearer.

I should like to stress, on the other hand, the signification of condensation.

One may interpret condensation as a structural mechanism of thought, by which it is attached to metaphor. And one is well aware of how much has been made of these links. It has rightly been remarked that for Freud condensation applied also to a transference and to an accumulation of energic charges. But the question remains: why does condensation prevail in the hysteric? I shall try to provide an answer to this question that is both clinical and theoretical. Every psychoanalyst has noticed the hysteric's *affective avidity*, which makes him a subject dependent on his love objects, in particular the mother. Mallet has noted the importance for the hysteric of the phantasy of death by starvation. Separated from the mother, losing her protection, the world appears to him like an immense desert where one runs the risk of dying from hunger and thirst. Of course, to speak of 'oral' hysteria has become commonplace: innumerable authors have commented on it. It is not at all my intention to shift, as has been done all too easily, the point of fixation of the Oedipus conflict in the hysteric and to substitute an oral for a phallic problematic. I am still convinced of the pre-eminence of the castration conflict in the hysteric and regard the oral pseudo-regression as a topographical regression. What is to be absorbed, following the displacement upwards, is certainly the penis, to which the vaginal way is forbidden, since it is already there in phantasy. But there is in the hysteric, at a level of intensity matching that of sexual disgust, a disgust that is at its

110

maximum when the desire for fellatio and possession by oral incorporation appears, a veritable psychical bulimia: bulimia of objects with phallic value, bulimia of affects in so far as the possession of that object is a warrant of love and the condition of obtaining the love of the object. What the feminine hysteric desires is not a penis, but a set of penile objects whose quantity or size never brings satiety, because satiety would suppress the desire for unsatisfied desire. Lacan is right to say that the hysteric desires unsatisfied desire. Castration now appears as the consequence of the phantasy of incorporating the penis, which, with its envied and feared size, cannot penetrate the vagina and whose dangers are transferred to the level of the mouth, where affective avidity is installed as a substitute for the object. *The hysteric lives by devouring his affects.* The tension of desire mounts, nourished by ever more highly valued phantasy objects, feeding – to use the appropriate word – the conflict with a megalomaniac ego ideal, aiming at a desexualization matching the cumulative sexualization of the most ordinary objects. Such would be the meaning of condensation. Conversion would aim at swallowing – literally – the excess, absorbing it into the body, just as the penis, absorbed and retained, takes the place of the child-penis desired in the phantasy of pregnancy. The transition from the vagina to the belly is a transition from phantasy to symptom of conversion. Of course, all symptoms of conversion are not related to the phantasy of pregnancy; but all the detailed operations can only be understood as part of an overall strategy that must contribute to the realization of that phantasy of being phallic-pregnant.[4] This problematic is valid for both sexes, each being unable to achieve, in reality, only half of this programme. All this is set in train in order to ward off the danger of being cut off, of separation.

2 Obsessional neurosis: regression from act to thought and displacement

Throughout Freud's works, obsessional neurosis is placed in a symmetrical and inverse relation to hysteria, a relation of complementarity that sets it up in opposition to hysteria, which nevertheless helps us to understand it.

In his early works 'The neuro-psychoses of defence' (1894), 'Obsessions and phobias' (1895), Draft K of the Fliess papers (1 January 1896) bearing the title 'The neuroses of defence' and the 'Further remarks on the neuropsychoses of defence' (1896), the same idea guides Freud throughout. Obsession is seen to carry out a work of dissociation between representation

---

4 This point of view may well throw light on today's changes in the symptomatology of the hysteric. Although manifestations of conversion are rare, the toxicomaniac note is rarely absent from clinical tables of hysteria nowadays.

and affect or, as he says again, between the idea and the emotional state. Here conversion does not occur. It is as if, instead of sliding on to the plane of the body, thus avoiding conflict, the obsessional neurotic found another means, that of dissociating the elements present in the conflict, then proceeding to a displacement of the representation or idea on to another idea, generally of secondary importance. This is, says Freud, a double displacement, in which *the present replaces the past and the non-sexual the sexual.* The essence of obsession is to be found in this work, which, instead of condensing, dissociates and displaces, and which, instead of converting by moving towards the body, on the contrary, 'rises' to thought, with a consequent sexualization of the processes of thought. It is by means of this replacement of the sexual by the non-sexual that aggressivity moves front stage, as if by a change of scenery on the stage of the unconscious. The succession of Freud's works will, in effect, pursue the theme of the obsession:

- *the disjunction of the relations of causality* with the elliptical distortion that ensues;
- *the omnipotence of thought;*
- *the predominance of the themes of death.*

I have stressed the presence in the obsessional neurotic, as opposed to the lacunary structure of the hysteric, of a metonymic language with successive linkings, in which the unconscious links can be read with great intelligibility, but in which they become incomprehensible for the subject by the double effect of isolation and of the eccentric position, so to speak, of the affect.

There are three interdependent points here: the action of displacement; the themes of aggression, hate and death; the omnipotence of thought. At first sight, the link that unites them is not clear. In order to discover and interpret it, one must resort to theorizations that have been made since Freud's time. Thus the work of displacement presupposes a split between representative and affect. In this apparently simple operation, one must introduce a power of separation that is none other than the one that Freud was to hypothesize with the death drive, which is above all a disjunctive force. It would be wrong to see the action of the death drive at the level of the sadism of anal regression. A sadistic anal regression that affects the drives is not the direct expression of the death drive, but its consequence. It is because the death drive has achieved the disintrication, the defusion of the aggressive and libidinal components, that aggressivity, *untied* so to speak from the mixture that it forms with the erotic libido, has a free field before it to proceed to the second expression of the death drive: the destruction of the phantasy object – the object that elsewhere it must at all costs preserve so that its destruction does not entail by the same token the failure of the reality principle and the movement towards psychosis, which the obsessional neurotic does not always escape. This work of destructive dissociation continues between act and thought, *in order to preserve the destruction of destruction itself.* At the level of the act, destruction would turn the obsessional neurotic into a psychopath or criminal. At the level of thought, the struggle between the destructive desires and the object exposed to its desires for preservation continues without cease, in order to save the enjoyment of its end in annihilating satisfaction. All the power is conferred on the mind, because all the libidinal power has taken refuge in it and deserted the act in so far as any act is presumed to be dangerous and destructive. On the other hand, death abolishes nothing, since ghosts live in the beyond and take their revenge by tormenting the living. There is no possible death, even in death. The last word must remain with endless conflict. Hence the importance that Freud accords in *Inhibitions, Symptoms and Anxiety* to the secondary defences, all of which concern the affect: isolation, undoing, retroaction. Isolation is to be understood here in a double sense, either disconnection of the kernels of conflict from the rest of psychical activity, or, from a more limited standpoint, isolation of the repressed representations and the affect from one another. The undoing that acts 'like a blowing away' to make it 'undo what has been done' continues in a ceaseless movement: undoing, then the undoing the undoing, and so on. It is pointless to discuss endlessly whether it is the representations or the affects that are 'blown away'. In the final analysis, what has to be prevented is their meeting. The inversion of pleasure, which leads the obsessional neurotic to seek satisfaction in the unpleasure of punishments inflicted by the superego, makes it clear enough that it is on the level of the affect that the struggle has to be waged.

And although the aim of the obsessional neurotic, as many authors have pointed out, is the pursuit of a phantasy of mastery, it is certainly an affective control, in which the sovereign ego will have triumphed over drives in narcissistic desexualization. That this control should lead to a mummification, to that state of indefinite preservation at the cost of a radical desiccation, demonstrates the triumph of death. The language of the obsessional neurotic's affects is, as Freud noted, that via media of destruction. What is important to note here is that it is still the same power of death that has been ceaselessly at work from the initial, apparently anodyne or innocent operation by which the representation was separated from the affect. And although I have said that hysterics live by devouring their affects, I would say that obsessional neurotics feed on their decomposed, cadaverous affects and on their phantasy representations. What perhaps prevents them from fully achieving their aim is that every obsessional neurosis is grafted on to a kernel of hysteria, whose evaluation marks the links between the obsessional neurotic and genitality.

I don't intend to dwell on the connections that may exist between the obsessional character and obsessional neurosis. I will simply repeat that it is abusive to link character and neurosis. An obsessional symptomatology may perfectly well co-exist with a non-obsessional character structure. It is only with the symptomatology that we should be concerned if we are to see the typical obsessional mechanisms at work. It is not a question of giving symptom precedence over character, or the reverse. What matters is detecting the mechanisms, whether they are operating on the symptom, the character or both the same time.

3 Phobia and anxiety

The hysteric, therefore, buries the condensation of the affects in somatic conversion, whereas the obsessional neurotic spirits them away in displacement and the omnipotence of thought. So it is hardly surprising if the study par excellence of the affect must be sought in that third way in which the subject no longer escapes the affect, but is tirelessly confronted by it.

The intermediary situation of phobia is well known. It is often linked by modern authors to hysteria – they speak of structures, of the hysterico-phobic ego – but it also makes many links with obsession. The transformation of phobia into obsession, described by Freud in 'The disposition to obsessional neurosis' (1913), groups together the obsessive phobias of classical psychiatric clinical practice, types of phobias involving libidinal regression (Mallet 1955) and those cases in which phobias and obsessions are closely linked. That is why the definition of phobia must be sought in itself.

In 'Obsessions and phobias' (1895), Freud stressed its essentially affective nature: *phobia is the psychical manifestation of anxiety neurosis*. For the affect of phobia is always that of anxiety – anxiety that is neither discharged and liquidated by conversion, nor displaced and isolated by obsession. Following a recurrent pathway, rather than fleeing into the body, the representative of the drive halts its course in the unconscious. Phobia is a 'limit-representation' (as Freud was to say in a letter to Fliess) – the last point to which the libido can cling before becoming pure athematic anxiety. Hence a certain moving form of phobia, capable of being displaced, for here, too, displacement operates, but in a sense limited by the affect, ever ready to dominate the phobia and, unlike the obsessional neurotic, to paralyse the infinite series of displacements that wipe away anxiety a little more with each operation. The phobia that accompanies anxiety forestalls the development of anxiety; it succeeds in circumscribing it around a central signification, only if it is an authentic phobia.

It is in *Inhibitions, Symptoms and Anxiety* that the analysis of phobia becomes clearer insofar as it is there above all that Freud completely analyses its relation with castration. Anxiety is linked not only to the danger of incestuous libidinal aspiration, but also to the expression of the destructive drives. The phobia is an attempt to resolve the conflict of ambivalence. The positive affects with regard to the object are in contradiction with the negative affects with which it is cathected. The old contrasted pairs in *Instincts and their Vicissitudes* are assembled here in the new coupling that the explicit formation of the Oedipus complex has established, all the more so in that Freud discovers the double nature, *positive and negative*, of the Oedipus complex. The affect of tenderness is preserved, whereas the affect of hostility is directed upon a substitute. But, on the other hand, the danger of retaliation appears: the fear of being aggressed by the object of the desire of aggression.

We know that, in the case of Hans's horse, this aggression is oral – fear of being bitten by him – and Freud discusses the value of this oral castration. In Hans's case, he opts for the substitution of one representation by another; in the case of the Wolf Man, he is much less sure. As we know, this discussion was the prelude to several developments to which Melanie Klein and her school made a noted contribution. For all these authors, there is no doubt that it was a question – and the very case of the Wolf Man shows this – of oral regression. To be devoured was identified by Freud with being loved by the father – and the Wolf Man does aspire to serve the father's coitus. But the demonstration on this point is too easy for the Kleinian authors, precisely because, in my opinion, the Wolf Man was in no way a phobic. Indeed, in his case, Freud speaks only of the history of an infantile obsessional neurosis. As for the structure of his patient, he says not a word. However, what he describes shows quite clearly that he was dealing with a psychotic structure. Thus the Kleinians' demonstration is falsified, for their analysis applies not to phobics, but to psychotic structures.

This leads me to say a few words about Bouvet's so-called pregenital phobias and about paranoid phobias (phobias linked to paranoid anxiety or the schizo-paranoid phase). The clinical existence of such states is beyond doubt; one sees co-existing in them badly structured, badly demarcated, extensive fears, accompanied by the experience not only of anxiety, but of depersonalization and strangeness. The mechanisms of defence provide poor protection for an ego perpetually submerged by unsustainable tension, threatened at every moment by collapse. Oral fixations (alcoholism, abuse of medication or toxic substances) stand out in this picture, sometimes accompanied by suicidal or delinquent acting out or temporary delusional activity. As all this shows, there is no longer anything in common between these states and the phobia described by Freud – and for very good reason. The confusion between phobic neurosis and borderline states or between phobic neurosis and traumatic neurosis or actual neuroses including phobias is frequent in clinical psychoanalysis. The Wolf Man is an example of this. We must now interpret phobia in this context, as Freud interpreted delusion in psychosis, that is, as a form of restitution: an effort made by the ego to circumscribe, to mark out, with the help of desperate cathexes, an anxiety that overwhelms the castration anxiety and which is, in fact, a fragmentation anxiety. Here again we see the vocation of the phobia as borderline representation.

What do these remarks contribute to the problem of affect? It seems to me that, in each of these cases, *a distinction between affect and representation is impossible*. It is an indissociable mixture that participates in them both, in which affect is its own representation. The depersonalization that draws the curtain on the representative activity shows this.

II Affect in psychotic structures

The situation of affect in the psychoses is determined by reference to a whole clinical practice that English-speaking psychiatry calls, according to established tradition, the *affective psychoses*: states of depression and excitation, as opposed to schizophrenic states. However, the place of affect will not be easy to define, for it is difficult to distinguish between affect and representation in the psychotic field. Furthermore, reference, unavoidable on this subject, to the works of Melanie Klein and her school make the distinction even more difficult.

1 The melancholic and manic psychoses

To begin with, let us remember that, after considering the psychoses as narcissistic neuroses, Freud restricted the term to melancholia alone (and, consequently, also to mania), keeping the term psychosis for the clinical forms previously referred to by this term.

Melancholia, the affect of mourning and pain

The relation established by Freud between object loss and depression dates from his correspondence with Fliess (Draft G: Melancholia). It was rediscovered in 1915, in *Mourning and Melancholia*. Mourning for the object results in the production of a painful affect of considerable intensity. Freud attaches to this painful affect an essentially economic significance. Hence the importance of the *work of mourning*.[5]

---

5 It should be noted that although the reference to work is slight in many places in the Freudian oeuvre, it is quite explicit here. Is this not the best proof that the economic point of view is a point of view on psychical work?

This work bears on the need to effect the libidinal detachment required by the loss of the object in mourning. But, in melancholia, by virtue of the fact of the narcissistic cathexis of the object, the loss of the object entails a loss at the level of the ego, the ego identifying, as we know, with the lost object and the object cathexes withdrawing into the ego. The ambivalence that characterizes these object cathexes then reaches the ego. Hate attacks the ego, as it would attack the loss object.

> The complex of melancholia behaves like an open wound, drawing to itself cathectic energies – which in the transference neuroses we have called 'anti-cathexes' – from all directions and emptying the ego until it is totally impoverished.[6]

This narcissistic wound to the ego, which enables it to bear these sadistic cathexes, goes hand in hand with the subjective feeling of pain. It is at this economic explanation of pain that Freud stops at the end of his work. He does not return to it until *Inhibitions, Symptoms and Anxiety*.

The melancholic's struggle takes place around thing-presentations in the unconscious, which are what is at stake in the conflict: love for the object insists that they be preserved despite loss, hate for the object demands that they be abandoned. What dominates this struggle is the impoverishment of the ego devoured by the object cathexes, irrupting through the open wound and giving birth to pain. The breaking down of the barrier of the ego by this excessive quantity of cathexes is comparable to the breaking down of the protective shield by a quantity of excitation that bursts into the individual. In this respect, melancholia is a *quasi-traumatic narcissistic neurosis*. The excessive internal quantities are equivalent to the excessive quantities that attack the subject during an instinctual thrust to which satisfaction cannot be given. But, in the second case, it is traumatic anxiety that results, whereas the impoverishment of the ego makes it a painful experience. The ego, as I have said, is devoured by the lost object, just as the cathexes are of a devouring, even cannibalistic nature with regard to this object.

This mutual devouring, this mutual tearing apart, is certainly what characterizes primary identification. I noted above the affective avidity of the hysteric and it is known how frequent depressions are for the hysteric; does this amount to saying that hysteria is to be confused with melancholia? Unlike the hysteric, it is not the object that the melancholic devours, but his own ego, confused with the object by identification. The shadow of the object has fallen on the ego, says Freud. Thus the struggle between love and

6   *S.E.*, XIV, p. 253.

hate that revolves around the object is essential for the survival or death of the ego. One might suggest that hate would deliver the ego that liquidated the object cathexes binding it to it, but there is a great risk of liquidating part or all of the ego in doing so. Love for the object entails the defeat of the ego, which thus follows the object into death.

It is important to note here that the struggle that the affects throw themselves into is pitiless and merciless. For the regression to oral sadism entails that the cathexes present are particularly intense, revealing an immeasurable passion. Pain is not anxiety. Is the narcissistic nature of pain sufficient to explain the difference? The threat that anxiety weighs on the ego is no doubt different from the one aroused by pain. With pain, the impoverishment of the ego due to the narcissistic haemorrhage attacks the ego in its very self-preservation. Its dependence on the object would incline it to follow the object in its loss, or to kill it a second time by killing itself. This is why it is necessary to complete the theory of the affect in melancholia by reference to the last theory of the drives, which will lead Freud to speak of the 'pure culture' of the destructive drives in melancholia. It is not simply a 'quantity of sadism' that irrupts into the ego, it is a destructive rage that demands vengeance on the ego identified with the object, and requires the ego to be reduced to the silence of annihilation, to the point at which all pain is abolished in the anaesthesia of stupor and amazement. Karl Abraham had already perceived this.

Mourning and Melancholia was written before the introduction of the superego into psychoanalytic theory. The struggle that Freud describes between two enemy parts of the same ego becomes clear only if we understand it as a struggle between the superego and the ego. We can then identify the painful nature of the affect that responds not only to the quantity of freed excitation, but also to the conflictual relations between superego and ego. A double game is set up that demonstrates the duplicity of the ego. On the one hand, the ego treats part of itself in the same way as the id would treat the object; on the other hand, the superego treats the ego in a similar way. At this point, we should draw a distinction in the superego between cathexes that properly belong to the object – which, in turn, properly belongs to the superego – and narcissistic cathexes that belong to the ego ideal.[7] In fact, what is remarkable is the fusion of these two aspects brought about by the nature of the object cathexes. In any case, it is the notion of a splitting within the ego that dominates the situation. This splitting becomes all the more important when we remember that we are dealing in melancholia with a narcissistic cathexis of the object. It is not

---

7 This distinction is useful in certain forms such as the 'inferiority depression' described by Pasche, in which the role of the ego ideal dominates.

surprising that the loss of the object entails this impoverishment of the ego, not only as a result of identification with the lost object, but also because the object is cathected in the field of narcissism. It feeds on the narcissism of the subject as it feeds that subject. *The Same eats the Same.*

As for the split between love and hate, it is important to recognize that it is the product of a disintrication between erotic and destructive drives. We know that in this case the forces of destruction, no longer 'bound' by the erotic libido, take the upper hand in the situation on being freed. The excessive narcissism of the depressed subject becomes a negative narcissism. The use of the superlative in self-depreciation shows the megalomaniacal satisfactions thus obtained (the melancholic says that he is the *greatest* sinner, the *greatest* criminal, etc.).

Melanie Klein saw the depressive position as an expression of those destructive tendencies in the child's attacks on the breast. Their effect is counterbalanced by the memory of experiences associated with the good breast. These experiences are constitutive of the love that the ego lavishes on the object and of the love with which it cathects itself. Melanie Klein's conclusions are in contradiction, however, with those of Freud. The emergence from mourning marks the triumph of the good objects over the bad, the triumph of the reparative tendencies imbued with gratitude over the destructive tendencies imbued with envy. For Melanie Klein, therefore, the end of mourning is linked to the preservation of the object and not to its liquidation. The possibility of displacing, of cathecting, other objects was related, according to Freud, to the liquidation of the cathexes of the object. For Melanie Klein, on the other hand, it is the preservation of the good object that is the condition of the end of mourning. Care for the object wins over the vengeance that the child intends to wreak on it. However important these divergences may be, one aspect should be noted on which Freud and Melanie Klein are in agreement. In melancholia, the split between object and ego, like the split between good and bad, separates total objects: a constituted ego and a unified object. The affects of love and hate, however brutal they may be, do not therefore have this shattered, fragmented aspect, uniting in each fragment erotic and destructive drives. Thus one may, in the case of melancholia, speak of an affective structure less fragmenting and fragmented than in schizo-paranoid forms. This might lead one to see those psychoses as more likely to be cured than is the case with schizophrenia. It would be fairer to say that, in those critical states, a choice – between death or life – is still possible, whereas schizophrenia is neither one nor the other, and both at once.

To conclude on the subject of melancholia, something should be said about the role of the devouring processes. Identification with the lost object must be understood in terms of a double process: on the one hand, object cathexes carrying the cachet of oral fixations cannot be expelled en bloc, they reject the vomiting that they might incur, they bite on the ego; on the other hand, the ego itself responds to this biting by constituting itself as consenting prey. It becomes the prisoner-gaoler of the prisoner it guards. It incorporates the lost object. But the work of mourning requires the dissolution of the object cathexes. What is at stake in the work of mourning is the digestion of poisons from the object. What is aimed at is the neutralization of the object's destructive powers, the triumph of the ego that refuses to share the destiny of the object. The distinction, proposed by Maria Torok, between incorporation of the object and introjection of the drives takes account of work carried out in two stages. It is as if, in certain mourning illnesses, the object were first incorporated and preserved in a mummified state, rather as certain animals ingest prey that they do not consume until later. The digestion of the object will take place only after the work of mourning, by feeding on the 'exquisite corpse' that it constitutes. The delights of this phagocytosis are consummated *a posteriori*. The mourning, too, is carried out later. Between incorporation and introjection, all the significant introjections pass through the filter of the incorporated corpse. This is why there can be no *jouissance* for the subject other than that of the torture that it carries out and which is caused by the ceaseless movement over the circuits of the cathexes of the included object. The exclusion of the object carried out by interpretative deconstruction will alone allow later cathexes to be accompanied by the *jouissance* that is proper to them, that which may be experienced without the colouring that is conferred on it by its filtering through the mummified corpse. It might be added, however, that it is if, between incorporation and introjection, the object continues, in a corpse-like state, to distil its poisons; these poisons undermine the ego, which can neither expel the prey nor consume it. It is then the work of delayed consumption that is produced by introjection. Unlike Maria Torok, I prefer to speak of introjection of affects, rather than of introjection of drives, for it is the recognition of the affects of mourning, a recognition equivalent to their resurrection, that is proper to the phase of the work of postponed mourning.

Mania, the affect of triumph and euphoria

The link between melancholia and mania leads me to stress certain points, without simply going over the preceding problematic once again. There is little doubt that the manic subject also undergoes a loss,[8] but then reacts to

---

8 This is usually the case, although the manic episode may occur after the sudden lifting of a situation of internal oppression due to an internalized object.

this loss by stressing the sense of triumph over the object. This feeling, as both Freud and Melanie Klein have noted, exists in an ephemeral way, often passing unperceived in mourning. Freud attributes this to surviving narcissistic satisfaction. Melanie Klein relates it to the satisfaction that the destructive drives derive from the object, thus subjected and dominated. Maniacal exaltation, the saturnalian orgy of mania would, therefore, be a funeral dance over the corpse of a hated enemy, reduced to powerlessness. Excessive euphoria would be related to the dysphoria that corresponds to it. It should be remembered, however, that the same features discovered in the case of melancholia are to be found here: object loss, ambivalence, narcissistic regression. The cannibalistic relationship to the object no doubt remains the most striking. But there is a paradox here: in melancholia, it is the assault of the destructive drives that accounts for the impoverishment of the ego, since the ego has identified itself with the lost object. It cannot be denied that the destructive drives that find expression in maniacal omnipotence are at work here. How does it come about, then, that this destruction assumes the form of an expansion, an enrichment of the ego? One might reply that in this case it is not the object that devours the ego, but the ego that incorporates the omnipotence of the object, whose capacity for absorption is unlimited. But we must insist on the fact that nothing can be assimilated from this absorption. All that is swallowed is spent or destroyed *ipso facto*, which forces the ego to seek endlessly other objects to consume.[9] The incorporated objects serve only to sustain the feeling of triumph by an immediate dramatic ingestion, using all the resources offered by this incorporation. The maniacal ego burns up all its reserves so that at no time is its omnipotence denied. It is a bottomless gulf. It empties as fast as it fills.

But why does this excess of object cathexis not create a sense of pain? It is no doubt because there is no desire here to retain the object, but rather a desperate consumption, which eliminates the ingested products as they are consumed. This economic explanation is no doubt inadequate.

One cannot escape the feeling that mania, while responding at the same level of repression as melancholia, is in a sense more ruinous than melancholia. Nowhere does negation prove to be more overwhelming. The maniacal subject no longer lacks anything, no longer has any illusions, because the very notion of illusion has been suppressed. Conflict has disappeared behind a strange disguise. For it is obviously not the erotic drives that have triumphed over the destructive drives in this case. It is as if the destructive drives had assumed the mask of the erotic drives, giving the maniacal

---

9 Lewin sees in the structure of mania a defence against the wish to be devoured and to fall asleep.

attack its carnival aspect. Parallel with this, the maniacal ego has disguised itself as the omnipotent object.

One may agree with Freud that the triumph over the object in mania is accompanied by a devouring by the ego not only of the object, but also of the superego. Thus pain would be linked to the effect not only of excessive quantity, but also of the intervention of the superego, which forbids the expression of hate towards the object, whereas hate invades the field opened up to it by the ego. In melancholia, the superego treats the ego as the ego (or the id) would have wished to be able to treat the object; so by the same operation it appeases the hate of the ego for the object and the hate of the superego for the ego. In mania, the superego is reduced to nothing by the omnipotent ego. The euphoria of the ego derives, therefore, from the fact that, having absorbed the omnipotence attributed to the object, it can by the same token swallow the superego born of the introjection of the object. Curiously, the affect of triumph in mania is even more demanding than the affect of mourning – it demands everything. Again there is a paradox here in that it is these destructive drives that may conceal, by neutralizing the superego, the true face of triumphant euphoria and that the erotic drives do not take part in this orgy. Love for the object, a resolution of the maniacal attack, will come, for Freud, from detachment from it; for Melanie Klein, from the reparation that the good objects will give to the debris that remain intact after these macabre Dionysia.

2 The schizophrenic psychoses

I shall be brief in this section, because of the fragmentary character of our knowledge of the schizophrenic psychoses. It is often said nowadays that Freud's denial of transference in schizophrenics is not acceptable. However, it would be truer to say that the transference of the neuropsychoses of transference psychoneuroses obeys different rules from the transference of psychotics, so much so that a distinction has to be drawn in the second case. The structure of the psychotic affects cannot, in my opinion, be regarded as identical with that of the neurotic affects.

Clinical psychiatry has long since recognized the double aspect of affect in schizophrenia, on the one hand affective indifference, on the other paradoxical affectivity expressed in acts stemming from the most explosive, most unexpected impulses. The link between affect and representation is perceived throughout the relations between act and hallucination. The affect is acted out; the representation no longer obeys the reality test. A whole section of psychical reality has been set up in the field devolved to repressed external reality. In a remarkable series of works, Bion has shown the role of the destructive drives in these processes.

122

If reality (psychical as well as objective) is so distorted in psychosis, it is because the death drives are constantly at work. Reality is hated, that is to say, not only is the inhibition of the affects by the ego ineffectual, but the affects are destructive by their nature. The attacks of the destructive drives are directed as much towards any awareness on the part of the ego as to what is happening inside itself or in the outside world. The attacks are aggressions against the linking processes that reside in the psychical apparatus. Henceforth there is no mastery by linking, no 'taming' of free energy can take place. The destructive attacks are directed against all the psychical processes: on the object, on the subject's body, above all on the subject's thought. By a paradoxical reversal, the affect is not only always infiltrated by hate, but hated *qua* affect.

Confronted by the kind of destructive aggressivity that the Kleinian authors attach to the schizo-paranoid phase and link to persecution anxiety, the psyche brings its earliest defences – splitting and projective identification – into play. It is as if it had no other option but to split the bad from the good and to reject the bad. I would remark at this point that although the term 'splitting' covers all such processes, it seems to me to be logical, as the Kleinian authors have realized, to distinguish between early splitting and later splitting. One might propose a similar distinction with that pertaining to repression: original splitting and splitting after the event. The splitting of the depressive position corresponds, as I have already said, to the splitting carried out on a total object and on a unified ego. The splitting of the schizo-paranoid position is a splitting that affects part objects within an undifferentiated, diffuse, limited and ununified psychical activity. The objects in it are presented as particles, to use Bion's term, a sort of conglomerate between object fragments and ego fragments. The splitting off attempts to unburden the psyche of those destructive forces by projecting the bad parts of the ego, expelling them outside the ego. It is not necessary to infer here a clear separation between ego and non-ego. It is only required to suppose that the bad parts must be rejected as far as possible from the living kernel of the good parts of the ego, far away, as Bouvet puts it. This attempt at banning bad parts, has the result of invading external objects and filling them with harmful qualities. But by this work it is fragments of the ego that are thus expelled, which has the result of weakening the ego and alienating it in those external objects occupied by the object–ego conglomerate. In one of her best works, *Notes on some Schizoid Mechanisms*, Melanie Klein has thrown much light on this narcissistic haemorrhage.

One might note a relative concordance between the conceptions of Freud and those of Melanie Klein. Does not Freud say precisely that in schizophrenia it is the object cathexes that are abandoned? The difference between these two conceptions is that for Freud the libido, thus disaffected, flows back on to the ego, whereas for Melanie Klein this expulsion of the object cathexes impoverishes the ego. One might bring these two authors together by stressing that the discrepancy between them derives from the fact that they are not speaking of the same psychotic stage and of the same vicissitudes of cathexis. At the terminal phase of the psychoses, we may observe this delusional megalomania to which Freud refers. But is this not due to the flowing back of the libido on to the ego and to the introjection, or rather the reintrojection of an idealized omnipotent object? The question may be asked. In any case, what matters is *the return of the excluded* into the psyche, as many of the persecutory phenomena of psychosis show. For Bion, the fragments thus expatriated try to repenetrate the ego, or to get closer to its living kernel, by violence. When they succeed, the damage that they do affects the activities of linking that may have tried to form. This 'construction' that I am borrowing from Bion has two merits – among others: the first is that one is made aware of the clinical fact that the problem of psychosis is that of the permanent threat of the fragmentation of the ego by rupture of its unity. This threat from the id prevents the ego's work of linking and controlling; it accounts for the experience of psychotic disintegration. The second is that one is shown that, from the point of view of psychosis, the differentiation between representation and affect is artificial. The psychotic particles are both ideational and emotional in nature. Any separation between feeling and intelligence does not apply here. Only the attempt at splitting off good fragments (to be preserved and incorporated) from bad fragments (to be destroyed and expelled) is operative here. This schema is close enough at many points to the construction of the psychical model established by Freud in 'Negation'. But, unlike Freud, Bion does not seem to take account of the original ego-reality that would be capable of determining the internal or external origin of excitations. However, in the treatment of schizophrenic confusional states, Rosenfeld has demonstrated the failure of the split between external and internal reality, succumbing to the attacks of the destructive drives at the boundary that separates them.

The fusion of representation and affect, idea and emotional content might offer a way into the problem of unconscious phantasy. Indeed it is difficult to assign to the latter a definite representative status. It is no less problematic to regard phantasy as a translation pure and simple of instinctual functioning (Isaacs). One is no doubt approaching the limits of a conceptualization which is based on the distinction between intellect and feeling. Taking refuge in the ineffable is of little help here. In my opinion, this question must be left in suspense, just as one refuses to allow oneself to fall into a trap. Nevertheless, I grant that the attempt to resolve unconscious phantasy is the representative verbalization offered in a positive affective situation. Indeed it is known that the schizophrenic, although intolerant of any dangerous approach, is incapable of accommodating himself to a neutrality that he experiences as hostility and to which he responds either by redoubled hostility, or by a wall of indifference. Thus where the work of the ego has failed in the separation of representation and affect, the work of the analyst takes up this work left in suspense.

Bion's theorization may seem abstract. However, there is nothing disembodied about his conception of analysis. Bion stresses that the field of analysis is that of meanings (of the concrete), myths and passions. In other words, the affect is at home here. But, on the other hand, the analytic relation must always be, in his view, maintained in an atmosphere of isolation. We should not misunderstand this term, which has nothing to do with the obsessional defence of the same name. What is meant here is that the analytic situation remains extremely particularized, different from any other, and must be referred, in the field of inalienable relations that bind the analyst to his patient, to the internal psychical reality, identified with everything that happens not only between patient and analyst, but also in the space that unites them, namely, the analyst's consulting room.

3 Paranoia

Just as I have situated phobia between hysteria and obsessional neurosis, I shall place paranoia between manic depression and schizophrenia.

Paranoia, which I see as the passion psychosis, is close to the narcissistic neuroses by virtue of the struggle around *an* object and the ego's struggle around that object. What it is at stake is considerable, since we know how often paranoia finds a resolution in the *crime passionnel*. All reality is attached to that object alone, to that object seen as alone desirable. Paranoia is close to the psychoses in the strict sense, by virtue of the threat of fragmentation, a consequence of the persecution anxieties that attack the ego and the object. The nuclear mechanism of paranoia is projection. It is the return of what was abolished from within, foreclosed, that marks paranoia – the return of the excluded referred to above. Freud, as we know, situated paranoia on the regressing path that goes from homosexuality to narcissism. Homosexual fixation in paranoia, unlike the destructive hate that affects the object, is in fact addressed to the reflected double that represents the object of passion. Projection is a solution to the conflict of ambivalence. Mallet has rightly stressed that regressing homosexuality had undergone in paranoia a masochistic regression. The aim of the paranoiac is not so much that destructive amorous possession of the object of passion as the self-destruction through annihilation of the image of the inverted double that is its subject. This brutal resolution is carried out in the murderous acting out in which the paranoiac intervenes as a subject in what assumes for him the value of a *re*birth. But, in fact, the essence of paranoia, we can hardly forget, is delusion. And delusion is an intellectual construction that must obey an implacable logic. The delusional reality of the paranoiac obeys the rule by which everything that is real is rational. The *ultima ratio* is discovered in delusion. Of course, to see it as a way of filling the gap of doubt is more than plausible. But the most disturbing phenomenon for human reason is this subversion that may affect it.

Affective logic, the logic of passion, has always presented a problem to thinkers. The mistake before Freud was to try to solve its enigma while remaining on the plane of conceptual rationality. Freud lifted the veil of this mystery as soon as he decided to approach the subject from the angle of desire: desire-delusion. Desire, as the original delusion, leads the subject out of the furrow. The essence of delusion is to constitute this new path, the tree hiding the forest of the old one, and Freud took its mechanism to pieces from the point of view of the affect: 'I do not love him – I hate him' (reversal into its opposite), 'I hate him, he hates me' (projection towards the Other) and, lastly, a third, what might be called *reflexive*, stage, 'Since he hates me, I therefore hate him, in order to defend myself'. To respond, by denying it, to the hate (love) of the Other as Same, such is the aim of the logic of passion. The accumulation of evidence of this affect, doubly inverted (into its opposite and towards the Other), must be assured by reason.

Here we must draw up a parallel that, it seems to me, has so far passed unnoticed. In the section of his study of the Schreber case in which he deals with the mechanism of paranoia, Freud speaks of narcissism. He sees in the narcissistic 'stage' a gathering together into a *unity* of erotic drives that, hitherto, had acted only in an anarchic way, as a mosaic in the individual. Narcissism gathers together those auto-erotic part drives into an individual-ized, indivisible eroticism, in which the body becomes the love object of the subject, before the subject is capable of cathecting another object, that of another person, as totalized object. This installing of a double as 'Other–Same', contemporary with secondary narcissism, shows clearly the intermediary situation of paranoia between fragmenting schizophrenia and melancholia, in which the object survives in the form of its shadow. The erotic affects are therefore unified here under the aegis of the individual's 'narcissization'. But it is important to date Freud's conception – that is to say, to stress its situation prior to the last theory of the drives. Elsewhere I have shown that Freud, turning his back on narcissism after *Beyond the Pleasure Principle*, may have given the impression that narcissism existed only in its positive, erotic form and that, in my opinion, it was necessary to re-evalu-ate narcissism in the light of the destructive drives. In other words, one had to admit the existence of a negative narcissism, in which the secondary 'gathering together' could be the object of an effacement such as can be seen in the negative hallucination of the subject. The paranoiac does not recognize himself in the image that the mirror presents. He cannot understand that the Other sees him as a despot, a tyrant blinded by passion, whereas his approach is quite logical. He cannot accept the criticism made of his egocentricity, when he is so concerned about the order of the world. In this respect, he is not entirely wrong. Freud is right to insist on the resexualization of the drives in the paranoiac's social life. Here again it is the return of the affect that strikes the psychoanalyst. The paranoiac wishes above all to be objective and not dependent upon his social relations. It is the Other that is interested in him. All he wants, he declares, is anonymity or recognition of his right to live in peace among his own people. This is true for all those who, without being paranoiacs, have sublimated the eroticization of their social relations. One now understands more clearly the importance of language for the paranoiac, his attachment to the precise use of words, his rigorous, almost legalistic syntax. Does not Freud say that the delusion of jealousy contradicts the subject, the delusion of persecution the verb, erotomania the object? It is not only language, but the whole of grammaticality that is at issue in paranoia. That is to say, paranoia is a process of resexualization of externalized secondariness in the field of social relations. Nowhere except in paranoia do words 'make love to one another'; they do so to such an extent that procreated verbal delusion engenders a neo-reality that conforms to its wishes. This is the prestige and mystery of logic, which enables archaeology to take possession of its own, by re-establishing itself in the place of what had expelled it.

Freud compared religion to obsessional neurosis and philosophy to paranoia. The world of the philosophers is so perfectly constructed that theoretical construction is, for the most gifted of them, an object of fascination and admiration. The role of the psychoanalyst is to deconstruct their system, by locating the traces of the excluded, of the affect exorcized by philosophy. No doubt Freud's discourse is nourished by the sources of western metaphysics and is a product of it. It cannot be denied that the distinction between feeling and intelligence is a major given of that philosophical tradition. With Melanie Klein, this tradition is, partly at least, denounced. Paranoia, the philosophical system and the Freudian theory are all three prisoners of ideology. This theoretical discourse cannot escape it either. Psychoanalytic ideology is like the individual's family romance. It is the idealizing construction by which one escapes the pressure of the drives and the constraint of the internal objects that one is subjected to. The psychoanalytic work, without claiming to attain that absolute truth from which all ideology is absent in the last resort, nevertheless takes its eradication as its horizon, a boundary that one knows to be unreachable, but which one posits as an orienting vector. The result is often disappointing, for every author then proves to be as intransigent and as rigid in relation to their theoretical construction as the paranoiac is in relation to his delusion. The theory of the

127

psychoanalyst, then, would seem to be a sort of narcissistic double; clung to as to their own identity.

III Between neurosis and psychosis

I cannot say very much here about the complex question of the borderline states. I shall simply offer a few remarks on some of the clinical forms that throw interesting light on the problem of the affect.

1 The neurosis of depersonalization

If there is a clinical form that evokes the aborted or transitional structure, on the edge of one of the completed structures that has been examined, it is the neurosis of depersonalization. I shall refer here to the work devoted to it by Bouvet at the twenty-first Congrès des Langues romanes, 1960. In it affect plays an important role, since it is what essentially characterizes the clinical syndrome through the polymorphism that it may cover. A sense of change in oneself and in the external world; an impression of strangeness, of alienation, experienced in an affective anaesthesia and apathy to the point of an atmosphere of coolness and death; loss of contact with objects and with the body; all manifestations that Bouvet summed up in the term 'sense of change', accompanied by an extremely painful affective state, paralysing the capacity for affective reaction (impression of desiccation or affective freezing), the whole being produced outside any characterizable delusional formation. It is not necessary to refer to this table to stress further the importance of the affects, which is obvious; the affects not only supplant the representations, but they seem to stifle them and prevent their very expression.

However, I should now say something about a number of paradoxes concerning this clinical constellation, especially from the point of view of the affect. On the one hand, there is an extinction of affective possibilities, as has been seen in apathy, anaesthesia and what Bouvet calls the 'barrier', whose protective role demonstrates its defensive value. On the other hand, there is the affective exacerbation manifested in the various changes that come about in one's feelings, loaded with disturbing or hostile projections about the ego and the world. Another paradox is that 'disturbing strangeness', which is not devoid of a certain pleasure and which is expressed in the feeling of a certain '*sweetness*'. Thus an affective bipolarity is expressed, as in the alternation of Bouvet's patient between horror ('It is horribly painful') and pleasure ('It's really sweet, I can tell you'). These paradoxes are to be found again in Bouvet's theory. He draws attention to the extreme affective

128

rigidity: the absence of variety in affective positions, together with a certain 'keeping one's distance', which does not accept variations in 'approach', as in drawing someone closer or distancing oneself from people. But, on the other hand, he also stresses that, on the contrary, compared with the psychoses, depersonalization will be characterized by playing different roles, by greater mobilization of alternating introjections and projections, without the solidity and fixity of the mechanisms of confirmed psychoses.

The transference will make it possible to bring out this ambiguity even more: on the one hand, the patient fears, to the highest degree, the experience of a painful affective dependence on the object, which is felt to be intrusive and mutilating, leading to a denial of any real experience with the analyst; while, on the other hand, this dependence will be necessary if the object is to be able to feed a perpetually inadequate narcissistic provision leading to a sustained affective demand. The fear of rejection goes hand in hand with the fear of contact.

The limits of this work force me to curtail the examination of the type of affect entailed in depersonalization as opposed to the neuroses and psychoses, and leave to one side, despite the artificial character of this separation, other features that merit discussion: oral fixation, the role of aggressivity and projections, the replication in the object relation, etc.

Most authors, Bouvet included, rightly link the structure of depersonalization neurosis to a narcissistic failure. Whether one invokes an original wound, or speaks of dependence on a narcissisic object, or the need for periodical and continual renewal of the subject's narcissistic provisions, it amounts to the same thing. Furthermore, the clinical configuration of the disorder suggests a disturbance of the narcissistic economy in the variations of the limits of the ego, but also, a fact that Bouvet does not seem to have stressed, a veritable narcissistic haemorrhage that the 'barrier' can hardly contain. Moreover, reference to a *loss* of the object rather than to a threat of castration certainly indicates that it is in this register that one should try to situate things, which in no way excludes the need to articulate both fields, that of object loss and that of the threat of castration. It is worth remembering that in his report Bouvet makes several references to the relations between depersonalization neurosis and schizophrenia and melancholia. But he is also right to show that what is in question is a relation with a *narcissistic object*, that is to say, an object relation of a narcissistic type.

What are the implications of these remarks with regard to the problem of the affect? As early as 1926, in one of the appendices to *Inhibitions, Symptoms and Anxiety* (addendum C), Freud discusses the relations between anxiety, pain and mourning, which I dealt with earlier. He remarks that although anxiety is the reaction to the danger entailed by the loss of the object, pain is the proper reaction to the loss. Although the model of pain as envisaged by Freud is that of physical pain, caused by an attack on the protective shield, the struggle against this break-in necessitates narcissistic anticathexes that empty the ego. Psychical pain involves the production of a hyper-intense cathexis of the absent (lost) object. And although Freud takes the trouble to add that 'the transition from physical pain to mental pain corresponds to a change from narcissistic cathexis to object-cathexis',[10] I ought in turn to add that this can only refer to the cathexis of a narcissistic object, following the link that has just been mentioned. The situation of depersonalization – halfway between anxiety and pain – is perhaps becoming clearer now. From anxiety, it retains a certain value as signal, which explains why it is triggered off when the danger of a possible object loss is announced. Of pain, it recalls the anticathexes as productions of a hyper-intense cathexis of the absent or lost object, as if that loss were not only experienced as a threat, but had in fact occurred. But, unlike the experience of pain, no representation of the said object ensues in a situation of distress, but a veritable emptying of the ego, which seems to want to join some unspecified object – in some indeterminate elsewhere – rediscovering in the objects of the external world, by the mechanisms of projective identification, the characteristics of hostility and alienation of the excluded object. 'Sweetness' could be explained therefore by this unspecified realization of the consubstantial confusion sought. The experiences of loss are not the only ones to provoke depersonalization, since Bouvet remarks that the danger of drawing close may play the same trigger role. One cannot speak of loss in the strict sense. But the danger is really the same, for what is feared in the act of approach is the risk of breaking into the ego, a threat to psychical corporal integrity. Here, too, the whole mechanism functions both as if it were an automatic danger signal of a break-in, setting in train the anticathexes and as if the break-in had already taken place, thus triggering off the flow of narcissistic libido towards the open wound, which would encourage again this emptying of the ego by the breach that the subject has opened up in himself.

It might be said that in every case a phase is so to speak occulted, scotomized, playing the role of an unconscious phantasy; the threat of loss experienced as a narcissistic amputation and the threat of a break-in experienced as a breach through which flows, as through a bottomless hole, the narcissistic haemorrhage that calls up other narcissistic cathexes. What strikes me as fundamental is the 'negativization' of the phantasy representation, allowing only pure affects to speak and transferring this phantasy representation to qualities projected on to objects in the external world. One can recognize here the role of the projective identification stressed by the Kleinian authors. But what characterizes the experience of depersonalization, as many

10 *S.E.*, XX, p. 171.

other authors, Peto and Bouvet in particular, have noted, is the recathexis of the object, which puts an end to the experience and which enables object relations of a very different style and even of a very different kind to be set up, than before the depersonalization episode, which brought about a purging of the subject's aggressive desires.

This explains the paradox of rigidity and movement, what can be expressed only in terms of narcissistic economy, marking alterations of balance and displacement of narcissistic, libidinal object energy. Loss (pain) and recathexis follow one another with their procession of associated reactions. It is a quest for the object and a flight before the object in a constantly unstable, precarious balance. It is understandable that no form is permanently fixed either in neurosis, which would imply a dominance of the object cathexes, or in psychosis, which would imply a narcissistic flowing back on to the ego, abandoning the phantasy objects and applying itself to the creation of the delusional neo-reality.

The narcissistic structure affect reveals that the danger whose existence it signals is no longer castration, but loss of the object, an attack on the ego and its consequences, either at the level of melancholic splitting, or at the level of schizophrenic fragmentation. As such, it is more diffuse, more invasive than the affect linked to an object structure. Side by side with this, its function as signal gives way to its quasi-automatic, economic function.

2 *States of object loss and recovery*

Although depersonalization neurosis causes this sudden, temporary break in the object relation, clinical psychoanalysis has revealed a gamut of more discrete states, ones linked to a related problematic. Most of them belong to the borderline states. They are characterized by alternations of object loss and recovery. It is as if, in these cases, the status of the internal object were constantly threatened, perpetually doomed to disappearance. Against this threat or following the survival of loss, various attempts at immediate object recovery at any price are set in train. Such attempts are absolutely necessary in the struggle against depressive or fragmenting affects and require a recovery by vicarious objects. These objects may be taken from the body or the outside world. We know that the aim of fetishism is to sustain the negation of the absence of maternal penis by the cathexis of what is linked to it metaphorically or metonymically. But what occurs here with regard to sex has equivalents on the level of narcissism. Two examples – hypochondria and toxicomania – will clarify what I mean. Hypochondria, whose link with the narcissistic libido was noted by Freud, illustrates this taking from the bodily space of an object whose cathexis has undergone a conversion from a psychical libido into a corporal libido. It is clear that the hypochondriacal organ catches in its net an object in danger of being lost, which is now contained. This observed object becomes in turn an object of scrutiny and persecution. It can neither be dropped nor assimilated. From the point of view of the affect a situation is set up that oscillates between precarious silence and malaise, an absorbing 'ill-being', evidence of a conflict between object libido and narcissistic libido, as between erotic drives and destructive drives. Such is the functional necessity of hypochondria, from the point of view of the affective economy, in the struggle against the feeling of narcissistic defeat brought on by object loss.

In toxicomania, we witness a similar situation insofar as the toxicomaniacal object aims to warn of or repair an object loss. The assurance that such an object may be rediscovered in the outside world and incorporated (unlike the hypochondriacal object which, so to speak, is 'excorporated') must be tirelessly verified. Toxicomania is necessary to the toxicomaniac in order to struggle against the feeling of affective emptiness.[11] Such patients complain of feeling completely emptied from the inside, as if they were in a state of permanent affective starvation. They hunger and thirst after objects and must *really* incorporate an external object capable of restoring them, in both senses of the term, that is to say, of feeding them and making good the effects of the destructive drives. The effect of these destructive drives is apparent in the emptiness that they leave after they have done their work, hence the need for a narcissistic reconstruction. What creates the problem is the impossibility of introjecting affects deriving from the relation to a psychical object, which necessitates recourse to some toxic substance. The choice of such a substance will be made in terms of its effects on the affect. Whatever may engender a state of affect – a sign of life – will be totally cathected against affective silence – a sign of death. Toxicomania is a struggle against what might be called narcissistic frigidity, a sense of affective poverty, rather as one might speak of physiological poverty where serious deficiencies are involved. But this revitalization is death-dealing.

Of course, toxicomania may take hold not against an affective void, but against affective pain, in order to neutralize its effects. However, I believe that the pain here is no more than a threat of affective extinction by exhaustion of the ego's ability to struggle.

It is clear that the roots of the object relation, the oral relation, are what are being touched on here. One might then conceive of interesting relations between hypochondria and toxicomania on the one hand, and anorexia and bulimia on the other.

---

11 Or perhaps of an excess of uncontrollable affect capable of destroying the object.

3 Psychosomatic and psychopathic states

The odd conjunction that I am making here is hypothetical, that is to say, open to discussion. Those who have more experience than I do of the patients to which the terms refer will no doubt question it. The metapsychology of the psychosomatic states is highly complex at present. Contributions from the French school (Marty, Fain, de M'Uzan, David) have noted among these patients the poverty of the representative element, the economic and functional inadequacy of their phantasies. Little has been written about the affect in these cases. However, one may infer from the works of these authors that it is not only the representative element that is inadequate in unconscious working out, but that the affect presents in these patients notable peculiarities. My experience, which is limited in this area, has shown that, with certain patients, the affect ought to be experienced *a minima*. When, after many years of analysis, the unconscious representative element had been recognized by patients, and was partly re-established in its functions (dream, phantasy), the affect, on the other hand, was much more difficult to mobilize. It was as if, in certain cases at least, *the affect was deduced from somatizations, or hypotheses after the event*, after some psychosomatic crisis. 'I had an attack, so I must have felt jealous of X.' In short, the affect in question had never reached consciousness; as soon as it was mobilized, it could be expressed only in a somatic storm. This storm was itself the cause of an affect, one of discouragement, sadness, the wish to abandon everything, which indicates the defeat of the ego, the ego's inability to prevent the attack, to master the affect by its non-occurrence. What is problematic here is this psycho (affect)-somatic (fit) conversion.

Unlike in hysteria, the link between desire and symptom struck me as being much looser than in hysterical conversion. One might run the risk of giving it symbolic value, but that would have no effect, no affect. That is to say, the interpretation would be received on an intellectual level, with no affective resonance. Parallel with this, the transference, though very intense, was fiercely denied. The analyst is perceived as a therapeutic instrument, with the role to remove the symptom, in order to allow the ego to re-establish its omnipotent mastery over the body. One guesses that this attitude goes hand in hand with the fusional movements linked to a fixation on a maternal imago that exercises a power of life or death over the body and affective sphere. The allegation of independence with regard to the analyst (or mother) goes hand in hand with a refusal to abandon the internalized imago that she represents. The imago and the ego hold one another prisoner. Any excessive approach, like any attempt at separation, is followed by a fit.

These observations suggested to me that the somatic crisis of the psychosomatics (or some of them) represents an authentic 'acting out', acting on the outside, directed inwards, for, as in acting out, the essential aim is the expulsion of the intruder (the affect) from psychical reality. It is this that leads me to compare the psychosomatic and psychopathic structures. The psychosomatic patient, then, seems to be a corporal psychopath, who treats his body in the way that psychopaths treat social reality, in an extremely relaxed manner, in which sadomasochism is in some way not only unconscious, but foreclosed.

Turning to the psychopathic structures, the importance, the sheer massiveness of the actings out, the contempt or unawareness that they show for external objects have often been remarked on. Here, too, one is struck by the constraining need to react by action. The action is intended to short-circuit psychical reality by the discharge of tension. It is performed with an absence of reflection that is quite striking and which casts doubt on the functioning of the reality principle in these patients: they do seem to obey only the pleasure principle, with consequent disagreeable effects on social reality. For them, social reality is over-cathected in relation to psychical reality, just as the body is over-cathected as against psychical reality in the psychosomatic. What strikes me about these patients is the relation of consumption that they have with regard to the objects (indifferent in themselves) that form a certain significant constellation. By throwing themselves desperately into the act, they devour the objects to be found in the field into which they have just thrown themselves. One has the feeling that the important thing for these patients is not to allow the affects to take their course in this situation, but to exhaust them in a single act. They cannot wait, or deceive their stormy, destructive hunger. The acting out finally brings a release of tension, whatever the consequences. Psychopaths are, therefore, comparable with psychosomatics, who inflict damage on their bodies in order not to allow psychical reality to be cathected.

A number of features differentiate the psychopath from the pervert. The broken line of object relations, the instability of the object in him, intolerance of frustration, responses that are immediate and undifferentiated, affective immaturity, the feeling that everything is owed to him and the ego's constant complaints about what others have made of him – all these features, so characteristic of psychopaths, hardly apply to perverts. The perverts, if indeed they can be treated as a single category, are in a sense the aristocrats of this great family, the refined product of a long genealogy. I have paid little attention to the affect of the pervert in this study. A number of works (by Rosolato, Castoriadis–Aulagnier, Masud Khan) have tried to throw light on this obscure part of the analytic field. The pervert's *jouissance* still remains a mystery, despite the fact that the child is said be polymorphously perverse. Like all *jouissance*, perverse *jouissance* is *jouissance* in action. His triumph is to publicize this *jouissance*, whereas it remains swathed in secrecy, despite the scandal that it needs in order to be revealed. Its relation to the Law is one of the points that link it to the condition of the psychopath. But the psychopath does not know how to be perverse, he cannot savour *jouissance* because the difference that separates him from the pervert is that between the gourmand and the gourmet. The pervert puts the finishing touches to his work and elaborates his *jouissance* in the scenario that is necessary to it. Perversion pursues the aim of embodying phantasy. That is why, it seems to me, the fulfilment of the perverted acting out necessitates the production of a theatrical performance.[12] In the perverted act there is an element of theatricality that is essential to perverted *jouissance*. The most seriously perpetrated perversion is marked by the seal of derision, on the part of the performer, as well as for the person who consents to participate in it. It is a sort of satyr play that must remain unknown, since only the pervert has the right to laugh up his sleeve. Who is he laughing at? Himself? Perhaps, but in so far as he denounces in his place the unmasked father, finally fallen from his role as noble father. The Law is simply the desire of the father, says Lacan. This is true above all for the pervert, who sees behind every father a hypocrite who, in secret, indulges in all manner of base acts, while severely punishing minor offences. And in every mother he sees a tart enslaved to the father, unless she herself leads him into shameless *jouissance*, while passing herself off as a holy woman, though one with strangely ambiguous gestures.

When the child discovers that his masturbatory auto-eroticism is forbidden, whereas the parents abandon themselves to a coitus whose *jouissance* he magnifies in phantasy, the only revenge that seems possible is perversion. But this revenge is cold, cruel and the *jouissance* that accompanies it is marked by denigration. For the pervert, a successful performance is to obtain the maximum *jouissance* through the part drives, whose function is to assume all the possibilities of genital sexuality. That is why he can succeed in what the non-pervert is incapable of doing (at the cost of becoming neurotic or impotent) and yet at the same time something will always be missing in his *jouissance*, despite his demand for unimpeded pleasure, the prolongation of organ pleasure, as against 'full object love'. Although the pervert's superego seems so contradictory, at once defeated by the completion of the perverse act and victorious by virtue of the penal sanctions that he seems to attract, it is perhaps because what he wants is that *jouissance* as punishment and that punishment as *jouissance*. Corporal punishment, inviting the Law to castrate him,[13] that is, to manifest its hypocrisy as Law, since the judges might equally well be condemned to the same penalties, were they not protected by their office.

12 Hence the comparisons that have been made with the role of the primal scene in the case of the pervert (McDougall). One may also compare it with the theatrical performances of great masochistic perverts (de M'Uzan).
13 Which it sometimes actually agrees to do (as in the castration of sexual perverts practised in certain countries).

This corporal *jouissance* and this corporal punishment bring us closer metaphorically to the converse and perverse structures. In the latter, to act in the body and to act in reality remain in a relation of strict symbolization with psychical reality, the unconscious, the repressed. In the psychosomatic and psychopathic structures, although the link here is much less precise, no subject is perceptible, the subject being cut off from all access to his unconscious. Thus conversion and perversion form a kernel coherent (in comparison with hysteria and obsessional neurosis) with the unconscious structures. Psychosomatic and psychopathic structures represent states of energic decline that tend to an economic discharge that may damage the individual's body and social status.

There can be no doubt that the price paid for these outcomes is evidence of the major fears felt by the ego, forced here to accept distortions, encroachments, mutilations or an essential impoverishment, in the sense in which the richness of affective life is compromised by its mode of functioning, its all or nothing character. There is an obvious split, then, between the critical and the chronic personality. In the final analysis, what characterizes both the psychosomatic and the psychopath is their absence of psychical symptomatology: that is to say, their normality. That is why the first are in the hands of doctors and the second in the hands of lawyers.[14]

4 Affective retardation

It is not in the spirit of psychoanalytic investigation to consider clinical practice from the point of view of retardation. So when I use the term affective retardation I am employing conventional usage to denote a particular characteral structure. Affective retardation is an apparently benign clinical picture. However psychoanalysts regards patients presenting affective immaturity with some reservation. They are well aware that the pitfalls presented by a psychical kernel constituted by dependence on the object and the idealization of that object may prove insuperable. What is striking in such patients is the maintenance, despite an apparent development in their professional and social life, of a style of object relations that has succeeded against all and sundry in maintaining its original ingenuousness: the eternally youthful physical appearance, the sensitivity, a certain sentimentality, the simpering ways, the affective claims, the total sexual and aggressive instinctual contra-cathexis reach surprising proportions here. Affective immaturity

---

14 I am well aware that these brief remarks on the perversions go little way towards grasping the essence of the relations between affect and perverse pleasure.

seems to depend on a narcissistic organization that must be protected from developing. The conflict between this narcissistic organization and instinctual demands culminates in keeping the latter secret. One is now in a better position to understand the phantasy of omnipotence that hides behind what one accuses of childishness. This omnipotence aims at keeping the object captive by affective 'blackmail'. Any demand on the part of the object implies either a relationship of a more mature type, or an instinctual satisfaction that is received as a narcissistic assassination. It is the child that one tries to wound by this demand. The instinctual cathexes of the object will be offset by anti-instinctual, narcissistic cathexes of idealized objects. Often the transitional objects will preserve their cathexis well beyond the phase of development in which they had a temporary functional value.

Perhaps even more than the sexual libido, it is the aggressive libido that will be carefully anticathected, probably because it is that which is experienced as the most dangerous in the object relation.

Indeed one guesses that what must be banished from the ego is a certain affective violence capable of destroying the object, as if a wish for criminal revenge were being satisfied here. What is the crime for which the object would be punished in this way? Although it is difficult to know for sure, one can guess. The major accusation brought against the object is freeing itself from the subject's tutelage in order to attend to its own tasks – tasks that, in the final analysis, prove to be instinctual satisfactions. The mother leaves the child at night in order to indulge in sexual relations with the father. The father does not grant all the affection desired in order to lavish it on his wife – or women. Affective retardation derives from this discovery and wishes to maintain the illusion of an encounter with an object that is an exception to this rule. At the same time, it accuses the objects of reproducing that childhood situation and forcing the subject to participate in what was the origin of a humiliating narcissistic wound. The wish not to grow up then becomes both fixation on a stage prior to the discovery of parental sexuality and also the revenge taken on the primary object through a dependence that achieves the loss of the object's freedom at the price of the subject's freedom. Of course, this object relation maintains the denial of the subject's drives. Affective retardation takes the idealized desire of the parent literally. 'They want me to be innocent so that I am not a witness of their instinctual life. They want me to be innocent in order not to feel guilty. I shall remain the eternal innocent so that they may feel eternally guilty. I shall make them feel ashamed of what they are, since they have not allowed me to be like them when I was only a child, even at the price of a mutilation of myself.' The interpretation of these structures in terms of Winnicott's conception of the 'false self' would be theoretically interesting.

Conclusion

The opposition between the field of the neuroses dominated by the problematic of castration, and the field of the psychoses dominated by the problematic of fragmentation (simple or multiple splitting) should not suggest that I am relativizing castration here and seeking a domain 'beyond' it. In fact, castration and fragmentation are to be understood in relation to one another. One might suggest as a common denominator the concept of *dismemberment*.

Dismemberment as loss of the sexual member and as separation from the members that make up the body. In fact, the threat of castration is a threat to narcissistic integrity and the possibility of becoming reunited with the mother. Indeed, the suspension of masturbatory activity has the aim of saving the organ by sacrificing *jouissance*, dooming it to a sort of functional paralysis in order to protect it from mutilation. Conversely, splitting is always splitting between a sexed part and antisexed part, in the case of a simple splitting. In cases of multiple splitting, each isolated kernel, each fragment of the fragmented body, is cathected with an erotic libido and represents the penis *in potentia*. Tausk reminds us that the corporal libido serves as a defence against psychical libido; the influencing machine is a genital organ, of course, but it is also an entirely libidinized psychical apparatus. The dispersal of the dislocated fragments is a ruthlessly perpetrated castration that reduces the whole phallic body to scattered fragments. Castration of the part object with its 'colossal narcissistic cathexis' (the penis) and narcissistic castration that fragments the body into a multitude of part objects: not only are the two registers not opposed, they define themselves in terms of one another.[15] Penile castration implies the reference to a narcissistically unified body; the fragmentation of the ego refers to the incorporated part object, the founding element of the subject's narcissism. Castration refers to the difference of the sexes, to sexual identity, just as fragmentation refers to the difference between the mother and the child, by which the child becomes an 'undivided whole'. We now understand more clearly the function of the phallus-bearing father, the locus of the difference between the sexes and the difference between the mother and the child.

15 I approached the relation between neurotic structure and psychotic structure in a work in which, in defining certain latent psychoses, I propose the concept of *blank psychosis* (J.L. Donnet and André Green, *L'enfant de ça*, Paris: Minuit, 1973).

4

Affect, the psychoanalytic process and the Oedipus complex

I Affect and the raw materials of analytic work

It is familiar ground that the work of analysis aims at inducing the patient
to give up the repressions (using the word in the widest sense) belonging
to his early development and to replace them by reactions of a sort that
would correspond to a psychically mature condition. With this purpose
in view he must be brought to recollect certain experiences and the
affective impulses called up by them which he has for the time being forgotten. We know that his present symptoms and inhibitions are the
consequences of repressions of this kind: thus that they are a substitute for
these things that he has forgotten. What sort of material does he put at
our disposal which we can make use of to put him on the way to recovering the lost memories? All kinds of things. He gives us fragments of
these memories in his dreams, invaluable in themselves but seriously distorted as a rule by all the factors concerned and the formation of dreams.
Again, he produces ideas, if he gives himself up to 'free association', in
which we can discover allusions as to the repressed experiences and derivatives of the suppressed affective impulses as well as of the reactions against
them. And, finally, there are hints of the repetitions of affects belonging
to the repressed material to be found in actions performed by the patient,
some fairly important, some trivial, but inside and outside the analytic situation. Our experience has shown that the relation of transference, which
becomes established towards the analyst, is particularly calculated to
favour the return of these emotional connections. It is out of such raw
material – if we may so describe it – that we have to put together what we
are in search of.[1]

---

1 *S.E.*, XXIII, pp. 257–8.

In this paragraph of some twenty lines, affect is mentioned four times – a sign of its preponderant presence whenever the question of the analytic situation arises.

To the category of affect corresponds: the *memory* of 'certain experiences', 'fragments of these memories in . . . *dreams*', '*ideas*', '*actions*', all these being reactivated by the relation to transference, 'particularly calculated to favour the return of these emotional connections'. One is placed by the analytic situation, therefore, in the presence of psychical material in which the 'presentation' of the past – the past combining with the present – occurs in a tissue of discourse characterized by heterogeneity. The analytic situation unites in its texture, in which the threads of yesterday and today intertwine, elements as different as ideas, representations, actions to which affects are joined. Affect, therefore, does not have a uniform function. Freud speaks in turn of 'affective impulses', 'affects belonging to the repressed material', 'emotional connections'. Thus affect has a function, depending on the context, being either an emanation of the drive (affective impulses), the motive force of an idea, the motive of an action, or again a set of relations that its connection with the transference object helps to repeat.

Although the aim of analysis is the lifting of infantile amnesia obtained by the lifting of repression, Freud, at the end of this article, was to concede that the recovery of memories does not always occur, resistance winning out over remembering. But he concludes that the analysis is not weakened for all that. The analyst's construction is validated by the patient's affect.

> Quite often we do not succeed in bringing the patient to recollect what has been repressed. Instead of that, if the analysis is carried out correctly, we produce in him an assured conviction of the truth of the construction which achieves the same therapeutic result as a recaptured memory.[2]

This truth effect is that of historical truth. A little further on, Freud makes the hypothesis that hallucination might be the return of 'something that has been experienced in infancy and then forgotten . . . something that this child has seen or heard at a time when he could still hardly speak'. According to this hypothesis the affect of experience is bound up with a hallucinated representation. Indeed, the absence of a possible encoding by language might explain its return in a hallucinatory form. It is remarkable that Freud ends his article by repeating the sentence that was to have such a

---

2 *S.E.*, XXIII, pp. 265–6. In his fine book, *La construction de l'espace analytique* (Paris: Denoël, 1970), Serge Viderman extended the notion of construction considerably, to the point of making it the keystone of psychoanalysis, inviting us to leave the circle of a historical reconstruction that is both uncertain and illusory.

future impact: such patients 'are suffering from their own reminiscences'. Originally, these words applied to the hysteric; he is now applying them more widely to delusion. It is no less remarkable that Freud did not cite, among the materials of the analysand's discourse, the phantasy, the discovery of which considerably changed the first conception of trauma and remembering.

Remembering and construction go hand in hand, insofar as remembering is the product of the analysand's construction. Now, since Freud, one may wonder whether the analyst's construction bears on the unconscious phantasy or on the actual event – whether the truth effect depends on the accuracy of the construction in relation to the event or in relation to the phantasy.

When Freud gives the example of cases in which analysis did not succeed in lifting infantile amnesia, it was because he had come up against the memory-screen, a representation blocking entry to the repressed, a sort of borderline beyond which it seems forbidden to go. Now rigorous analysis does not allow, if one resorts only to the analysand, to draw a distinction between screen-memory and phantasy.[3] Their structure is the same – both are constructed out of disarticulated fragments of perception, brought together to form a 'psychical stage', with a set or a scenario, an element of private theatre. Thus the controversy as to whether the construction bears upon memory or phantasy is, in the final analysis, pointless. What needs to be stressed is that one must not be so naive as to believe that real experience gives rise to affective reactions of greater intensity than those produced by phantasy.

Traumatic events are interpreted in phantasy terms; the trauma is all the more violent in that the ego is less able to perceive the reality of the event. Conversely, phantasy activity turns the ordinary real experience into a traumatic experience. Distinguishing between event and phantasy would amount, during the first phases of development, to trying to dissociate the indissociable.[4]

---

3 In the letters to Fliess (Draft M, 25 May 1897 in *S.E.*, I), Freud describes the structure of the phantasy and its link to memory: 'Phantasies arise from unconscious combination, in accordance with certain trends, of things experienced and heard. These trends are towards making inaccessible the memory from which the symptoms have emerged or might emerge' (*S.E.*, I, p. 252). The processes of amalgamation and chronological distortion lead therefore to a 'construction' that may be compared with the analyst's construction. It should be noted that, in this text, Freud accepts the existence of a formation of symptoms on the basis of the construction of impulses (*Impulsbildung*).

4 This implies, it should be said, no pre-eminence from the genetic point of view. On the contrary, psychoanalytic practice sends us back to the primal phantasy known as the *primal scene*.

The affective power of phantasy is at least the equal of that of the real. Phantasy and affect support one another. Evocation of phantasy arouses an upsurge of affect (one has only to reread 'A child is being beaten'), which often leads to a reshaping of the affect in a more anxiety-arousing way or one closer to the undisguised realization of desire. Affective tension solicits the phantasy, which is already in itself an outcome of discharge, a 'link' with that free energy in search of representation. The phantasy is elaborated on a kernel of memory, but the phantasy is in turn transformed into memory, combining with other fragments belonging to memories from different periods and mixing with it the content of other phantasies. This 'construction' is a mixture in which prohibition and wish-fulfilment are combined, filtered through different layers, real events and phantasy events. What matters is the organizing effect of this result of psychical work.

However, after bringing memory and phantasy more closely together as compared with the real in the affect effect, a limit must now be set on this closeness. Real and phantasy are *each separately* producers of affect. But the traumatic effect of the affect originates precisely, as every analyst knows, when the real confirms what might be called the presentiment of phantasy.[5] When Freud says that the perception of the mother's genital organs, bringing castration out into the open, has an effect on the child comparable with what occurs in the adult following the fall of a throne or altar, he is not exaggerating. If the only possible response to this visual trauma is the splitting of the ego, of which fetishism shows us the scar, then indeed the affect must have had a drastic effect to bring the ego to consent to such a self-mutilation by disavowal. Here one sees the operation of one of the major effects of the affect, one that has not been sufficiently stressed: *belief*, or perhaps one should say *faith*.

Freud's various writings on religion reach their limit at the gates of faith, which often resist analysis. The maintenance of the splitting is such that there is no shortage of believing analysts – whichever religion they belong to – just as there are irreproachable scientists who attend more or less regularly church, temple or synagogue. So securely preserved is the domain of illusion, from belief to fetish, to the omnipotent protective father or to the consoling mother.

When the experience of the real confirms phantasy, one is confronted by an *event* that links perception and affect, which the defence will be able to dissociate. The traumatic effect derives here from the 'unfortunate meeting' of phantasy and perception. Without the phantasy of castration, the perception of the mother's genital organs would mean nothing more than the recognition of a visual difference. Without the 'sexual theory' of sadistic

---

5 It is perhaps against this conjunction that what Lewin calls 'screen-affects' are formed.

coitus, according to which the mother is castrated by the father or castrates him, the perception of the vagina could not have such dramatic affective consequences. It should be remarked in passing that the phantasy of an internal maternal penis – the father's penis in the mother's belly – solves nothing. Vaginal castration coincides the absence of a member 'lost' on the way, with its rediscovery in the other, in which the parasite feeds on the power of its host. The horror of castration gives way here to fear of penetration – a phantasy no less fearsome than that aroused by the mother's evident lack of a penis.

Thus the series formed by phantasy, memory-screen, memory and perception links and unlinks these various terms and makes them indissociable. In any case, before embarking on construction, the analytic work must carry out the *deconstruction* of the composite psychical fragment offered by phantasy, the memory-screen and the formations of the unconscious. It is when this work is completed in a satisfactory way that one observes a parallel work on the affect in the transference.

This reshaping takes place through a quantitative and qualitative change in affects. Since the ego is now able to reintegrate the unconscious fragment of representations and affects, it extends its power over the conquered terrain. Having fallen under the jurisdiction of the ego, the quota of affect is, so to speak, an integral part of the functional structure that characterizes it and no longer threatens this organization. As for the quality of the affect, it recovers its true identity. From the qualitative point of view, the affect would rediscover its vocation after the lifting of repression. Unpleasure is brought back to its true representation: evocation of the loss of the object or loss of object love, loss of the member, loss of self-esteem. Or, again, where pleasure was presented under the disguise of unpleasure, where pain was satisfaction turned upside down and addressed to the superego, Eros reaffirms its original rights and removes the masks. One should not neglect however the separating effect of the destructive drives, which, by means of resistance, maintains the repressed in segregation. Indeed, as soon as awareness is achieved, a new resistance is set up in opposition to any later breach. The outcome of treatment depends on the balance-sheet of this work of Penelope.

This happy development is rarer than one would like. If such results are neither so complete, nor so frequent, this does not diminish the fact that this outcome is the criterion of analytic work that has reached its conclusion.

II Schematic typologies of discourse

What does this favourable outcome of the analytic work consist of? What are the cases in which such an outcome does not occur?

At this point in my investigation, I might be permitted to call upon my own experience. But at what level of experience? Of course, one can draw up a contrasting nosographical picture of good and bad cases, neurotics and psychotics. But such an approach is probably too general, too removed from the psychoanalytic work. Moreover, every analyst can recall the case of psychotic patients who have benefited more from analysis than certain neurotics, whether they were cases of character neurosis or transference psychoneurosis.

The criteria of health and illness are certainly imprecise and inadequate for my purposes here. Analyses of 'normal' persons (training analyses) are not, far from it, those that give the impression of the easiest analytic work.

One may question, too, the structure of the transference. Transferences may be described in which the ambivalence remains moderate, the affects subtle, the aggressions partial or temporary, the defences supple and mobilizable; here the interpretations have been capable of integration, leading to a true transformation of the psychical economy. On the other hand, there are transferences in which ambivalence is extreme, the affects stormy, the regressions massive and lasting, the defences rigid and self-supporting; here the patient remains blind or deaf to interpretation, the analysis leading only to the superficial, precarious transformations, unless the balance-sheet is quite simply negative, marked by an unfavourable change that would justify the greatest caution at the moment of deciding in favour of an indication for psychoanalysis. We find in this opposition Bouvet's description of genital and pregenital structures, which has been continued in recent observations by de M'Uzan.

I shall now contrast the three types of analytic session and draw certain conclusions.

Type 1

The session is dominated by a heavy, stormy atmosphere. The silences are leaden, the conversation is dominated by *present concerns*: the presence of the analyst, who cannot for a single moment be placed in parentheses, the presentness of the conflict that dominates the life of the analysand, the presentness of reality and the outside world, which imprisons the analysand and stifles speech. That speech is quiet, monotonous, as if bound by the presence of the body that is being expressed through the voice. The discourse is uniform, a descriptive account in which no reference back to the past is detectable; it unfolds like a continuous stream, allowing of no interruption. This captive speech sets out to entrap the analyst. The analyst feels as much a prisoner of the analysand as the analysand seems to be of his body. One proceeds to a spectral analysis of this discourse, in which one can detect only gloomy uniformity, enunciated rather like a recitative or incantation. What reaches the analyst is a thick, gelatinous substance. One is reminded of Freud's phrase 'libidinal viscosity'. The diversity of the registers to which Freud refers in the article quoted earlier melt into a common mass, in which any distinction between affect, thing-presentation and word-presentation is arbitrary. The transference projections are presented with an unshakeable certainty that cannot be questioned, and thus give access to greater awareness or to the repetition compulsion, which, in a different analytic situation, might allow a better interpretative approach. The reverie seems bloodless, impoverished, unworked out. Dreams are recounted; the analysand seems concerned above all to restore in the session the affective atmosphere of the dream. The enigma that is the dream is caught up in the secondary working out that gives primacy to the dream as narrative and event, over the dream as work on thoughts. When the affective atmosphere grows tense in the course of the session, it is discharged in one go, without any representative connotations being able to be linked with it. Everything is pure present. Can one speak here of transference resistance? It seems rather that one must speak of a 'stuck' transference, which emerges from its slime only to explode without producing any insight. Sometimes, on the other hand, once the discharge is over, and the affect seems to have been voided, the patient's body becomes even heavier: the analysand is a dead weight on the couch.

It should not be thought that such an analytic relationship is decathected by the analysand. On the contrary, it is hyper-cathected. The analytic session has long since been expected, feared and wished for. For the analysand, the analyst is an iron lung that enables survival outside. The analyst's absences lead to a position of retreat on the part of all the cathexes, a libidinal hibernation until the sessions are resumed. The parasitical transference may exhaust the analyst's efforts at empathy and lead to a counter-transference of disengagement in which the analyst tries to extract himself or herself from the transferential quagmire.

This untypical caricature, which I have exaggerated on purpose, is that of the transference in which the affect takes the place of all possible forms of representation. A transference with a dominant physical presence, it allows only the most limited work, limited for the analyst to a policy of presence. If the analyst wishes to avoid certain narcissistic catastrophes, he must be particularly careful, in the manifestations of his presence, about anything that might reveal traces of a negative counter-transference.

Type 2

In this type, the session is dominated by an extreme mobility of representations of all kinds. No sooner is the patient lying on the couch than he has a great deal to say. Reflections deriving from the previous session, everything that he has experienced since then, everything that occurs to him during the present session. The associative work goes on, the tongue is loosed, speech rapid, almost torrential. The analyst is submerged under a flood of words; these form groups of highly ingenious thoughts, usually accurate enough in themselves, but which might equally well be part of a lecture or piece of writing. The images crowd in, from the recent past or the most ancient past, anticipating the future. Everything is grist to the mill: relationships with spouse, friends, colleagues, current work, readings sacred or profane – that is to say, works relating or not relating to psychoanalysis. The analyst ought to be attracted by a patient who gives so much. Yet the analyst has the feeling that his or her analytic process has not been put into gear. The typhoon of representations whirls around, placing him or her at the eye of the storm, the place where the air does not move. The flow of representations, which is like a flow of ideas, gives the impression of being quite arbitrary psychical productions. That is to say, the patient might equally well say the opposite of everything that he has said, without changing anything fundamental in the analytic situation. The formations of the unconscious are marked, when the patient analyses them, with the same seal of sterile abundance. The analysand is expert at finding the associated threads of a dream, a phantasy, a slip of the tongue, a parapraxis. All this leads nowhere, for the analysis glides off the couch like water off a duck's back. The unconscious cannot get a grip on anything; the transference remains without moorings. Here the transference is volatile, free as the air. The analysand is a marvellous association machine – and it works perfectly. The presence of the analyst is quite superfluous. Were he or she to leave the room quietly, it would not be noticed by the analysand. In other words, the psychoanalytic process has not even begun and the transference has simply not occurred. Any effort on the part of the analyst to point out the nature of this situation is wasted, because it is immediately accepted by the analysand, that is to say, what the analyst says immediately becomes the object of associations and interpretations, which may well be correct, but have no impact.

The caricature that I have just sketched is, like the preceding one, exaggerated. It is the extreme form of a type, but one that nevertheless exists. It is easy to locate the defence here, namely, in the continuous elimination of affects, which, as soon as they appear, are caught up in the representative network.

It would be easy to find Bouvet's descriptions in this opposition between type 1 and type 2. Transference resistance, resistance of the type of experiencing too much, resistance of a hysterical kind in type 1; resistance to the transference, resistance of the type of understanding too much, resistance of an obsessional kind in type 2.

What strikes me as significant in this opposition is *the defence against representation by the affect and the defence against the affect by representation.* It is as if, by operating the unconscious defence mechanisms, the ego had the power to bring about the relative separation of affect and representation, so that in no case can they co-exist in the chain of discourse.

One cannot ignore the counter-transferential consequences of situations presented by patients who produce sessions of types 1 and 2. Although it is true that the analyst must be capable of sympathy and empathy when confronted by these indications of psychical pain, of this excess or inadequacy of affect, one cannot, without falling into an idealizing view, expect him or her to be able to confront such trying situations impassively. Of course, the analyst is well aware of the masochistic, and therefore aggressive, provocation that hides behind sessions of types 1 and 2. The repetition compulsion of patients producing such sessions is aimed at renewing, on the part of the analyst, the rejection that they expect from him or her. And no doubt the analyst who possesses sufficient control of his or her affects will be alerted to the trick that the patient would like to play on him or her. But knowing something and being able to act on it are different matters. The analyst's affective control, however well analysed, cannot measure up to every situation. Of course, if these situations are too frequent or too intense and the analysis of the counter-transference does not counter them sufficiently, it is the analyst's task to carry the analysis further. But one cannot, without falling into an ideological myth, expect the analyst to be superhuman, with all affects completely in control. If the analyst is capable of confronting every analytic situation, as should be the case, the problem of the indications of the analysis no longer arises.

What do analysts do with their affects? Although the answer often given to this question entails splitting – they control them in their professional work and give free rein to them in their private life – it remains problematic in practice. How can one, at the same time, require the deepest empathy, affective identification and control of response? Not to lay down limits to each of these is to turn the analyst into a magus, a speliologist of the psyche, a high priest of words. It is to encourage the phantasy of analytic omnipotence, capable of dealing with any unconscious structure. The analyst's expiatory or reparatory masochism does not necessarily have, *de jure* or *de facto*, curative effects on the analysand's masochism. It seems to me desirable that the analysand's masochism should induce in the analyst a feeling of *limited expectation*, a sign of awareness of his or her power and of the boundaries within which that power operates. Although the affective play will take place along those boundaries, at least it will not spread out over the whole field with a view to displaying the intrication of demands for regressive satisfactions and his defensive operations.

According to this view, affective control does not mean affective impassiveness, but an appeal both to affective liberation and the desire to overcome that does not give in to fascination with what has been freed.

These considerations concerning difficult analyses, at the limits or beyond the power of the analyst, must be compared to the affective suppleness, the mobility of insight, the acceptance of variations in register to be found in analysable subjects. In such cases, analytic practice is no longer a burden, but the exercise of a function entailing its own satisfactions as well as renunciations, its own privileges as well as obligations. Love of one's calling may then make analytic practice an enriching affective experience, both for analysand and analyst. Affects go in both directions, from the couch to the armchair and back. The role of the analyst will then be to ensure the cathexis of their communication.

Type 3

The essential characteristic of the session is to engage the analyst's hearing as an effect of the patient's desire to be heard. The patient's discourse begins from the moment that something occurs to him as a possible opening, which, in the course of the session, will be expanded or restricted according to the moments of tension or relaxation of the transference situation. The analyst is present for the patient, but this presence, the motive force of speech, will have no need either to be averted or circumvented. For whom does the analysand speak? No doubt for the analyst, but also for the Other that he represents, for himself and, possibly, for nobody and for nothing. He speaks in order to *say* something, but I would rather say that he speaks in order to speak. Far from seeing this as a pejorative distinction, I see this project of speech as, on the contrary, fundamental to analysis. The analysand speaks in order to set up the process of a chain of signifiers. Signification is not attached to the signified, to which each of the spoken signifiers refers, but is constituted by the process, the suture, the concatenation of the linked elements.

One should be under no illusion that there is anything here that identifies the process of signification with a narrative structure. On the contrary, the line of the discourse, the one that the censorship does not impede in any major way, is fundamentally broken and discontinued. Here one may see a double articulation similar to the one that Martinet describes for language. The syntagmas of discourse are articulated within themselves and between one another, but the breaks in discourse can turn it into a discourse that is unintelligible to the listener seeking its conscious signification. The second articulation is that which, invisible at the level of conscious discourse, is to be deduced by the analyst during the analytic work. To do this the analyst takes account not only of the flows of discourse, but also of the breaks, the blanks, the lacunae in each syntagma and between the syntagmas. Silence says as much as speech. What is revealed by this process of concatenation is a heterogeneity in the time of the discourse and in the constitutive forms of discourse. Elements belonging to the past refer to the present. The present returns associations from the past, sending the ball towards anticipations of the future by reference to a project. The unity of time is broken, the signification of the past, like that of the projected future, is perceived in fragments after the event. All interpretation provided by the analysand may be offered as something already signified awaiting its signification. In this sense, interpretation[6] is always retrospective, as is the perceived signification: 'So this is what that meant.' The (unconscious) signification never belongs to the present, only conscious signification can belong to it. And this is precisely what the process of the session puts into question. The certainty of the affect experienced in the present is questioned. The process of the session is sometimes painful because it may reveal a profound betrayal of the conscious identity, but the rule of analysis is to accept this implicit challenge. The unity of the subject is broken up, split. The elements by which the process proceeds are heterogeneous modes of discourse. The analysand speaks and links by word representations, thoughts, which he thus transforms, through language, into perceptions, via verbal memory traces. Suddenly a vision belonging to the past rises up in him; sometimes it seems to be formed extemporaneously and is revealed in *statu nascendi*. At the most unexpected moment of discourse, the analysand is caught by surprise and an affect appears. This affect may be verbalized, expressed through words, but usually the analysand will insist on the inadequacy of language to describe it, whether it is a source of pleasure or unpleasure. This affect relaunches the analytic process, orients the representations towards other representative contexts, directed on to the analyst, whose presence becomes more material, or on to a pregnant childhood image, some feature taken from the object. The analysand then remembers a dream, his account of it is followed by a description of daytime fragments, the unveiling of dream thoughts that make it possible to gain access through an analysis of the dream-work to the latent content of the dream. Here the functioning of the dream-work is consubstantially linked to the desire of the dream and to its latent content. The economy of the dream and its symbolization go hand in hand. The analysis of the dream is accompanied by a certain amount of motor activity on the couch, a hand plays with the wedding ring, fiddles with a tie or slips between a particular item of clothing and the belt, whereas the other hand is hidden behind the patient's back. There then appears beyond the affect a sense of change in the patient's body: an impression of strangeness, of change in the consistency or weight of the body, a change of the corporal schema:

---

6 But the interpretation cannot be based on signification alone. 'The analyst cannot say what would make most sense because it is not only meaning that decides what will or will not be heard. It is not enough that the interpretation carries meaning; someone else must receive it at the same time with as little alteration as possible. At every moment, the analyst must be aware of the affective state of the patient' Viderman (1970), p. 48.

a stretching of the legs, paraesthesia in the hands and lips, etc. The analysand now feels that he must communicate what he is experiencing and how inadequate words are compared with this never experienced, this never said. The analyst's interpretation links the successive effects by reminding the patient of the process that led to this resumption of speech by the body. This new awareness may lead to a resumption by the ego of the fragments that had escaped it and over which it may exercise control. The analysand's discourse is a polyphonic discourse. It is inscribed on several staves, from the highest to the lowest. Various voices are mixed in it, some resembling a pure language game activated by its own movement, others coming from the vibrations of the body, astonishing, disturbing, familiar and strange.

Although words have always served to bind together the various registers of discourse, their value, depending on the moment, has been very unequal. Their linking power has proved effective as long as a certain level of cathexis was contained within certain limits. On the one side, verbalization demonstrated the omnipotence of language; on the other, it revealed its powerlessness. The *linking* power of language was undermined by the affect, which resisted being linked in the form of a representation. When the body 'joins the conversation', as Freud put it, the chain might snap and the energy of cathexis be released in the form of a free affect, with no representative link, even that of a representation of the body. But what is remarkable about the process is the partial, temporary, reducible, irreversible character of that loosening of the concatenation. Eros, who resides over the concatenation and whose energies are cathected in the ego, regains the upper hand when the force swings temporarily from the side of the drives, which break the linkage.

The analytic work is safeguarded by the analytic process, which continues between body and thought. These functional differences in the power of language as against the productions of the body demonstrate that however great the temptation may be to reduce the structuring process to a formalization, attention must be paid to the substance, the raw material on which this formalization is carried out. The more crude the material is, the more it belongs to a previously unworked substance; the more precarious the power of language proves to be, the more fragile and open to destructuring influences the work seems.[7] The drive, that 'mythical, proud and

---

7 It may be thought that, however raw this material may be, it entails *in potentia* the possibility of language and, therefore, from the beginning, a potential structuring. That is my opinion. One then has to consider the effects of structure, the structuring process in action. This position would seem to me to be more dialectical than the one that would defend the idea of psychical structuring as the result of the interaction of two spheres, hypothetically different in structure – the affect and language – which would appear to go out to meet one another. It is at the heart of a register of more extended heterogeneity that these problems might find a solution.

indeterminate being', is the measure of the demand for work made on the psyche as a result of its link with the corporal. The drive is already in itself work carried out on the body. The more its psychical representatives testify to that work, the more language will be able to reach an accommodation with it; on the other hand, if that original work is defective, if the body is able to take possession of itself by an unexpected assault of discourse, language reveals the chink in its armour. *Language can work only on an already worked material.* The analytic session enables the analysand to experience, in protected conditions, both that failure in the work of language and the ability of language to take that work further and to do it better than previously. Representation and affect will be the necessary mediators of that elaboration: representation on the side of thought, affect on the side of the body.

A distinction should be drawn, however, at the heart of the representations, between thing-presentations and word-presentations. Thing-presentations properly belong to the unconscious, by virtue of their very structure. The visual sphere has more affective resonances than the auditory; it is closer to the affect.[8] Between word-presentation and affect, thing-presentations form a bridge between intellect and feeling.

Thing-presentations are particularly open to the work of transformation by virtue of their very plasticity. This malleability of the imaginary is governed by the influence of the affect, subjected to the pleasure–unpleasure principle, and by that of word-presentations, which aim to establish relations between the elements represented whose functioning is made possible by language.

Thing-presentation is the pivot of the work of the unconscious, as of the analytic work. Modern investigations have amply shown the various avatars of psychical structures in which phantasy organization, formed out of thing-presentations, is defective. In the final analysis, one finds once again the role of phantasy in the psychical economy. It is surely no accident that the phantasy may at the same time be the object of a logical approach (see 'A child is being beaten') and an economic one (see the works of the psychosomaticians).

III The Oedipus complex and the ordering of discourse

In the first part of this chapter, I considered, with Freud, the success of analysis on the basis of an essentially historical criterion: construction. The

---

8 Affect is provoked in the auditory sphere; but it is in the visual sphere that the first formation of the affective reaction occurs. The phantasy both presupposes the object and constitutes it at the same time. But the important thing is that this double operation should take place by snatching the representation from raw material that both lends itself to it and opposes it, seeming to challenge the rights that the representative organization assumes with regard to signification.

relations between the construction of the repressed that bears on lost memories and the construction of the repressed that bears on unconscious phantasies were discussed. In any case, the success of the analysis was linked to a real or mythical history whose content the analyst succeeded in re-establishing.

In the second part, taking up Freud's description in 'Constructions in analysis' of what is offered to the analyst by the analysand, I contrasted three extreme types of session: type 1, dominated by the affect; type 2, dominated by representation; type 3, in which affects and representations together form the text of the session in a movement that is the process of analysis. Here the success of the analysis derives from the establishment of that process. There is no reason why the three types should not alternate in the course of the same analysis. But only type 3 will be the one in which the analytic work of *working through* is carried out. In short, the criterion of success here lies not so much in the construction of the content of the text as in the construction of the text itself, in its writing as formations of traces. The text has become by this fact, unlike in types 1 and 2, interpretable *de jure* and *de facto*. The meaning of this second approach is now seen to be more structural than historical.

In fact, history and structure are interdependent here. For where the historical construction (mythical or real, but in any case truthful) was built up, it was by means of the possibilities offered by the text, the legibility of the writing, the preservation of punctuation, the underlining of certain passages, the varied typography, the ordering of the paragraphs, etc.; all the things that go to the making of a text.

Conversely, the process of writing; its deciphering in the course of its development, its *'obscure clarté'*, to use Corneille's words; the legibility that made it possible to find once again articulations on the first and second levels; the sense of life flowing through the text, which exposes its veins and limbs, all this is evidence of a history – that is to say, of a temporal linking of after-the-event reshapings that do not contradict that linking, but which help to fix its true order, to distribute events according to all the places that they occupy not in chronology, but in historical truth.

One finds here once more the contradictions of the structure–history opposition, since, in the final analysis, history is structure. It has been remarked that the composition of the signifiers synchrony and diachrony was based in both cases on a common reference to *chronos*, time: simultaneity or successivity. Similarly, I would say that at the level of the signified, structure and history both entail a reference to structure: transversal structure and longitudinal structure.

In fact, the analysis of the syntagmas also depends on the order of distribution of its elements – which can be changed only within precise limits, as Chomsky shows. Structure and history are doomed to refer to one another.

Thus confronted by an analysis that offers a whole variety of desirable elements to be joined together in the process of discourse, one will not be surprised to encounter in a key position the structuring factors of the Oedipus complex: marked difference of sexes, distinct paternal and maternal imagos, identification established on a secondary mode, recognition of castration, presence of sublimations, limited phantasy, etc. Whereas in analyses in which there are many sessions of the first two types, the destiny of the Oedipus complex remains ill-defined: the difference of the sexes is vague, the masculine and feminine imagos often confused, just as the paternal and maternal imagos are merged into a 'phallic personage', to use Bouvet's expression, the identifications are made in a primary merging mode. Castration seems to give way to fears of fragmentation, phantasy activity is ill-defined, phantasy no longer being identified as such and confused with a projective vision of the world, when it is not lacking altogether.[9]

And so we come back, it would seem, to Bouvet's distinction between genital and pregenital structures; however, the distinction here is based on different criteria: those of Oedipal and pre-Oedipal fixations.

The difference may be considered unimportant: it is more important than it seems. Although genitality is the reference by which the various structures are distributed, one might criticize the analyst for taking the role of spokesperson and defender of a normality that is all the more mythical in that he or she is the last to be able to embody it when leaving his or her chair. On the other hand, if the division operates from the Oedipus complex, things are quite different. For the Oedipus complex is what specifies the human condition. It is both structure and history: structure because it allows no definition of the subject outside the sexual difference that unites parents to one another and unites him to his parents in a reticular situation; history because sexual difference is duplicated by the difference between the generations. To the break that divides the sexes corresponds another break, that which separates the child from his parents.

What, then, is the pre-Oedipal stage? How can one speak of prestructure

---

9 Type 2 may seem to contradict this schema. A vigilant defence against the affect may well be evidence of the danger of allowing the appearance of a psychical layer whose characteristics would be those that have just been described. Of course, every analysis operates successively and simultaneously on these two registers. Broadly speaking, the evolution of the affective transference follows a curve that goes from the analysis of a superficial Oedipal structure, to a layer of pre-Oedipal conflicts, ending in a final phase in which the Oedipus complex is given a new interpretation that preserves what has preceded while superseding it. This process goes hand in hand with a concomitant evolution of affects that reach maximum intensity and crudity in the analysis of the pre-Oedipal phase and end with a more subtle, more controlled expression during the final phase of the analysis of the Oedipus complex.

or prehistory when these are apprehended only from the point of view from which one speaks of a structure or a history. Since Melanie Klein, one no longer ignores the early stages of the Oedipal conflict. It matters little that Klein advances Oedipus's age; what matters is the quasi-contemporaneity of the Oedipus complex and birth. It is important, then, to distinguish between the Oedipus complex as structure and the Oedipal period in which the structure assumes its most obvious, most crystallized and also most complex form, since, as Freud reminds us, the Oedipus complex is always double: positive and negative.

Thus prehistory and prestructure are evaluated only from the point of view of history and structure. Conversely, history and structure yield their semantic or organizational value only when confronted by what they are not yet, but might be, or what they have been, but can no longer be.

How can one not confront these questions when contrasting pre-Oedipal affects and Oedipal affects? How can one not consider this distinction in terms of a model of dual or triangular relations? When the tertiary mediation is present by its lack, can one conceive of the so-called primary affects in their overwhelming massiveness without considering the possibility of using them or controlling them? Can the distribution of the affects be described in terms of the double modalities of the positive and negative Oedipus complex without the reciprocal balancing of one affect by the other and of the two objects to which the affect is destined in the network of triangular relations? Similarly the affect–representation relation is given in a quite different way in the relations of the dual pre-Oedipal period and in the relations of the triangular Oedipal period. In the first case the affect–representation combination is difficult to split; in the second, affect and representation may be referred to as distinct realities. Hence castration, which entails at once a representation (that of the severed sex) and an affect (the horror of remembering it), the vicissitudes of repression (in the broad sense), which allow the stress to shift from one of the two elements on to the other.

I shall not say very much about the pointless discussion of the hypothetical affects of the prenatal period – and hardly more about the birth prototype. It is clear that affects are felt intensely during that traumatic experience. However, that experience must be related to the state of the ego at birth. The absence of differentiation between ego and id allows one to speak only of physiological discharges that have as their psychical correlative a certain experience that can only be conjectured, but it would be erroneous to call it an affect, since no ego registers it. And if wishing to go as far back as possible into the prehistoric mist, one must distinguish between *the affective experience of birth and the phantasy of conception* (primal scene), thus distinguishing between the birth of the individual and the birth of the subject. In any case, one may speak of affect in the proper sense of the term only if there is an ego to experience it. Short of that or beyond it (in the cases of ego collapse), one will have to refer to another notion than that of the affect, though it hardly matters what it is called providing the distinction is made. Thus in my opinion affect is bound up with a certain relationship between the ego and the id.

One is led to consider therefore the phases of the ego's formation. Like Glover, it is possible to conceive of this 'birth of the ego', to use the title he gave his last book, as the result of a gradual integration of the primitive nuclei – a conception, provided one added maternal cares, close to Winnicott's. One may also, like other authors, conceive of a primitive ego endowed with innate functions. Since it seems to me to be difficult to proceed to a realistic construction – which direct observation and the works of Spitz have tried to constitute – I prefer Melanie Klein's metaphorical model, articulated with that of Freud.

One knows that, according to Melanie Klein, the split between good and bad breast establishes the object relation, within the framework of the schizo-paranoid phase. In a later work, Melanie Klein postulates precursory elements of the depressive phase in the schizo-paranoid phase. Does this mean anything more than that an intuition of the totality of the object emerges very early on? Personally, I shall postulate an intuition corresponding to the unity of the ego, although this intuition is far from being actually fulfilled. What is more, the good–bad (breast) duality implies, if only on account of their being linked together, a reference to a latent third party apprehended in terms of the two-sided reality of the totality of the object and the unity of the ego. This absence of totality–unity is a quasi-presence, if only in its negative apprehension. One can say, to simplify matters, that this is a metaphorical link, a field of exchanges, without which the good–bad opposition has no significant value and can refer only to a succession of states unrelated to one another.

The fulfilment of the unity of the ego, concomitant with that of the totalization of the object is a paradox for psychoanalytic theory. For it is at that very 'moment' when the ego is unified that it splits into good and bad ego. In a similar way, the mother-breast as total object replaces the breast as part object, good and bad mother referring to the mother's presence and absence, her life and death. It might be thought, therefore, that the good and bad ego refer to a third term, the mother, as long as she is present or absent, living or dead. We know how the alternate affects of satisfaction and aggression are then transformed into another form dominated by the experience of mourning that profoundly alters the affective tonality. To the 'stage' that I am conjecturing corresponds the importance of repression, which must try to rein in the bad ego, in order to preserve the object from destructive attacks. *The opening to the Oedipal phase makes it possible to link the absence of the mother to the presence of the father, who alone possesses the right to enjoy the mother.* The effective triangulation allows the sex to take on the specification of sexuality. The part objects have lost nothing of their virulence and effectiveness. However, the reference to the penis gives castration its full meaning. Through castration, all the external experiences associated with privation, frustration, the *lack* of part objects are signified after the event. All previous history is remoulded into a new version in the light of castration.[10] Castration will bring about this distribution of the affects between the two parental objects, modulating and dividing them: love (and hate) for the mother, hate (and love) for the father, in the double form of the Oedipus complex.

Furthermore, the affects of the drives with inhibited aim, whose intervention I would situate very early (in the phase of the separation between mother and child, the inhibition of the aim preventing the return of fusional experiences of too massive a kind), are completed by the transformation of sensuality into tenderness and of aggressivity into hostility. Thus the Oedipal phase preserves its importance by virtue of the structural mutation that it carries out. Finally, the formation of the superego, the 'heir of the Oedipus complex', marks the encounter, beyond the father, with the Law. This is the last structural mutation that allows the transformation of earlier relations into relations between the agencies, the id, the ego and the superego. Here the 'negative' affects are differentiated according to new parameters. They cease to be reactions to the prevention of satisfactions, responses to the non-fulfilment of wishes, and become *values.* The recognition of the vagina at puberty completes the full recognition of the difference between the sexes and the complete detachment from the parents.

This historico-structural view may provide a better understanding of the Oedipus complex as both structure and phase. The pre-Oedipal and pregenital phases entail, even at the heart of dual-type relations, a reference to a third party. It seems to me, therefore, that the mother–child or ego–object differentiation should be understood as the precursor of the incest prohibition, which is expressed here by the metaphorical prohibition of a return to the mother's womb, the basis of the prohibition omophagy.[11]

Thus the historico-structural model is based on *difference* and *differentiation.* Difference between the child as undivided entity and the mother; the sexual difference between the parents. The differentiation in terms of ego and id,

---

10 As de M'Uzan has very well realized. However, it should be noted here – but this goes beyond the limits of this work – how castration is already present in the experience of lack and how it proceeds from it.

11 For it is not only the child's cannibalistic drives that are in question in the relation to the breast, but also those of the mother, which aim at the integration into the maternal body of its product, by a fusional desire of narcissistic completeness, to which the child is not alone in aspiring.

then between ego, id and superego. Differentiation within the ego, which allows the differentiation of the affects – and that between affects and representation. The primary affects are primary affects–representations that contemporary psychoanalysis interprets as unconscious phantasies.

The original affects are linked to *the mother's body*, just as the secondary affects are linked to *the Law of the father*. Thus the affect is always caught between body and law, between the law of the body and the body of the Law.

The interpretation of the body and of the law is a permanent one. From the moment of birth, the mother lends her body to the child, more for its survival than for its enjoyment. Although the mother is, as Freud says, the child's first seducer, she is quite unaware of it. And when the father's desire lovingly inscribes the law in the register of the legal code, thus condemning transgression, transgression strikes the body and inflicts constraint upon it. Mere privation of liberty entails it. Capital punishment is destruction of the body.

This chapter, which began with the question of the aim of analytic work, must end – after this long detour – with the same question. The 'psychical maturity' of which Freud speaks requires further explanation. It is no doubt affective maturity, but what exactly does that mean? Although it is difficult, if not impossible, to express an opinion on the matter without falling into the mirages of idealization, one should not avoid the question altogether.

To reach psychical maturity amounts for me to the possibility, however over-estimated in relation to our actual psychical functioning, of as far-reaching an analysis of the Oedipus complex as possible – not an analysis of the Oedipal phase, as described by Freud, but of the Oedipal structure that comprises the positive and negative side of this complex and involves the pre-Oedipal phases of the Oedipal conflict.

Primal repression is opposed to exhaustive remembering; the analysis of the formations of the unconscious come up against the uncrossable limits of primal repression. But it is that very limit that allows the indefinite relaunching of the analytic process. It is not, therefore, simply by rediscovering contents that this maturity will be achieved. Nor is it achieved by identification with the analyst. For if analysts – even though they are supposed to have no need of identification – are known, at the end of the analysis, in their psychical reality, providing they are freed of transference projections and become, for their analysands, beings among others, why identify with them? Would the analyst be any better than anyone else?

As psychoanalysts are only too well aware, the true acquisition of psychoanalysis is . . . psychoanalysis, that is, the ability to analyse psychical activity. Now this treasure of psychoanalysis, which is the exercise of that ability, is in dialectical relation with the affect. Only that faculty is capable of leading to psychical maturity and yet psychoanalysis implies that a certain psychical maturity pre-exists the ability to psychoanalyse.

In truth, one arrives here at the limits of psychoanalysis: on this side, as condition of its taking place at all; on that side, as postponed effect of its action.

Symbolic activity is possible only within certain economic limits. The psychical apparatus, like any piece of machinery, can only deal with certain quantities. The truth of the Oedipal structure is not in question, whatever the vicissitudes of certain of those quantities, of which madness is one example. But the alteration of the structure by analysis is subject to certain restrictions.

Thus, although psychical maturity and control of the affects go hand in hand, it is achieved only by following the limits laid down for 'analysability'. One may, if one so wishes, prefer some other, quite different criteria, which will not entail the criterion of the maturity–immaturity distinction, or that of control–uncontrollability. It is a choice that no longer concerns the analyst. Whatever the analyst may propose, it is not a social model or paragon of Stoic virtue – God knows, analysts are not noted for it- but the acquisition of the power to analyse, which implies a desire to control the affects. It is perhaps a superannuated ideal. This control, it has to be said, is not an affective control, but a *play*[12] of affects, providing the grip of the affects is not total, massive, irreversible. The play of affects is the same play that governs the distribution of feelings in the Oedipus complex and which allows their reciprocal balancing within a structure.

If one affect could be designated as a value, it would certainly not be Olympian serenity devoid of illusion, but humour. Freud, as one knows, did not lack it. Unfortunately, the same cannot always be said of those whose mission it is to continue his work – whether as a result of being worn down by time or the effects of selection.

---

12 One may extend this category of play here and give it a paradigmatic value, as does Winnicott (*Playing and Reality*), for whom the whole purpose of analytic work is to facilitate this capacity for play.

Part III
Theoretical study: affect, language and discourse; negative hallucination

5

Affect and the two topographical models

The diversity, entanglement and complexity of the problems seem to make any attempt at theoretical unification, if not impossible, at least hazardous. Nevertheless, I think it ought to be attempted.[1]

I The paradoxical situation of affect in Freudian theory (quantity and quality)

Depending on the texts, one finds in Freud two different definitions of the affect, whose compatibility presents a problem. In the first, the affect designates essentially a *quantum*, a quantity or sum of excitation 'capable of increase, diminution, displacements and discharge, and which is spread over the memory-traces of ideas somewhat as an electric charge is spread over the surface of a body'.[2]

The electro-physiological orientation of the definition is not in doubt. Freud is here, at the outset of his work, still imbued with the preoccupations of his biological period. 'The project for a scientific psychology', not yet written, would be constructed around two hypotheses: the neurones and moving quantities. Here, then, affect corresponds to an energic allocation, that of a mobile, variable, transformable, dischargeable quantity. The free or bound state of this energy specifies very different kinds of functioning (primary and secondary processes). Later, the state of binding or unbinding will reflect the action of opposed instinctual groups: Eros or the destructive drives. Are there one or two new energies present, according to its link to

---

1 Certain repetitions are inevitable here. However, by situating them in the broader context of general discussion, I hope to avoid giving the impression of mere repetition.
2 *S.E.*, III, p. 60.

Eros and the destructive drives? Should one consider that, depending on the case, a single energy is bound or unbound? In the latter case, by what or by whom? Is the tendency to unification or to separation exterior to the energy, subjecting that energy to its action? One would then have to consider Eros and the destructive drives as endowed with properties that are placed well beyond the general attributes recognized as belonging to the partial drives. Might their active principles (binding–unbinding) be of a quite different kind of energy? If so, one is now postulating not two energies, but three: an undifferentiated energy and two other energies, one binding, the other unbinding – unless one regards them as intrasystemic transformations that allow the energy sometimes to bind, sometimes to unbind under the action of either the unknown active principles of Eros or the destructive drives. Laplanche has rightly observed that the organization of the states of binding ought to refer us to different types of binding according to whether one is dealing with the binds of the primary process or with the binds of the ego.

The metapsychological problems raised are considerable. For, beyond their instinctual functioning, the principles of psychical functioning (Nirvana, pleasure–unpleasure, reality) are at work. Beyond the pleasure principle, one finds the repetition compulsion, which refers us to instinctual functioning. The repetition compulsion must be related to Eros (the binding tendency) and to the destructive drives (the unbinding tendency). The repetition compulsion, revealing the most essential instinctual functioning ('the conservative character' of the drives), is caught between a return to the most radical previous state (total abolition of tensions to zero), the effect of the Nirvana principle and the preservation of the pleasure principle, forced to subject itself to the reality principle, of which it is one of the essential functions. What is being dealt with here is not facts, but aporias. The repetition compulsion, which works in the service of total inertia, to death, is a metapsychological myth – a metaphor. The clinical facts, on the other hand, present us with a compulsion to repeat the fixation conflict: this conflict is loaded with anterior and posterior resonances. Thus the castration anxiety enters into resonance with anal and oral castration, but also with the loss of the love of the superego. In any case, what is repeated is certainly the resurgence of an experience by which the libido is bound, structured in a binding manner around a phantasy or a memory. These are now fixed in the unconscious and will tend to be reconstituted in other contexts. However compelling the clinical facts may be, what accounts for them are metapsychological myths. Thus the hypothetical return to the inanimate, the ultimate destination of the repetition compulsion, preserves its heuristic value. What one finds here is the weight of the destiny of the quantities of energy, sometimes exhausted in discharge or restored to the unbound state, sometimes subjected to another type of link, that which is required by submission to the reality principle and whose quantitative reduction is a pre-condition.

The pleasure principle lies at the centre of the discussion. Not enough attention has been given to the crucial turning point, after the arrival of the second topography, which led Freud to dissociate the unpleasure–tension and pleasure–discharge pairs and to recognize – how late in the day! – that the qualitative nature of pleasure or unpleasure was distinct from the quantitative aspect of tension. Of course, it has been observed[3] that it was indispensable to distinguish between the *states* of pleasure–unpleasure, eminently affective experiences, and the *principles* of pleasure–unpleasure. But, in any case, what is important to retain is that the quantitative aspect of the affective phenomena cannot ignore its qualitative dimension.

One now comes to the second definition of affect. Freud gives a number of different definitions of it, all more or less identical. One may distinguish in affect:

1   A *discharge* particularly oriented towards the inside of the body. External orientation of the discharge may exist, but it is secondary and non-specific;
2   *Feelings* of two types:
     (a) Perceptions of internal movements;
     (b) Direct sensations of pleasure–unpleasure that give the affect its specificity.

This definition, different from the first, may be analysed thus. The affect is split into two sides:

1   A corporal, above all visceral side;
2   A psychical side, itself split into two:
     (a) Perception of *corporal movements*;
     (b) *Sensations of* pleasure–unpleasure.

In short, the psychical side of the affect is split in two:

     (a) An activity of self-observation of the corporal change that is the result of a specular activity on the body: function of psychophysiological introspection, centred on the self-perception of a movement inside the body;
     (b) A purely qualitative aspect: pleasure–unpleasure.

---

3 See Schur, *The Id and the Regulatory Principles of Mental Functioning.*

This definition calls for a few remarks. In it the affect is given as a corporal and psychical experience, the first seeming to be the condition of the second. The corporal experience is produced on the occasion of an internal discharge; this discharge reveals a sense of the existence of the body, insofar as it snatches the body from silence. It testifies to a high level of corporal cathexes, tension that is released in discharge. Here the body is acted upon and not acting, passive and not active, spectator and not actor. *The body is not the subject of an action, but the object of a passion.*

One has imperceptibly passed from a physiological dimension to a psychical one. Beginning with the objective phenomena of discharge, one has arrived at the subjective phenomena that have brought us from the corporal sphere to the psychical sphere, which is given to us in the experience of observing the corporal experience. *The affect is gazing into the moved body.* This split, essential though it may be, between the internal motion of the body and awareness of that motion, tells us nothing, apart from the experience of duplication that it gives rise to. To say that the body speaks has no meaning unless one refers to the reading of the phenomena to which the affective experience may be subjected. Identification with the subject of experience implies that I feel his body as if it were mine. Meaning begins to emerge as soon as I am able to hear *my body speak* or my 'body-speaking'. The splits may occur along different planes:

1 my / body-speaks;
2 my-body / speaks;
3 speaks-my / body.

In any case, three terms are brought together:

- that which indicates my property (my);
- that which is the object of this property (body);
- that which denies that property (*it* speaks).

The subject–object relation shows then that the object eludes the subject and lives its own life, thus revealing the subject's inability to hold it in subjection. The subject may then consent to this disappropriation or reject it. The affect may be accepted by the ego or rejected by it. But so far I know nothing of the affect, since if my body speaks, if it is even spoken more than it speaks, as analysis clearly shows, *as long as I do not refer the experience to quality, I lack the essence of the affective experience.* At this point there intervenes the gamut of pleasure–unpleasure states. It is significant that at this point, having reached the essential of the experience of the affect, I can say nothing more about it: it is pleasant or unpleasant. The overlapping of this differentiation by acceptance or rejection by me (the ego) is inadequate. The ego may also accept unpleasure and reject pleasure. Another overlapping by the good–bad split brings us to the same observation, just as the reference to the object or to the aim of the affective experience frames the latter more than accounts for it.

What this qualitative reference reveals most clearly is that the affect is then susceptible to developments and transformations: inhibition of the quality of unpleasure; development of pleasure; and, conversely, a fusion of the various qualities of pleasure and of the various qualities of unpleasure, or fusion of pleasure and unpleasure; more or less complete transformation of pleasure into unpleasure, or vice versa. In any case, each turn of the bipolarity includes the other actually or potentially, and is never given totally in isolation. The neutral state exists only potentially, it is always in the situation of an ideal point capable of turning into one or other of the polarized extremes. I might add that this double pleasure–unpleasure bipolarity is valid only for the consciousness, the unconscious ignoring both quality and contradiction. For the unconscious, only pleasure exists, anything serves to satisfy the drive and to provide an outlet for pleasure. Unpleasure appears only by way of repression. The contrary of pleasure cannot exist in the unconscious. It will be seen later that the replacement of the unconscious by the id may throw light on this difficulty, which seemed insuperable.

In the second place, this analysis of the affect in terms of Freud's second definition reveals the particular position of the ego with regard to the affect. The affect is caught between the body and consciousness. The self-observing activity of the ego registers the change occurring in the corporal movement and the quality of this change. On one side, a silent body, living as far as life is concerned, but dead for consciousness. On the other, an acute consciousness of the affect. But if experience reaches a certain intensity, consciousness sees its ability to register it overwhelmed. Up to a certain threshold, the affect wakens the consciousness, widening its field, whether in the direction of pleasure or unpleasure. Beyond a certain threshold, the affect disturbs consciousness; one is 'blinded by passion'. Below a certain threshold, the discharge is deprived of affect, the affect is not registered. Beyond a certain threshold, the affect submerges the activity of consciousness to such an extent that the subject falls into dissolution, even loss of consciousness. The consciousness of the affect is limited by two unconsciousnesses. Where, then, is the unconscious?

This insistence on the two limits of the affect, the body and consciousness, might make us think that the unconscious is alien to the affective experience, which would be paradoxical to say the least. All clinical experience would suggest the opposite. The manifestation of the affect in the course of the psychical processes constantly reveals that when it emerges, like the devil out of its bottle, that is just when one perceives an appeal from the unconscious. Something has been activated either on the inside or on the

165

outside, which is expressed by a disturbance of the subject's organization and breaks the barrier of repression. Through the affect, the unconscious is manifested as that which seizes the ego, questions it, subjugates it.

What cannot be settled by this affective irruption is the congruence or incongruity of the affect with the unconscious content. Nor can one wager on the positive or negative value of the affect (pleasure or unpleasure) in relation to the accompanying situation. Pleasure may emerge by means of the disguises of condensation or displacement; it is not linked to the conscious context that accompanies it. Similarly, unpleasure is the disguise by means of which pleasure is manifested. Here, too, a direct translation by simple inversion of sign (unpleasure = pleasure) is impossible, for unmasked pleasure also refers to distorting displacements and condensations. What matters is *the break in affective silence through the constricting affect.* Thus the greatest importance will be attributed to the element of surprise that accompanies the affect. At that appointed moment, in that odd, unexpected situation, the unconscious is revealed through the affect. With the affect, it is the Other that insists by its intrusive presence. The gloss ceases, the discourse is broken and gives way to the irrepressible affect. The non-ownership of the body by the consciousness, the powerlessness of the ego, which cannot control the affect, becomes all too evident. 'I am affected, therefore I do not belong to myself.' The explanation comes after the event.

So far the context in which the affect appears has been dealt with in an abstract manner. Of course, it goes without saying that the provocative agents of the affect may be located in the real and in the imaginary. That evocative perception, that embryonic phantasy, that word heard have unsuspected affective repercussions. There is no question as to its origin. I would say, however, that it is not the only one. For me, there are affects that emerge from inside the body, by a sudden elevation of cathexes, which emerge without the help of representation. Of course, one may, if one looks hard enough, find·perceptual and representative vestiges that one is tempted to attach to the affective eruption. But one does not escape then from the feeling that this link is artificial, secondary, in every sense of the term. Everything suggests that the movement that begins in the body has undergone a reinforcement of the cathexes emanating from the drive, and that the affects thus produced have desperately sought representations to which they have tried to attach it, as if to contain in the psyche the tension that would tend to be discharged directly in action.

One can see, therefore, the difficulty in relating the two definitions of the affect. The first, that of quantity, is consubstantial with the unconscious, since it deals with the energic allocation of representations. The second, that of quality, seems to leave little place for the unconscious. In the first case, the affect is not only unconscious, but *above all* unconscious. In the second, the affect is the privileged topic of physiology or experimental psychology, on the one hand, and of phenomenology, on the other, but it defies psychoan-alytic investigation.

I would like to introduce an additional notion here. Lacan has insisted in his works on the effect of captation by the imaginary (mirror stage). The effect of the image is to catch the subject in a state of otherness. If I am sen-sitive to my image in the mirror, it is because through it I force myself to confront the dimension of otherness by which *I am another for myself.* I love myself or hate myself as I love or hate the object. Conversely, the object that I love or hate induces in me those affects only because in the object it is I that I recognize – or 'fail to recognize' (*méconnait*). What Lacan is stressing about the role of the image, of representation, seems to me to apply partic-ularly to the affect. *The affect is an object of hypnotic fascination for the ego.* Bewitchment by the affect is what, in analysis, maintains it in a position of dependence in relation to narcissism. All awareness is barred by the con-scious affect, which cannot be questioned as such. The analytic process can be established only if the affect is capable of being questioned, only if the affect is regarded as suspect beyond the weighty presence to self that it induces – in short, when the affect is taken in its contradictory bipolarity (pleasure–unpleasure, good–bad, love–hate, etc.).

It is important to note that whereas the reality principle is a principle determined by a single term (reality), the pleasure–unpleasure principle is doubly determined by the pleasure–unpleasure dichotomy. In short, the reality/pleasure–unpleasure opposition, depending on which of its terms it is referring to, leads to different remarks. There is no internal contradiction in the sense of the real, except that the term reality covers internal psychi-cal reality, as opposed to the reality of the external world. Ideally, psychoanalytic work ought to reach the point where internal psychical real-ity is perceived with the same objectivity as the reality of the external world – not as the subject wishes it to be, but as it is. This is, it has to be said, an asymptotic task. But as far as the pleasure–unpleasure principle is concerned, this dichotomy enables us to conceive this principle as *a princi-ple of primary symbolization*, by virtue of its ability to divide and categorize – and therefore to structure – affective experience. The initial rejection of one of the terms (unpleasure), which results in the purified ego-pleasure, gives way to the later conscious–unconscious division by the repression of what was once accepted as pleasure and which ceases to be so at a certain moment, because it threatens the organization of the psychical apparatus.

One is led, therefore, to regard the pleasure principle as a transition-prin-ciple. Insofar as it entails the instinctual discharge of pleasure and the abolition of tension, it is at the service of the destructive drives and looks in the direction of the Nirvana principle. Insofar as it aims at the preservation of pleasure, the safeguarding of the pleasure principle, it looks towards the reality principle, which alone can ensure its preservation. The primary symbolization of the pleasure principle is stretched, therefore, between *the asymbolia of nothingness* (the Nirvana principle) and the secondary symbolization (the reality principle). The *unity of pleasure* is caught between the zero that it is tempted to rejoin and the link that one calls concatenation, which entails the quantitative and qualitative reduction of the primary affect in the interests of the cathexis of the chain in which the secondary (reduced) affect takes its place in the network of thing- and word-presentations.

In the final analysis, the affect as quantity and the affect as quality are indissociable from one another. The distinction between the objective aspect (quantity) and the subjective aspect (quality) may lead to relatively independent developments, but the two dimensions must link up again. Although it is true that maximum pleasure tensions may be desirable and minimum unpleasure tensions feared, a high quantity of pleasure or unpleasure is always experienced as a threat to the ego and to the psychical apparatus. Below a certain threshold, combinations of pleasant and unpleasant tensions are possible. Similarly, a minimum of affect, pleasant or unpleasant, must always be preserved, if a state of psychical death is not to ensue.[4]

My reflection leads me to consider the situation of the drive and the agency that is both its depository and its representative, the id. This situation of the id enables us to understand the drive and the affect, on the one hand in relation to this non-psychical on which it is built, and on the other in relation to the ego and secondarization. In other words, what is found here once more is, on the one hand the affect, by the automatic transformation of libidinal energy into the id, which, by its quantitative and qualitative characteristics, cathects the ego *en masse*, as by a surprise attack; and, on the other hand, the affect that is introduced into the ego, without its consent, of course, but by a limited breach, leaving the ego the possibility of displays and ripostes, through the repression and defence mechanisms, and which will include the affect in the chain of the representations of the drive. But this requires us to pause first at the problems presented by the drive.

II First topography: affect and the unconscious (language and discourse)

It seems logical, when one wishes to study the relation between affect and representation, to begin by examining the meaning of the concept of drive.

---

4 The question of the independence (and interdependence) of the relaxation–tension and pleasure–unpleasure dyads, between which Freud hesitated (see above), might gain in clarity if the ambiguity that it conceals were seen to derive from the fact that, whereas pleasure is linked either to tension or to relaxation, unpleasure is always associated with tension.

1 Drive

The problem of the situation of drive in relation to the somatic and the psychical is one of the most confused in Freud. The first quotation that comes to mind is one in which Freud defines drive as 'a concept on the frontier between the mental and the somatic'. But he adds at once: 'as the psychical representative of the stimuli originating from within the organism and reaching the mind, as a measure of the demand made upon the mind for work in consequence of its connection with the body'.[5]

The ambiguity of the definition increases as we progress in its formulation. For it is a definition with three branches.

First, *a borderline concept between the psychical and the somatic*. It is the concept that is the borderline, not the drive, let it be noted. This means that we cannot use the traditional conceptual instruments, which normally use terms that fall on one side or the other of this boundary.

Second, *a psychical representative of excitations coming from inside the body and ending up in the psyche*. The drive is a psychical representative of corporal excitations. Is one to conclude from this that the drive belongs to the order of the psychical? If so, the situation of the concept at the frontier between psychical and somatic would no longer be justified. The stimuli, as such, are unknowable, have no direct psychical expression. They are of an absolutely natural order, but they are not fixed. They make their way to the psyche – and it is on arrival, as if crossing a frontier, that they become psychical *representatives*, delegates or ambassadors in another country. The drive, then, is the result of a journey that ends in 'psychization'. The drive, its motive force, is that invitation to a journey. But the passengers, the stimuli, are not, on arrival, in the same condition that they were at their departure. Just as ambassadors often adopt the way of life, even the appearance, of persons of the country to which they have been sent, so the stimuli born in the organism disguise themselves in forms proper to psychical activity. But they remain representatives of those stimuli. In any case, the change from the organic to the psychical only occurs at the crossing of a frontier. The drive is not so much a place as a circuit.

Third, *a measure of the demand for work that is imposed on the psyche as a consequence of its link with the corporal*. Unquestionably, this last branch is the most difficult part of the definition to understand. The psyche is the object of a demand for work, for working out, for transformation.[6] The body, linked to

---

5 *S.E.*, XIV, p. 122.
6 *Travail* (work) comes from *trabaculum*, the machine used to tame large animals, either by shoeing them or by practising surgical operations on them (Littré). Robert devotes six and a half columns to the word. It should be noted that, originally, from the twelfth to

the psyche, demands something of it. The psyche is, so to speak, worked by the body, worked in the body. But this demand for work cannot be accepted in its raw state. It must be decoded if the psyche is to respond to the body's demand, which, in the absence of any response, will increase its demands (in force and in number). The psyche must acknowledge receipt of this demand and work to satisfy it. The drive is the *measure* of this demand. The drive makes it possible to measure this demand. Obviously the most obscure point is the nature of the link between the psyche and the corporal. According to the Freudian conception, the psyche governs the body only in so far as it meets its demand. Nevertheless, the stress in this third branch is placed not on the quality of the psychical representative of the excitations born in the organism, but on the quantitative *appreciation*[7] (the measure) of work to be carried out, whose energic nature is hardly in doubt. For even in cases in which it is simply a matter of transcribing the demands of the body, only an energic transformation will make the demand intelligible. Here two hypotheses may be sustained. In the first, one may conceive that instinctual pressure gives birth to the representation, as if the representation were born from that work. In this case, the 'origin' of the representation would be of an economic nature. But one may also conceive of the instinctual excitations soliciting representations and co-opting them so to speak. In the second case, the 'origin' of the representations would have to be sought in the symbolic order, as endopsychical equivalents of external perceptions, ghosts of perceptions, that is 'phantasy traces'. Freud does not choose clearly between either of these two conceptions.

The notion of the borderline concept comes into its own here insofar as it is our conceptual instruments that prevent the conceptualization of the event that takes place at the psychosomatic or somatopsychical crossroads. The two hypotheses entail different conceptions. The first is successive: from the body to psychical activity. The second is simultaneous: the

---

the sixteenth centuries, the definition is the following: 'State of him who suffers, is tormented'. The meaning evolved up to the eighteenth century. The notion of work appears to be linked to *force*. Energy, force and work are interdependent. This short-circuiting shows that Freudian theory merely follows the spirit of the language, when the drive is presented as a force, a quantity, energy that must be transformed by an apparatus, with a result in view. A human being in travail is a situation of pathos, pain, which must be transformed by a series of mediate operations. The difficulty derives from the fact that Freud adopts a double language in this definition: beginning on the level of concept, he continues on the level of description. The homogenization of these two discourses is what is problematic, as in many works that open up a new field to theoretical and practical reflection.

7 'Measure' is also implicitly qualitative. For it is the appreciation given to 'measured' (*mesuré*) or excessive (*démesuré*), that is to say, unacceptable to this demand.

encounter of corporal excitations, coming from below (or within), and psychical excitations coming from above (or from outside), which produces at the crossroads of their union a new element, the drive. Drive splits once again into affect and representation, no doubt under the impulse of the anti-cathexis that causes the counter-thrust to oppose the instinctual thrust.

Many others (Strachey, Laplanche and Pontalis, Schur) have noted Freud's ambiguities and imprecisions on the subject of the drive. Sometimes Freud describes drive in purely energic terms: the cathexis attached to a 'representative'.[8] Similarly he expresses the notion of an idea 'which is cathected with a definite quota of psychical energy (libido or interest) coming from an instinct'.[9] Sometimes he identifies the drive only with the psychical representative, by virtue of the fact that one can only know the latter.

Here one should recall an important distinction: that between psychical representative of the drive and ideational representative. The first term, the result, I suggested, of 'psychization', is a representative-delegation, of a non-representative nature. It is not a representation in the psychological sense of that term. It comprises what will be the ideational representative (which is a representation) and a quota of affect. I would see this as a mixture, whose elements divide only under the influence of repression. This mixture is, of course, 'more psychical' than the drive at its source, but much less so than the ideational representative. It seems that Freud more or less invokes a succession of transforming operations from the most organic to the most psychical, the end of the process of 'psychization' occurring in word-presentation. Thus, for Freud, the word psychical has a sense that must be constantly relativized. Psychical is to be understood only through a relation, the relation with the somatic, a relation whose quantitative and qualitative ratios vary.

Thus, moving through Freud's oeuvre, one finds the same ambiguities about the place of the drives in the id and their 'psychical expression' as were found at the outset, but they are much more openly admitted. In the *New Introductory Lectures*, the text in which the id is defined in the most complete way, Freud writes: 'We picture it as being open at its end to somatic influences, and as there taking up into itself instinctual needs which find their psychical expression in it, *but we cannot say in what substratum.*'[10]

This admission of ignorance is repeated in *An Outline of Psychoanalysis*: 'It contains . . . above all, therefore, the instincts, which originate from the somatic organization and which find a first psychical expression here [in the id] *in forms unknown to us.*'[11]

8 *S.E.*, XIV, p. 148.
9 *S.E.*, XIV, p. 152.
10 *S.E.*, XXII, p. 73 (my italics).
11 *S.E.*, XXIII, p. 145.

All this shows very clearly the inadequacy of the traditional semantic limits that designate the psyche in its relations to the somatic. The psychical expression of the drives, especially when it is the *first* psychical expression, has nothing to do with representation, the idea or, more generally, with any notion implying a definite separation between the representative element and the energic affective element. Here, too, one finds that collusion between the symbolic and the economic, an indissociable collusion that has no profoundly distorting effect on the spirit of Freud's work.

2 Desire

If one moves from the concept of drive to the model of desire, it will be seen that they share a similar problematic. In both are found the conjunction of a given of the order of the memory of a perception and a given of the order of the 'impulse', that is, a force in movement, a moving quantity.

Consider what Freud says of the experience of satisfaction in *The Interpretation of Dreams*:

> An essential component of this experience of satisfaction is a particular perception (that of nourishment, in our example) the mnemic image of which remains associated thenceforward with the memory-trace of the excitation produced by need. As a result of the link that has thus been established, next time this need arises a psychical impulse will at once emerge which will seek to re-cathect the mnemic image of the perception and to re-evoke the perception itself, that is to say, to re-establish the situation of the original satisfaction. An impulse of this kind is what we call a wish; the reappearance of the perception is the fulfilment of the wish.[12]

Desire (wish) is defined, therefore, in terms of movement, of thrust. The definition of desire as 'psychical' is subjected to this disturbance, this movement within the psychical apparatus. Desire refers us to a category that usually expresses this relation to movement. The controversies around the various possible translations of the German term *Trieb* reveal that, in French, *pulsion* (drive) is preferable because it expresses directly the notion of thrust or constant force – the thrust which, with source, aim and object, constitutes the installation or circuit of the drive. Can it be said, then, that the movement of desire, is mobilized by the 'driving' force of the drive? But how can one maintain their differentiation?

12   *S.E.*, V, pp. 565–6.

Indeed, although one may recognize in the motion of desire the energy that animates it, and which would seem to belong to the drive, it does not exhaust the concept of desire. It may be said of the desires that they may be condensed and displaced. This cannot be said of the drive, but only of its objects and also, to some extent, of its aims. Thus the symbolic polarity would belong to desire, the economic polarity to drive. The economic at the level of desire would have to be sought at the level of the motive force of the impulse, and not in the cathexis of the memory trace (the rediscovery of the satisfaction that is missing). In order to find the symbolic in the drive, one must look at the representatives and derivatives of the repressed. One now sees that the two divergent stresses are in opposition. The reference to desire will be linked to the reference to the unconscious, insofar as it is the locus of repressed representations, and the seat of symbolic processes in which the role of condensation and displacement are valorized. The reference to the drive will be linked to the reference to the id insofar as it is the reservoir of energy, in which the unity of collective desire, indeed the limit of any organization, is precisely what is lacking.

At the intersection of the two one will place the primary processes – common to the unconscious and the id. But the property of the primary process in the two topographies is to link in themselves an energic pole (tendency to discharge, mobility of energy), a symbolic pole (condensation, displacement, use of symbols in the restricted sense) and a categorial pole (ignorance of negation, absence of doubt or of degree of certainty, insubordination to the givens of space and time). The primary process is a mediation between energic stress and symbolic stress. Depending on whether it is framed by the id or the unconscious, one or other predominates. My task is not to simplify obscurities or contradictions in the theory by drawing it one way or the other, but to conceive of these ambiguities as a new horizon that Freud lays down and which breaks with traditional thinking.

3 *The unconscious, the repressed, representations*

The unconscious dominates Freudian theory from the earliest works undertaken on the neuro-psychoses of defence (1894), to the modifications of the second topography. The concept was undeniably at its height in 1915, the year of the *Papers on Metapsychology*. As has been seen, it was in the articles on 'Repression' and 'The unconscious' that the most explicit account was given of the relations between the affect and representation, and in which the discussion around the unconscious affect is confronted head on. One has seen how the definition of the concept of drive contains *in potentia* all the theoretical difficulties in question. One can hardly insist too much on the fact that this discussion is dated, that is to say, it is not the last word in Freudian theory on this point. At that time, the unconscious and the repressed were identified together: the repressed constitutes the unconscious as a system.

I shall return to that text on the unconscious only as a reminder of the topographical context of the different types of representation: 'The conscious presentation comprises the presentation of the thing plus the presentation of the word belonging to it, while the unconscious presentation is the presentation of the thing alone'.[13]

Consequently, in the order of the unconscious, the link between affect and representation can only be the link between affect and thing-presentation. This elective affinity of the affect for thing-presentation, what might be called the *cell of the unconscious*, must emphasize even more, if there were any need of it, the affective resonance of the imaginary. If the unconscious is that 'other stage', it is because a spectacle is played out there, a spectacle that affects the subject. In that place, the relations between affect and phantasy, a visual scenario, or rather a visuo-affective scenario, is formed.

As for the phantasy, although the exegesis of this formation of the unconscious gives rise to analyses as diverse as those of Melanie Klein and Freud, or those, closer to us, of Susan Isaacs, Sandler and Nagera, Lebovici and Diatkine, Benassy, Laplanche and Pontalis, it seems to me that, in the final analysis, the heart of the question requires a structural distinction. Just as Freudian theory distinguishes between primal repression (*Urverdrängung*) and 'after-pressure' or secondary repression (*Nachdrängen*), so one must, in a structural approach, separate the primal phantasies (*Urphantasie*) from (secondary) phantasies. Primal phantasies (primal scene, seduction, castration) are in an ordering position, linked by elaboration to 'sexual theories'. By means of the primal phantasy, what might be called the representation–affect complex is constructed, unless it is deconstructed by post-repressions, then reconstructed in other formations. The primal phantasy seems, therefore, to act as the matrix of the unconscious. Primal repression will bear on the maintenance in a state of primary repression of what is linked to the primal phantasy. The primal phantasy will be constructed out of perceptual elements borrowed from the real, elaborating the most discrete traces.[14] These traces will be organized as primal phantasies and, as they are being constructed, will undergo primal repression, which will thus maintain them in the unconscious, where they will govern the secondary repressions (attraction by the pre-existing repressed). The laws of the primary process will

13 *S.E.*, XIV, p. 201.
14 The question remains as to whether the construction of the primal phantasy always derives from these representative elements. I shall come back to it later.

govern later elaborations that will constitute the formations of the unconscious (secondary phantasies, dreams, slips of the tongue, forgetting,
parapraxes, etc.).

4 Language

Now the relations between the primary process and the secondary process
have to be considered. What follows in Freud's text on the unconscious provides some extremely useful comments on this matter.

> The system *Ucs.* contains the thing-cathexes of the objects, the first and
> true object-cathexes; the system *Pcs.* comes about by this thing-presenta-
> tion being hypercathected through being linked with the
> word-presentations corresponding to it. It is these hypercathexes, we
> may suppose, that would bring about a higher psychical organization
> and make it possible for the primary process to be succeeded by the sec-
> ondary process which is dominant in the *Pcs.*[15]

Such a statement confirms what Freud always maintained from the
'Project' (1895) and especially since the 'Formulations on the two principles
of mental functioning' (1911). It is as if the replacement of thing-presentation by word-presentation that corresponds to it were the result of decisive
work. This mutation is the one that presides over the transformation of
object-presentation by the representation of object relations, that is, the
conditions that make it possible to correlate it with its presence or absence.
This transformation is reminiscent of the development that Freud theorizes
in his article on 'Negation' (1925). The judgement of attribution is limited
to affecting the object with its (good or bad) affect, which entails its admission or rejection, its introjective incorporation or its projective
'excorporation'. The judgement of existence must decide whether this
object is or is not, *independently of the affect that accompanies its presentation*
(good or bad). In the first case, only Eros or the destructive drive are at
work; in the second, Logos and Ananke ally themselves with Eros in order
to defeat the destructive drives, for the subject who maintains only the
pleasure–unpleasure principle towards and against everything is exposed to
grave danger. On the other hand, one knows that the pleasure principle
returns to the heart of the reality principle through phantasy.
    The destiny of the affect is linked, therefore, with this mutation. Since the
'Project' – again! – Freud attributes to the inhibition of the affects by the

15 *S.E.*, XIV, pp. 201–2.

ego the ability to decide whether the cathexis of the object is hallucinatory in nature, or whether it corresponds to its perception in the real. In a parallel way, it is by energic reduction, that is to say, the possibility of filtering quantities of energy and manipulating small quantities of energy, that the work of thought is carried out. Language has the aim of making the processes of thought conscious, the cathexis that accompanies it transforming thoughts into perceptions. The fate of the affect, therefore, is in the preconscious and conscious processes, to be inhibited quantitatively and qualitatively. No work of thought is compatible with excessive quantitative rises and qualitative intensities. Otherwise, an affective logic is established that uses in the paranoiac's passion all the resources of condensation and displacements in a sequence of excessively 'meaningful' illuminations.

One must not go so far as to believe that the total elimination of affect is necessary to thought. That degree of formalization may be compatible with the formal sciences, of which mathematics is an obvious example. As far as the sciences of man – or, if one so prefers, the sciences of the subject – are concerned, the affect plays the paradoxical role of a return of the repressed of psychical reality, which leads to a relativization of our intellectual constructions. Savage thought – that of the primary process, that which cannot fool the intellect – cannot be eliminated.

The last remarks lead on to some observations on language, on the theory of the unconscious structured as a language (Lacan). I shall not return to the comments that I made on the work of Lacan and his school. Let me say to begin with that one cannot simply dismiss such a theoretical construction by taxing it with intellectualization, any more than one can confuse the role played by language in Lacan's conception with the one that it plays in Freudian theory. What is in question in Lacan's theory is the relation of the subject to the signifier, and the production of the effect of meaning by the structuring process whose mark is borne by the human mutation.

Thus, by relating the processes of the dream-work to the language processes (condensation and displacement on the one hand, metaphor and metonymy on the other), Lacan is certainly concerned with the study of the primary processes and not with the secondary processes. That the language of the unconscious is not simply language is obviously accepted. In fact, what is at issue in Lacan's theory is only the study of concatenation (the signifying chain). Here I should mark the boundaries of my agreement and specify the points of disagreement.

The Lacanian conception of concatenation is based on the concept of the unconscious, but it takes into consideration only the representations of the drive. I have already stressed the danger of levelling down representations by confusing the distinction between thing-presentation and word-presentation, and ending up treating thing-presentations as word-presentations, that is to say, to regard as negligible the relation of thing-presentation to affect and, in general, to its energic cathexis (the affective load). Such an approach is justified, according to Lacan, in the distinction to be made between the representations,[16] which alone would be repressed, whereas the affect would be subjected only to suppression. I think I have done justice to that objection. I have also shown the sensitivization of thing-presentation by the affect. But above all, with Freud, I have drawn attention to the fact that language does not have the same functional properties when linking thoughts, representations, affects, acts and states of one's own body. It does not seem to me to be legitimate, in the process of concatenation, to give identical value to such propositions as: 'I have been thinking about my conversation with my friend Peter. He has opened my eyes as to why I find A. attractive' . . . 'I thought that you [the analyst] must have spent your holidays with your family, playing with your children, as I always wanted my father to do with me, and was looking forward to your return. . . . As I'm speaking to you now, I feel uncontrollable hostility, for which I can give no good reason. I suddenly feel anxious – I feel I want to smash that knick-knack on your mantelpiece. . . . I can hardly speak. It's difficult to explain. I feel I'm being transformed inside my body. It's as if my hands are detached from my arms and I can no longer feel them. Things in this room are getting vague. The noise from the street seems muffled. I can't hear you breathing any more . . . Where are you? . . . My body feels like a dead weight, lifeless. Everything seems strange. My legs are getting longer. There's a black veil in front my eyes.' Although the analyst decodes what is presented in the analysand's words, he or she is also sensitive to the prosody of discourse, to the strangulated quality of the voice, to pauses, to the quality of the silence that separates propositions, to the work that is taking place in the analysand through his speech, in his psyche and in his body. The analyst may perceive the physical signs of anxiety or depersonalization, hear the breathing quicken, see certain surface veins pulsate, notice that the patient is blushing or making small nervous movements. At the end of the session, the analyst may note that the patient looks temporarily confused, as if trying to adjust to reality, and, on the way out, makes some significant parapraxis, such as opening the wrong door or switching on the lights in the staircase, even though it is flooded with daylight. Language has moved from being a particular way of developing thought to an over-saturated communication, overwhelmed in its activity of suturation. In the first case, language has imposed its own structure; in the second it is in the grip of ever more affective, ever less differentiated cathexes.

I shall distinguish therefore between language that refers only to itself in its own

---

16 The reference here, of course, is to ideational representatives and not to the psychical representative of the drive.

structuring order and presupposes reduction and homogenization to the verbal signifier, forming and subjecting the linear process of verbalization, and the discourse in which the concatenation receives the impressions coming from the heterogeneous signifiers (thoughts, representations, affects, acts, bodily states) and from variable energic cathexes expressing qualitatively and quantitatively different states of tension, tending to discharge. On this question, I should like to remark that the most verbal, the most abstract speech is the result of a discharge. This is not at all the same thing as knowing the associations of a thought and recounting those associations to the analyst. Not only because, once the thought is spoken, it is said by the Other to the Other; not only because saying it gives rise to a new associative network; but also because the spoken thought is a thought that is being discharged. These differences in the cathexis of thought, this energic upsurge that invades language and may destructure it to the point that it becomes unintelligible and refers, on the analysand's admission, to the unsayable, mark the return of the corporal raw material into language. It is the cathexis of formalization by substance. *The affect is the flesh of the signifier and the signifier of the flesh.*

This heterogeneity of the signifier is described by Freud in a seldom quoted passage from 'The claims of psycho-analysis to scientific interest' (1913). Referring to the various sciences for which psychoanalysis may have an interest, Freud begins with philology:

> For in what follows 'speech' must be understood not merely to mean the expression of thought in words but to include the speech of gesture and every other method, such, for instance, as writing, by which mental activity can be expressed. That being so, it may be pointed out that the interpretations made by a psycho-analysis are first and foremost translations from an alien method of expression into the one which is familiar to us. When we interpret a dream we are simply translating a particular thought-content (the latent dream-thoughts) from the 'language of dreams' into our waking speech.[17]

But then Freud becomes even clearer:

> The language of dreams may be looked upon as the method by which unconscious mental activity expresses itself. But the unconscious speaks more than one dialect. According to the differing psychological conditions governing and distinguishing the various forms of neurosis, we find regular modifications in the way in which unconscious mental impulses are expressed. While the gesture-language of hysteria agrees on the whole

17 *S.E.*, XIII, p. 176.

with the picture-language of dreams and visions, etc., the thought-language of obsessional neurosis and of the paraphrenias (dementia praecox and paranoia) exhibits special idiomatic peculiarities which, in a number of instances, we have been able to understand and interrelate. For instance, what a hysteric expresses by vomiting an obsessional will express by painstaking protective measures against infection, while a paraphrenic will be led to complaints or suspicions that he is being poisoned. These are all of them different representations of the patient's wish to become pregnant which have been repressed into the unconscious, or of his defensive reaction against that wish.[18]

Thus, according to Freud, the language of the unconscious is deducible only through the multiplicity of these dialects. But it is impossible to refer this language to language without considerably extending the sphere of language to everything through which psychical activity is expressed: gestural language, but also writing, body language, etc. All this suggests an opposition between the language of the linguists, a formal system combining linguistic elements – phonemes, morphemes, words, syntagmas, whole sentences, on the basis of a single homogeneous element – and the language of psychoanalysts, which is made up of a heterogeneity of the signifier, which derives from the heterogeneity of the raw materials of psychical activity and which I should prefer to call discourse.[19]

The marked insistence with which certain contemporary orientations of psychoanalysis valorize representation as against the affect is closely bound up with an intellectual attitude whose aim is to draw psychoanalysis towards the symbolic pole and to distance it from its economic pole. It is quite clear, from the authors who advocate this orientation, that it is a question of developing that side of psychoanalysis that is concerned with the 'noble' (linguistic) element and of distancing it from the 'vulgar' element (energic cathexis, the affect). The prestige of representation derives no doubt from the fact that, being laid down in the inscription of the memory trace, it refers to the psychical activity whose development has certainly had the most important consequences for mankind: memory. Now it should be remembered that, according to Freud, the affect also has a memory function, as is abundantly shown in anxiety. Although the theoretical conception that sees the affect as the memory of former acts, hysterical attacks, may be subject to caution, the triggering of anxiety as memory of a former danger

---

18 *S.E.*, XIII, pp. 177–8 (my italics).
19 Lacan frequently uses the term *discours* (discourse), as in, for example, 'the unconscious is the discourse of the Other', without however drawing the distinction that I have proposed and which seems to me to be essential.

seems unquestionable. What is remembered by the affect is not only the representation of the dangerous situation, but the affect that accompanied it and whose return is feared. It is not only the affect that is attributed with the memory function; the drive, too, is conceived as a form of memory. As a hypothesis, one might say that part at least of the drives would seem to be 'precipitates of the effects of external stimulation, which in the course of phylogenesis have brought about modifications in the living substance'.[20]

The link between language and memory, a particular case of the link between representation and memory, does not preclude the affect also having a memory function, although this is less precisely defined.[21]

After Freud, the Kleinian authors have brought memory and affect together. In a passage from *Envy and Gratitude*, Melanie Klein stresses this relation when speaking of the unconscious phantasies concerning the breast.

> All this is felt by the infant in much more primitive ways than language can express. When these pre-verbal emotions and phantasies are revived in the transference situation, they appear as 'memories in feelings', as I would call them, and are reconstructed and put into words with the help of the analyst. In the same way, words have to be used when we are reconstructing and describing other phenomena belonging to the early stages of development. In fact we cannot translate the language of the unconscious into consciousness without lending it words from our conscious realm.[22]

Affirmations of this kind are to be found throughout the writings of the authors of the Kleinian school, such as Rivière, Isaacs and Segal in particular.[23]

Beyond the Kleinians, almost the entire British school of psychoanalysis stresses the value of lived experience as opposed to the functions of language (see Winnicott, Masud Khan). The discussion now brings us to the question of unconscious phantasy. For the Kleinian school, phantasy is the quasi-direct expression of instinctual functioning. The unconscious phantasy of the Kleinians is the heir to the psychical representative of the drive in Freud, this representative (which is not a representation) and which we have supposed to be an indissoluble mixture of affect and as yet indistinct representations. That is why the translation of the unconscious phantasy into words is met with incredulity by Melanie Klein's adversaries. The truth is

20 *S.E.*, XIV, p. 120.
21 Modern research in cerebral pathology seems to support this view. See Angelergues (1964).
22 Melanie Klein, *Envy and Gratitude*. London: Tavistock, 1957, p. 180.
23 'The nature and function of phantasy', in J. Riviera, *Developments in Psychoanalysis*. London: Hogarth Press, 1952.

that they misunderstand what she is saying. Klein is not claiming to restore what actually takes place inside the young baby. How could she? She is simply trying to convey in adult language and imagery the processes of the psychical layers, in which the representative activity that it transmits to us cannot exist as such. However, the representation of the unconscious phantasy and its interpretation form the communicating bridge enabling us to understand those layers in the transference situation. Rather than try to think the unthinkable, Melanie Klein proposes a version for adults, the opposite, one might say, to those literary texts that are rewritten for children.

Kleinian theory has been criticized for plunging us ever more into that primitive hell and reducing the wealth of psychical functioning to a few crude mechanisms. Such a view is rather unfair. The work of Bion is evidence that, on the contrary, the developments of Kleinian theory may lend themselves to a highly elaborate conceptualization, based on a double synchronic and diachronic scale of psychical phenomena, beginning with the elementary forms of psychical life in which the 'elements' are of an ideo-affective nature.

Since Freud, few authors have, like the Kleinians, understood the need for a psychical theorization that shifts the stress from the unconscious to the id. Parallel with the enormous development of works on the ego – which are not always of the best – Melanie Klein has given us this psychoanalysis of the id, or at least of what Freud left unexplored in that agency.

5 From the unconscious to the id

Without exaggeration, one may speak of Freud's growing disaffection with the notion of the unconscious in the second half of his work. What in the early discoveries of psychoanalysis was one of the finest jewels in its creator's crown, became gradually devalued. So much so that in 1939, in *An Outline of Psycho-Analysis*, no chapter was particularly devoted to it and from being a system it passed into the rank of adjective. The unconscious was no more than a psychical quality. This shift had begun a long time before. Going back, from *An Outline*, one finds confirmation in *The Ego and the Id*, in which the id dethrones the unconscious.

But if one looks for the reasons that motivated this transmutation of values from the first to the second topography, one must, in my opinion, find the source in *Beyond the Pleasure Principle*. As soon as it was revealed that the repetition compulsion is situated beyond the pleasure principle – that it obeys a blind determinism; that it is, in a phrase often repeated by Pasche, like 'the instinct of the instinct', that is to say, like that which is most essential in the principle of instinctual functioning – the very concept of the unconscious was called into question. Before the repetition compulsion, the

181

unconscious was defined as another stage, the locus of repressed representations, governed by the laws of the primary process, open to intelligibility – even though one applies to it the logic of a particular causality that is not the logic of the secondary process, that which governs the unconscious system. But by opening up the unconscious to this intelligibility by methods of adequate interpretation, the formations of the unconscious yielding the secret of their organization, it was the whole pathological organization that had to cede with them, with the exception of cases of massive fixations.

It was not that the unconscious was in the least docile. Its relations with the conscious remained clearly relations of superior to subordinate, even of master to slave. From primary to secondary, in importance as well as in precedence. But if the discovery of the unconscious served only to throw light on the genesis and structure of the formations by which it is manifested without any practical change, the discovery called for serious corrections.

The most profound reason for the turning-point of 1920 is not to be sought in traumatic neurosis, nor in the child's play, nor in the transference (or at least not in its general, undifferentiated acceptation), but in the negative therapeutic reaction. What the experience revealed was really the limit of interpretative power. In other words, it was not so much that the unconscious revealed itself to experience more opaque or less intelligible than before, but rather that the intelligibility to which it yielded by its inverted form in interpretation came up against an obscure force that tended to undo the combined work of the analysand and the analyst.

It has not been sufficiently demonstrated how much of the concept of the unconscious was closely bound up with a *solely erotic* problematic. I mean by this that repressed Eros is expressed in its disguises, its lacunae, its *enigmas*. Whether there is a conflict between Eros and the self-preservation drives or whether Eros is split into object libido and ego libido, this conflict presupposes that the active, dynamic agent, the factor for positive change, always lies in Eros. Eros interpreted could in some way follow the happy ways of sublimation. Were it to follow obstinately in the ways of infantile sexuality, then the only consequence would be the maintenance of a perverse position, which from the outset had been placed beyond the reach of psychoanalytic treatment. In short, the action of Eros was always positive, despite its profound indocility, because the unconscious was structured – that is to say, positively interpretable through the concatenations of basic logic. It did not go as far as psychosis itself, yet it was just as difficult to approach by analysis, which could not pass itself off as the 'elegant solution' of a blocked question posed to the unconscious, as was shown by Schreber's delusion.

What was learnt from the negative therapeutic reaction was that beyond a conflict, however bitter, between sexual drives and self-preservation drives, then between object libido and narcissistic libido, in which interest for the object and interest for the ego are in opposition, another type of conflict was revealed, that between the life drives and destructive drives. For the first time, after twenty-five years of psychoanalytic practice, the evidence had become clear. The progress of analysis was not hindered by the neutralization of two forces, each by the other, but by the destructive (and not only competing) effects of one force on the other after their disintrication. Like Pasche, I must insist on the distinction between repetition compulsion and destructive drives. The repetition compulsion is a fact of *any* instinctual functioning, whether it belongs to the life or the death drives. It is a factor of stagnation and regression. But the regressions in question may also be due to a massive fixation in which the erotic drives are, so to speak, anchored. The disintricated destructive drive destroys all the mechanisms of concatenation, of linkage, beyond the pleasure principle. For that is where the analysis of the negative therapeutic reaction leads – not to a return to a blocked or cemented fixation, attached to a form of pleasure, however masochistic, but to an undermining, a demolition, which prevents psychical energy being linked in an organization that, like any organization, enters the field of the life drives. The negative therapeutic reaction, insofar as masochism maintains an audible discourse in it, is still under the reign of the pleasure principle. The negative therapeutic reaction is the fact of a situation in which no benefit from analysis is to be attributed to the ego by virtue of the demolition of earlier work by a force of dissolution that attacks any attempt to bind psychical energy. Here are opposed the two last terms of the conjunction–disjunction, link–separation conflict, as two states of psychical representations and energy affected to the drive.

Agreement with (or rejection of) the last theory of the drives may amount therefore to a recognition of this second force (second in the chronology of the theory, but first in the importance that Freud accords it) of destruction. Depending on whether one accepts its role of despecification, of differentiation, or interprets its purpose as a return to a mode of negative pleasure (masochism), one adopts or rejects Freud's theoretical point of view.

But the question cannot remain blocked at the level of this alternative. It would seem that if one wanted to be coherent with oneself, the rejection of the last theory of the drives ought strictly speaking to be accompanied by a rejection of the second topography. For the concept of the id, insofar as it replaces the concept of an unconscious (in the final analysis, always organized, structured), tends precisely to recognize at the heart of that agency those blind, opaque forces, inaccessible to exploration, still more 'savage' than those that were detected at the level of the unconscious, which were even more resistant to domestication. Subjected to obscure influence, they tend to tear one another to pieces in discharge and cancel out one another's effects. The major difference between the id and the unconscious is not only

183

of a quantitative order.[24] Indeed, it is not enough to say that the id is more irreducible than the unconscious, since it is basically of the same structure. The mutation carried out by the leap from unconscious to id must be found elsewhere. In order to draw the line of development in Freud's thought, one might say: 'Where the unconscious was, the id will be'. In order to trace the line of development in the psychical apparatus and to denote a structural mutation, perhaps one should also say: 'Where the id was, the unconscious will be'. The major difference between the concept of unconscious and the concept of id derives from the fact that at the level of the first the destruction drives have no place, whereas at the level of the second not only is their place determined, but their role is held to be dominant. Such seems to me to be the pertinent feature that unites and separates the unconscious and the id.

If my hypothesis is correct, namely, that with Melanie Klein there begins a psychoanalytic theory elaborated in terms of the importance of the id, then we should discuss the relation between the Freudian conception of primal phantasy and the Kleinian conception of unconscious phantasy. It is clear that the two conceptions do not work very well together: Melanie Klein's unconscious phantasy is understood as the psychical equivalent of instinctual activity. For Freud, primal phantasy is the primary organization of the unconscious. It is, in fact, sensitization to the primal phantasy that sets repression in train and constitutes the unconscious. In their turn, the first regressions organize the post-repressions, by attraction in the pre-existing repressed. The primal phantasy, therefore, is the central theme that the organization of the unconscious preserves in an unconscious state and whose effects urge the individual to displace his or her interests and activities as far as possible from that theme, while seeing it return again and always in the field of those displacements.

Can this view be expressed in Kleinian theory? One might conceive that unconscious phantasy, according to Melanie Klein, as primarily a phantasy activity, linked to the vicissitudes of the experience of satisfaction (good or bad breast) in the context of part object relations referred to a fragmented, polynuclear ego. In my opinion, it is at the moment when the concomitant unification of object and ego takes place that the fundamental primal phantasy − the phantasy of the irreversible destruction of the breast-mother object, followed by mechanisms of reparation set in train by mourning − is formed. Furthermore, the phantasy of the combined parent − the Kleinian equivalent of the phantasy of the primal scene − constituted in the primal

---

24 It should be stressed that the 'nature' of the sexual drive as described by Freud up to the second topography (demand, tendency to discharge, inaccessibility to the reasons of the real) cannot avoid resorting to the last theory of the drives, which includes an explicit reference to an unbinding actively at work.

phantasy, is not unrelated to that absence of the object. The bad object is the absent object, the object about to be lost. From that point on, two registers come together: the phantasy of the absent object, attacked precisely for its absence, and the phantasy of the combined parent, in which the absent object is the prey of the Other, thus escaping the subject absolutely. The subject can neither hate the object without running the risk of destroying it, nor accept its absence, which implies its abandonment to the Other third party, on whom is projected all the destructive aggression of the primal scene. Only the analysis of this phantasy, which implies, it should be noted, consent to separation from the maternal object and the idea that this object can in turn experience satisfaction – that is to say, find pleasure with another good object (the Other third party) may lead the subject out of this impasse. As long as the absence of the object arouses hate and the fear of destruction; as long as the complementary phantasy of that absence is that of murderous aggression between the object and the object of the object (the Other third party); any displacement towards a fourth object is impossible. This fourth object is really what Winnicott describes as the transitional object, an opening to the field of illusion, a decisive displacement of the object initially caught up in the shared corporal space of infant and mother, towards that potential space *between* mother and child – the first not-ego possession.

This role that I am assigning to *absence* is crucial in all psychoanalytic theory. It is the absence of the object that causes the affect of unpleasure; the representation of satisfaction and of the object that conditions it. Again it is during that absence that the tension becomes the spur of phantasy. It might be useful at this point to introduce the notions of mourning and response from the object. On this matter, the role of the environment, unmentioned by Freud, ignored by Melanie Klein, has been brought out by Anna Freud and Winnicott. The temporary, limited absence of the object, which allows the threshold reached by tension not to go beyond the tolerable, has undeniably structuring consequences, insofar as that absence is a factor of elaboration for the ego. On the contrary, too long an absence of the object, too postponed a response or one given in conditions that do not bring satisfaction, causes the tension to exceed the subject's tolerance and conditions the appearance of phantasies that are destructive both for the object and for the ego.[25] The instinctual invasion then disorganizes the fragile kernel of the ego's structuring, going beyond unpleasure to the point of becoming psychical pain. The response that does not bring satisfaction may well, in my opinion, be the origin of the precocious superego, generating primal guilt, that is attached not only to experienced destructive aggressivity, but to the

25 The determinants of this absence have meaning, it should be said, only by being articulated on the mother's desire.

mere manifestation of the drive that can no longer, either *de jure* or *de facto*, be a source of satisfaction other than negative.

These remarks are worth thinking about. The excessive valorization of the environment would no doubt lead us to take psychoanalysis in the direction of orthopedagogy. The underestimation of its role would bring us rapidly to the opposite danger, that of an extreme constitutionalism, explaining differences of behaviour in terms of unequal innate endowments of life or death drives.

Thus although the Freudian theory of the complementary series may seem eclectic, it is the only one to provide a useful working hypothesis.[26] But although it is clear that, whatever the etiological factors, what matters is the intrapsychical elaboration of conflictual experiences. One meets here once more the difficulty in deciding between the respective roles of the memory of trauma and the organizing phantasy, that is to say, the primal phantasy.

To conclude, one might propose that Freud's primal phantasy is an unconscious phantasy, in that it is part *of* the unconscious, whereas the unconscious phantasy of Melanie Klein is an activity of the id. Thus the contradiction between the one and the other would no longer be absolute. To that unconscious phantasy, in its Freudian version, would correspond a representative structural organization; in which the subject may occupy all the places; in which the subject is nowhere in his place, because he is employed everywhere distributing them. To the unconscious phantasy in its Kleinian version would correspond a primitive instinctual activity of discharge, combining, with the minimum elaboration, instinctual source, object and aim, in the antagonism between the life and death drives. In the Freudian version, representation and affect will be distinguishable, the modification of the affects entailing a representative reshaping, just as a change of the representative table arouses other affects. In the Kleinian version, affects and representations are not distinct as such and are apprehended in the form of that undecanted mixture. Clinical experience would seem to support this way of seeing things.

III Second topography: affect and the id (the affective economy)

The ego is where the affect is manifested. The id is where the forces that will bring it to birth come together. Of the various descriptive definitions that Freud gives of the id, the most eloquent is the one to be found in

---

26 I agree that there is a great deal to be done before we can move from the useful to the operational.

Lecture XXII. It is remarkable to find again on the subject of the id the same formulations that Freud used to designate the unconscious or the primary process. But greater stress is placed on certain orientations, such as the opening to somatic influences, the importance of the economic factor, the vocation to discharge.

Since the first formulations concerning the unconscious and the primary process, a certain balance had always been maintained, in Freud's writings, between a symbolic pole (condensation–displacement), an economic pole (tendency to discharge, variations in quantity) and a categorial pole (space–time relations, contradiction, etc.). With experience, Freud seemed to break this balance in favour of the economic pole: 'The economic or, if you prefer, the quantitative factor, which is intimately linked to the pleasure principle, dominates all its processes. Instinctual cathexes seeking discharge – that, in our view, is all there is to the id'.[27]

This marked insistence on the function of discharge is a characteristic that the id shares with affect. In fact, it is through the instinctual cathexes that the relation between id and affect may be understood.

What Freud calls called automatic anxiety is the product of a direct mutative transformation of libido at the level of the id, no doubt by a process of discharge. The problem here is whether the tensions discharged at the level of the id are capable of assuming a strictly affective form or whether they are pure quantities. Freud adds, in the text to which I referred, that the displacements and condensations that occur in the id thanks to the mobile state of energy and its tendency to discharge ignore 'the quality of what is cathected'. He adds: 'what in the ego we should call an idea'. Quality, therefore, is attached to content here. Thus in relation to the *unconscious*, an important modification has occurred: *nothing is said about the representations of the drive*. At the level of the unconscious, the representation–affect duality found its place. At the level of the id, only contradictory instinctual movements are present. The structuring reaches its extreme point here, beyond which is *chaos*. This structuring of the economic pressures will, at the very least, end in discharge. But that discharge is of a quite different kind, by virtue of the fact that it has as its counterpart the completion of that structuring whose secret nature remains mysterious to us. The fundamental organizing structure is that of the opposition between *life drives and death drives*. Freud even goes so far as to write that *the id has no organization*, that it obeys only the pleasure–unpleasure principle. Laplanche and Pontalis have described with great clarity the differences between the id and the unconscious.[28] It is quite clear to me that the motivating factor that led

27 *S.E.*, XXII, pp. 73–4.
28 *S.E.*, XXII, p. 74.

Freud to radicalize what was newest in his discovery and which he called the repressed, the unconscious, the primary process, is the reshaping brought about by the last theory of the drives.

The sense of the conflict has changed: it is no longer a struggle between a sexual, repressed, unconscious pole and a non-sexual, repressing and conscious pole; nor is it a question of an opposition between an object pole and a narcissistic pole. It is now a question of a double conflict: on the one hand, between an unorganized or weakly organized instinctual pole and, on the other, a pole differentiated from the instinctual one and better organized, between the forces of binding and forces of unbinding in each of these two spheres.

Nothing of the earlier acquisition is rejected on the subject of desire or sexuality. What is changed is the placing of the concepts. The unconscious, the repressed, the primary process are relativized according to two orders of reference: on the one hand, the Oedipus complex as a knot of intersubjective relations; on the other, the psychical apparatus as system of intrasubjective relations. From this point of view, the Eros–destructive drives dyad is what at the same time holds the theoretical structure on its feet and serves to mediate between Oedipus complex and psychical apparatus.

This articulation between complex, apparatus and instinctual conflict seems to me to form the theoretical framework that makes the second topography an epistemological whole that is more fruitful than that of the first topography, although Freud's writing is less illuminated by the fires of brilliant discovery (revelation is behind him, it is now a question of constructing).

The consequences from the point of view of the affect must be separated from this rehandling. The id can be the seat only of phenomena of tension and discharge. These instinctual tensions and discharges are not strictly speaking either conscious or unconscious as such. The most one can say is that the antagonism between the life drives and the death drives gives these states of tension and discharge a connotation either of fusion, binding, linkage or of defusion, unbinding, unlinkage, sustaining states of partial reunification or partial disintegration. The boundaries between id and ego being much vaguer than those between unconscious and preconscious, there is a whole area of exchanges between the products of the id and those of the ego, exchanges that take place in both directions. But the barrier of the ego, even if no strict boundary constitutes it, is crossed by a network that accepts into the ego only 'domesticated' fragments of id. These instinctual movements carry within them contents, distinct representations as such. *My hypothesis is that these fragments of the id are made up of a material that makes any division into affect and representation impossible.* The tension–discharge dyad, however, is under the domination of the pleasure principle; it is therefore impossible to suppress the qualitative aspect of the productions of the id.

What is more conjectural is the role played by the representations. In fact, it should be stressed that just as the id is a place of exchanges between impressions received from the outside world and those coming from inside (id–superego), the id is also a place of exchanges between impressions from the soma (organic sources of the drives), and impressions coming from the ego.

In effect, the id comprises:

1 innate elements that have always been unconscious;
2 acquired elements, which have become unconscious and have crossed the ego without leaving any trace;
3 acquired elements, deriving from the id, which have reached the ego, been rejected by it and returned to the id in an unconscious state.

Depending on whether one is speaking of the deepest, most inaccessible layers of the id or of those most in contact with the ego, the representative element will take on a different signification. The work of differentiation will relate to a certain decantation between affect and representation, under the influence of the proximity of the ego; where a raw fragment, in which affect and representation are mixed, was originally present, a splitting distinguishes them.[29]

At the level of the id, the affect, indistinguishable from representation, is unrepresentable. It is looking for representations. Many authors have insisted on the fact that the affects in question are not verbalizable; this is due not to resistance, but to the very nature of the phenomenon.

What is called automatic anxiety (affect), the result of a discharge *in situ* at the level of the id, which breaks into the ego, is in fact an *affect–representation*, in which no distinct representation is conceivable. Such effects are non-representative. They have an essentially economico-traumatic signification. Through them is expressed the threat that weighs on the organization of the ego. The psychical apparatus can no longer bind that free energy that dissolves the organizations linked to the ego. It is pointless to say that they are situated beyond the possibilities of analysis, *qua critical affects*. It is readily understandable that if to the pressure of *need* is added the tension set up by the non-satisfaction of the need, no desire is possible. The demand is that of the satisfaction of an indistinct *need–desire*. The tension must be more or less tolerable for the subject to be able to operate the hyper-intense cathexis of the object capable of appeasing the tension by satisfaction. This cathexis would intervene only at the initial phases of the experience – that

---

29 I can see no other possible explanation for this split than the intervention of primal phantasies. As for the nature or precise structure of these phantasies, a whole new book could be devoted to it.

is, at its desire stage – or when relief has begun to attenuate the tension, when certain signs of the presence of the object are in view.

Freud borrowed the term *es* [it, rendered into 'English' in Strachey's translation of Freud as id – translator's note] from Georg Groddeck. This borrowing occurred at the time of a profound metapsychological mutation marked by the introduction of the second topography. But on the admission of Groddeck himself, the borrowing was only of the term, not of the concept. I think that an examination of Groddeck's conceptions might be useful because they seem to influence or coincide with other psychoanalytic conceptions among Freud's contemporaries. This influence is still continuing for many an author. Groddeck had the merit of making some profound observations and coining some felicitous expressions. Whoever recalls statements like: 'There is no such thing as an I; it is a lie, a distortion, to say: "I think, I live." It should be: "it thinks, it lives"',[30] or, more succinctly still: 'I am being lived by the It',[31] cannot but be struck by their modern resonance. But behind these propositions is concealed a perception of the 'It' quite alien to Freud, as Groddeck does not fail to point out when he accuses the founder of psychoanalysis of lacking intellectual audacity.

For, as soon as these propositions are advanced, one is confronted by a mystery, 'the greatest mystery in the world', which Groddeck resolves in quasi–religious terms. 'I have no answer to the question of what the It is', he admitted in 1920, but in many other places he does more than hazard an answer. He formulates it in terms that one may rightly call metaphysical. If on certain points Groddeck's and Freud's formulations seem close to one another – on the impersonality, the timelessness of the id (It) and also on its absence of spatial limitation, its immutability – even a superficial examination will show their divergences. To remain close to Freud's formulations, it should be noted that for Groddeck the It 'encompasses the unconscious and the conscious, I and drives, body and soul, physiology and psychology. As far as the It is concerned, there is no frontier between physical and psychical. Both are manifestations of the It, modes of appearance'.[32]

Later, Groddeck was to conceive of a new division, comprising the conscious, the unconscious and the vegetative. This third term could only serve to mark off its difference from Freud's id, whose domain is much less extensive. 'I repeat', he says in the same text, 'that I see the It as the sum of all the life forces making up an individual.'[33]

I shall confine myself to stressing the differences between Freud and Groddeck insofar as Groddeck's position and the current of thought to

---

30 Groddeck (1977), p. 254.
31 Ibid., p. 132.
32 Groddeck (1969), p. 96.
33 Groddeck (1977), p. 212.

which his work gave rise may be followed right up to today. There the 'It' appears as an organizing, totalizing principle of the human being, although it may be differentiated in a multiplicity of Its. It determines the construction and destruction of everything in the living being. It transcends all its manifestations, for it is neither born nor dies with what it engenders. It cannot be linked to any particular determination, since to link the part to the whole of which it forms a part and to see the whole in each part, according to the Goethean principle, is the aim that must guide our minds and which is itself a manifestation of the It. Furthermore, the opposition between life and death drives (for Freud, at the heart of the id) has no place in Groddeck's theory, which transforms this opposition into a union. Thus the Goethean 'die and become' is carried out.

The It is, so to speak, fully itself before birth, before sexual division, in the foeto-maternal totality. This explains why, after sexual division, there is a compulsion to return to that initial Edenic condition, a yearning to restore that completeness, that aspiration to perfection that animates the It. We come close here to Rank and others, as we came close to Ferenczi in the lack of distinction between body and psyche. That such a conception of the It is concerned with the affect goes without saying, since it is the most 'affective' of the conceptions of the id. For if Groddeck sets great store by symbolization, it is not because (like Freud) he is locating at the level of the It some fundamental processes that would constitute the matrices of symbolization as well as being the expression of symbolization itself; it is because the It is an obscure demiurge capable of the most immediate intuitions and the most complicated operations.[34] It is no longer a question of acting on such a master, but merely of serving it. It is no longer a matter of analysing, a vain enterprise where the It is concerned, still less of interpreting, but of submitting oneself to it, while speaking its language, which is that of affect: 'To enter into the patient's personality is a demand that has to be made of the doctor.' And this empathy goes far.

> The doctor must try and sympathize with what may have gone on in a patient's mind before he decided to produce a high temperature with the help of some germ, to make tumours grow, to allow certain microbes to enter his body and stay in his brain for years so that they will be able to destroy this brain sometime; what might have caused him to torture himself with pains, anxieties, compulsive worries; he will find an answer in himself for all these and a thousand other things.[35]

---

34 See in particular Groddeck (1969), p. 95, where Groddeck gives a lyrical description of the achievements of the It.
35 Groddeck (1977), p. 214.

Thus, by its power of symbolization, its absolute power in the symptom and in language, in organic illness and in sublimated human productions, the It organizes the experience of illness and of health.

We are really brought back to the notion of a 'God nature', words that Groddeck used in the title of one of his first works, *Hin zur Gottnatur* (*Towards God Nature*, 1912). Groddeck's clinical descriptions show us that force at work, obscure and thinking, occult and omniscient, ignoring the difference between psychical and corporal, applying the same determinisms to both, crossing without difficulty the 'wall of biology', which gives the impression of an essentially religious power at work. At least, Groddeck's formulations encourage us to think this: the It is the great mystery, the 'miracle'.[36]

In his first epistolary contact with Groddeck, Freud was well aware of this. At the time of Groddeck's temporary conversion to psychoanalysis, Freud wrote to him on 5 June 1917:

> Why do you plunge from your excellent vantage point into mysticism, cancel the difference between psychological and physical phenomena, and commit yourself to philosophical theories that are not called for? . . . I am afraid that you too are a philosopher and have the monist tendency to disparage all the beautiful differences of nature in favour of tempting unity. But does this help to eliminate the differences?[37]

For, it should be stressed, such a unitary, totalizing conception of the It deprives this concept, in my opinion, of all efficacity, for not only do the differences disappear, which makes it possible to avoid the whole economic question in the study of psychical structuring and the production of symptoms, but it also avoids the whole conception of conflict, since instinctual antagonism is dissolved in the unification of 'die and become'. The relations between the agencies are no longer apprehended in the tensions that govern them, the It becoming the ultimate, final cause.

If I have dwelt at some length on Groddeck's somewhat mystical conception of the It, it is because it seems to me to represent one of the swings of the pendulum, the other being represented by the North American formulations.

In the post-Freudian psychoanalytic literature, the Freudian concepts of ego and id have enjoyed varying fortunes. One knows what became of them

---

36 'Man my scientific object begins at fecundation. And what is constituted at that point I call man's It. The term must denote all that is indeterminate, inderterminable in that being: the miracle' (Groddeck 1969, p. 95).

37 *Letters of Sigmund Freud, 1873–1939*, trans. Tania and Joseph Stern. London: Hogarth Press, 1961, p. 324.

in the theoretical current stemming from Hartmann. The hypothesis of a free sphere of conflicts, ego apparatuses, innate and value adaptive, was well received in North America and even among some British authors. In 1967, Max Schur defended a new conception of the id in which this instance is also endowed with a certain autonomy and adaptive value. The id, succeeding the undifferentiated id–ego phase, becomes the product of an interaction of innate, maturing factors, linked to experience. The id, like the drives, is phylogenetically and ontogenetically the product of maturity and development. 'I maintain', says Max Schur, 'that certain autonomous apparatuses serve the development of the id as well as of the ego.'

The ego, the central organ of adaptation, must take account of instinctual demands. According to Schur, it is the id that first has the task of elaborating instinctual demands *from an adaptive point of view*: the id is a precursor of the ego. According to this author's thinking, there is no strict boundary between id and ego, any more than there is between physiological needs and their unconscious mental representation as drives and desire. The pleasure principle is the regulating principle of the psychical apparatus, working, in the final analysis, in the service of adaptation. Far from being the agency resistant to all domestication, irreducibly tending to discharge and satisfaction, it becomes, in this new conception, the first adaptive level, which, so to speak, does half the work of the ego.

Although it is true that Freud stressed this somatic rooting to which I have referred, the physiological–psychical differentiation raises quite as many problems as its theoretical counterpart: the hypothesis of the biopsychical *continuum*. No doubt the presence of condensations and displacements at the heart of such a structure is evidence of a certain degree of organization. One does not solve the problem by installing at the level of the id a pre-id, as Schur seems to postulate. The contradiction to be considered is that of an agency without organization, but capable of crude symbolization in the figures of displacement and condensation; it is no doubt an insoluble contradiction. The solution may be the opposite of that advocated by Max Schur. It would consist, as against psychological realism of genetic inspiration, of adopting a metaphorical theorization of structural inspiration. The term structural must be taken in a different sense from the one used in the American works referred to. In other words, it is heuristically profitable to institute in the continuum postulated cuts, mutations that indicate orders of organization of a different structure:

- order of structure of the soma: asymbolic;
- order of structure of the drives: primary symbolic;
- order of structure of the ego: secondary symbolic.

These different orders of structure are connected–disconnected. That is to say, although each sphere possesses its own organization, disconnected from that of the others, they are also united by relations of connection. From this point of view, the order of structure of the drive is at the crossroads of the somatic and the psychical, stretched between a possible annihilation of its symbolic organization and a secondary symbolic differentiation. *The drive is between body and a language.* It is neither of the order of the first, nor of the order of the second, but may, depending on the circumstances, make itself undifferentiated or differentiated, not so much in continuity as in discontinuity.

The id, then, is an unorganized organization, structure and non-structure, the locus of work that is ceaselessly done and undone. In the best cases, this work may be resumed and pursued by the ego; at worst, the ego is dissolved in the somatic. The unconscious, the repressed is, at the heart of the id, its most organized fraction, at the frontiers of id and ego, a locus of exchange between representations and affects. What characterizes it, as Freud says, is the tendency to discharge and the economic point of view.

As far as the affect is concerned, much has been said since Freud about whether the affects were states of discharge and tension. In fact, these discussions have meaning only if one relativizes them in terms of the agency from which the affect derives. Under the regime of the id, tensions are followed by discharges, in a massive, crude way. Under the regime of the ego, the inhibition of the primary processes changes the direction of the tension. The tension becomes a state of inhibition of the discharge, a temporary retention that, for different aims, tries to bear the weight up to a certain limit. Beyond that limit, the discharge is produced all the same and the affect resumes its specific aspect at the level of the ego, as Freud describes it. But this discharge usually remains limited. Although it may seem to threaten the ego and its organization, this discharge functions nevertheless to the extent that the affect remains caught in the ego's chain of productions, co-existing with unconscious and preconscious (thing- or word-) presentations.

This brings us to a reconsideration of the economic point of view. Freud gave a partial, univocal theorization of the economic. He always linked its effects to action of a quantitative order. The quantitative point of view is pre-eminent in the psychical apparatus, since Freud gives the tendency to discharge the major function in reducing the quantity to a zero level, in order to return to the state of repose that existed prior to the disturbance. However, this conception leads to ambiguities, insofar as Freud speaks in turn of the tendency to *absolute* reduction (zero level) and of a *relative* reduction (lowest possible level, constant level) of tensions. Only the exigences of life oblige one to be content with the solution of the lowest possible level, short of being able to achieve complete discharge, that of zero level. The economic point of view cannot but be affected by this ambiguity. In my opinion, the economic point of view is not limited to the tendency to discharge, any more than to the notion of quantitative relation (calculation of the quantity). Another property, not mentioned by Freud, seems to me to be essential, namely, *the transformation by work on libidinal energy. Although the psychical structure cannot allow itself the luxury of complete discharge without risking psychical death; although it must be content with the lowest possible level; although it is forced to retain a necessary quantity; the action from the economic point of view presupposes that the energy reduced to quantities that the psychical apparatus can tolerate is the object of a work of transformation whose transition from free energy to bound energy is one of its major tasks.* It is this work that is responsible for the transformation of somatic energy into libidinal energy, among others, and it will be responsible for the transformation of the drives into psychical representation of the drives, as it will be responsible for the division into affect and representation, and later for the distinction between thing-presentation and word-presentation. It is also the economic point of view that will be seen at work in the processes of cathexis and anti-cathexis. It is the economic point of view that, at the level of the ego, will provide the energy for the ego's defence mechanisms. Again, it is the economic point of view that will preside over the vicissitudes of the drives: inhibition of aim, displacement, desexualization.

In other words, one cannot envisage action from the economic point of view in terms of restraint or understand its effects in a univocal, homogeneous way. The economy of the psychical life in Freudian theory governs the relations between the different cathexes proper to the different agencies. The cathexes of the id, the ego and the superego cannot be calculated on the same scale. For what specifies these different agencies is perhaps above all their energic regime: the massive or limited character of the cathexes, total or partial mobilization, tendency to extension or to limitation, etc.

To a greater degree than representation, affect is linked to the economic point of view. Not only because the notions of threshold (and therefore of quantity), tension and discharge are to be found there, but also because affect represents the instinctual element of the drive that is most resistant to transformation, that which does not enjoy as varied a play of permutations and combinations as the representations.

This leads me to make certain remarks on the conception that derive from Lacan's works. It is no accident if one is found here face to face with a theory that has always valorized the unconscious, word-presentation, language to the detriment of the id, thing-presentation and affect. Similarly, in Lacan, the economic point of view is stuck to theory or subjected to a mutilation that makes it no more than a shadow of itself.

In a strange way, Hartmann and Lacan, apparently poles apart from one another, are closer than might be supposed. Hartmann eclipses (or tames) the id to the benefit of an autonomous ego and defends a conception of psychical life in which the apparatuses of the ego belong to the cognitive sphere, in which the function of the *signal* plays a major role. Lacan eclipses the id to the benefit of an unconscious structured as a language, constituted by the effects of the signifier, whose grammaticality the id would reflect, subjecting the imaginary to the *symbolic*. I am quite aware of the difference between signal and signifier, or between signalization and symbolization. What strikes me is that both cut themselves off from the dimension in which the structure is threatened with death because of the action of the destructive drives. The death drive in Hartmann is transformed into aggressivity; in Lacan it is the mark of absence in which the signifier happens.

That Hartmann and Lacan say nothing of affect is hardly surprising, since, for the first, affect is what challenges the supposed autonomy of the ego; for the second, affect is subjected to the play of the signifier. My analysis of Freud's approach, from the *Studies on Hysteria* to *An Outline of Psycho-Analysis*, shows the inalienable place occupied by affect. Its omission in theory seems to me to be the sign of a foreclosure whose effect, as one knows, is always to return to the subject by way of the real.

These versions of the id indicate the wide range of interpretation to which this unthinkable concept has given rise. When Freud decided to introduce the id into theory, he was giving in to the pressure of clinical facts and to a sense that there was a gap in theory. Between 1893 and 1921, Freud was preoccupied above all with finding sense in psychical phenomena, where traditional thought saw only nonsense. This gave birth to the unconscious. From 1921 to 1939, Freud's main preoccupation was understanding why, where there ought to be sense in that continent that he had discovered and explored, sense fell short. No doubt he was coming up here against the wall of biology. But he tried in all his formulations concerning the id to remain prudently optimistic. Alongside him and after him, the fruitful ambiguity of the id was dissolved. The 'unthinkability' of the id would be raised to the level of mysticism or reduced to the level of biology or language. Thus Groddeck's conception clearly shows that the It is everything and the rest nothing. In a note dating from 23 August 1938, Freud writes: 'Mysticism is the obscure self-perception of the realm outside the ego, of the id'.[38]

On the other hand, certain authors have been able to accept the view that the id was the mode of self-perception of mysticism. The id becomes an internalized mother–nature, living in close contact with the living spirit of natural things, the locus of a sort of immediate, wordless dialogue with the world. The 'Groddeckian' inspiration is to be found in authors who would not explicitly claim allegiance to him: before Groddeck, there was Jung; contemporary with him, Ferenczi, the author of *Thalassa*, and Rank, the

---

38 *S.E.*, XXIII, p. 300.

author of *The Birth Trauma*; after Groddeck, there are those who have extended empathic and intuitive communication to a limitles degree, to the detriment of the process of communication. For all these authors, language is 'superficial'; words are pale, bloodless shadows that say nothing of the reality of things, which only direct, immediate, infra- or supra-verbal apprehension can make visible in all its luminous radiance.

It is easy to understand why, by an inevitable swing of the pendulum, theory would go to the opposite extreme. Affect would be completely valorized; any reference to affect would be regarded as taking refuge in occultist, obscurantist thought, something from which science could expect nothing. The implicitly religious ideology of theoretical currents that claimed an explanatory value from affect would then be denounced. This position would merely substitute one ideology for another, for the solution to these difficulties cannot be found in the exclusion of affect. Yet it is this exclusion of affect that exposes these various approaches. Thus there are those that reduce affect to its physiological aspect. Another form of exclusion is to propose a linguistic model of the unconscious based solely on the representations, promoted to the rank of signifier. All these approaches seem to me to be mutilating. The choice that is offered between mysticism and linguistics cannot solve our problems. In my view, the solution lies in a deepening of the notion of *work*: work on the givens of the external world and the traces that it leaves in the psychical apparatus; work on the productions of the internal world, which the apparatus must deal with, no doubt with much more difficulty than the first; work that psychoanalytic practice presents to our view and invites us to carry out.

IV Second topography: affect and the superego (renunciation, idealization and affective extinction)

In the course of this study, I have said very little so far about the relations between affect and the superego. This might seem surprising, since part of the discussion concerning the unconscious affect entailed for Freud an analysis of unconscious feeling of guilt. It is as if Freud could not but refer to such a feeling and yet had to criticize the term as incorrect. As a result, he preferred the term 'need of punishment'. To describe the fact more accurately, would it be enough to change the word?

The difficulty of the problem stems no doubt from the peculiarities of the superego. As one knows, it is of the same nature as the id. Its cruelty is explained by that natural relationship. When regression reaches the id, it affects the superego. Obsessional neurosis and melancholia, those illnesses of the superego, show this quite clearly. It is not enough to stress that relationship to refer the superego to the id. For, although it is true that the superego

197

is directly connected to the id, part of it belongs to the ego, particularly in anything concerning inhibition and control of the affects. Of course the structure of the superego is not simple, since modern authors have rightly distinguished in this agency between the superego strictly speaking and the ego ideal. Furthermore, it has been proposed that a distinction should be drawn between the ego ideal and the ideal ego. This separation of the functions of censorship and prohibition from the 'ideal' functions has been noted, but not sufficiently explained. By means of the functions of censorship and prohibition, the superego prohibits the affects of pleasure, which, being unable to obtain parental approval, or what the subject imagines that approval to be, triggers off unpleasure. It then becomes necessary to forbid the representations, the desired aims, which are likely, given the promise of pleasure that they imply, to run the risk of this disapproval, and therefore to provoke unpleasure. The subject's pleasure comes up against the Other's unpleasure.

The renunciation of satisfaction governs repression therefore. What was previously accepted by the ego must be refused, rejected, condemned and repressed. Of course, the sexual is the privileged object of repression. But we must go back further towards the love of the object if we are to find its roots. By object love, I mean of course the pleasure that the object may give, but I also mean, when the primordial object is at issue, security, protection, care, attentive presence. The renunciation of the object, therefore, is much more total, more extensive, than the renunciation of sexual pleasure. But, on the other hand, sexual pleasure is what gives structuring signification to the object. This renunciation of the object occurs very early on in the mother–child relationship. Every mother, however attached she may be to her child, is also attached to other cathexes: the father, the interests of the ego, etc. However dear her child may be to her, the competing demands of these cathexes prevent her from being exclusively attached to him. The incest prohibition operates from birth. The fusional experiences with the child, which have a certain integrating and maturing value, cannot be either too intensively prolonged or always arrive at the moment when the child seems to demand them. The absence of the object is unavoidable. We know that affect is never so intense, so painfully felt as when the object – or its representation – is lacking. For the experiences of lack are experiences of rejection by the object, ones in which the object is known in hate.[39] The mother demands that the child be capable of waiting, of bearing the tension, of proving that he can be 'good'. In the end, the child consents. On several occasions, in particular in *Moses and Monotheism*, Freud stresses that this victory of the ego over the id can only occur if, by way of compensation for

---

39 Object *of* hate, but not hated object.

this renunciation, a narcissistic reward is accorded by the superego. The child demands that the exploit that he has accomplished by his docility be recognized; he demands that the object acknowledge his renunciation and, in place of the anticipated pleasure, acquire a pride in what he has done, which the object duly confirms.

This negative satisfaction of a narcissistic nature is the matrix of a structure of primary idealization. Even before this behaviour is actually experienced, the ego ideal, whose aim is to free itself from the hazards of satisfying the object, functions in a precocious manner. 'To be their own ideal once more, in regard to sexual no less than other trends, as they were in childhood – this is what people strive to attain as their happiness',[40] says Freud in his first text on narcissism (1914). The links existing between the prohibition of the affect of pleasure and the appearance of desexualized narcissistic affects, the sources of a sublimation, now become clearer. It will be observed that, in such cases, one has succeeded only in substituting one affect for another. In my opinion, the movement sketched here may, in certain conditions, go too far. It is no longer a matter in these cases of proceeding, by control of affects, to the replacement of one drive by a drive with inhibited aim (tenderness replacing sexual pleasure), or to a narcissistic orientation thwarting the orientation to the object (pride in this renunciation compensating for the lack of satisfaction), but of succeeding in a total indifference to the object insofar as the object is the condition of pleasure or unpleasure. An excessive idealization then leads the subject to a total ascetic renunciation, in which the whole psychical apparatus is oriented towards the objectal and affective vital minimum. One may consider that what is hoped for is an affect of triumph in the success of this project of emancipation. At most, it will extinguish all affect, even narcissistic satisfaction, in order to achieve a total affective neutrality. Of course, such cases are rare, because they represent the extreme figure of a whole series, one in which the elimination of all affect leads to a sort of psychical cadaverization. The ego ideal thus succeeds in satisfying negative narcissism, which dissolves the image of the subject in an affective void.

This vicissitude of affect in neutralization is not the only one, or the most frequent. Usually what one is dealing with, halfway to that result, is masochism. It is seen not only in moral masochism, but also in the obsessional neurotic's superego, in that of the melancholic and the paranoiac. It is here that the unconscious feeling of guilt, like unconscious pleasure, appears dramatically. Is it a true affect, sealed up in the unconscious? Freud hesitated to say so openly. What is obvious is that the triple dimension, economic, topographical and dynamic, is present in any of these pathological states. Indeed, there are considerable instinctual tensions, agencies set up against

40 *S.E.*, XIV, p. 100.

one another, absolutely opposed desires. The dimension of the conflict is at its height. To eliminate the unconscious affect in these structures does not seem possible. In *Inhibitions, Symptoms and Anxiety*, Freud insists on the fact that the superego unmasks the duplicity of the ego, which finds a disguised satisfaction in the exercise of its defensive functions. In *The Economic Problem of Masochism*, he was to stress that the masochist punishes himself for the pleasure that he derives from his masochism, thus fooling the superego. How could the superego punish anything other than disguised, unconscious pleasure? *Civilization and its Discontents* referred to it quite openly.

Thus, just as I have stressed, with Freud, the existence of unconscious affects at the level of the id, I shall now postulate the existence of unconscious affects at the level of the superego. What should be made clear here is that the presence of affects in the superego and the id does not imply that they exist in the same form as in the ego. This does not mean, however, that the affects must be conceived as mere quantitative tensions. The unconscious affect, whether in the id or in the superego, is inconceivable for consciousness, since the quality of the affect can be understood only in relation to consciousness. But the unconscious, too, can be understood only in relation to consciousness. It is never apprehended as such, but deduced through the formations of the unconscious. It is remarkable that all the formations of the unconscious are accompanied by affects, all the more surprising in that these affects do not 'go' with the representations that they accompany. The affects that are most directly in relation to the superego are those linked to the protecting influence of the object; they go from the presence of the object, the sign of its existence, to its visual perception and its voice. The role of the auditive perceptions in such cases is constantly stressed by Freud.[41] Beyond the Parousia of speech, announcing prohibitions, writing introduces a new mutation which renders the presence of the superego anonymous. Identification is the resolution of the Oedipal conflict. Identification with the ego ideal is its accomplishment.

Between these elaborate forms and what has been called the precursors of the superego (Ferenczi's morality of the sphincters, Melanie Klein's precocious superego), a permanent play of exchanges takes place. Thus the ego ideal exceeds the possibilities of the ego by an exigency that it borrows from the persecution of bad internal objects. The badness of the subject is relentlessly tracked down, its inadequacies are denounced, its lacks reified, its hypocrisy displayed for all to see.[42] Here, again, seeing the torments that the

---

41 Rosolato has fully brought out the role of the voice in psychoanalytic theory.
42 We should remember here the role of shame is more specifically attributed to the ego ideal than to the superego, which is rather the generator of guilt. I describe these developments in my work on moral narcissism.

superego and the ego ideal inflict upon the ego, one cannot but be convinced of the existence of the unconscious affects that are thus being fought against. However, this infernal vision would have us believe that superego and ego ideal are for the ego mere subjects of torment and anxiety, that anxiety of the superego described by Freud in *Inhibitions, Symptoms and Anxiety*.

We attribute a fundamental role to the ego ideal in the elaboration and transformation of the affects, of whose sublimation only partial aspects can be observed. It is the ego ideal that valorizes and fashions the derivatives of the primary affects. It is the ego ideal, too, that gives the project its form and destiny. Although it is true that the extreme exigencies of the ego ideal, the heir of primary narcissism, may reduce this realization to nothing, one must denounce the analytic aim that claims to 'adjust' the patient's ideals to the possibilities that are on offer – calculated solely in terms of the limits of psychoanalysis. For the ego ideal contains, in itself, the psychoanalytic subject's whole dimension of the possible.

I shall recall once again a truth stated by Francis Pasche concerning the superego. The ego can live only on condition that it is loved by the superego. The reconciliation with the superego, as outcome of analytic treatment, is a given of experience. It entails the renunciation of the ego ideal's and the ideal ego's megalomania. Suicide, says Freud, occurs when the subject feels abandoned by the protective powers of destiny. In that case, the break is consummated between an ego handed over to *Hilflosigkeit* and a superego, forever disappointed by the ego, that refuses help and protection. Here the castration anxiety gives way to the death anxiety. However far people may try to carry their wish to be done with God's judgement, they can only re-establish the divinity in other substitute figures, which must in turn take the place of the dethroned gods.

Do not forget that Freud regards the cult of the various religions as a re-establishment of the power that their images have lost in reality. The religion of the father appears when the father has been stripped of these omnipotent rights. This excessive power accorded his sons must be paid for by a sacrifice. These remarks have lost nothing of their contemporaneity.

V Second topography: affect and the ego (negative hallucination)

The last theory of anxiety led Freud to conclude that the ego is the seat of the affect. In this study of the relations between affect and the ego, I do not intend to consider all the affects that the ego may experience, but confine myself to those that are specific to the ego, that is to say, to its narcissistic organization.

Federn has described a 'feeling of the ego', closely bound up with variations in its limits which are responsible for its states of expansion or contraction. Despite the interest of his views, especially in the domain of psychosis, I believe that Federn's work has tended to substitute a phenomenological view for a metapsychological theorization. This tendency is still to be observed in a number of works inspired by the observation of children in which the paraphrase of a phenomenological description in metapsychological terms takes the place of theorization. There can be no doubt however that every metapsychology of the ego must include the genetic dimension. In this respect, the relations between ego and affect are an important chapter in that study, even when one confines oneself to the affects proper to the ego. All authors agree with Freud in stressing the ununified character of the primitive ego dominated by the drives of the id. All authors also agree that the stress should be placed on the fundamental role of maternal care in the primary structuring of the ego. However, if one does not wish to slide towards genetic psychology, which is certainly not without interest but is a different field from psychoanalysis, one must first define the domain of the ego with a view to locating the specificity of the relation to the affect. It is useful, but insufficient, to recall the triple servitude of the ego to id, superego and reality.

The specific structure of the ego relates to its topographical situation: at the crossroads of external and internal reality. It is this insurmountable fact that divides it into two irreconcilable parts: the pleasure-ego and the reality-ego. One should not be too hasty in concluding that, by locating it in the pleasure-ego, one has thus defined the relation of affect to the ego. Its relation to external reality is imbued with affect, not only because reality is constantly cathected by projected affects, which goes without saying, but because the sense of the familiarity of the real necessitates that the real be treated affectively in a positive way. An external reality, perceived as unfriendly, hostile, dangerous, because of the bad objects that it contains, and also because of the diffuse tonality that it gives off, cannot be a field of perceptual information serving the tasks of the ego. No doubt this amounts to saying that the ego must itself be felt as friendly, benevolent, safe, for the relation to reality to become established. But nor should one fall into total subjectivism, or encourage an idealizing vision of the real. There are horrifying realities, and the ego that is not sensitive to them and which remains unmoved by them is no less alienated than the one that gives in to panic at the sight of them. Although, in the final analysis, external reality remains unknowable; although the mediation of our perceptual instruments will always set up a screen between it and us, nevertheless something remains knowable to us – and that is what is so surprising, of course – something that engages us in the real.

This sense of familiarity with the real is directly linked to the affects of the ego, to precisely the extent, as Widlöcher showed, in which the omnipotence of the phantasy may counterbalance the constraint of the perception of the inevitable, the necessary, the *fatum* that governs the course of things. In any case, it is clear that this affective cathexis of external reality as basic cathexis cannot go beyond certain thresholds without disturbing the exercise of the perceptual functions.

The ego as the agency of psychical reality raises other difficulties, one suspects. Freud defines the ego as an organized whole, possessing a constant cathexis, which differentiates it from the primary processes. Many contemporary authors (Hartmann, Erikson, Jacobson, Winnicott, to mention only the leading ones) have admitted being unsatisfied by the Freudian theoretical conceptions of the ego and have added the self or some equivalent metapsychological construction. They have justified their approach in terms of the need for a reference to the sense of identity. However, it seems to me that this has not added much to our understanding of the ego. The Freudian conception of narcissism seems to me to offer unexploited resources. The introduction of identity into metapsychology is based on the affect concerned with the unity of the ego, to its sense of self-belonging. Although it is true that clinical experience brings us more and more into contact with cases in which the clinical picture is dominated by existential unease, anxiety before the sense of not knowing who one is or what one is, should one not try to explain these states with the help of the existing metapsychological instruments before creating others? In 'Neurosis and psychosis', does not Freud indicate that the ego, in order to avoid a break, will ward it off by distorting it, admitting chinks in its unity 'and even perhaps by effecting up a cleavage or division of itself'.[43] How can one not link this disturbed sense of identity with identification? In fact, what has guided these authors was perhaps a desire to give back to the ego part of the functions with which pre-analytic psychology had endowed it: a sense of unity, self-control, self-belonging, essential individuality, etc. Such authors have chosen to forget that Freud spoke advisedly of the ego as the agency that has meaning only in its relation to the other two, that an important part of the ego – and God knows how much – is unconscious, the rest for ever so and that the identification is double. In other words, everything that Freud challenged with such vigour surreptitiously returns, with the self, to take up its place once more. However, it would be quite wrong to defend the opposite thesis of the absolute powerlessness of the ego: *Inhibitions, Symptoms and Anxiety* shows an ego less powerless that it had seemed in *The Ego and the Id*. In the later work, he denounced the *Weltanschauung* that had rushed in to exploit what were seen as the inadequacies of the Freudian ego.

Yet what Freud regarded as an avatar of the ego, splitting, turns out in fact to belong to its very structure. The ego is split by its double orientation,

43 *S.E.*, XIX, pp. 152–3.

external and internal. The ego of psychical reality is itself divided between contradictory identifications. It is from this point of view that, in Lacan's words, 'the ego appears as the locus of the subject's imaginary identifications'. The image that the ego has of itself cannot therefore coincide with the subject's self, by the fact of the otherness that inhabits it. It cedes alternatively to the vertigo of triumphant megalomania and hopeless despair, to which there is no remedy.

Melanie Klein's theorization takes account of these variations: splitting, introjection and projection are fundamental structural mechanisms. The splitting of the ego is that activity of division by which primary symbolization is established, separating the good from the bad. This splitting is necessary if the integrations required by the unification of the ego are to take place. That is to say, the ego's object relations depend on the affective context, traces left by the experiences of the good objects in the ego. It is clear that the struggle against the affects of persecution that oppose the work of unifying the ego make the ego a place of conflict and constant affective storms. Any success in the integrating experience creates an affect of triumph over the traces left in the ego by the bad objects. However, it must not be forgotten that this experience of fusion of the kernels of the ego is possible only at the price of a rejection of part of the ego, expelled by projective identification. This means that the ego can evolve only by cutting off part of itself. When, in the depressive phase, the co-existence at the heart of the ego of its two parts, the good and the bad ego, is compatible with the pursuit of integration, it will be at the cost of the work of mourning on the object, which entails the need to cede to the reparation of the destruction that the ego has suffered. There then come into play the conflictual identifications with the good and bad object, with their specific affects of triumph or defeat. Of course, one should take into account the results of the other defence mechanisms, omnipotence, denial, introjective identification, etc. In any case, alienation of the ego is inevitable to the extant that the states of the ego as primordial experiences and states of the ego as results of defensive operations are superimposed and interlinked. The result is this state of the ego in representation that it acquires of itself, constituting secondary narcissism and the affect that connotes this representation after the mourning for the object. Where an indissociable compound took the place of affect and representation, without distinguishing between them, the self-perception of the ego splits off from the affect, but not without each affecting the another. Identifications are the result of incorporations of objects and introjections of affects bound up with the experiences of those objects. The capacity to be alone (Winnicott) in the mother's presence marks the accomplishment of that affective self-representation.

Thus there is a distinction between representation and affect on the one hand and, on the other, an indissociable mixture capable of separating into its component elements. By this separation, the effects of affects will be linked not only to internal states, but also to situations: that in which the presence of the object may be evoked in representation; that in which the perception of the object leads to an affective change. On several occasions, I have the stressed this importance of the perceptual–representative system where the object is concerned.

I shall conclude this chapter by examining the perception and representation of the subject. Lacan has described the mirror stage and marked by an expression that has since often been quoted the affect that accompanies it: the child's jubilant assumption. Clinical experience teaches us that this experience of the mirror is subject to other vicissitudes. I should like to say something about that lack of self-representation as shown in *the negative hallucination* of the subject. Where the image of the subject ought to appear in the mirror, nothing appears. All that is visible is the frame of the mirror, on which no trace is inscribed. It is then that the subject experiences the absence of self, the lack emphasized by the fact that the non-presence of the image is seen as an attack on secondary narcissism. What is lacking in the subject is not a sense of his existence, but ocular proof of it. This absence of any representation of the subject is accompanied by a rise in the anxiety affect, which may be compared with anxiety about loss of the object. Here representation and affect are dissociated, together with the disappearance of the power to see the representation. What is lacking is not the sense of existence, but the power of representation. The affect is experienced with maximum intensity, being unable to rest on any representation, since the mirror sends back only its own reflection. The empty frame evokes another void, the void of the Other. The other that I am no longer appears. The subject is referred back only to his corporally experienced presence. What does the affect that is manifested on this occasion signify? Is it that anxiety of the void, similar to the perceived absence of the mother's penis? This, which is highly likely, is not enough. This *aphanisis* of the subject, by which his image is given back to death, is responsible for this anxiety, of course, but it means something else. The anxiety affect expresses the effort on the part of the ego to reach a representation of itself at all costs. He seeks himself elsewhere, everywhere, around himself, outside himself and finds no palliative to this excess of presence. He tries to rejoin that lost image that is missing, and it is that impossibility of finding himself again that is responsible for the anxiety. He is lacking to himself, for this empty reflection is experienced not as pure absence, but as a *hallucination of absence*. It is because the image is covered over with a hallucination of lack that the subject tries, beyond that hallucination, to find his representation again. The affect is evidence of that effort to regain his image, beyond the mirror, on the other side of the mirror. It is from that break, which makes him powerless to weld together two parts of himself, that the affect surges, marking the failure of

205

the attempt. The splitting here is absolute: between representations and effect, but also between representation of internal self and his absence of projection in the mirror.

These remarks may guide us in appreciating the effects of the loss of the power to bring together an internal representation and its perceptual counterpart. One can now understand more clearly why Freud was forced to introduce into the 'Project' that inhibition of the ego that makes it possible to differentiate at a very early stage between object hallucination and its absence in reality. When the hallucination has a bearing on the self-image and its absence in reality, positive hallucination will cover that intolerable lack. The affect, in the case of negative hallucination, itself totalizes the power of representation. It takes the place of self-representation, acknowledges what is missing in its place and arouses the horror that accompanies that acknowledgement; the subject will try, beyond the acknowledgement, to inscribe a representation on the reflecting surface at all costs. It is because he fails to do so that he will be unable to make up for it by summoning up a hallucinatory Other, which he will not recognize. However identical it may seem, it cannot at best be anything more than a double, a shadowy, lost half that returns from hell to persecute him.

This is a paradigm of psychoanalytic treatment. The resolution of the transference will coincide for the patient with the recognition of that image as his own, not as abominable as he feared, but not as flattering as he would have hoped. It no doubt takes courage and humility to consent to recognize yourself as others have always seen you.

6

Draft for a theoretical model: the process

I Affect, history, structure

A theoretical conception of the affect cannot escape historico-structural confrontation. This confrontation may be detected in psychoanalytic theory itself, as well as in psychoanalytic practice. One may posit a double opposition depending on the parameters of history and structure. On the one hand, the opposition between primary affects and secondary affects, the terms designating the primary and the secondary having to be understood in their historical and structural ambiguity. In the sense of a diachronic succession, the primary precedes the secondary; in that of a synchronic simultaneity, the primary co-exists with the secondary, the whole reflecting a double systematic differing in its mode of organization. By primary affect I shall denote both the earliest, the least elaborate affects, and the affects relating to a mode of organization that is opposed to a mode of secondary organization. Furthermore, it might be noted that the affect is always given in a constitutive bipolarity; thus to the pleasure–unpleasure dyad correspond other dyads, such as good and bad, enjoyment (*jouissance*) and pain, love and hate, right or wrong.

To the three points of view that constitute the Freudian metapsychology (dynamic, topographical, economic), others have been added: the genetic point of view and the structural point of view. In my opinion, these additions are not justified in so far as the history–structure opposition is present in each of the points of view that make up the metapsychology. If Freud did not differentiate them explicitly, it was because they formed part of the implicit approach of any theorization of psychoanalysis. However, one is obliged to separate them artificially in order to show, in relation to the affect, what each of them contains.

1 Affect and history

No notion is more directly linked to the historical dimension than the affect. When one thinks of what remains irreducibly childish, not to say infantile, in us, one thinks of the affect. Psychoanalytic investigation oriented towards the study of development attaches itself to affective development first. Two misunderstandings must be noted here. In my opinion, psychoanalysis cannot claim to offer an exhaustive view of development, it is not a theory of personality, as is sometimes maintained. Its object is more limited, more specific. Even if the second topography seems to extend the field of the first, the object of psychoanalysis remains centred around the investigation of what Freud called in the 'Project' the 'inner world', that of psychical reality, that is to say, desire and the drives. If other systems than the unconscious or the id are considered by psychoanalytic investigation, it is always insofar as the conscious, the ego and the superego are linked to the unconscious and to the id and considered in terms of them.

The second misunderstanding, which is not unrelated to the first, is that the historical point of view as envisaged by psychoanalysis cannot coincide with the psychological conception of development. This conception is presented as a process of cumulative integration, which is linear in view. This would be to take little account of what properly belongs to the Freudian discovery, namely deferred-action structuring ('afterwardness', as Laplanche proposes to call it) and the repetition compulsion.

I cannot deal at length with the role of the notion of deferred action. Let us simply recall a few formulations that I have developed elsewhere:[1] the moment of experience and the moment of meaning do not coincide. The meaning of an experience is so to speak in suspense, the experience lacks meaning. The moment of meaning is always retroactive. When the experience is remembered, the meaning may seem to coincide with it, but usually it is a later elaboration that has become attached to the original experience. The experience is accompanied by a quite different 'meaning', and was in a sense framed by a 'sexual theory' that accounted for it. One might almost say that experience and meaning call out to one another, but never meet. Experience runs after meaning, but never finds it. Meaning is acquired when the experience has been lost forever. Furthermore, the affective intensity of the experience cannot simply lead to meaning, which requires a process of affective selection and a certain degree of detachment. Similarly, the detachment that accompanies meaning is what orients the search for the retrospective rediscovery of the conditions of the experience, without ever

---

1 'La diachronie dans le freudisme', *Critique*, no. 238, 1967.

fully reviving it. It may be objected that certain facts plead for the opposite thesis: in a fruitful affective moment everything becomes clear. In my opinion, the moment of this encounter always has something of the echo about it, the moment when fragments from the past, scattered, disconnected, but belonging to another temporal sequence, are brought together.

One comes here to the second point of the psychoanalytic theory of history: the repetition compulsion – insofar as it concerns the affect. Although one cannot forget the psychoanalytic theory of the stages of development of the libido (oral, anal, phallic, genital), one must insist on the fact that this convenient schema may be at the origin of the most regrettable confusions, by which psychoanalytic theory is thrown back to a traditional conception of individual evolution. The theory of the stages entails its counterpart: the repetition compulsion, the essence of every instinctual phenomenon. If, therefore, one postulates an affective evolution that goes from the most crude to the most subtle affective expressions, one must also remember that every crossing from one stage to the next is never achieved definitively and that, as experience shows, the return of the most ancient affects is possible at any time.

However, one usually conceives of affective life in terms of a schema that seems to me to be incomplete and incorrect. One always postulates a direction to evolution that would always move from primary affective violence to a gradual affective attenuation, the result of maturity, affective maturity. Without insisting further on the normative aspect of such a view – which the facts disprove: *crimes passionnels* and suicide are less frequent among children than among adults – I shall recall a few examples taken from Freud. In the *proton pseudos*, the 'first lie', described in the 'Project', Freud notes the two stages of repression bearing on the two scenes, each having been accompanied by an affective and sexual discharge. 'We invariably find that a memory is repressed which has only become a trauma by *deferred action*. The cause of this state of things is the retardation of puberty as compared with the rest of the individual's development'.[2]

Freud postulates the existence of a presexual sexuality: 'The word "presexual" means "prior to puberty before the appearance of the sexual products"'.[3]

In the search for the determining factors of the *proton pseudos*, he attributes the first repression to the precocity of the sexual discharge. It is the postpubertal sexual discharge that, by association, transforms the memory of

2 *S.E.*, I, p. 356.
3 Letter to Fliess of 15 October 1895, in J.M. Masson, editor and translator, *The Complete Letters of Sigmund Freud to Wilhelm Fliess (1887–1904)*. Cambridge: Harvard University Press, 1985, p. 144.

the first discharge into a trauma. But it is clear that the diphasic evolution of sexuality, which disconnects infantile sexuality from the sexuality of adolescence reveals a new aspect. Whatever the quantitative intensity that accompanies the presexual discharge, the postpubertal discharge is quantitatively much greater.[4]

This observation leads me to re-evaluate our conceptions of the evolution of the affects. Although the affects of the infant, the baby, seem undeniably to be of a singular violence, it would be wrong to say that their evolution will move constantly in the direction of decrease. It seems to me, on the contrary, that the pubertal mutation is concomitant with a considerable intensification of the affects. This quantitative rise is accompanied by a decisive qualitative transformation. It is after puberty that sexuality assumes its full significance. When a young boy speaks openly, during the Oedipal period, of marrying his mother and sleeping with her, the sexual phantasies that may underpin infantile masturbation can hardly be compared with the phantasies of his adolescent older brother (who regards what his younger brother says with condescension) and which accompany a masturbation in which he enacts sexual acts that he would like to perform with the object of his love at that time. The emotions of the younger brother, however Oedipal they may be, are far from being the equivalent, quantitatively or qualitatively, of the emotions of the older brother. The Oedipus complex is doomed to failure, not only because of the prohibitions that forbid desires, but because of its sexual prematurity. To speak in these circumstances of repetition of affects must entail an important corrective. They may be the same affects that re-emerge in postpubertal sexuality as those in the prepubertal period, but their quantitative and qualitative transformations forbid any reduction of one to the other. Traditional psychology laid down a coincidence between sexuality and genitality, whereas psychoanalysis discovered infantile sexuality; yet it would be erroneous to confuse the two. On the nature of this presexuality, it is difficult to be dogmatic. I shall simply say that proof of the *undesirable* character of these desires is to be found in the defence mechanisms that they give rise to.

Just as I have distinguished between primary and secondary affects, I must also distinguish between primary and secondary defences. Throughout his work, Freud attempted, without ever making it explicit, a historico-structural systematization of the defence mechanisms. Traces of it can be found in the letters to Fliess.[5] One may remember the discussions on the subject of

---

4 One can see how quantity may play a double quantitivo–qualitative role: on the one hand, it summons up previous quantities, on the other, it transforms memory into trauma.

5 See in particular Draft H of 24 January 1895 (*S.E.*, I, p. 211); letter 46 of 30 January 1896 (*S.E.*, I, p. 229); letter 52 of 6 December 1896 (*S.E.*, I, p. 236).

repression, conceived as one defence among others, or as a structural mechanism of unparalleled importance. In hysteria and obsessional neurosis Freud found evident examples of the role of condensation and displacement. In 'Instincts and their vicissitudes', he dated 'turning round upon the subject's own self' and its opposite as prior to repression. The role of projection in paranoia was recognized from the outset; its theorization is given in the study of the Schreber case. The introjection of the lost object is bound up with the process of mourning and melancholia. In *Inhibitions, Symptoms and Anxiety*, Freud complements the defence mechanisms met with in obsessional neurosis: isolation, undoing what has been done, reaction formation. Lastly and above all, in one of his last works (1939), Freud crowns the whole edifice with the splitting of the ego. In 1936, Anna Freud described these defensive operations, almost getting as far as the splitting of the ego without mentioning it.

It was to be the works of Melanie Klein, nourished by contributions from Abraham and Ferenczi, that were to bring the primary defences – splitting, introjection, projection (complemented by projective identification), disavowal, omnipotence – into the light and open up new horizons in the interpretation of the most regressive clinical forms. Defences against what? it has been asked. Against the affects no doubt. For Freud, these affects were linked, as he was to make clear in *Inhibitions, Symptoms and Anxiety*, to the loss of the object, to the loss of the love of the object, to the loss of the sexual organ, to the loss of the protective powers internalized in the superego. For Melanie Klein, the primordial danger, the counterpart of the death anxiety, is the fear of annihilation. I shall not adjudicate between the opinions of Freud and Melanie Klein. Their divergences merely throw light on one another and stem from the different material that constituted the object of their reflection. In fact, Freud and Melanie Klein do not hold radically different opinions. For Freud, what is threatening is the instinctual invasion, coinciding with an increase of tension, which the defence mechanisms fail to contain. What is threatened is the organization of the ego, whose power of linkage cannot control that torrential energy. For Melanie Klein, what is threatening is the unlinking of the death instincts that are psychically manifested in the death anxiety or fear of annihilation. What is threatened is the embryonic ego, which runs the risk of succumbing to the attacks of the bad objects loaded with destructive aggressivity. Is there an unbridgeable gap between these two conceptions?

Side by side with this genetic vision of the defence mechanisms, we must consider the structural dimension that corresponds to them. One may, with Laplanche, believe that the major prohibitions – of incest and parricide – have this function. But one may also defend the opinion that this structural dimension is just as much represented by the principles of psychical functioning that are concerned with the affects: the Nirvana principle and the pleasure–unpleasure principle.

211

The aim of the pleasure–unpleasure principle is above all the disappearance of unpleasure. It will be defence mechanisms, then, that will strive to obtain this result at a more or less high price. Whether the reality principle succeeds or co-exists from the beginning with the pleasure principle, the main point is to mark their connection. Freud speaks of the sovereignty, the primacy of one over the other. That is to say, he observes their agonistic and antagonistic functioning. In any case, the affect must be regarded as being held 'under surveillance': it must be given satisfaction, but it must not be given complete satisfaction, lest it come to dominate the psychical processes. On the other hand, the undertaking of the psychical apparatus to free itself of all affective constraint is fraught with grave dangers. For, under an idealizing influence, the ego may – being unable to avoid unpleasure – wish to be free of affective slavery by renouncing all pleasure. There then follows, when the aim is almost attained, a feeling of psychical emptiness, of affective death, which is not pain, but beyond pain, which reaches as far as the feeling of existing. Hence the shifting conflictual game of an ever unstable equilibrium between the principles of psychical functioning.

2 Affect and structure

The pleasure–unpleasure principle, by virtue of the very fact that it is a principle and not the reflection of a range of states, plays the role of an organizer in psychical life. Its intermediary situation must be stressed. It is the heir of the Nirvana principle, which leads the subject to aspire to the total abolition of tensions, their reduction to the zero level, that is, to total affective silence. The pleasure principle must be content with the reduction of tensions (above all of unpleasure) to the lowest possible level. In earlier works, I have given examples of the operation of the Nirvana principle in certain clinical narcissistic structures. But the action of the pleasure–unpleasure principle is a double one. Although it aims to escape unpleasure, it also aims at obtaining pleasure. With this view in mind, it orients the course of the psychical processes towards the search for pleasure and its preservation. When it is oriented towards crude pleasure, as Freud shows, it is at the service of the death drive, the total exhaustion of Eros in discharge, leaving the field free to the death drives. But insofar as the role of the pleasure principle is also the preservation of pleasure, another principle, its heir, the reality principle, must assist it in this aim.

This brings us to the genetic aspect of the question: must one necessarily think that the reality principle succeeds the pleasure principle, or can one not maintain that the two co-exist from the beginning? This was the solution proposed by Laplanche and Pontalis, who seem to consider that a distinction must operate between the drives of self-preservation, which are sensitive from the outset to the reality principle by virtue of their hereditary equipment, and the sexual drives, which are inaccessible to the reality principle and which are governed solely by the pleasure principle. In that case, there would be no real transfer of sovereignty from the pleasure principle to the reality principle, but conflictual co-existence from the outset. How, then, is one to account for the transition from the first constellation of pleasure to its later forms? According to Laplanche and Pontalis, it is made possible by the accession to the Oedipus complex and to the identifications that govern access to reality. It is no longer a question of external reality, whose field is structured according to its own ways, but of psychical reality, which deals with desire and the unconscious.

Of course, the notions of reality and pleasure are not simple in Freud's work. An analysis of the texts shows us how Freud distinguishes between an original 'reality-ego', whose function is to distinguish between the internal and external origins of excitation, an original 'pleasure-ego', which introjects all that is good and rejects outside itself all that is bad, and, lastly, a definitive reality-ego, which acts according to the reality test, aiming at finding once again in the external world the real object, the one that corresponds to the originally satisfying object.

The aim of this parenthesis is to remind us of the difficulties of too simple a genetic conception, by which the reality principle derives from the pleasure principle. In my opinion, the solution is not to opt either for the genetic or the structural conception, but to accept their double hypothesis. What, at the level of the Freudian work, may seem to be a contradiction may, in the end, be a fruitful ambiguity in the polysemia of psychoanalytic theory.

As far as the question of the affect is concerned, what matters is, once again, the quantitative–qualitative complex that it forms. We should stress here that although the genesis of the affect is dependent on the presence or absence of an external perception, and although the course of its development entails an internal corporal discharge, as well as an external motor movement, the order of the affect is that of psychical reality. Just as it is necessary to draw a distinction between the order of desire and the order of need, the first deriving from psychical reality, the second from physiological reality, a similar distinction must be made in which the affect is assigned its psychical place. This place, for anyone dealing with the psychoanalytic conception, cannot be situated in the body, still less in the outside world. The affect is an integral part of the drives governed by the pleasure–unpleasure principle.

This dual organization of the pleasure–unpleasure principle is so strong that one of these terms is inconceivable without the other. There is no pleasure, however full, however complete, that does not have in its shadow possible unpleasure. There is no unpleasure, however desperate, that does not leave a glimpse of the search for pleasure. The principal dichotomy is articulated with other dichotomies, good and bad, pleasure and pain, love and hate. On these dichotomies are articulated others, inside and outside, internal world and external world, psychical reality and reality itself.

All that we know of the pleasure–unpleasure principle is learned through the formations of the unconscious. Whether symptom, dream, parapraxis, slip or forgetting, each reveals a complex made up of representations and affects. But none of them shows this more clearly than phantasy. Psychoanalytic practice has taught us to look in the analysand's speech for the phantasy that is consubstantial with it. The conscious phantasy is itself an element of that discourse inviting the search for the unconscious phantasy that it masks. The discovery of this unconscious phantasy is carried out on the basis of the process of joining that links the elements together: word-presentation, thing-presentation, affect, bodily states, act. When discourse suspends representations, it is continued by an affect that signals the existence of a veritable gap in the succession of representations. *The affect appears to be taking the place of representation. The process of concatenation is a chaining up of cathexes in which the affect has an ambiguous structure. Insofar as it appears as an element of discourse, it is subjected to that chain, includes itself in it as it attaches itself to the other elements of discourse. But insofar as it breaks with representations, it is the element of discourse that refuses to let itself be linked by representation and arises in its place. When reaching a certain quantity of cathexis, a qualitative mutation occurs; the affect may then snap the chain of discourse, which then sinks into non-discursivity, the unsayable. The affect is then identified with the torrential cathexis that breaks down the dikes of repression, submerges the abilities of binding and self-control. It becomes a deaf and blind passion, but ruinous for the psychical organization. The affect of pure violence acts out this violence by reducing the ego to powerlessness, forcing it to cede to its force, subjugating it by the fascination of its power. The affect is caught between its chaining up in discourse and the breaking of the chain, which gives back to the id its original power.*

These strained forces that have been freed may turn either to the object or to the ego; place themselves at the service either of Eros or of the destructive drives. The whole range of clinical structures illustrates the states of passion that correspond to them: Eros of the ego in triumphant megalomania, negating the object and death; suicide, which destroys the object in the ego and the ego that is confused with it; the passionate desire for amorous possession of an object conceived as alone desirable, to the detriment of the most elementary self-preservation; implacable hate of the object aimed at its absolute mastery and destruction, etc. Psychoanalytic clinical practice will show us behind each of its positions its inverted double:

negation of the ego's powerlessness, of the hateful ambivalence of love, of the narcissistic cathexis of the object, of the love that lies concealed in its folds, etc. But, in the final analysis, it is the result that shows which side of the scales is tilting.

An echo of these infernal powers of the id reaches consciousness in the form of affect. It is understood that the role of the ego and of the defence mechanisms is the chaining up of the affects, which means not their neutralization, but their subjection to an organization. The primary process is a primary organization, perhaps even what might be conceived as the organization of the id; the secondary process is a secondary organization, the organization of the ego.

Let those who fear that such a conception may lead us to some apology for the reason that corresponds to a denunciation of the passions be reassured. The powers of the id, as is known from experience, are the most untameable; they remain, as the course of things shows, the first powers. The transformation of the Erinnyes into Eumenides is a legendary projection. The rights of the city triumph over blood, but within the city lethal forces will reappear that will tear it to pieces. The city, and the human world with it, may perish from their conflicts. The only hope, as Freud expressed it at the end of his work, is the triumph of Logos and Ananke over Eros and the destructive drives. That is to say, in the final analysis, a mutation of Eros. Where the id was, the ego must be. The meaning of this proposition ought to be that Eros can triumph over the death drives only if Eros becomes the Eros of Logos and if Logos becomes the Logos of Eros.

When it penetrates the conscious field, when its blossoming has not been stifled at birth by repression, the affect breaks the screen of consciousness. It embraces the ego in pleasure as in pain, and sometimes leaves no room for any other psychical activity, so much does it infiltrate the domain that it has managed to take over. In this subversion of the ego, the subject appears as other. He no longer recognizes himself in the state that is invading him. Even in the pleasant affects that a feeling of 'being oneself at last' may give him, this feeling assumes its full value only to show the difference between the self of the happy moment and the Other – a break marking the difference between the extraordinary and the ordinary. *The affect is the epiphany of the Other for the subject.* The double emerges from the shadows and takes the place of the ego, an ego that dilates and extends to the surrounding world or contracts into the retreat of its own dereliction. The old background of childhood is reborn, the old man comes back to life, the successes or failures of the intellect appear derisory before this constricting presence of the Other. The terrain conquered by the affect, whether it is accompanied by a state of pleasure or pain, drives the threatened subject to the brink. The subject may be damaged in this affective irruption, whether of pleasure or unpleasure. Beyond certain limits, the affect becomes a power of loss, even in elation, orgasm, triumph.

The whole of our individual evolution, our morality, the mountain of censorship that has made us what we have become, has constantly valorized control of our affects. Although certain extreme affects have remained lawful – the pain of mourning a loved object, joy at the satisfactions that come from the love of the object – everything reminds us that we tolerate these affects only when they are harnessed to the superego. What does one ask of the psychoanalyst, if not control of one's affects? Paradoxically, one will also ask for empathy. But what kind of empathy can be the one that wisely knows how to confine itself to its own observation, when it has to question oneself on the experience that it entails? In the final analysis, this affective control is only control of the id and the drives, control of our wild, passionate childhood.

So am I advocating, like some contemporary prophets, a return to innocence, providing innocence is that 'spontaneity' endowed with all the creative virtues? Is one recommending a plunge into the fountain of everlasting youth, which will give us back our first nature? I shall see that quest as merely one more illusion in which the oppressed consciousness is fooled. The sleep of reason engenders monsters, said Goya. Thus resurgent Eros will not be, whatever may be said about it, a chubby cherub, and his arrows, if they are to reach their target, will be tipped with virulent poison. And, in any case, this is to ignore Thanatos, Thanatos the invisible, the innumerable. There is no need to exorcize phantasies and await the day of liberation. That dawn will never come. For, although the unconscious is timeless, the primary affects (despite the faces of madness) are irremediably lost with the objects of our childhood. Only disappointment at their loss tirelessly revives, a disillusion for which one will endlessly seek consolation.

The human condition is affective alienation because it tirelessly reconstitutes that forgetting, and the recollection of the animal that man has been does not cease to be and can no longer be forever, at one and the same time, Logos and Ananke. Affective alienation is the price of their advent. That debt will never be paid back to us.

And yet is not the aim of a psychoanalysis to give back to the person submitting himself or herself to it the greatest recoverable part of its lost affective wealth? To put Logos to this service of that aim and to urge Ananke to be resigned to the fact that *everything* cannot be reconquered by this quest is one of the paradoxes of this impossible profession.

The dyad formed by Logos and Ananke derives from Eros and Thanatos. Logos, like Eros, is a power of life, of binding, Thanatos and Ananke a power of separation. The contradiction is impassable. Only compromise is possible: compromise between acceptance of life and acceptance of death, acceptance of orgasm and acceptance of castration. The recognition of the vagina as the destination of sexuality is a recognition of origin and end. For the mother is, as Freud says, generatrix, companion and destroyer, or, again, the mother herself, the beloved and the earth mother, towards whom 'the silent goddess Death' carries us in her arms. For whatever the hour may be when we shall rejoin her, it does not belong to us to fix it. It belongs to us only to be mature. Ripeness is all. Freud loved to quote those words from the greatest Shakespeare, that of *King Lear*, which Freud is a little for us.

II A hypothetical theoretical model: the process. Locus of affect

The aim of this work is not to close a debate, but to open up perspectives. From the outset I was aware of the fact that the problem of affect, through its very specificity, was leading us to the most general problems of psycho-analytic theory, practice and technique. At an early stage I formed the project of a work on models in psychoanalysis. I then became all too aware that my thinking had not advanced enough to bring such a vast undertaking to a conclusion and decided to limit myself to the problem of affect. Now, near the end of my work, it has occurred to me that I should attempt a hypothetical theoretical model. Time alone will tell whether it measures up to the promises that I have claimed for it.

Contemporary psychoanalytic thought is concerned to find a theoretical base for the acquisitions of post-Freudian psychoanalysis by constructing theoretical models. Here and there various authors have proposed sketches or examples of such models (one thinks of Guttmann, Klauber, Arlow and Brenner, Wisdom, Sandler and Joffe, Zetzel, Moser, Zeppelin and Schneider, Bion). The extreme diversity of the axes of reference and doubts as to the legitimacy of their use would not allow me to examine them without also examining those doubts, and this would take me well beyond the bounds of this book. But the indicative value of this movement of thought seems to me to be too important not to mention it. A 'new tendency' is emerging, whose traces are still discreet, around the question of meaning in psychoanalysis (see Rosen 1969b and Wolheim 1969).

Discussion has an important place in my work. I have given it that place because I believe that it is from the encounter between a clash of views and the spark that is generated by *praxis* that new ideas, those right 'conceptions' of which Freud speaks in the quotation that I have placed as an epigraph to this book, are born.

My interlocutors in the discussion have been above all Hartmann, Melanie Klein and Lacan. I have rejected Hartmann's system, for it really is a system and not a limited theoretical contribution, that is to say, a reformulation of Freudian theory. If I were trying to explain the reasons for this rejection, over and above the examination of detail in the problem of affect, they would no doubt be sought outside psychoanalysis, in the effect, in the United States, of the interrelations between psychoanalysis and the behavioural sciences. In the preface to *Language and Mind*, Chomsky writes:

> Modern linguistics shares the delusion – the accurate term, I believe – that the modern 'behavioural sciences' have in some essential respect achieved a transition from 'speculation' to 'science' and that earlier work can be safely consigned to the antiquarians. Obviously any rational person will favour rigorous analysis and careful experiment; but to a considerable degree, I feel, the 'behavioural sciences' are merely mimicking the surface features of the natural sciences; much of their scientific character has been achieved by a restriction of subject matter and a concentration on rather peripheral issues. Such a narrowing of focus can be justified if it leads to achievements of real intellectual significance, but in this case, I think it would be very difficult to show that the narrowing of scope has led to deep and significant results.[6]

I believe that these remarks apply, in the case of psychoanalysis, to the result of the interrelation between the behavioural sciences and a fraction of North American psychoanalysis, of which ego psychology is the fruit. This feeling is fairly widely shared in France, even though one may recognize the interest of the contributions made by many North American authors who seem unable to dispense, in the most favourable cases, with paying lip service to Hartmann's thought.

This leaves the work of Melanie Klein and Lacan – work that may no doubt be criticized, each in its own way and for diametrically opposite reasons, but work that stimulates reflection, even to the point of excess, with the result that they arouse excessive reactions in the opposite direction. It would be casuistical to defend the fecundity of Melanie Klein's work – it has no need of such a defence. Because I belong to a particular tradition of thought, Lacan's work spoke to me, and no doubt not only because of that. I have tried to evaluate the significance of that work and the influences that it has had on those who have learned from it (and it is by no means sure that Lacan's pupils are those who have best testified to its interest), by refraining from any other consideration. I have taken as a postulate that if that work were based on a practice of psychoanalysis that seems to me to be incompatible with the fundamental requirements of its exercise, that work

6 Chomsky (1972), p. xi.

would bear the mark of it. It is from this point of view of critical openness that I have approached it, without claiming to have exhausted its resources, but trying to define what is essential in it and comparing it with what is essential in Freudian thought and with the contributions of, in my view, his most interesting successors. One has seen how this work, when dealing with the problem of the affect, reaches what I think is its limit.

In the final analysis, my delay in confronting the question of models has been of service. Not only because the problem of the affect, which is more circumscribed, solicited an urgent response, but because a problem of method was revealed to me in all its heuristic implication. In confronting the problem of affect, what I had in mind was to reveal the effects of an exclusion in a theoretical system. For me, it was not a question of finding a place for it in this system, but of exploring the resources of that exclusion in order to propose a different solution. For me, it is not a question, then, of complementing or reshaping the Lacanian model, but of offering an alternative to it. Let us see how.

Let us begin with the most general model of Lacanian thought (schema L):[7]

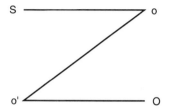

The condition of the subject, says Lacan, depends on what is being unfolded in the Other. 'What is being unfolded there is articulated like a discourse (the unconscious is the discourse of the Other.)' The justification of this graph, clearly drawn by J.-A. Miller, derives from the fact that this relation to the discourse of the Other is mediated through the relation of the ego to its imaginary projection (*o–o'*). Mediated means that such a relation is the necessary condition of that accession of the subject to his symbolic structure, both as means and as obstacle. It is here that the function of reduplication takes its place: the position of the *oo'* relation is coupled on the *o* side (the object of imaginary projection) by that of the subject S and on the *o'* side (the mirror image), by that of O. These last two terms are not posited *in praesentia*, but on the contrary *in absentia*: the first as the undoing of the subject in the signifying chain, the second as key of the system (locus of truth, or rather of the signifying system).

7 Lacan (1977), p. 193.

Let us note that in this schema neither the third term of the symbolic/imaginary/real triad, nor retrospective effects are featured. The Real will find its place in the modified schema of the quadrangle called schema R introduced in Lacan's article on psychosis,[8] and undoing in the seminar on 'The Purloined Letter' with which the *Ecrits* opens.[9]

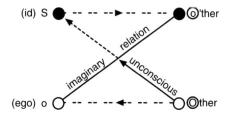

Lacan's conception, on the author's own admission, rests fundamentally on the postulate that tends to install narcissism at the centre of his reading of Freud.[10] Indeed, it is significant that the place of the real in schema R is superimposed on the line of the imaginary relation, the relation that constitutes the very limit of the field beyond which the symbolic operates.

Faced with this conception, which gives narcissism that regal function, the work of Melanie Klein, among others, is characterized by the fact, as I have pointed out on a number of occasions, that narcissism is, in its specificity, remarkably absent, to the advantage of the object relation. Following the Lacanian graph, one might transcribe Melanie Klein's theory in two successive graphs, the first designating the schizoparanoid position, the second the central depressive position, thus:

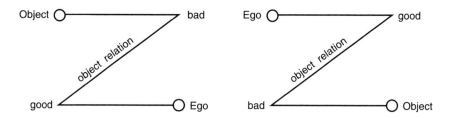

8   Lacan (1977), p. 197. See my commentary (1966a).
9   Lacan (1966), p. 53. We should note that in the second schema the positions of *o* and *o'* are reversed, without explanation.
10 'The specular relation to the other, by which, in fact, I originally wanted to give back its dominant position in the function of the ego to the theory, crucial in Freud, of narcissism, cannot actually subordinate the whole phantasizing revealed in analytic experience only by interposing itself, as the schema shows, between a place this side of the Subject and that beyond the Other, where speech inserts itself, as the existences that merge into speech are entirely at the mercy of its faith' (Lacan 1966, pp. 53–4).

For the convenience of our discussion, I am no doubt forcing the facts a little far in this transcription. Perhaps I should simply say that I am trying to emphasize the structuring role of the good–bad dyad in the two phases. But whereas the first has the aim of reaching the constitution of the ego through the object, in the two tensions of the life and death instincts, the second aims to preserve the object threatened by the same tensions at the level of the ego, for the pursuit of their mutually structuring effects.

In my discussion of the problem of the affect, I have developed at some length the arguments that seemed to me to justify my interest in the theoretical systems of Lacan and Melanie Klein, and my reservations about them. In the introduction to this book I also declared that I would be guided by a critical reading of Freud's work by his successors *and* of Freud's successors by an interpretation of his work.

What I am proposing now is neither a combination of the two systems examined, nor a synthesis, still less an attempt to go beyond them. It will be rather an expression of the meaning that I give to the *return to Freud*, which for me does not mean stagnating in Freud's thought, but *aufhebung* (preserving while going beyond). What I shall attempt will be nourished not only by those two master oeuvres, but also by the dialogue that they have sustained with their contradictors. In the case of Melanie Klein, I am thinking of the critiques of Glover, Winnicott and, in France, those of Pasche and Renard, Lebovici and Diatkine, Torok and Abraham, Laplanche and Pontalis. As for Lacan's thought, some criticisms were devoted to it in psychoanalytic works some years ago: among them, one might mention those of Stein, Lebovici and Diatkine, Pasche, David, Marthe Robert, de M'Uzan, Viderman, Anzieu, Laplanche and Pontalis, as well as my own.[11] However, I shall keep the general structure of Lacan's schema L. What seems to me to be important in that structure is, on the one hand, the role of the *detour*,[12] and, on the other, the fundamental position accorded to conflict (mediation conceived as means and as obstacle). I also posit that conflict can be apprehended only through detour and reduplication, the conditions by which it is manifested. Furthermore, I shall give that schema its economic and dynamic connotations, in the exercise of the function of oscillation.

---

11 To these should be added the contribution of certain recent readings of Freud, no doubt more or less stimulated by Lacan's work, which have had the merit, not only of drawing psychoanalysts' attention to points that have been ignored in Freudian theory, but also of nourishing our critical reflection on Lacan's thought.

12 I am using 'detour' here in its most general sense. In the context of analytic theory, I prefer it to 'difference', since it implies the notion of return.

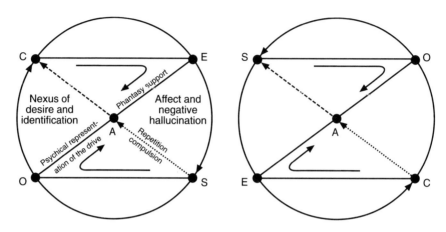

Schema of the process

This schema brings together four terms – *conjuncture, event, object, structure* – connected by a circuit. What matters above all is their articulation, which, as well as the four terms themselves, I shall now try to justify.

By *conjuncture*, I mean a certain constellation, whatever its origin or nature, as it appears at a particular time. The conjuncture is that pre-articulated set of circumstances that elude the subject's grasp, insofar as the subject cannot display his structure in it, but also in so far as it will put his structure to the test. The conjuncture is that by which the structure is manifested, though it cannot leave its mark on the structure. It is a condition of the revelation of structure. Structure does not pre-exist it, nor is it engendered by it. It is the precondition of the manifestation of structure. Conversely, structure cannot be expressed otherwise or elsewhere than in the context of the conjuncture. This context is profoundly multiform – effect of the constitution of the subject (in the naturalist sense of that term), circumstances of his conception and birth, his parents' desires for him, the biological and social situations in which he finds himself – insofar as the conjuncture belongs to a causality that marks his subjectivety. None of this eludes topological location. That locus is that of the psychical apparatus in which the conjuncture is inscribed, but in so far as the structure does not inform it and is not formed by it. For this to occur, the mediation of the event and the object will be required.

By *event*, I mean that which stands out from the conjuncture, the moment when space becomes circumscribed, opaque or suddenly lights up, when time becomes concentrated, intensified, whether it becomes frozen or rushes on. It is what in English is called 'experience', and which is untranslatable, for it is not what we mean in French either by *expérience* or by *vécu*.[13]

The same profound disparity as I indicated in conjuncture is also to be found here. The external world has no monopoly of events, any more than what is experienced must necessarily be situated in the internal world. What matters is the break in the tissue of the conjuncture from which the event emerges. In this category may be subsumed the experience of lack, of object loss, of the revelation of seduction, of castration, of the primal scene, which drive the subject to fabricate phantasies or memories, from the moment when the project becomes crystallized, from the discovery of the game (*fort-da*) from auto-eroticism, from aesthetic 'seizure',[14] from the 'symptomatic attack', from the moment of awareness, etc. Freud's hesitation between the theory of trauma and the theory of phantasy may be superseded by this reference to the event, understood in its most general sense.[15] Of course, what is found here again is the contradiction between conjuncture and structure in the situation of the event; in the structure, the event is not intelligible. But, on the other hand, the structure does not contain the event; the event emerges from the conjuncture and introduces into the structure an obligation to reshape it; the structure will, at one and the same time, have to feed on the event and get a grip on it, which it can do only by absorbing it or by profoundly transforming itself; it is at this point that the object intervenes.

By *object*, I mean the effect of the encounter with the event that emerges from the conjuncture and the structure. The imprecision of the term object in psychoanalysis is no doubt what lies at the centre of the discussions that this concept raises. Freud, Melanie Klein, Winnicott, Hartmann, Bouvet and Lacan give it different interpretations. In 'Constructions in analysis', at the end of his life (1937), Freud writes: 'Psychical objects are incomparably more complicated than the excavator's material ones and we have insufficient knowledge of what we may expect to find, since their finer structure contains so much that is still mysterious'.[16] From the beginning of his work,

---

13 See Deleuze (1969), pp. 175–80: 'The event is not that which happens (accident), but that which is most purely expressed in what happens, that which makes sign to us and is expecting us: it is meaning . . . The brilliance, the splendour of the event is meaning'. But it is also to say that meaning is manifested through the mediation of brilliance and splendour.

14 To use Moebius' term, quoted by de M'Uzan.

15 Let me quote Deleuze (1969) once more. He speaks of that 'jumping on the spot of the whole body, which exchanges its organic will for a spiritual will, which now wants, not exactly what happens, but something *in* what happens, something that conforms to what is to come'. I remark elsewhere that in the analysis of 'something that happens' the stress should have been laid on the *happening* of something, rather than on this something itself (see 1967b).

16 *S.E.*, XXIII, p. 260.

Freud conceived the object as divided into a constant fraction and a variable fraction. Later, the shattered object appeared in all its many metamorphoses or co-existing expressions: object of the drive, part object, object of the external world, split object of fetishism and, lastly, object in relation to historical and material truth. This plurality of contexts in which the object appears is, for me, less a conceptual limitation than a fruitful source of reflection. Modern psychoanalytic practice has tried to base this multiplicity in the context of the object relation. Lacan spoke quite rightly of the object as *cause* of desire, at the same time the condition of its appearance, its raison d'être and its finality; its how and its why. For my part, I have defended the idea of the existence of the part-object and the total object. By total object I did not designate the object of totalization, the locus of a unity, but everything belonging to the object that is not accounted for by the relation to the part-object. I situated the various functions of the part-object, a product of the drives that finds expression in organ pleasure and the function of the total object, which can be reached only by the aim-inhibited drives, situating the contradiction in the conception of the drive itself (1967c). But in modern psychoanalytic theory and practice the status of the object is much more extensive. It is apprehended in its relation to the ego. The ambiguity that affects this term (part of the psychical apparatus and expression of individuality and singularity) usually makes it necessary either to introduce an additional concept (the self), or to transfer to the object certain properties belonging to the subject.[17] In the second are to be found both the fundamental idea that the constitution or construction of the subject depend in man, owing to his prematurity, on objects to which he owes his life, and the modern notion by which the object is that which divides up and limits a field in the very operation of division that isolates both field and object.

I should like to stress two features that properly belong to the object in the psychoanalytic conception. The first property of the object is to be constituted by desire and/or identification. It is the locus of both being and having, says Freud: 'Children like expressing an object-relation by an identification: "I am of the object." Having is the later of the two; after loss of the object it relapses into "being". Example: the breast. "The breast is a part of me, I am the breast." Only later: "I have it" – that is, "I am not it"'.[18] The relation of succession mentioned by Freud is less important, it seems to

---

17 It is clear that the opposition between internal object and object in the external world is very approximate. Thus Winnicott insists throughout his works on the relation between internal object and internalized object coming from the environment, the latter itself being distinct from the external object.
18 Posthumous note 12 July 1938, *S.E.*, XXIII, p. 299.

me, than the conjunction of both effects in the object – witness Freud's contradictory statements on identification, both appropriation and substitution of the loss of the object or its lack. The untying of that knot into its constitutive threads will occur at the stage of the Oedipus complex. I shall postulate that this untying presupposes the double possibility of both terms of the alternative. This is certainly how one must understand primary identification, the role that is played in it by incorporation of the object and the importance given to projective identification by the Kleinian authors.

In his works on female sexuality, Ernest Jones posited, as a solution to the female Oedipal complex, a double outcome: renunciation either of desire or of the object. Lacan's stress on the object as cause of desire and the fortune of the notion of object relation have led me to conclude that in the context of psychoanalytic theory the *cause* of the object or the *relations* forged between it and the psychical structure might well suggest that it is as if *desire* (*or the object relation*) *becomes as object.* Not only desire of desire, but untying of the object of desire and desire as object: desire as mode of transformations that affect not only the object or objects, but 'produce' the object *qua* object. At this point, I cannot say very much about this last feature, but I shall return to it elsewhere. It is clear that this work of transformation belongs to the combined effects of event and structure.[19]

By *structure*, finally, I mean that which belongs to the most general concept in psychoanalysis: the Oedipal structure. It is by means of the Oedipal structure that one arrives at the definition of the subject in psychoanalysis as constituted by his relation to his parents in the double difference of difference between the sexes and difference between the generations, organized by the primal phantasies. The structure is understood only in the forms taken by the Oedipus complex in human productions, cultural and natural, institutional or individual. The peculiarity of the structure is that it can never be apprehended as such, but only by its effects; it is, as has been said, an *absent cause.* In psychoanalytic theory, it is by means of the psychical apparatus that its effects are evaluated. But although I have also defined the conjuncture by its effects on the psychical apparatus, as such, I said, it bears no mark of the structure, whereas the structure revealed by the conjuncture – which is its condition of possibility – refers us back to the psychical apparatus insofar as it is the 'locus' by which it becomes 'visible'. In this way, I hope, my reference to clinical structures as forms of the Oedipal conflict

---

19 The object–event relation is a complex one of course. In no case must it be thought of as a stimulus–response dyad. For if the event reaches the object, and even forces the object to influence its structure and expose itself to the test of the conjuncture, in other circumstances the object calls to the event, solicits it, summons it and changes the conjuncture.

will be more easily understood. Similarly, in the field of psychoanalytic practice, I shall contrast the analytic situation as conjuncture and the transference as structure.

Affect, then, is situated on this model at a point that constitutes for me the pivot of the system. It is at the place of an encounter between the effects of the tensions aroused by the object and the event. It is not only the limit of their effects, but, at one and the same time, a zone of interpenetration and a point of turning back. Whatever happens, at the level of these effects, the affect is a time of revelation that makes it a central reference in the psychoanalytic field. On the side of the event, what emerges to constitute the affect is the support of the phantasy; apprehension of the phantasy, that is to say, a power of fear and anticipation, a place where desire is betrayed, a time when it is unmasked and distorted. On the side of the object, what goes ahead of the affect is the psychical representation of the drive, that by which the drive is knowable – psychical representative of the drive, not ideational representative. The point at which the vectors amass their effects is the affect, as force (*quantum*) and as subjective experience. As force, the affect is what sustains that linkage of the ideational representatives, what relaunches their associations, what provides the energy necessary to the operations of the psychical apparatus. But Freud also says that this energy resides *between* the cathexes. The affect, then, has this conjunctive–disjunctive role, a function of 'penetration of the signifier'. When, under the effect of the tensions of which I have just spoken, the affect is discovered in its manifestations – its subjective epiphany – its peculiarity is *to recover, abolish, replace representation. Its most striking effect is negative hallucination.*

Over the last few years, I have often stressed the structural importance of this concept. Perhaps I should make it clear that negative hallucination is not a univocal negative concept referring to an experience of lack or deficit. Negative hallucination is not the absence of representation, but *representation of the absence of representation* – though the sense of the term representation here is not that of 'second best', since it entails a distancing of the subject, who is, by definition, absent. It is much more a condition of possibility of representation than representation itself. Negative hallucination is the reverse side of which the hallucinatory realization of desire is the obverse.

In March 1919, Freud finished 'A child is being beaten', began *Beyond the Pleasure Principle*, which he finished in May of the same year, and then (or at the same time?) went back to an old manuscript that he had taken out of his drawer, 'The "Uncanny"', which he may well have been thinking about as early as 1913.

Thus those three works are closely related. It is worth noting that in 'A child is being beaten' the whole dialectic of the phantasy centres around a play of permutations between representations of scenes and affects that are attached to them, as is clear in the grammaticality of language – 'a child is being beaten' – whereas 'The "Uncanny"' frames the representation by the reflection on semantics and pure affect. An alliance is being forged here between pure affect and phantasy: 'There are many more means of creating uncanny effects in fiction than there are in real life'.[20] The detour of the phantasy certainly seems to be the condition of this production of affect here. But beyond or short of fiction, the unconscious phantasy is itself that detour. In the same text, Freud relates how he experienced that affect of disturbing strangeness in the prostitutes' district of an Italian provincial town: having beaten a hasty retreat, he found himself coming back to it twice, involuntarily, by a new *detour*. What does this mean if not that the representation is no more than the avatar of the projection of the eye as look and of the look as eye that looks at it: object of desire as object. In the final analysis, the uncanny is 'the entrance to the former *Heim* [home] of all human beings, to the place where each one of us lived once upon a time and in the beginning'.[21] That is why I have placed on the side of the object not the ideational representative of the drive, but *the psychical representative of the drive*, without distinguishing between its constitutive elements. Nowhere has Freud better articulated the themes of fragmentation and castration in the concept of dismemberment. Now this articulation passes through the retroactive effect of the *repetition compulsion*.[22] For the structure is not a fixed, unchangeable, predetermined whole. But its possibilities of movement are limited by the maintenance at its heart of the fundamental articulations in which a certain play is permitted that finds its limits in the preservation of the fundamental organizing constituents of the Oedipal structure: the primal phantasies.

The role of the line that joins object and event is now clearer: it is a factor both of conjunction and disjunction between its structure and conjuncture, subjected to the impact of the repetition compulsion, in which that compulsion meets a limit that may either contain it or give in to it – a barrier between the mother's body and the individual's body, between the id and the ego, between the organic expression of the drives and their psychical representations, but also a barrier of language and the law.

Thus constituted, this model will pivot around its axis in an alternating oscillation. Through the event, the conjuncture will force the structure to become manifest. Through the object, the structure will act on the conjuncture. To that outward movement will correspond a return. Through the

---

20 *S.E.*, XVII, p. 249.
21 *S.E.*, XVII, p. 245.
22 I have considered elsewhere the relation between the phenomenon of the double and repetition compulsion (1970). I would simply note that the first mention of it occurs in 'The "Uncanny"'.

object, the conjuncture will dislodge the structure and take its place, modified by the preceding stage. Crossing the event, the structure will find its
original place.

This oscillation round its axis shows us the importance of the value of 'the
return' (or 'turning round') in psychoanalysis. Here, as so often, the plurality of the semantic contexts shows us that the term is applied to the most
primitive operations of the psychical apparatus,[23] as also to the most polished
expressions of the unconscious.[24]

Now, in psychoanalytic theory and experience, the affect is the privileged
place of the return: turning round against oneself and turning into its opposite in the duality of the pleasure–unpleasure principle.[25] *On the basis of the
structure, as combining a source, a thrust, an aim, an object, and of the double return
(reversal into its opposite and turning round upon the subject's own self), I shall propose a theoretical model of the psychoanalytic field in which the subject is defined as
process.* Process (*procès*) is to be understood both in the sense of movement,
development, progress, and in the (legal) sense of an outcome to a conflict
as decided by a judgement after due examination of it. I prefer this term to
that of psychoanalytic process (*processus*), which renders only one of the two
senses, omitting the other. Its application is not restricted, in my view, to the
theorization of the analytic field, but also to one's experience through the
analytic situation and the transference.

If I have given this place to the affect, it is indeed because psychoanalytic
experience teaches us that, although it is the absence of [*Jouissance*] 'that
makes the universe vain' (Lacan),[26] it is through suffering that the truth of
the subject is attained. Freudian pessimism? Twenty-five centuries before

---

23 I have explained elsewhere (1967c) the metapsychological significance of the double
reversal.

24 It is by the message that 'the subject is constituted, which means that it is from the Other
that the subject receives even the message that he emits' (Lacan 1977, p. 305). It is in the
inverted form of this 'sending back' that the unconscious is marked. The article in which
this quotation appears, 'Subversion of the subject and dialectic of desire', seems to me to
be Lacan's most important one. I commented upon it in Piera Aulagnier's Saint-Anne
seminar of 29 April 1968.

25 'What a queer thing it is, my friends, this sensation which is popularly called pleasure!
It is remarkable how closely it is connected with its apparent opposite, pain. They will
never come to a man both at once, but if you pursue one of them and catch it, you are
virtually compelled always to have the other as well; they are like two bodies attached to
the same head. I am sure that if Aesop had thought of it he really would have made up
a fable about them, something like this: God wanted to stop their continual quarrelling,
and when he found that it was impossible, he fastened their heads together; so wherever
one of them appears, the other is sure to follow after'. Socrates' last words to his friends
on the day of his death. Plato, *Phaedo*, in *The Last Days of Socrates*, trans. Hugh
Tredennick and Harold Tarrant, London: Penguin Press, 1993, p. 112.

26 Lacan (1977), p. 317.

Freud, Aeschylus accepted the popular Greek wisdom that says 'one has to suffer to understand'. That does not mean that one should suffer for the sake of it, or seek out suffering with the aim of understanding it, but that however much one may wish that it were otherwise, one knows from experience that suffering is the main spur that drives one to understand – and also that the best use that one can make of suffering is to understand. To understand in order to understand, to change oneself or to change the world.

Analysis is not a culture of suffering, but a process that aims at control of the affects of suffering by 'detachment' from the drives that are its cause, that two-headed body of pleasure and unpleasure.

Detachment can only be achieved at the cost of painful feelings of loneliness and abandonment experienced by the primitive animal mental inheritance from which detachment is effected and by the aspects of the personality that succeed in detaching themselves from the object of scrutiny which is felt to be indistinguishable from the source of its viability. The apparently abandoned object of scrutiny is the primitive mind and the primitive social capacity of the individual as a political or group animal. The 'detached' personality is in a sense new to its job and has to turn to tasks which differ from those to which its components are more usually adapted, namely its scrutiny of the environment excluding the self; part of the price paid is in feelings of insecurity.[27]

Suffering divides us, it activates everything that is already divided in us, but it also urges one to gather oneself together, in order to find the temporarily reconstructed unity that accompanies the emergence from suffering. But division remains.[28]

Thus psychoanalytic theory considers conflict as unavoidable, but aims at making its inevitability fruitful. From fragmentation one is sent to castration.

That primal fragmentation, in which the matrix of a split unity is already prefigured, is not only fragmentation of the parts; it is dispersal of matter, *diasparagmos*. It is the place that I wanted to give to heterogeneity. Each of the terms in my schema of the process refers back to it: the mobile variability of the various contexts of the conjuncture, the many faces of the event, the fragmented status of the object, the difference of the various

27 Bion (1963), p. 16.
28 Laplanche (1968) has brought out the close relations that link the masochistic pleasure derived from the postponement of satisfaction, and the ordeal of increased tension that this entails to the effectiveness of the reality principle. It is significant that Bion (1963) has added to the two great Freudian and Kleinian points of reference – love and hate – a third, on the same level as the others, knowledge.

elements that make up the psychical apparatus. Out of that varied universe a world has to be made. Heterogeneity and dispersal are so many elements of stimulation and distraction. They force meaning to work – and discourage it. And also, when the horizons seem blocked on every side, they are an invitation to the possible, that which, from the point of view of structure, is its invisible necessity.

III The economic and the symbolic: force and meaning

The thought that has guided me is the indissoluble interdependence of force and meaning.[29] Force cannot but be conceived as an oriented vector, endowed with a direction, therefore a meaning. Meaning is inseparable from an aim towards which it is directed and moved by internal violence, therefore by a force.

Analysis constantly compels us to forge this conjunction of force and meaning, but also to separate them. I distinguished between them in the categories of the economic and the symbolic. To the category of the economic, I attached 'moving quantity', the motive force of distributions, exchanges, transformations. To the category of the symbolic, I attached representation, nourished by the vital forces of the instinctual body, which entails language and thought. This transition is possible only if one supposes that the drive, even in its most elementary forms, possesses an organization whose principles of psychical function govern the various forms it takes. Conversely, although the economic transforms forces, it also elaborates values. By value, I certainly do not mean an individual's superior qualities, but what for him or her has value: avoidance of unpleasure, the search for pleasure, above all, but also control of the affects. Analysing Michelangelo's *Moses*, Freud concluded that the artist's aim in representing the character's extraordinary musculature, the evidence of his exceptional strength, was to suggest the

---

29 After the publication of my report, I came across the following passage by Viderman. It comes from a chapter devoted to the transference, 'Sens et force', in his book *La construction de l'espace analytique* (Paris: Denoël, 1970): 'There is no meaning in the analyst's discourse that is not borne by a force that is that of the economy of the affect; there is no interpretation that has any impact that is not itself borne by the affect that gives it its own force of impact, which means that the interpretation is never of the order of pure meaning . . . Meaning and force form a dyad linked by a relationship of objective uncertainty that is not the perfectible imperfection of theory or technique, but represents one of the irreducible aporias of the analytic situation, by which the phenomena displayed in its field always lose in meaning what they gain in affect, and vice versa' (pp. 315–16). However divergent the interpretations that Viderman and I give construction may be, I go along entirely with the notion of the interdependence of force and meaning.

control of that strength. Moses does something superhuman: he performs 'the highest mental achievement that is possible in a man, that of struggling successfully against an inward passion for the sake of a cause to which he has devoted himself'.[30]

Similarly, the symbolic cannot be operated unless a force feeds the process of transformation by which it is constituted. Hence the importance of the work of the symbolic. Brute strength must be worked in order to be operational. 'Small quantities' of it are necessary conditions for the functioning of thought. Without it, no 'work of thought' is possible.

Force and meaning are interdependent because they are complementary, unthinkable without one another. For they are not merely opposed. To the very extent that force creates a *ratio of forces*, it is symbolic. Insofar as meaning is always caught up in a *conflict of meaning*, it is economic. Rather than an opposition, it is rather a Janus couple, a dyad whose terms are not symmetrical, but in which each may be divined in the other.

If the affect is the witness of wild, ineliminable thought, present at the very heart of the most abstract, the most rational processes, the final refuge of the affect is rationalization. The fact that nothing, neither in its content nor in its form, allows us to distinguish it from reason, shows that the only attitude that it ought to inspire would be to let the discourse continue, until such time as its own movement, the one that forges it, undergoes the test of its challenge.

But we are a constituent part of this *living discourse*.

---

30 *S.E.*, XIII, p. 233.

Postface*

To conclude, a few theoretical points and a few hypotheses. At the end of this work, I cannot help feeling that many of the problems raised remain in suspense and that much of what I have said may call for a fresh examination.

Here are a few of the questions that the work has reflected afterwards on the reflection that has produced it: the end of a piece of writing is not its closure, but the revelation of the point from which it ought to have set out.

A – Psychoanalytic speech

Let me refer to the shared experience of psychoanalytic practice. The fact that the mainspring of what takes place in psychoanalysis is put into operation by the combined effects of the speech of analysand and analyst has given rise to controversy in discussions among psychoanalysts. For reasons that cannot be analysed here, such discussions have often taken the form of a double monologue, rather than of a dialogue. It may be of the nature of speech that it is split and divided into a double locus, without there being any need for the two parts to be joined together. This evocative image of the topographical relations of the psychical apparatus is striking enough, but it may well hinder a recognition of the question of speech in psychoanalysis. One must not be afraid to remind oneself of the evidence; it will bring us closer to the heart of the question than a premature theoretical development.

Analytic speech is speech delivered lying down. This is a paradoxical position, associated with sleep, relaxation, idleness or making love, but scarcely with speech. Second, analytic speech is speech addressed to *a hidden*

---

* This postface was originally the oral presentation of a pre-published report at the Congrès de Psychanalystes de Langues romanes in 1970.

addressee. Contravening the rules of verbal exchange, which is usually delivered face to face, analytic speech reaches its addressee in recurrent mode, as a result of his or her position and silence. But this mode has a double consequence: on the one hand, speech cannot in any way be regulated according to the effect that it is having on the addressee, to his or her reactions, even if they are unspoken, and, on the other hand, this speech must traverse a void (constituted by the absence of facial communication), in order to reach the addressee. This void then ceases to be a mere medium transmitting the message and gives rise to a double effect: on the one hand, it produces a reflection of the polysemic enigma that it has engendered in the addressee on to the transmitter and, on the other hand, this void is reproduced in the speaker, an expression of the gap between the enigmatic source of speech and its finished product. Let us say, to simplify, that the usual system of relations between transmitter and receiver has superimposed upon it another system, usually concealed in ordinary verbal exchange, between the source of the emission and its object, whether a product emitted in the statement or its addressee. Here, besides the possible plurality of meanings engendered by this deployment of speech, there opens up the breach of a number of affective phenomena, which are as surprising as they are unexpected. The major paradox of these phenomena is that they occur in a situation in which analysands feel caught in an impasse: if they speak, they observe their own undesirable reactions, which they would like to be able to consider, in every sense of the word, as *secondary* to their speech, but if they do not speak, these effects are manifested with an intensity that makes them even more important. From this ambiguity, contradictory conclusions have been drawn. For some, since the manifestations were produced in a context of spoken exchanges and that silence, far from being exclusive, was never more than a particular case, they have been introduced into the whole set of relations and avatars of a capture of the subject by his speech. Others, on the contrary, since silence is the state in which the embarrassment of the subject is most manifest, have preferred to opt for the thesis of the superficial nature of language, to the benefit of what seemed to thwart the project of speech, to refer the question back to the state of psychical activity in which verbalization might be excluded.

But, in the final analysis, whether the question is taken at one end or the other, their common denominator is still that speech and its effects are the fruit of a development. One is always dealing with a speech that is wandering or flowing, which witnesses the production of manifestations that exceed its possibilities in the sequences that the context of the analytic situation tries to encourage. Speech delivered lying down, speech hidden from its addressee – the two features by which I have just distinguished analytic speech – are reminiscent of writing, of the text, as understood by modern literary theorists. But although Freud sometimes speaks of the unconscious as a text, for the psychoanalyst, this text requires attention only to see it constituted in his or her ear, if I may put it like that. For me, the question lies between the act of constituting text in the speech and the locus (therefore the mode) of its constitution, by which it is sent back to that which it is not. In any case, for the psychoanalyst, the umbilical cord of the problem is that difference of structure and nature between the emission of the text of the speech to an addressee and its recurrent return to that which destines it to be the object of such a destiny, beginning with its anchorage in the body.

One must return, therefore, to the encounter determined by the context of the analytic situation between speech and its affect effect. What seems to me to be heuristically of little interest is to account for it as *an adding to or a subtraction from speech*. For what is most striking in this event of analytic speech is, in that affect, the encounter with an alien phenomenon with facial speech. It is not that in principle facial speech cannot experience it, but it is able to eliminate that intrusion or make it an object of adventitious curiosity, to prune it, dilute it or to enslave it in order to make it conform to the practices of communication, all manoeuvres that allow whoever makes the strange discovery of this experience to fall back more or less quickly on their feet, or to turn heel and drop the whole enterprise. The point that has to be discussed, therefore, is that of the constraint on hearing at the advent in speech of what indicates in that speech the unavoidable gap, not only in relation to the content of its message, but in relation to the very act that leads it to become spoken. For all these reasons, and not to include the affect effect in speech, or to exclude it, it seems preferable to me to state that the context of the analytic situation invented by Freud may be defined as *an extension of the field of discourse*, on condition nevertheless that it is made clear that discourse is not to be confused with speech, but requires that the semantic specificity that it acquires by the *event* that is analytic treatment, forces us to redefine its use in analytic theory.

B Affect and instinctual impulses

Such was my position at the outset. I shall not go over the various stages in the exegetical work of reading Freud that confirmed me in my view, though it was my previous reading of Freud that had enabled me, in this necessarily brief account, to formulate the problem clearly. I shall do no more than mention the 'Papers on metapsychology', out of which certain individuals have made a great deal, not out of Freud's work itself, but out of Freud's hesitations concerning the complex question of the status of the affect. I do not intend to go back over that; to enter into such detail would divert me from the questions still outstanding. I should, however, like to return to Freud's own discussion of the question in *The Ego and the Id*. Two facts strike me in this text. The first is Freud's description of internal perceptions: multilocular (divided into a large number of boxes or compartments), ubiquitous, possessing opposed or antagonistic qualities. It should be noted that Freud does not give in to the temptation of a phenomenological description, but tries, whatever reductions this might entail, to remain analytic. Yet he, usually so precise, ends up calling the affects that 'something' that precedes what will become conscious under the qualitative aspect of pleasure or unpleasure, though this consciousness is not necessarily given them. When censorship, defence or repression set up obstacles to them, these sensations and feelings are manifested not as sensations, '*although the something that corresponds to them in the course of excitation is the same as if they did*'. In the final analysis, he concludes:

> Actually the difference is that, whereas with Ucs. *ideas* connecting links must be created before they can be brought into Cs., with feelings, which are themselves transmitted directly, this does not occur. In other words: the distinction between Cs. and Pcs. has no meaning where feelings are concerned; Pcs. here drops out – and feelings are either conscious or unconscious. Even when they are attached to word-presentations, their becoming conscious is not due to that circumstance, but they become so directly. (author's italics).[1]

It would be wrong to believe that this correction of a possible interpretation of unconscious affects in *The Papers on Metapsychology* is some chance shift in Freud's thought. In 1895, he made a similar observation. In the last lines of the 'Project', considering the problem of the cathexis of the *motor image* in its relation to movement in thought–action relations, Freud confirmed its *sensorial* nature. He says of these motor images: 'And they are not associated with word-presentations, but, on the contrary, they themselves serve in part the purposes of that association'.[2] But what struck me in that text of 1923 is this enigmatic sentence: 'If the way forward is barred, they do not come into being as sensations, although the "something" that corresponds to them in the course of excitation is the same as if they did'.[3]

Two solutions present themselves here. The first has been followed by most authors in the modern psychoanalytic literature. Faced with the obscurity of the problem, the tendency has gradually emerged to speak of *object cathexes* rather than of memory traces and affects. Although this replacement

---

1 *S.E.*, XIX, pp. 22–3.
2 *S.E.*, I, p. 387.
3 *S.E.*, XIX, p. 22.

has often had happy results, I have preferred a second solution: to maintain Freud's distinction between affect and representation. However, in doing so, I would stress that this duality does not mean that the offshoots of the drive have a uniform status in the unconscious. As far as affect and representation are concerned, the adjective unconscious referred to the notion of *the heterogeneity of the raw materials of the unconscious*, a heterogeneity whose character is neither incidental nor accidental, but constitutes its very texture. At least this option, whatever theoretical difficulties it may have given rise to, had the merit of not dissolving the importance of language, to which Freud showed constant attention, in the indeterminate nature of cathexis.

Comparing Freud's formulations on the unconscious and the id, I have been confirmed in this hypothesis. It was not possible for me to consider here all the problems that relate to the transition from the first to the second topography, even were I to limit myself to questions relating to the unconscious and the id. In Lecture XXXI above all I have noted how Freud stresses the economic over the other two poles, which I have called the symbolic and categorial. Freud makes a new place there for contradictory impulses, 'contrary impulses exist side by side, without cancelling each other out or diminishing each other'.[4] Laplanche and Pontalis note quite rightly, but they draw only discrete consequences from it, that 'the idea of an "inscription" of the instinct, previously lent support by the notion of "representatives", though not rejected outright here, is not reasserted'.[5] One can see how this 'lapse of memory' on Freud's part singularly weakens the idea of an unconscious structured like a language, this thesis being based almost exclusively on the ideational representatives of the drive. The idea of an id as correspondent of grammaticality at the level of the drives is a Lacanian hypothesis difficult to sustain. Indeed in the cut that separates the drive from the organic function it inhabits, Lacan installs the drive's 'grammatical artifice, so manifest in the reversions of its articulation to both source and object';[6] he refers to a schema of the drives as described in the first topography, without considering the new perspective brought to the earlier formulations by the agencies of the second topography. 'Impulse', a controversial term, I know, does not apply only to the unknowable aspect of the drive, since Freud also links it to affect in 'Constructions in analysis', where the heterogeneity of the materials that the analytic work brings to light appears more obviously than anywhere else.

It is on the basis of discrete traces of much more far reaching revisions of Freudian theory that I have proposed to extend the register of psychoanalytic

4 *S.E.*, XXII, p. 73.
5 'Id', in Laplanche and Pontalis (1973), p. 198.
6 Lacan (1977), p. 314.

signifiers to include the act and bodily states, giving them a form of existence in the relations of the unconscious and the id, which may be
understood as vicissitudes of these instinctual impulses. Although all correspond to cathexes, it is this very diversity that has led me to make this
addition to conceptual reflection. However, if the native state of the drive is
the impulse, a considerable problem is posed. How is one to conceive of the
relation of the said impulse with the representations? I am well aware how
lame may seem the conciliatory hypothesis that I proposed for a structuring
of the unconscious in relation to the id, within all three agencies, but with
a particular regionalization in the neighbourhood of the oldest. Freud
reminds us that, in Scripture, it is not a sin to be lame.

Two solutions are offered here, between which it is difficult to make a
definite choice. Either one has to admit that a representation results from
work, whose characteristics are not known to us, on perceptions of the outside world, revised by the unconscious but constituting in a sense a category
independent of the line of internal perceptions of corporal origin, or one is
of the opinion that, partly at least, the representations derive from an equivalent work of somatic entrenchment by the drives, the id possessing in a
sense a 'power to represent' deriving from the precursors of affects, which,
by a work of energic decantation, would arrive at this mysterious result.
Although Freud himself seems rather to adopt the first solution, modern
psychoanalysts often decide in favour of the second.

The rather unlovely term 'psychization' has been used in this area. It is
undeniable that it harbours a great deal of obscurity, quite as much as the
Freudian proposition of Lecture XXII, according to which, 'on its path from
its source to its aim the instinct becomes operative psychically'.[7] Effective
means that it takes effect, is active, in a new field. For such is its contradiction, not only because it is a borderline concept, but also because it
combines two profoundly different terms: an organic source apprehended in
the form of an instinctual excitation and an object apprehended by perception. However, I must add to this simplifying view of things. It is not in the
idea of a gradual appropriation of the real outside the solipsistic world that
a coherent theoretical response may be found. On the contrary, a crucial
moment of psychical structuring is that in which *the body takes the place of the
external world*[8] (where it becomes, in Freud's words, *the ego's second external
world*).[9] In an earlier work,[10] I proposed the hypothesis of an inhibition of

---

7 *S.E.*, XXII, p. 96.
8 *S.E.*, XIX, p. 55.
9 *S.E.*, XXIII, p. 162.
10 'Le narcissisme primaire, structure ou état', *L'inconscient*, no. 1, pp. 127–57; no. 2, pp.
    89–116, 1967. See also *Narcissisme de vie. Narcissisme de mort*. Paris: Editions de Minuit,
    1983.

the aim of the drive, in favour of which this change would be implemented under the auspices of the double return (reversal into its opposite, turning around on the subject's own self) and what I called primal decussation.

C – Status of the primal phantasy

But if one is confronted by the drive and its native element, the impulse, the question still remains as to what psychically structures it. In the present state of psychoanalytic theory, the answer to that question can only be conjectural. It will come to us via a concept whose status is itself conjectural: the phantasy. A debate has grown up around the phantasy between those who hold the traditional conception and those of the Kleinian school, who see it as the psychical equivalent of instinctual functioning. This debate, which is as impassioned as it is sterile, has led me to wonder how it is that Freud recognized the importance of the phantasy, especially in the first topography, only to a relatively limited extent, as compared with the place that is given to it today. However far we may wish to carry our hypotheses on the construction of the psychical apparatus and however attentive we may be to the economy of the concepts, we cannot, in my opinion, be satisfied with a genetic point of view, which gives us an image of development based on a cumulative process, whatever flexibility one may bring to that schema by introducing such notions as structurings, destructurings and restructurings. Questions still remain as to what is structurable, what is structure *in potentia* and what is structuring potential. Various answers have been given to these theoretical questions. As opposed to those who have concentrated this dialectic in the field of the ego and those who have situated it in language, I have opted for the solution of the Oedipus complex and have recognized the primal phantasies as mediators in the advent of the Oedipal structure. It now seems to me that the answer to the question about the limited place of the phantasy in the second topography was to be found only in Freud's insistent reference to the phylogenetic memory traces; in my opinion, the primal phantasies represent the actualization of the memory traces, possessing a double power, economic and symbolic, in the psychical apparatus. The primal phantasies are not representations, still less contents, but mediations. Contrary to everything we might expect of the rules of traditional logic, they are *that by which representations and contents occur.* The latter would seem to be manifested as the results or effects of the primal phantasies, making it retroactively possible to infer their operational function, which is essentially one of induction. This induction necessitates, however, a release that is always to be expected of the conjuncture and the event, these providing the minimum necessary to the maximum effects of induction.

Being unable to provide all the theoretical justifications, which would go beyond the limits of this book, I have had recourse to experience on the one hand and, on the other, to epistemological reflection on the status of the subject in his relations with his parents. Laplanche and Pontalis see the primal phantasies as above all phantasies of origins.[11] What I find more striking is the articulation of their logic. The primal scene, seduction and castration are in effect conjoined and disjoined in the Oedipal structure to which they refer. Since Melanie Klein, we understand better, through the phantasy of the combined parent, the link between the projective effects of instinctual activity, which is as dangerous as it is uninterrupted, and this relation to the Other, alternately bringing desire and identification into play in the primal scene. The subject must enter the play of generation, the generation of his own phantasy existence by the intrusion of what is excluded in him and of those who by excluding him force him to include himself in it. Through the experience of seduction is recalled – both after the event in relation to the primal scene and before the event in relation to its later evocation which transforms the memory of it into trauma – this premonitory constraint of adult sexuality, this obligation to participate in the pleasure of the parents, to allow this premature, anticipated sexuality to penetrate him. By the time seduction has introduced him to sexuality, castration operates a partial totalization of previous phantasies; this totalization is concealed by what it reveals; it provokes a recoil, as if both to see better and to see less of what is the child's share in the pleasure of his parents, according to which he regulates his own. In other words, depending on his or her sex, the child pays the cost of an operation in which the inadmissible reappears: in such a relation there is always one sex less or one sex too many. Everything has to be thought out again.

But what I am gathering together in this way in order to articulate it now derives its power of structuring only to operate according to two essential theoretical axioms: discontinuity and fragmentation. It is precisely because it cannot be totalized that there is a motive to attempt a totalization in the field opposed to the phantasy, that of the ego, at the level of the secondary processes. To confine myself to these remarks would bring us back to a theoretical conception compatible with the first topography, minimizing the emphasis that I noted in the second. The return to the impulse seems to me to be necessary in so far it is a break in dynamic equilibrium, topographical and economic. Solicitation, demand, urgency, it calls for repression only because there is oppression. The impulse is badly in need of representative co-option: it interjects phantasy into an appeal, but the phantasy remains 'invisible'. It is visible only in the effects that it has

---

11 'Fantasme originaire, fantasme des origines, origine du fantasme', *Les temps modernes*, no. 215. Article reprinted, Paris: Hachette, 1985.

induced: the hallucinatory realization of desire, which conceals time, but whose repetitions will have the extreme advantage of constituting the traces of the object to come.

We now have a better understanding of the relations between the impulse of the second topography and the motor image of the 'Project': the latter partly serves the aims of the associative activity. What was true for word-presentations is even truer for representation in general. Representation emerges not from the phantasy alone, but from the encounter of impulse and phantasy. This is what I wanted to denote by the obscure and unsatisfactory expression *mixture of representation and affect*.

In the interlacing of impulse and phantasy, force and meaning are exchanged and appropriate one another. From this chiasma originates the libido in the strict sense of the term; where the impulse brings energy, whether expended or pent up, the phantasy acts as a vector orienting and directing, constituting libido in a double way, through the object and through narcissism. If one accepts Freud's thesis of the primal reality-ego, its differentiating capacity is confined to the origin of excitations. However, it is not unthinkable that critical situations, which are inevitable, cause a partial covering over of one field by another. Is not the proof of this that Freud assists this system, whose partial efficacity is compromised, by the inhibition of the preconscious ego on the internal representation of the object? The state of distress, therefore, necessarily results in the cathexis of perceptions by anxiety. It will be these decathected, but largely revised remainders that will constitute the support of the phantasy. The phantasy puts the energy of the impulse to good account as if it provided it with the necessary means for its phantasy formulation. It should be remembered here that the indispensable agent of this formulation is always an experience of lack. But the impulse alone can do nothing with this lack, which is the precondition for the production of the impulse, which, in turn, increases lack and constraint in the interpretation of which the phantasy will be the outcome. If the body takes the place of the external world, then it is easy to understand how the kernel of the phantasy may be a perceptual remainder, *though without for all that acceding to representation, which will be the result of the phantasy*. That is why it seems to me it to be pointless to discuss phantasy in terms of an expression of instinctual functioning or as an organized scenario, for the phantasy is in a latent state of organization, this latency coming to an end only under pressure from the impulse.

D – Repression and the phantasies

I have maintained the hypothesis that the psychical representation of the drive owed its splitting into representative and affect to the function of repression. But this does not mean that I adopted the thesis by which primal repression becomes the essential concept of psychoanalytic theory. In an earlier work, I defended the notion of double reversal, which combined the Freudian terms of reversal into its opposite and turning round upon the subject's own self. However, I cannot go into detail about it here. This double reversal precedes the dialectical stage of repression. In my opinion, it is after the closure of the double reversal that the functional capacity of repression becomes clear. It is one thing to posit primal repression as directing agent of the unconscious, it is quite another to make it the founder of the unconscious. I posit the hypothesis that the suture of turning round upon the subject's own self and reversal into its opposite, which assists the separation of the child and the primordial object in the experience of the loss of the breast, is the determining condition of repression. Such a break is responsible for the mutation undergone by the remainders of perceptual experiences under the influence of phantasies. Phantasies, let me repeat, do not arrive uniformly in a representative form, but, being necessary to the constitution of representation, in their encounter with the impulse. Retroactively, it is to phantasy that I would be inclined to attribute the role of implementing repression. It is as if, therefore, the consequence of this operation were to draw the phantasy into that closure and to hold it prisoner in the repressed. But, and it is here that things become complicated, if the primal phantasy must never arrive at its clear formulation, not only because it takes the form of an image, but also because of its consequences, the whole work of the unconscious is dominated by it, in a paradoxical constellation. Any activation of the phantasy entails an excessive anticathexis of the unconscious, which leads as a preventive measure to the retreat of preconscious cathexes and the maintenance of unconscious cathexes, or the replacement of the preconscious cathexis by the unconscious cathexis. In any case, all that could result from the repression is a strengthening of the unconscious cathexes, which can only accentuate the pregnancy of the primal phantasy and which consequently tend to redouble their efforts to give the phantasy an expression less and less removed from its aim, whereas prohibition cannot, by drawing the preconscious contents into the pre-existing repressed, authorize its explicit formulation. It will be noticed that such a problematic will necessarily be contained within the limits of the repressing agency/return of the repressed ratio without which there is no place for the hypothesis that ought to account not only for the withdrawal and the mutual co-options of representations in the unconscious, but also for the nature of the economic transformations that govern it. The only solution offered to this system, which tends more and more to circularity, seems to me to be the fragmentation of the primal phantasies into secondary phantasies, which are organized in a representative form. In my opinion, this *modulation* would alone be capable of producing the derivative representations whose relation with their phantasy organizer and the disguise necessitated by the crossing of the *Ucs.–Pcs.* barrier, will allow their admission to consciousness and their analysability. For such a solution is unthinkable in the context of the first topography; only deferred repression ought to correspond to it and it is precisely this that is at the base of the vicious circle. It seems that a force of distinct separation as such may account for it. This, in my opinion, is one of the best illustrations that I can give of the importance of revaluing the first topography and the first theories of the drives together with a revision of the second topography and the last theory of the drives. So the collaboration and antagonism of the last instinctual categories, those deriving from Eros and the destructive drives, take on a particular interest.

This solution is paradoxical insofar as the operation, which in a sense consists of debiting the sum of primal phantasy as currency, has the effect both of making that phantasy treatable by the secondary phantasies and of preserving still better its inductive function. Repression, which offered its services as a gaoler of the primal phantasies, now becomes their preserver. But, on the other hand, the work on the secondary phantasies, following the vocation of the primal phantasies, whose absence of totalization as a result of fragmentation and discontinuity I have already stressed, turns the mobility of the displacements of libidinal energy to the account of condensation and displacement. That repression as a vicissitude of the drive serves the 'representability' of the drive, to use Tort's term,[12] I am all the more willing to agree in that support can be found in that force of separation capable of producing them. For, so far, no text has accounted for this absence of any reference to representation and the affect in the works in which Freud deals with the drives and their miraculous appearance whenever repression is mentioned. All that we are allowed to know is that *all representations derive from perceptions and are repetitions of those perceptions*, as Freud maintains in several places, in particular in his article 'Negation'.[13] They derive from and are repetitions of perceptions, that is to say, they are the product of their elaboration, but, as Tort judiciously says, 'the starting-point remains the instinctual impulse' and the problem that of 'a particular quantity of excitation'.[14] The representability of the drive is psychical representation of excitation–excitation expressed as a form of the psychical manifestation of a force. Is one to conclude from this that the appearance of the ideational representative and the affect, from the beginning of the 'psychological process', would suggest a more properly psychical origin for this new

12 'A propos du concept freudien de "représentant"', *Cahiers pour l'analyse*, no. 5, 1966, pp. 37–63.
13 *S.E.*, XIX, p. 237.
14 'A propos du concept freudien de "représentant"', *Cahiers pour l'analyse*, no. 5, 1966, p. 51.

acceptation of representation? The thesis that I have proposed on the primal phantasy dispenses me from any such obligation and spares me any embarrassment that I might feel if I decided that the origin of affect had to be referred exclusively to the body, which is contrary to the observations of psychoanalytic practice and theory.

In fact, the elucidation of the notion of representation suffers from our habits of thought. When using the word representation, one cannot help referring implicitly either to a notion of content or to a notion of image. But the psychoanalytic sense of the term refers to neither of these and I find myself in agreement with Laplanche and Pontalis that a thing-presentation, for example, is not a representation *of* the thing, but an associative whole that relates to this or that feature of the thing or even to the field in which it is situated, and that its specificity is to be a cathexis figure of the traces left by this configuration. In the gap that separates the direct *memory images* of the thing and the *memory traces* derived from it, we find a similar gap to that between perception and representation. The trace lives solely from the recrossing over a line that reanimates it and constitutes its manifestation. This pathway of the cathexis is not left to chance, but is oriented by what Freud calls *Zielvorstellung* (translated by Strachey as 'purposive idea', and by Laplanche and Pontalis as *représentation-but*). As I remarked above, *représentation-but* is not *représentation du but*, and the translation proposed by Laplanche and Pontalis makes the difference clear. But when those authors try to answer the enigma that the term purposive idea tries to express by locating it the place of the unconscious phantasy, I wonder why Freud did not refer to it explicitly. The purposive idea is not a scenario, but an aspiration that, with the satisfaction sought by the drive, has the same relation of intercalation as the one that I placed between memory trace and memory image in the correlative field of thing-presentation. The difference between my interpretation and that of the authors of the *Vocabulaire* stems from their understanding of the term unconscious phantasy. For, although it is true that it would be wrong to make an absolute split between unconscious and conscious phantasy, in terms of a difference of nature, it seems to me that their pole of reference lies much closer to the relations of the phantasy with the conscious rather than with the unconscious. One may accept the idea of the purposive idea as unconscious phantasy, but only on condition that one sees the unconscious phantasy more as an orienting vector than as a representative agency, until such time as it becomes a representation of what is the anticipated canvas of the imaginary realization of the satisfaction sought. I am more interested in considering, at least in some of its aspects, a notion used by Freud in the 'Project': the motor image, whose paradox, yet another one, is that there is nothing of the image about it, but that it is an evocation of movement. This evocation is not so much a representation of movement as an induction to the act intended by the movement. This moving sensoriality will be found in another form when language has the function of recathecting the thought process. This is what Freud expresses in the 'Project' by this forthright proposition: 'We do not really speak, any more than we really move when we imagine a motor image'.[15] This is the moment to return to that conclusive remark in the 'Project' to the effect that motor images 'are not associated with word presentation, but, on the contrary, they themselves serve in part the purposes of that association'.[16]

E – Language for Freud

Freud's treatment of language is so scattered throughout his work that it is difficult to grasp any unity of conception. However, one may detect four fundamental themes:

1   Language serves as a mediator to help us to bring back to consciousness everything that we were previously conscious of, but which has been transformed into a memory trace, this memory trace having to be hyper-cathected in order to regain consciousness. Consciousness operates on the very place of the memory trace. Thought, therefore, must rediscover the path of perception and it is the function of language to give it back this lost quality. If this conception of language seems somewhat simplified, it is because what is essential – the destiny of the perceptions in the unconscious – is only allusively named. The mechanism common to the various aspects of the operation is cathexis, in its inscriptive or retranscriptive form.

2   Between thing-presentation and word-presentation there are economic, dynamic and topographical relations: in the sufficiently limited relations of contiguity (given the proximity in time between them or by regression), word-presentations may be treated as thing-presentations. Thus communication between the visual and auditory spheres is established at the level of a relative osmosis of different types of cathexis. Freud even goes further in fact, since word-presentation may serve as raw material for the constitution of an 'organ speech'.[17] But their essential operational value derives from the fact that word-presentations are *limited* and *exclusive*.[18] This implicitly posits the question of the properties of the raw material linked together and the modes of linkage. The counterpart

15   *S.E.*, I, p. 367.
16   *S.E.*, I, p. 387.
17   *S.E.*, XIV, pp. 197–9.
18   *S.E.*, I, p. 365.

of the limitations and exclusivity of the linked elements lies in the high level of cathexis, that is to say, of the processes of linkage.

3   Language is apprehended as a 'revealer' of the processes of thought. The processes of thought are displacements of mental energy, whereas mental energy proceeds on its way to action.[19] We should note in the 'Project' an allusion to a concept that might have been thought outdated a few years ago, but which has now been raised to the forefront of epistemology, namely, *practical thought*. It is by this *actualization* that consciousness is given to thought, for consciousness functions, according to Freud, by means of 'systems so far remote from the original perceptual residues that they have no longer retained anything of the qualities of those residues'.[20]

4   The restriction of motor discharge operated by thought leads to a transformed form of internal action: an experimental mode of attempted seizure, investigation and capture of the data of the external world, by displacement of small quantities of energy. Here two remarks should be made. On the one hand, quantitative reduction facilitates the linking of the elements displaced and subjected to the risks of a function of which modern warfare has provided an illustration. Thus we see how a certain form of radar picking up information is itself picked up. On the other hand, a fraction, if not the whole of the remainder of the unreduced quantity is cathected in the system of linkage and raises its level of cathexis. The crucial consequence of this is that thought is originally unconscious not only in the descriptive sense, but also in a systematic one. What Freud expresses by supposing that thinking 'went beyond mere ideational presentations and was directed to the relations between impressions of objects, and that it did not require further qualities, perceptible to consciousness, until it became connected with verbal residues'.[21]

Freud conceived thought, if I may be permitted this approximate comparison, as a sort of empty whole always ready to be made present by different modes of excitation, cathexis, discharge. But what matters is the mode according to which the acts of the cathexis are performed, the topographical situation of the place of the cathexis and its regime. In *The Interpretation of Dreams*, he took care to make clear that 'what we regard as

19   *S.E.*, XIX, p. 190.
20   *S.E.*, XIV, p. 202.
21   *S.E.*, XII, p. 221. A statement previously contained in the 'Project for a scientific psychology', Part III (*S.E.*, I, pp. 360ff.) and in *The Interpretation of Dreams* (*S.E.*, V, pp. 574, 611, 617) and, later, in the *Papers on Metapsychology* (*S.E.*, XIV, p. 202), in *The Ego and the Id* (*S.E.*, XIX, pp. 19ff.) and in *An Outline of Psycho-Analysis*, pp. 162–4.

mobile is not the psychical structure itself but its innervation' – today one and, no doubt, Freud, too, would say, its cathexis. But Freud's thought goes further.

> We can avoid any possible abuse of this method of representation by re-collecting that ideas, thoughts and psychical structures in general must never be regarded as localized in organic elements of the nervous system but rather, as one might say, *between* them, where resistances and facilitations [*Bahnungen*] provide the corresponding correlates. Everything that can be an object of our internal perception is *virtual*.[22]

It seems that the whole difficulty derives from the fact that Freud needed the mediation of the dream to discover the unconscious, that is to say, not only to speak about it, but to articulate it operationally. Confronted by the enigmas of his first attempts at psychoanalysis, he needed to find the common place between analysand and analyst in the dream. Now, although *The Interpretation of Dreams* brought to maturity certain of the hypotheses in the 'Project', it did have the indirect consequence of occluding many of them, which Freud was to bring out later bit by bit. The great ambiguity of the 'Project', produced in a staggering flash of inspiration, is to have amalgamated as yet unmastered theoretical presuppositions of a historico-genetic order, together with hypotheses on psychical functioning, in which file past, as in some strange carousel, 'representatives' of his conception of the nervous system, views on the infantile psyche (probably deriving from observations of his first children), thoughts on the treatment of the neuroses, indications of his transference on Fliess and traces of an exceptional self-analysis of his own processes of thought as he formulated his discoveries, of which the writing of the 'Project' is not only the product, but the object. For all kinds of reasons, which it would take too long to go into here, the discovery of the unconscious through *The Interpretation of Dreams* may have gained in rigour, but it lost something in extent and depth – if I may be permitted such a scandalous thought – when compared to the promises of the 'Project'. But if we had not had *The Interpretation of Dreams*, we may never have had the opportunity of thinking about the 'Project'.[23]

What may be conjectured is that Freud is caught, as far as the representation–language–thought relation is concerned, in the following contradiction: it is as if cathexis is stretched between a *precathexis by desire* and

---

22 *S.E.*, V, p. 611.
23 On the relations between the 'Project' and *The Interpretation of Dreams*, see my article 'De l'Esquisse à l'Interprétation des Rêves', in *La Nouvelle Revue de Psychanalyse*, no. 5, 1972.

hyper-cathexis by the attention that is turned on the clues of quality, which, in the end, are merely clues of discharge.[24] The dialectical spring of this tension is that by a translation of the attention that is paid to the clues of quality in the process of opening up, the attention cathects an activity that is both associative and prospective. The perception of quality gives way to the perception of the change, which is best suited to establish the difference between perception and representation. In other words, in psychoanalytic treatment, the diversion of attention and its incapacitation by free association lead to a freeing of energy that is converted only to proceed to a marking of the links between the co-ordinates of precathexis (what Freud calls concordance and resemblance with perceptions) and the facilitations, that is to say, the perceptions of change. The role of the verbal associations repeats this process by making it present and making manageable (that is to say, intelligible and interpretable) for us the way in which it proceeds.

At this point, I come up against an obstacle in the pursuit of this development, insofar as Freud's conception of thought remains astonishingly bold and modern, whereas his conception of language, despite several dazzling strokes, shows its age, belonging as it does to a time before the remarkable progress made in linguistics. This delay is more noticeable here than in any other concept of Freud's theory, whether the drive, representation or cathexis, where no striking novelty has forced such a broad requestioning on us.

F – A few thoughts on modern linguistics: the heterogeneity of the psychoanalytic signifier

A little reflection took me away from language; a great deal of reflection has brought me back to it. It is difficult for a psychoanalyst to clear a way through the enormous mass of linguistic works that began at the beginning of the century. However, I would submit a few remarks that have occurred to me, well aware of how arbitrary such a choice may be. I am not going to claim that they are the ones that, for linguists, are the most important, but only those that have made me reflect most.

Saussure's proposition that *in a language there are only differences*[25] has enjoyed an enormous fortune. But it seems to me that the proposition is capable of developments that might be of interest to the psychoanalyst only if it is articulated above all with the notion that the linguistic system (relations between the terms *in absentia* in a virtual mnemonic series)[26] refers to

24 *S.E.*, I, pp. 325 and 360.
25 Saussure (1974), p. 120.
26 Ibid., p. 126.

a series of *heterogeneous associated fields* (heterogeneous by sound and by sense) and above all with the observation that *the ideational and material content of a sign matters less than what is around it in the other signs.*[27] The constitution of the signifying chain ought logically to feel more than is usually noticed the effects of mutual irradiation of the sign, which shows that although the placing in series imposes an order, it revives more than it tames what might be called the effects of propinquity – and one knows that they are not always of the best. Saussure cannot help stumbling on the problem of value: let us note in passing that he establishes a parallel with economics whose aim is – I summarize – the determination of the characters of the unit by differential articulation.

Extending Saussure's thought, Charles Bally has opposed analysis and synthesis: *uncommunicated thought is synthetic, that is to say, global, unarticulated.* This statement leads only to a negative definition: *synthesis is the ensemble of linguistic facts contrary in discourse to linearity and to monosemia in the memory.*[28] Having conceded that dystaxia is the usual state, the correlative of polysemia, which means that the discourse would bear in itself the marks either of resistance to linearity or of a return to synthesis at the heart of analysis, Bally must give up any idea of showing, as he previously maintained, that the discordance between signifiers and signifieds is the rule and proceed to their reconciliation;[29] the associated operations that govern it being *demarcation* and *identification*. This impasse is due to the idea that the factor opposed to analysis, uncommunicated thought, is nebulous. However, that traces of dystaxia, or non-linearity, are felt at the very heart of linearity, would logically imply that between linearity and the nebulousness of uncommunicated thought, other modes of structuring might intervene in which the relation between polysemia and monosemia would be more strictly established. This is not possible because all linguistic research is mobilized in the direction of a unitary demarcation. By demonstrating its double nature, Martinet shows that he is still attached to demarcation:[30] the first articulation at the level of the monemes (the true word units) and the second articulation at the level of the phonemes, the first being that of the signifying units, the second that of the distinctive units. One must insist on the fact that this double articulation presupposes a profound conceptual and material heterogeneity and that it is this heterogeneity that represents its originality. One can see how the determination of the unit slips between the fingers before the multiplicity of referents. Heterogeneity attains its full status in Hjelmslev's

27 Ibid., p. 120.
28 Bally (1932), p. 144.
29 Ibid., p. 187.
30 Martinet (1965).

opposition between *form* and *substance*, itself duplicated by that of *expression* and *content*, and in the more complex relations between *connotation* and *denotation*. The duality is met in a new form in the work of Benveniste: following all the fundamental positions adopted by the linguists, the Saussurian insistence on virtuality is also present. But here virtuality is represented in person, if I may put it like that, in a study on the nature of pronouns, considered by the specialists themselves as a major work.

The I and the you are in opposition to the he or she insofar as the first two establish a relation between the indicator and the *present* agency of the discourse, whereas the last represents the unmarked member of the person correlation. Benveniste says of the third person: 'It is a function of syntactical "representation", which extends in this way to terms caught in the different "parts of speech" and which thus respond to a need for economy, by replacing part of the statement and even an entire statement by a more manageable substitute'.[31] Since absence (the unmarked member of the correlation to the person) 'represents' itself, it necessarily makes itself present, thus creating another splitting. One finds here again, inside language, a relation of comparison that Freud established at the level of the relation between representation and language.

Splitting assumes a more radical aspect in the works of Jakobson, especially in the distinction between subject of the statement and subject of the utterance, and in the determination of the two great axes of language: metaphor and metonymy.

Then came Chomsky: the richness of his thinking derives from the fact that he was able to bring together two streams of thought. According to the first, it is the properties of the systems of the laws that govern it that make clear the specific nature of the organization of a language and, according to the second, those properties have an endlessly generative capacity. The present splitting, in the opposition between surface structures and deep structures, brings Chomsky closer to Freud than any other linguist.[32]

These disparate references ought to help us to elaborate, on the basis of Freud's work, a modern psychoanalytic theory of language – and Freud always recognized the extreme importance of such a theory – rather than a psychoanalytic theory based on language. I can do no more here than lay down the main stages of such a reflection, for at a number of points one encounters a problematic that converges with that of psychoanalysis.

---

31 'What must be regarded as distinctive of the "3rd person"' is the property of 1) combining with any object reference; 2) never being reflexive of the agency of discourse; 3) comprising a fairly large number of pronominal or demonstrative variants; being compatible with the paradigm of the referential terms *here, now*, etc.' (Benveniste 1966, p. 256).
32 Chomsky (1972).

It is now the moment to speak of Lacan's conception. One may be surprised at the importance that I have accorded it, given that the affect has no place in it. But it is for that very reason that I saw it as an illustration of a methodological paradigm, leading to the construction of a theoretical system whose force and richness of thought are beyond dispute, although its truth, based on the exclusion of the affect, is not. From Lacan's theory I shall retain two propositions. The first of these strikes me as self-evident: *the signifier is that which represents a subject for another signifier.* The second is that *the subject receives the message from the Other in an inverted form,* which presupposes the misunderstanding (*méconnaissance*) of the inscription of knowledge in the discourse of which it is the function of the Other to make it attain its structure. It is untrue to say that Lacan does not take the drive into account. The trouble is that he uses the same term, through its lack, to cover the signifier, the drive and the Other.[33] Now 'the Other as previous site of the pure subject of the signifier holds the master position'.[34] The whole question is summed up in fact in the implications of the unification of the signifier, if only in its splitting of the chain in which it is inscribed, linking one to the drive and the other to speech. For it is this unification that seems to me to be debatable, as the whole Freudian exegesis shows. Whether it is at the level of the ideational representatives of the drive, in the gap between thing-presentation and word-presentation, and a fortiori in the gap between ideational representative and the affect. Freud's essential preoccupation, the distinction between two types of excitation and between two modes of discharge in the psychical processes, melts here like snow in sunshine.

However much Lacan insists on the splitting of the subject, unity returns in his unitary conception of the signifier. This heterogeneity is in no sense incidental, for systemic plurality is central to Freud's theory. It is as a consequence of this that I have proposed the concept of *the heterogeneity of the signifier,* a heterogeneity *of substance and of form.* The first is inferred allusively by the comparison with the figure in the analogy of the magic Block, the second by the various types of representatives, the affect included, that make up the unconscious.

The same remark goes for the Lacanian conception of lack; for what is the object of all contemporary psychoanalytic research is precisely the differential study of the effects of various types of lack, which does not exclude their articulation. Here I have indicated the path that might be taken by a problematics of dismemberment as a relation between castration and fragmentation. And if we must respond in spite of all opposition to the question of the basis of the articulation of the chain, it is to the concept of *moving*

33 Lacan (1977), pp. 316–17.
34 Ibid., p. 305.

quantity that I would refer, for of the two postulates in the 'Project' (the other being that of the elementary particles relating to the representative element), it is the first that matters to Freud, as his letter to Fliess of 25 May 1895 (no. 24) makes clear. But it is of the nature of such a concept to resist unification insofar as that moving quantity generates the systems that it feeds and which, in return, fix its regime, engendering not only functions, but structures whose originality is the relation of conjunction and disjunction that is established between them. Blanchot reminds us that out of the mouth of the poet Bacchylides Apollo says to Admetus: 'You are only a mortal; so your mind must entertain two thoughts at once'.

G – The linkage of discourse

Plurality of systems, plurality of sources and starting points of meaning (the drive is the id's mode of perception, which means that it is to be related to perception such as the ego apprehends it), plurality of forces and regimes, plurality of the forms that govern the signifiers, all this has led me to recall that the various types of signifiers do not obey the same mode of linkage.

The notion of linkage, in which the affect may find its place *qua* signifier, seemed to me to offer a solution to these difficulties, in conformity with the Freudian spirit: linkage at the level of discourse, as product of preconscious and unconscious, but linkage constantly threatened by id discharge cathexes, untreated by the ego, of which the old notion of actual neurosis recently revived by de M'Uzan provided an illustration. Freud's theorization was no doubt defective, but its individualization was well founded.

To the series described by Freud, word-presentation, thing-presentation and affect, I have added, as elements of discourse, terms relating to the categories of act and one's own body. This seemed to me to be authorized by 'Constructions in analysis' and to be supported by all psychoanalytic experience accumulated over the last few decades. The series thus completed presupposes a polygraphy of the unconscious and is opposed to the linearity of language. It makes polysemia interdependent not only with the signifier's non–identity to self (the signifier necessarily referring to the ensemble of other signifiers), but with its correlate: substantial heterogeneity.

One can see how the existence of an unconscious signifying chain thus becomes, to say the least, problematic. The linkage belongs to discourse, since the very specificity of the unconscious seems to me to be linked to that reticular polyphony and polygraphy, whose characteristic is to make possible the co–existence of the various states of unconscious material. It is the linkage of discourse that refers retroactively to the network of transformations of which, in the form of a chain, it is the product. This heterogeneity on which the signifier's non–identity to self rests is not a circumstantial given, but a theoretical necessity to make the effects of structuring intelligible. The task of these effects is not so much to constitute fixed structures as to establish relations of co-existence and compatibility between the symbolic order and the economic order, of which the observable result is the endless relaunching of the process of psychical activity. This is certainly what will be expressed in theory by the idea of the work of transforming the drive. For the drive can be envisaged only from a double historico-structural perspective. If its constitution (source, thrust, object, aim) belongs to structure, its destiny links it unavoidably to the history of a transforming elaboration. That which we are allowed to know about it already bears its traces.

The whole reference to language as founding lever of psychoanalytic theory comes up against the observation that *language can only work on material that has already been worked on.* The error of Lacanian theory derives from the fact that it takes such work as a given. In psychoanalytic treatment, however innate human linguistic possibilities may be, this work has to be done, and done again as if it had not been done, even though it is because it *has* been done that the work of treatment is possible. Linguists have taught us that it is of the nature of the sign to be repetitive, and Freud enjoins us to remember that 'all presentations originate from perceptions and are repetitions of them'.[35] Only this repetition includes the difference implied by the psychical work that will serve as a prelude to the new differential repetition in the rediscovery of the object. In that elaboration, I have posited the hypothesis of the role of phantasy, but this calls for an additional comment on the concepts involved, in particular on inductive thought, about which logic itself is highly embarrassed. The fundamental attribute of representation is to make a sign, to attract our attention and suggest: there has been a phantasy. But the most disturbing thing is when this warning operates in a negative way, where our option – and nothing in the final analysis allows us to be sure – suggests that it is nothing more than a failed hope, the promise of a phantasy that has remained in suspense. Confronted by a dissolving instinctual power, which affects the psychical economy and now proves to be an obstacle to inductive thought, repression finds its limit. Everything would be simpler if one did not have to make such a choice. But it is not up to us to decide on the simplicity that facilitates our task.

A great deal of work remains to be done on the relations between the Freudian concept of binding (*Bindung*) and what I have called linkage (*concaténation*), as against the linearity of language. Linkage seemed to me to be its temporary stage. I situated affect in the chain as the replacement of representation, as the flesh of the signifier and the signifier of the flesh, in

35 *S.E.*, XIX, p. 237.

homage to the thought of Merleau–Ponty, who suspected the dangerous character of a theorization of the unconscious based on language. In order to go further, perhaps we should go back to the model, proposed by Freud in the 'Project', of *side-cathection* insofar as it can act as *an inhibition of the course of quantity*[36] by facilitation (*Bahnung*). The theoretical difficulty of the notion of facilitation derives from the fact that it combines effects of correlation by a deflection on to elements not originally targeted by the cathexis and the facilitation by energic movement, the result being *an inhibition of moving quantity* that maintains it in the indispensable medium, an operation correlative with the reduction of excitations from the external world.[37] It is here that we find the key sentence from the 'Project': 'Thus quantity in φ is expressed by *complication* in ψ'.[38]

It is perhaps at this point that we will be able to understand the power both of *structuring* and *dissociation* possessed by representation: the capture of energy in an associative network, on condition that it puts back into circulation a remainder of moving quantity destined to be carried into other associative networks, without exhausting the power of a force that is only partially erect. The moving image serves the associations and will again serve in the connections with verbal memory traces. And even when pain is avoided, the field of unpleasure, far from being overcome, acquires a communicative function. If at the level of the primary process representation and affect are signifiers of equal dignity, the secondary processes require such an attenuation of the affect that it seems to be excluded. But it is by *the return of the excluded* that the affect will appear as a demand for representation, echoing its previous withdrawal of cathexis, with the aim of preventing the development of the affective intrusion. The affect contradicts both the work of dissociation carried out by representation and the totalization of the phantasy of omnipotence. It is the spur, whether it concerns defence or desire, to *relaunching* the structuring operations of the psychical apparatus, of which splitting is the major form, with its essential consequence, projective identification, insofar as it is itself devoted to the return of the excluded. Nowhere is this a better show than in 'A child is being beaten'. The scene observed in reality produces no more than excitation. To reach the affect in a phantasy, one must pass through the detour of an indifferent person beaten by an undifferentiated adult. When the explicit cast of characters appears in the Oedipal drama, the father beating the subject, then we are confronted by 'a high degree of pleasure', but this 'enactment' is usually unconscious. The phantasy swings into action and

---

36 *S.E.*, I, p. 323.
37 *S.E.*, I, p. 313.
38 *S.E.*, I, p. 315.

has 'strong and unambiguous sexual excitement attached to it, and so provides a means for masturbatory satisfaction', though at the cost of a father figure representing the father himself and children known to the child rather than the child himself.[39]

No doubt the psychoanalytic conception of affect sins by default, stressing the negative effects of affects more than their positive effects. This stems no doubt from the material on which it is based, the cause of this shift that mobilizes our attention on to the affects rejected by the ego as against those that are accepted by it, to use Mallet's excellent distinction. One ought to let affect speak. Unfortunately, affect appears only when the other parts of speech have exhausted their possibility of speech, hence my difficulty in speaking about it, in carrying my explorations into that sphere of *conation* to which Arthur Valenstein has drawn our attention. It is in the work of Bion that I have found the best formulations on the intrication of *thinking* and *feeling* in the relation that he makes between *preconception* and *presentiment*, a conjunction that is all the more interesting in that this author places *knowledge* at the same organizing level for the psyche as the traditional Kleinian categories of love and hate.

If defences seem to me to be directed most often towards affects, either because their quality appears inadmissible in the eyes of repression, or because their quantity threatens the psychical organization, one experiences resistance in the relation to knowledge. What is striking in the resistance is the way in which, similar to the signifier's effects of radiation, it infiltrates ever more closely the rest of the psyche, beyond the localized aspect of the conflict. It is not only resistance to saying something, but also resistance in the saying and by the saying, as Donnet puts it. For the paradox of representation is that when the signs of a total repetitive identity of perception offer themselves to the abused consciousness, at that moment appears the pure affect of the series 'already seen' (*déjà vu*), 'already heard', 'already experienced', 'already recounted'. And, similarly, when reality responds without defaulting to the perception that was expected of it, there emerges the 'something missing' to which David has devoted one of the finest articles in the psychoanalytic literature of recent years.

The enigma of these questions is the reanimation of a thought extracted from the absence from which it drew its active force. As Donnet says: 'The postulated existence of a trace makes one wonder not only about the wiping out of the trace, but about the trace of that wiping out'.[40]

---

39 *S.E.*, XVII, p. 179.
40 'L'antinomie de la résistance', *L'inconscient*, no. 4, p. 69.

H – Negative hallucination

I now find myself in the situation of having to explain to myself the place that I have accorded negative hallucination. One may well be surprised, given its rarity as a clinical phenomenon, at the function that I am attributing it. Here the gap between practice and theory is patent. Let us look at it more closely, however. In the second contribution to the theory of dreams, Freud considers not hallucination as a clinical phenomenon, but what might be called *the hallucinatory fact*, common to wish-fulfilment, dreams and hallucination, and he adds in a note: 'I may add by way of supplement that any attempt to explain hallucination would have to start out from *negative* rather than positive hallucination'.[41] I feel unable to decide whether the addition concerns the clinical phenomenon of hallucination or the hallucinated fact. However, I have chosen the second hypothesis and propose to explore its theoretical advantages, which seem to me to support fundamental notions that Freud sketched out, though he did not develop them fully: the non-excitability of uncathected systems, the inertia principle, the lowering of tensions to zero, etc. I have thus refused to limit negative hallucination to a defence mechanism, in the more or less limited sense of the term.

One finds an explicit mention of negative hallucination by Breuer in the study of Anna O . . .,[42] where Anna O . . . seems to ignore the presence of a consultant brought along by the physician a few days after the death of the patient's father. Negative hallucination is always linked to what Breuer and Freud called *absences* (hallucinatory absences being a secondary condition). Breuer notes that 'the affect had transformed the patient's habitual daydreaming into a hallucinatory *absence*... Any sudden distressing affect would have the same effect as an absence'.[43] The context of the Breuer quotation must not distract us from its meaning. Indeed, Freud keeps the term absences, which he returns to five times in the first of the *Five Lectures on Psychoanalysis* in 1910.[44] It is on the basis of these remarks that 'profoundly nostalgic phantasies' are discovered. It is pointless to wonder whether absence is the consequence or the cause of the phantasy. It should be noted, however, that hypnosis was necessary to bring them together. *Absence* crops up again in Freud's posthumous notes of 1938[45] as a substitute phenomenon 'en attendant quelque chose qui ne venait point' (in French in the original: 'waiting for something that was not coming').

41 *S.E.*, XIV, p. 232.
42 *S.E.*, II, p. 27.
43 *S.E.*, II, pp. 42 and 43.
44 *S.E.*, XI, pp. 12–13.
45 *S.E.*, XXIII, p. 300.

The frequency of these correlative states of phantasy activity made me think that they represent in some sense processes of recathexis, not of withdrawn representative cathexes, but of an exclusion of processes of cathexis, in which negative hallucination operates. I have noted elsewhere (*Le narcissisme primaire*) the function of negative hallucination in the his-torico-genetic model, hypothetical and metaphorical, which serves as reference. From a structural point of view, I understand negative halluci-nation not as *absence of representation*, but as *representation of the absence of representation*, which is expressed clinically by an excess of affect, whose effect in relation to its representative correlate may be compared to the effect of aggressivity when it is disintricated from erotic libido. Formulated theoretically, this amounts to saying that *negative hallucination is the reverse side of that which hallucinatory fulfilment is the obverse*. As a result, its role extends over a much wider area than the narrow context of unconscious represen-tation, since its field of action is able to extend over all forms of representativity.

Not without reason, psychoanalysts feel somewhat mistrustful of negative concepts, sensing in them a surreptitious return to the logic of the con-scious. This reticence might have been less marked if the specific fecundity of the concept of negativity in psychoanalysis had been more clearly explained. The heuristic interest of negativity in psychoanalytic theory is to be placed in a context in which it is inferred from the result of a *covering* operation. In Freudian semantics, negativity is neither the process by which the contrary of the affirmation is posited, nor its antithesis, nor its liberating 'annihilation'. It is what is appreciated as absent cause retroactively deduced from work that refers to a reality that is both *covered over* and *displaced*, and in which the activity of thought is always given in concrete terms. We appre-hend absence, if only under the paradigm of the absent cause, in the threefold concrete domain of myth, passion and meanings, to use Bion's felicitous terminology. But in order to conceive of psychoanalysis, the detour of covering over and replacement takes a negative form.

'I never thought about it': throughout Freud's work this proposition returns again and again as the seal of what is 'made in the unconscious'. 'I never thought that such a thing could be thought without thinking about it.' 'All you had to do was think about it', one might say. Its echo would be rather: 'It was not enough to think about it for that not to be thought.' In fact, it is at the moment when the words 'I never thought about it' are spoken that it is admitted that it would have been better never to have thought about it, then or now – or, it is hinted, ever to have embarked on psychoanalysis. This may be thought on its own, therefore, and it is at that moment that the affect surges up. In more than one place, Freud notes this strange phenomenon of the disappearance of the image by speaking, as if, he says, 'a sweeping away' had taken place. But for this to happen there must be a mediation of the object, namely, the analyst, the event produced by free association in the circumstances of the analytic situation, coming as a structure in the transference relationship. This production of affect and this sweeping away are reminiscent of light coming from a distant star, which, by the time it reaches us after its journey in space, has ceased to shine in a star already dead, of which the psychoanalytic situation produces the inverted figure.

I – Process as model, living and experienced

I have established the conjunction of negative hallucination and affect. In contemporary psychoanalytic theory this conception links up with the classical idea of the appearance of affect with the withdrawal of the cathexis of representation. I wanted to carry this point of Freudian theory further in the light of modern theoretical approaches. Affect seemed to be the pivot of a system at the time and place of the encounter between forces deriving from the object and the event. I proposed as a contribution to the theory of the object two features, namely, that the object is given in an alternative of occurrence and intercurrence, desire and identification. The result of these combined effects is that *the object of desire may bring desire as object*, a problematic linked with identification in which *the subject has to situate himself or herself in the difference between the object of desire and desire as object*. It seemed to me that the introduction of the *event*, whose function I have tried to specify, had the purpose of raising the contradiction between phantasy and memory, the stress being placed not on the real, but on the disturbing role that it displays. The effects of this encounter reverberate through the mediated relations thus established as far as the *conjuncture* and the *structure*.

The conjuncture is the determining condition of structure, the structure that necessitates the intervention of the conjuncture for the establishment of its effects. The psychical apparatus is the ensemble of relations that, through the primal phantasies, makes us witnesses of these strange effects of the structure. The structure could be nothing other than the Oedipal organization as relation to a double difference: between the sexes and between the generations.

The articulation of this theoretical ensemble into a model has been borrowed from Lacan, who has rightly stressed the functions of *detour and mediation as means and as obstacle*; however, I have not adopted the terms that he uses to unite them in his schema, which, in my opinion, reflect a narcissizing interpretation of Freud's thought.

In a study of great interest, Georges Canguilhem classifies the models into two categories, thus designating sometimes a grouping of analogical correspondences between a natural subject and a manufactured object . . . and sometimes a system of semantic and syntactical definitions established in a mathematical language concerning the relations between the constituted elements of a structured object and their formal equipment.[46]

One can see at once that in psychoanalysis neither a model of the first type, which occurs most often in biology, nor a model of the second type would be suitable. No doubt the whole tendency of Freud's work goes against the choice thus formulated between *biomechanical and logico-mathematical terms*. If one tries to grasp in a still more general way the meaning of the oppositions that I have just indicated, one finds a traditional contradiction in the history of ideas, that between life and concept. To clarify the problem, I would refer once again to a study by Canguilhem, in which he deals with two questions. The first considers life as universal organization of matter, the principle of living forms; the second examines the experience of the individual human being. 'By life, one may understand the present participle or the past participle of the verb to live, the living and the lived.'[47] This simple introductory proposition takes us to the heart of the debate. In it is found the opposition between language and affect, that is to say, between formalization and the 'lived' (experience) – and their mutual confrontation. 'In knowledge, do we proceed', asks Canguilhem, 'from intelligence to life or from life to intelligence?' What one has here once more is the opposition between the structural and the genetic point of view in psychoanalysis. It is the impasse of the conflict that opposes those whom one suspects of intellectualism, because they affirm the primacy of the structures that govern the principles of developmental transformations; and those suspected of empiricism by the first group, who assign the essential role to evolution, development, differentiation. Whether one likes it or not, only a further work of reflection, in which the notions of structure and history are given their specificity in psychoanalysis, will enable us to emerge from these fruitless oppositions.

Canguilhem's reflections give us an opportunity to recall once again how Freud's work disturbs the traditional problematic. And nowhere is this more evident than in affect. What I have called the paradoxical situation of affect in Freudian theory is abundantly apparent here. That Freud should have referred by the same term, give or take a connotative variation (quota of affect and affect), to an *application of energy* and a *subjective experience* is perhaps what is most difficult about it. But what must retain our attention is that

46 Models and analogies in biological research, in Canguilhem (1968), pp. 305–18.
47 Canguilhem (1968), p. 335.

Freud did choose that term and assumed not only its hypothesis, but its contradiction. Thus it is by linking moving quantity (it is not possible to grasp the principle of the movement) and the fundamental subjective states of pleasure–unpleasure that the psyche will offer itself as a work of transformation of the interrelations between one and the other. And it is precisely to the extent that the whole theoretical context of the concept of representation would be evidence above all that these are mediations that are fruitful by their effects – but powerless to retain all the energic force in themselves – that the question of psychoanalysis posits problems not so much at the level of the combinatory of representations, as at the level at which the capturing fixation leaves force at liberty, a force that can be used only for an endless *relaunching* of the transforming operations. As such a relaunching, by the work of thought, moves away from the sources that gave it birth, it sees the product of its exclusion re-emerge repetitively. But here, from being enigmatic, the question may become dramatic, when the cause of the linkage, the moving quantity, is expatriated and manifested in discourse as that which refuses to allow itself to be bound by linkage. If the affect takes the place of representation, all the relation ratios around it may infiltrate it and the range of the process widen instead of contracting. On the other hand, in an extreme case, as it crosses the filters through which this compatibility with representation is assured, the affect may stand out, attracting to itself all the violence of discourse, whereas putting the meaning into perspective frees the living force, which distributes its planes and is inverted into a relief in which the freed energy extravasates, this energy overloading any relation ratio to the point of making it impossible, either by tearing it apart or by petrifying it.

Freud never went beyond the questions that he raised in the 'Project', but he did try, and that is something, to tame them, that is to say, to take that oscillation between *discharge functions* and *transference functions* over intercommunicating vessels as far as it would go.[48] Some may reproach me for lifting a corner of the veil that Freud wanted to draw over the indecent nudity of a thought whose ink burnt the paper on which it was written, and even for finding a somewhat concupiscent fascination in it. It has given me enough trouble to make me feel absolved of this violation of an optical taboo.

In his article 'The Moses of Michelangelo', Freud is making a confession about himself when he declares that Moses, in overcoming his own passions in order to take up a mission to which he had dedicated himself, was embarking on the most formidable psychical exploit of which man is

48 *S.E.*, I, p. 312.

capable. But the figure who inspired this reflection is a man who narrowly avoided having the tables of the Law fall on his head. In legendary tradition, the passion was at first God's and took the form of storm clouds and rumbling thunder. Between these signs of sacred fury and divine speech echoed the cry of the ram's horn, that Chofar, who attracted the attention first of Reik, then of Rosolato, who rediscovered the original pole of 'complaint, affliction and immense jubilation',[49] which led to the Voice. Moses communicates the content of the Law orally before Yahweh inscribes it in stone – and it is on his descent from Sinai after God's inscription and before the worshipping of the golden calf that he breaks the Tables in anger. In the end, it will be on other tables of stone, carved by Moses on Yahweh's orders, similar to the first ones, that the Ten Commandments will be fixed forever.

As to what was sealed on the first Tables, one will never know. And yet it is what one tries to discover with each patient whose analysis one undertakes. To sit in a chair and listen to patients is not really very difficult. What is more difficult is to love the truth as Freud loved it, that is to say, as one loves a sexual object.

49 Rosolato (1959–69), p. 296.

Postscript 1: Free reflections on the representation of affect[1]

I have chosen to approach the theme of the representation of affect in an attempt to take up once more certain of the ideas that I have expressed on this subject and to evaluate not only the relations between representation and affect, but the representative function of affect, in other words, to discover whether one can attribute to the affect a function of representation and how that function of representation may become part of our conception of the psyche.

I do not know whether I shall succeed in bringing more order and clarity to the subject, so difficult is it to define the nature of affect and to situate it in the unconscious. The true difficulty lies in its use of modes of thought that are fairly far removed from consciousness and the rationalizations of consciousness.

For me, it is no longer satisfactory to remain at the point at which my earlier work had brought me, namely, to distribute affect into two categories, one integrated in the chain of representations, and therefore having a value as signal, the other being a factor of traumatic disorganization, which takes up again the two forms of anxiety described by Freud in *Inhibitions, Symptoms and Anxiety*. I should like to attempt an investigation that would go deeper. However, one must be aware that all reflection on representation must set out from the idea that the Freudian oeuvre is our representation. It is our representation because we operate on it in exactly the same way that representation operates on sense impressions; one constantly makes it drift into post-Freudian theoretical systems; and one is always obliged to go back to it, as if it were both an

---

1 Transcription of an oral presentation to a symposium on representation at the Paris Psychoanalytic Society, 1984. Reprinted in André Green, *Propédeutique. La Métapsychologie revisitée*, Seyssel: Editions Champ Vallon, 1995.

unknown object of reference and the starting point of the drift as representation itself.

But if one takes this seriously, one thing should come as a surprise, namely, the fact that the relations between representation and affect are the object of an extended reflection on a short period in Freud's work, mainly in the *Papers on Metapsychology*. This reflection continues as far as the threshold of *The Ego and the Id*. I say to the threshold of *The Ego and the Id* because Freud was to move away from it in the course of that work: the whole of the last part shows more than neglect, I would say disdain, of this problem, even when he refers more and more to the affect as a phenomenon.

This has struck many of Freud's commentators. When one compares the definitions that Freud gives of the unconscious and those that he gives of the id, one finds a number of elements common to both, but one is also struck by certain omissions. He is not just missing things out: he is also adopting positions, as when he declares that 'there is no notion of content in the id', that is to say, as a consequence, no notion of representation in the sense of ideational representative.

How is one to explain this? I suppose that at a certain stage in the course of his theoretical work, Freud no longer felt the need to situate the problem of the unconscious in relation to the consciousness. Now, for Freud, the problem of representation lay essentially in its relations with conscious activity. It is as if Freud is now, I do not know whether self-confident is quite the right word, but in any case determined to turn his back on this question of the relation between the unconscious and consciousness. It must be acknowledged that he rids himself of the problem of the unconscious, however shocking that might seem to our ears today, when the unconscious is no longer more than a psychical quality, which is what he clearly states in *An Outline of Psycho-Analysis*.[2]

Then perhaps the question shifts and, even if one keeps the reference to the unconscious, it can no longer be posed in terms of content, a notion

---

2 In other words, what makes it possible to apprehend the non-conscious psyche is not to be sought in the direction of the representations (even those of the affects), but rather in the direction of the instinctual impulses. One can see that the stress has been displaced in the direction of movements as strong as those of the drives. However, since in any case it is a question of designating aspects of the psyche outside consciousness, one will continue to refer to the unconscious in a metonymic way, agreeing to apply the term psychical to that which concerns an order of facts further removed from consciousness, a reality that is defined above all by instinctual dynamism considered as a force in movement animated by the directions of binding and unbinding and whose relations with earlier perceptions and representations becomes what is at stake in the id's relations with the ego. The unconscious does not remain the same as it was in the first topography, since it is no longer limited to content (the repressed), but also annexes part of what contains it (the unconscious defences). (Note of 1995.)

quite inadequate to define the nature of what is envisaged, as much in relation to the unconscious as in relation to the id.

The move to the second topography is contemporary with an effacement of the role of representations and an ever more marked inclination to invoke the instinctual impulse.

I shall take by way of example a quotation from 'Constructions in analysis', for if one is to rethink representations it must be in the terms in which Freud understood it in that text. He writes:

What sort of material does he put at our disposal which we can make use of to put him on the way to recovering the lost memories? All kinds of things. He gives us fragments of these memories in his dreams, invaluable in themselves but seriously distorted as a rule by all the factors concerned in the formation of dreams. Again, he produces ideas, if he gives himself up to 'free association', in which we can discover allusions to the repressed experiences and derivatives of the suppressed affective impulses as well as of the reactions against them. And, finally, there are hints of repetitions of the affects belonging to the repressed material to be found in actions performed by the patient, some fairly important, some trivial, both inside and outside the analytic situation. Our experience has shown that the relation of transference, which becomes established towards the analyst, is particularly calculated to favour the return of these emotional connections. It is out of such raw material – if we may so describe it – that we have to put together what we are in search of.[3]

Here the references to representation are allusive, since it is a question of memories and ideas that crop up during a session. On the other hand, the reference to the affect is repeated three times. This does not at all mean that, like Freud, I, in turn, am trying to distance myself from representation, on the contrary. I shall say quite simply that it was a question of seeing how the problem had changed in nature in relation to the concepts defended in 1915.

Freud observes that what was at issue in the material comprises at the same time what is most ancient, what is least representable and the contrary reactions associated with it. This is a characteristic feature of the affect: it is capable of expressing at the same time as the movement of the drive the reaction caused by that movement in an opposite direction.

In the history of psychoanalysis there was a turning away from representation, especially under the influence of the English School and it seemed

3 *S.E.*, XXIII, p. 258.

that the notion of object–relation was much more convenient for the analyst. The question is why representation returned to the foreground. It is, I believe, thanks to the works of the psychosomaticians. It is about the notion of mental functioning that the question of representation acquired a new interest. The question bears not only on the presence or absence of representations, but on their functional value for the psychical apparatus. And it is this that gives legitimacy to my reflections, because what is at issue here is the evaluation of my own psychoanalytic work when it concerns representation and my conception of it.

Before going any further we should return to Freud's position in 1915. Indeed, as Alain Gibeault has reminded us and as all the commentators on Freud remind us, what one has here is Freud delivering a quite extraordinary blow in an attempt to sustain the hypothesis of the dissociation of affect and representation, and the possibility of separate destinations for each of them. However, since what interests me today is the representation of representation at the level of theoretical language, I see Freud using a double language here. That is to say, when he speaks of representation, he treats it according to philosophical tradition, whereas when he deals with affect he uses a different language.

Representation is treated under the double aspect of philosophical thinking, namely, the reproduction of something that has belonged to perception and the replacement of the form that it has taken: reproduction and replacement. But, obviously, what he adds to it is that an associative process is at work here, what a particular philosophical school, associationism, had already defended. Freud takes up this associationism, but, in the end, to defend the opposite position from associationism. In other words, it is not a question of knowing how representations are linked together, but how, at an earlier stage, they are unlinked in order to be linked together again. Associationism conceives only of a cumulative approach in which, one might say, association is constantly enriched. On the other hand, when Freud speaks of affect, he is using physiological language, terms involving not only energy, but also corporal innervation. That is to say, Freud does not treat these two elements identically. The difference is expressed in terms of their relation to memory traces. He declares that affect is a process of discharge, whereas representations are the concern of memory traces. But, from that time on, one sees Freud confronted by the difficulty of conceiving of the existence, the form I should say, of the unconscious affect. It is a problem that he did not resolve until 1923; but until then Freud was hindered by a prejudice that is both philosophical and psychological. Why was this?

This derives precisely from the fact that, up to 1915, the question of unconscious representation was purely and simply linked to its disappearance from consciousness and that it was no longer a question, for him, of rediscovering the missing representation at the heart of a succession of unconscious representations, which, of course, is what tends to encourage free association. What is important to notice is that, until 1915 at least, representation does not change its nature because it is unconscious. It exists simply in the state of disappeared representation, hence the difficulties in explaining what the unconscious is without falling into the trap of the hypothesis of another consciousness. But the fact is that representation does not change its nature in relation to conscious representation because it is topographically linked to the unconscious. There then follow discussions on the question of the functional hypothesis and the economic hypothesis, the change of status, or the inscription in two different registers. In any case, there is a persistence of representation in the unconscious.

For affect, the solution that he proposes seems to me to be less satisfactory at first sight, but, on further reflection, one of extraordinary force. Considering the various vicissitudes of the quantitative factor of the instinctual representative, under the effect of repression, Freud considers the possibility of a drastic repression of the drive, since he says that it may be that no trace of it exists any longer. Here one might be tempted to think that Freud is referring to the ideational representative. I do not think that is at all the case. I believe that Freud wishes to speak here of a much more definitive phenomenon of eradication of the instinctual representative, that is to say, of the most inchoate, the closest to the earliest representative of the drive. I would willingly link what is in question here with something that has always struck me as enigmatic, which appears in that strange title of 1926, *Inhibitions, Symptoms and Anxiety*. It is a scarcely sketched out addition to the metapsychological reflection of 1915: the entry of inhibition where the excessive eroticization of a function entails by way of response an amputation of the ego, accompanied in a muted way by extinction of instinctual activity. In my opinion, this is already there in embryo when Freud speaks of this vicissitude of affect.

Other problems face us concerning relations between affect and representation. One question concerns the reduplications within the representative system. That is to say, representation is a reduplication; in itself, thing-presentation is a reduplication. Now, in the representative system, there is reduplication of reduplication insofar as the system of thing-presentations is relayed, accompanied or taken up again by the system of word-presentations. As for the affect, it has only a single system of expression at its disposal. Another problem concerns a major difference: the representation–perception coupling introduces the dimension of deception and doubt. At the beginning, Freud's whole work is haunted by the distinction between perception as an objective guarantee of reality, and representation as deceptive effect that runs the risk of damaging the psychical apparatus. Hence the problem of deception, of the existence or non-existence of the represented object, or of the judgement of existence or non-existence, is absolutely inconceivable in terms of affect. The affect never doubts its own existence. This means that, when confronted by an affect that presents problems as to how it is to be dealt with, how it is to be integrated into the psychical apparatus, I can resort either to affective extinction, or to its reversal into an opposite affect, or to its projection on to another (there are other solutions that I shall mention a little later), but even if I wonder about the true nature of my feelings, their existence is not put into question, for to do so would be to question my very existence. Hence no double relay, no snare.

Lastly, there is a third differential characteristic that seems to me to be of the greatest importance: representation operates only in absence, in presence the activity of perception prevails. Representation presupposes the evocation by non-perception, with the bracketing out of the perceptive pole. The entire analysis is based on the constancy of the setting, so that representations may arise. The affect, on the other hand, operates in both cases; in presence and absence.

Why was this concept of representation in 1915 ignored by Freud later? Because, little by little, and already in 1915, the perception–representation problematic had failed. Since then, in the Metapsychological supplement to the theory of dreams, developed in the *Papers on Metapsychology*, Freud had sought for criteria that would guarantee the perception of reality, but he was forced to admit defeat. This capitulation took the form of reality testing. In other words, the perception–representation problematic could not be based on functional differences alone and Freud was forced to introduce here an a priori, namely, reality testing. From then on, the perception–representation problematic loses much of its interest. But it becomes more complicated, since reality testing does not function automatically and without failure, as psychosis shows. There may be repression of reality and failure of reality testing. Even when there is no major disorganization in the ego, perception may very well register reality and yet in no way conform to its demands or submit itself to it, as in the experience of splitting in fetishism.

It is of limited interest, therefore, to consider things in relation to representation.

Can one still say that the reference to the memory trace will never the less retain some solidity insofar as it involves the memory? We find in the *Introductory Lectures on Psycho-Analysis* a commentary by Freud on the affects, in which he says that they are part of a system of memory traces, to which he assigns a phylogenetic origin, residues of ancient, well adapted acts that have been internalized. So much is this the case that the true opposition is not, therefore, between a historical perspective, reserved to representation, and something immediate, belonging to the affect, but rather to the development of two histories. I will say a history convertible by representation and a compact history, for it is probable that behind these phylogenetic experiences Freud is referring to individual primal experiences. It is also in the *Introductory Lectures* that one finds the most interesting definition of affect, and the one that, in my opinion, is capable of getting us out of our usual modes of thought. He declares there that the affects are not elementary things, but, on the contrary, extremely composite products that introduce two factors:

1   processes of innervation and discharge;
2   sensations, these sensations being themselves distinguished from perceptions of movement when the affect goes into operation, and direct sensations, qualitatively distinct from pleasure and unpleasure.

Why is this construction important? Because if, with Freud, one continues to think that unconscious phenomena are devoid of quality, and if representations are therefore expressions of what is called thought, but a thought devoid of quality, the affect at the unconscious level will manifest by the innervation–perception of movement dyad, since one has withdrawn quality. At the level of sensations, Freud distinguishes between perception of movement and the direct, qualitatively distinct sensations of pleasure–unpleasure associated with it. At the conscious level we have the perception of movement, which Freud separates from the quality of affect. And it is this, in my opinion, that gives all its strength to the instinctual impulse, insofar as it cannot exclude reference to movement and this, I believe, is what the 1915 theory of representation tried to understate.

In the *Papers on Metapsychology*, what mattered to Freud at the time that he was examining the various forms of repression was to distinguish between two stages:

• the first, which he calls substitute formation, and
• the second, that of symptom of formation.

With substitute formation, Freud sees displacement as the means by which representation plays its full role, as is shown with phobias and obsessions. Let us take the example of the Wolf Man: Freud says that, when the instinctual representative fell on the wolf, displacement occurred and there was a substitute formation that made possible quite peaceful relations with the father. The quota of affect is transformed into anxiety. Then, in a second stage, there is symptom formation: phobia.

However, when Freud turns to hysteria, the substitute is corporal innervation and the substitute formation coincides with the symptom formation: the two stages are combined into one. In other words, if from the point of view of the thought mechanisms of consciousness one can easily make a link between the notion of an ideational representative of the drive and the idea of a substitute, one is following one's habit of conscious thinking and is not too disturbed. But what must be taken into account is that, for Freud, this substitute formation can have nothing to do with representation in the classical sense of the term and be corporal innervation.

Why does this pose a problem? Because the operation of substitution in representation has a quite clear source and this source is the external world. Freud says as much unambiguously: 'all presentations originate from perceptions and are repetitions of them'.[4] So it seems quite natural to us that the action of substituting for representation refers to this transformation of reality that comes from outside, whose model is placed outside. One has no difficulty in admitting that there is never an exact reproduction, but always a transformation in relation to an apprehensible external source. But what becomes of this when the operation of substitution concerns something as unthinkable as the notion of corporal innervation? I believe that at this point one must conceive things in a different way from the way in which one apprehends them intuitively. One always speaks of affect in terms of complement, of connotations. One says: there is representation and then one must not forget the affect that accompanies it. But what makes us so sure that the affect has this accompanying role? And why not think, on the contrary, that *the profound nature of the affect is to be a psychical event linked to a movement awaiting a form*? Once this form is found, the dissociation between affect and representation can take place. But what does this dissociation depend on? Instinct, Freud tells us 'has become detached from the idea'.[5] In itself, representation has no autonomy. One never says: 'Representation is detached from the drive'.

What one has here is a consideration of cathexis. One might suppose at this point that this detachment actually consists of the transference of one form to another form, opportunities for which are constantly provided by the external world – which constantly feeds the affect to enable it to mobilize part of its dynamism in psychical events that have the power to constitute poles of fixation that will be able to be broken down into more primitive elements and later recombined.

So the question that I am asking is this: since there is a use of diversity, not an appeal from forms, but an invitation made to forms to be captured by the drive by means of its affect representative, what is the unifying factor? Is there a spontaneous unification? My growing impression is that this factor of spontaneous unification cannot exist anywhere else but in repression. When one reads what Freud says of repression, it is as if it plays the role of

4 *S.E.*, XIX, p. 237.
5 *S.E.*, XIV, p. 152.

a selector. Repression is not confined to anticathexis; it also carries out a permanent surveillance of meaning, in which associations are formed. Sometimes its vigilance is deceived, but this associative work is constantly placed under the eye of repression, so that what is reassociated can never again create a trauma for the psychical apparatus.

Rereading the 1915 article 'Repression', there is no longer any doubt in my mind that it is absolutely necessary to distinguish between the psychical representative of the drive and the ideational representative. Freud does not always make this clear, but sometimes he does. When he wishes to specify that he is speaking of the psychical representative of the drive *qua* ideational representative, he places a note to this effect in parentheses. Reading the article more closely, one has a strong impression that, when Freud speaks of the quantitative factor of the drive, he is referring to the movement that ani-mates the psychical representative of the drive. This poses an extremely important epistemological problem, namely: when speaking of the ideational representative, there is a reference to a model, even if one is inca-pable of saying what exactly this model is (I am referring to perception as the source of representation). When one relates representation to percep-tion, it is not at all essential to know exactly what the content of the perception is. What is important epistemologically is to know that there is a reference to something perceived. On the other hand, one can take Freud's definition of the drive and read: 'An "instinct" appears to us as a concept on the frontier between the mental and the somatic, as the psychical represen-tative of the stimuli originating from within the organism and reaching the mind, as a measure of the demand made upon the mind for work in conse-quence of its connection with the body'.[6] What one is dealing with here is a completely different epistemological status of representation, in the sense that there is no model. But the psychical representative of the excitations that come from inside the body and reach the psyche is in no way repre-sentable. In other words, one is faced with a conception of representation – and here Freud's thought is revolutionary – without any reference to what is represented, for the psychical excitations coming from inside the body cannot be the object of any representation. In Freud's system of thought, there may be a difference between a representation 'of' and a representation 'for'. By that I mean that the function of 'for' representation is not situated in relation to something that is outside it, and certainly not in relation to a form; it is a function of delegation that may be revealed to itself only by an encounter with a form. Indeed one will notice that, in this definition of the drive, Freud establishes something that I should say was more than a dual-ism; there is not simply the borderline concept between body and mind,

6 *S.E.*, XIV, pp. 121–2.

there is an implicit outline of what he calls the mind, as if one were speaking to another. With the mind part of the definition of the drive, it is as if the body were addressing someone else inside the psychical space.

The point that I wish to make and which may not seem to be entirely clear is that the question of the affect–representative is linked to identification. If one regards the ideational representative as coming from the external world, one must situate the affect–representative at the level of the affective induction of the other. The drive, as a spontaneous force, ignorant of itself, can come into existence, be manifested in a thinkable way, only by mediation. This mediation is the other; it is representation that opens the way to the specular, but this mediation may also take the circuit of identification. There is a reference to 'Mourning and melancholia', in which Freud speaks of primal identification and its relation to the lost object. It is clear that there is no longer any question here of representation. In the case of melancholia, Freud is careful to draw a distinction between representation and identification, when he asks the question: 'What part of the mental processes of the disease still takes place in connection with the unconscious object-cathexes that have been given up, and what part in connection with their substitute, by identification, in the ego?'[7] The fact that the ego is able to identify the lost object shows that there is a treatment of the other that consists in its absorption by identification and which is situated outside representation, which concerns only object cathexes that have been left outside this identification.

When considering the very regressive forms which have to be dealt with in analysis, one cannot fail to observe that, apart from the difficulty that one gives oneself in interpreting object cathexes, one comes up against this structure of the affect linked to an identification that does not know what it is the identification of. I am thinking of those patients who live in a sort of inviolable affective hideout, which they call a black hole. It takes a lot of time to understand that this black hole is not just something that they remove from psychoanalytic investigation; it is the space in which they are themselves enclosed and that, for them, there is an enormous danger in leaving it. This danger may be the loss of an inner object whose relations with narcissism are not easy to establish. It is clearly not a question of primary narcissism *qua* form, nor of auto-eroticism. It is close to what Tustin describes as 'encapsulation'. Such subjects feel that if they left this space they would be in mortal danger because certain objects inside them would be free to attack them from the inside and that their only protection is to find themselves in that identification with an object that is not nameable, in which they imprison themselves inside themselves. Furthermore, they

7 *S.E.*, XIV, pp. 255–6.

express the humiliation of needing the other. This feeling is quite fundamental, for it expresses a rejection of the drive; fear of the drive is not rejection of
the drive. The analyst is witness to a sort of emptying of the body by the drive.
The drive no longer lives in the body, but it cannot disappear for all that. The
drive is then transferred on to the other. It is the other that disposes of the
whole of the drive. Furthermore, in that projection, the drive loses its libidinal qualities and becomes pure power. It is probably an effect of the
unbinding; when the drive is unbound, when this emptying of the body by
the drive takes place, this drive can only go and inhabit – I don't know
whether the phantasy of the other or the shadow of the other would be the
right term, for no doubt it is something that vaguely evokes a representation –
however, *in extremis*, it has no form and is entirely *in potentia*. The drive
cannot be thought; one is forced to have recourse to mediations; in the broad
sense, they are representations. One can work only through these mediations,
but it would be a big mistake to confuse mediation with that which is mediated. One is now obliged to give oneself an image of the drive that is different
from the representations on offer in current theory. The drive appears to me
to be more and more like a sort of *psychical hand*, one of whose most fearsome
destinies being what has been expressed in the notion of mastery. In those
cases in which it seems that the forms of representation are not being
cathected, the dynamic potential of the drive does not have as its aim to take
what is the very activity of the drive in its most fundamental manifestation, but
to prevent the other from taking it, which is a reversal of its aim.

From the point of view of this 'prehensive' conception of the drive, the
works of Tustin seem to me to be of great interest. I am sometimes rather
reticent concerning theorizations about children, but I should like to say
that I do find these works interesting, not because they define some stage of
development, but because they have the merit of bringing out the constituent elements in the analyst's conceptualization. If one is able to conceive
of the constituent elements, one will be better placed to reflect on what is
being transformed. For the constituent element brings out the importance
of manipulation. Autistic children create something that they call *shapes*.
These shapes have nothing to do with the representation of external objects;
they are, says Tustin, asymbolic, shapes that these children concoct, which
they can transform, but not plan ahead. She relates these shapes to tactile
hallucinations. And, indeed, what seems important is the notion of impression. In order to give some idea of the function of these shapes, Tustin says:
'Forget your chair. Instead, feel your seat pressing against the seat of the
chair. It will make a "shape". If you wriggle, the shape will change. Those
shapes will be entirely personal to you'.[8] These autistic shapes are impres-

8 Frances Tustin, 'Autistic Shapes', *IRP*, 11, 1984, pp. 281–2.

sions. Their essential function is to create experience out of corporal sensations. These corporal sensations do not have the ordinary quality of corporal sensations; they are the emanation of something felt, which, at bottom, is really experienced as a corporal *substance*, the separation with the object giving the experience of a loss of substance at the level of the body.

The notion of confusion seems to me . . . to be totally confused. For if there is confusion, why is there, at the moment of separation, an impression of loss? When there is confusion, there is a state that is sensitive neither to addition nor to subtraction. It must be something quite different. Indeed it is a matter of *difference*. The aspiration at all costs to rediscover the sensation of contact is accompanied by a complete intolerance to asymmetry, to contrariety, to what isn't quite 'right', in the sense of corresponding accurately. Now representation in the usual sense is exactly the opposite: to resort to representation is to show that the representation isn't entirely 'right' in relation to the perception or to the object of desire. These observations call for an extension of the field of representation. But let us return to the formulations of Freudian theory.

At the level of consciousness, reduplication takes place since one has word-presentation and thing-presentation. At the level of the unconscious, where is the reduplication? There is only thing-presentation. Is it that the thing itself provides the reduplication? No. I believe that it is the affect that is the reduplication of the thing-presentation, the object-presentation. And, finally, what is the affect, what is it the representative of? To answer this question, one must turn to the very end of Freud's work, to something that is rarely referred to, as if one hardly dares speak of it. I mean the theory of the drives, by which the sexual drives are turned into life drives. And yet this occurs at a time when Freud gives the greatest field to the sexual drive, when he integrates everything into it – drives of self-preservation, narcissism, object drives – and even adds something else, which he calls Eros or life drives. How is one to conceive of the relation between these two formulations? In *An Outline of Psycho-Analysis*, he concludes the chapter on the theory of the drives with this remark:

> The greater part of what we know about Eros – that is to say, about its exponent, the libido – has been gained from a study of the sexual function, which, indeed, on the prevailing view, even if not according to our theory, coincides with Eros.[9]

Would the affect be this representative of the life drive in the sexual function?

9   *S.E.*, XXIII, p. 151.

I shall end with a few general remarks.

If one can consider that psychoanalysis, by its mode of thought, turns tradition upside down, it is no doubt because it forces us to conceive of causality in a way that overthrows our capacities of reasoning and even those of psychoanalysts. Whereas one is used to beginning by asking the right questions in order to find their appropriate answers, psychoanalytic experience forces us to proceed in a different way, that is, one has to understand that one is dealing first of all not with enigmas, but with answers that precede any question. These answers are solutions to questions that one is not capable of conceiving and whose formulation eludes our understanding. This is because our way of asking questions is always in that area beyond the answer with which one has been confronted, that is to say, with the beginning of a questioning that conceals the character of answer to what is presented to us as an initial enigma.

In other words, one begins the question at the level of what is already an answer and because one is incapable of conceiving of the order of the facts that determined the original answer, the whole series of questions and the answers given to them leaves an interrogation in suspense.

What do these formulated questions and the answers that they have brought with them tell us about the implicit, unformulated, perhaps unformulable question of the phenomenon, taken as a point of departure, considered as an answer? It seems to me too easy to regard the succession of questions and answers simply as a snare, a sort of Utopia, a screen. Instead I shall consider that the function of the axes, the nervures, the selective choices of any *a posteriori* system of questions and answers is to manifest the character of *a priori* answer of the phenomenon under consideration and to see in it how it makes the question possible – to consider retroactively the initial question as an echo having no answer that can be found, and yet one that has already been given. In other words, one has to see the first phenomenon, to which I have given the name of answer, as always having a transgressive character. The question thus concealed will lead to conception of thought, not as questioning, but as the result of a transgression. I am thinking not so much of the notion of prohibition, as of that of the boundary: what is there, what exists and questions me, is there only because it has not been able to stay in its place. So it is confused with the movement of cathecting life, not only '*Wo es war soll ich werden*', but 'If I come, where was it?' There where I could be only by representing myself. This infernal circle derives from the fact that I can question everything, except my own life.

That is why sexuality eludes us in its role as life's answer. Yet one wonders about its effect on everything that is not sexuality, or about that which inside it moves, meets obstacles, is subverted, transformed. A psychoanalyst does not ask questions in order to know why sexuality is there, or whether it might not be. And it is there that one forgets what is one's sole possible approach to life, because it alone links the forms assumed by both the most fundamental spontaneity of the human being and his or her need to couple with another, which is the condition of maintaining human existence. And it is no doubt also because there is no sense in going straight to the primal question of the why and how of life, without employing a mediation or thread that one would pull out of a tangled web. How can one be sure that one has pulled the right thread? One may well doubt it. Others are offered: reality, thought, God, etc. How does it come about that one regards one's own as the most effective one? It is because with human sexuality as the clue to the life drives, this clue will never entirely coincide with what it is supposed to represent. For what sexuality says is that, from the point of view of human life, each of us is never more than a half of it, marked as it is by sexual difference. What is lacking is a clue to the life drive, the life of another.

And yet sexuality loses nothing of its function as clue, that is to say, of that which is supposed to account for the whole of life. It is then that one understands that the series of questions and answers concerning the stops, obstacles, diversions, deviations, extinction, effusions of the sexual drive are answers from which one elaborates one's first thinkable questions, and the answers that one thinks ought to be given them.

As to the questions that one cannot formulate from their status as first answers, it is not enough to say that the cause lies in the obscurity, the muddle, the ungraspability of life. This is only part of the mystery. What is lacking in the formulation of this question is the fundamental link between the sexual drive and its object, of which one must be content, at best, with a representation. Representation of the other, representation even of the sexuality of that other who comes so miraculously to marry for better or for worse the forms of the subject that are revealed in that encounter.

If the conjunction of the two clues gives us a glimpse by means of the representation of one of them of what the life of one of them might be, one will still remain totally in the dark as to what the life of the other might be. That is to say, the question of life will always remain unknown if its clue, sexuality, teaches us that it always implies another, of whom one knows only the answers, without being able to say to what question.

274

Postscript 2: The representation of affects (and their consequences for our understanding of what we call psychical)

ANDRÉ GREEN

> For feeling has to him imparted power
> That through growing faculties of sense
> Doth like an agent of the one great Mind
> Create, creator and receiver both,
> Working but in alliance with the works
> Which it beholds.
>
> Wordsworth, *The Prelude, Book II*

It is customary for everyone starting to write on affects from a broad per-spective to recall that there is no present satisfactory theory of affects, and to say that all the same the census of the theories is by the present time more or less around a hundred.

Such a field of research is so full of possible confusions that it is important to examine carefully definitions and basic assumptions. For instance, one can compare the different statements of Laplanche and Pontalis, Fine and Moore, and Rycroft, written in approximately the same year,[1] which show significant differences of perspective.

The twofold theory

Instead of building a realistic portrait of affects, one has to give priority to the problems which hamper our understanding because of our difficulty in organizing our conceptions. Therefore accepting that our description has to give up the aim of similarity to what it is dealing with, I prefer to use con-ceptual tools whose value makes it possible for us to link what one supposes

---

1 Laplanche and Pontalis (1967-1973); Fine and Moore (1967); Rycroft (1968). See in these three works the entry: affects.

are fundamental aspects born from our thinking about affects from a psychical point of view. One will then try to build a representation of affect which may stand as a psychical construct. In fact what I am assuming is that there is no possibility in the present state of our knowledge to use directly biological or psychological data for the erection of so-called scientific models because first a psychical model is required from which one will – or will not – be able to derive other models of a more general range.[2]

This idea is shared by others (Grinberg 1986[3] and indirectly Bion), though their conclusions differ from mine. It is always commendable to start with a reference to clinical experience. Surely it encourages us to deal centrally with affects. How could one define transference without focusing on affects? However one will soon remark that the fundamental affects differ from one analyst to another, and this finds its explanation in the fact that psychoanalysts connect affects with different basic assumptions.

Psychoanalytic theory is twofold: it is the theory of psychoanalytic practice and it is also the theory of psychical activity in general. As it is impossible to assume that what is analysable in the psychoanalytic situation can account for the psychical activity in general, the basic assumption is that the analytic situation creates favourable conditions for the emergence of what is fundamental in psychic activity in general. Therefore one must be very cautious about assuming a correspondence between the two targets of theory. The theory issued from practice has to draw its main core from what is the essence of psychoanalytical experience in order to form the basis of the fundamental concepts of the general theory, and, conversely, the fundamental concepts of the general theory have to be in close connection with the essentials of psychoanalytic practice. To be more clear: one should deal exclusively with what *only* psychoanalytic experience can achieve in what has to be known. The information gathered outside the analytical situation should not be integrated to psychoanalytical theory without close scrutiny of its reliability in relation to the parameters of psychoanalytical thinking. In spite of these warnings one has to admit that the challenging new theories do not obey these requirements. Either those aspects that are highlighted do not seem to relate to the basic principles which are supposed to be at the roots of psychical activity according to psychoanalytical thinking, or the features of psychoanalytic practice are interpreted with conceptual tools which

---

2 I am here thinking of the impressive attempt of the late Jerome Sashin to apply René Thom's catastrophe theory to affect. I have paid homage to his work in a lecture to celebrate his memory at the Boston Psychological Society and Institute on 25 April 1992.

3 The paper was presented at the 2nd Symposium of European Federation of Psychoanalysis, Divonne 1986. In the same issue the reader will find other contributions on the topic by Joseph Sandler, René Diatkine and myself, with a summary of the discussion by Quinodoz.

do not fit with psychoanalytic principles but are borrowed from neighbouring fields with a considerable loss of explanatory power when trying to understand what is specifically psychoanalytic in them. Of course there is still room for debate between diverse psychoanalytic interpretations, forcing one to admit that one is not in a position to decide which theory is good and which has to be rejected.

It is currently stated today that for all sorts of reasons, Freud's metapsychology has to be abandoned, only his clinical discoveries deserving to survive. As my own position is contrary to that recommendation I shall not enter into that discussion. Whether one agrees with Freud or not, a psychoanalytic theory of affects must take a stand on the existence of unconscious affects, on their relationship with conscious affects, and on the other components of mental life, a point left unclear by Freud.

The observation of affects in infants

Though there is a general consensus that affects are rooted in the very beginnings of mental life I do not believe that a developmental approach is really helpful in solving our difficulties. I am aware that many colleagues, if not the majority, will not agree with this assertion. Due to space limitations my statements run the risk of being considered as overschematizations; nevertheless I shall try to explain my reasons.

1   Observational procedures with children are unable to give us an idea of what goes on in the psychic processes of the internal world especially those belonging to the unconscious. Moreover they have less access to these psychic processes than what can be drawn from the examination of adults. The approach is essentially behaviouristic when it is not closely linked to the psychoanalysis of children.
2   The facts discovered by such methods have great value for a psychological approach to the infant but are of less significance for the understanding and elaboration of psychoanalytic theory. Unfortunately for psychoanalysis the researchers (sometimes even psychoanalysts) draw from the discovered facts of observation, which seem to me of little significance for psychoanalysis, theoretical implications which are of momentous importance for psychoanalytic theory. The changes they propose imply radical transformation of our body of knowledge along lines which are not psychoanalytical, but only psychoanalytical-like. This results in an increase of the normal gap which exists between the two fields of theory: theory born from psychoanalytical practice and theory as knowledge of general psychic activity, orienting the former in a direction far away from the basic principles of psychoanalysis.

3   The findings, most of the time, seem to contradict psychoanalytic concepts only superficially. They invite us to a greater hermeneutic analysis
of their contents instead of declaring them unfit. These observational
studies obviously have a weaker explanatory power than psychoanalytic
theory in spite – or maybe because – of its remaining ambiguities, mysteries and enigmas – most of them being prematurely given up and
replaced by oversimplifications. It is noteworthy that many of the so-
called new views born from infant observation such as self relatedness or
intersubjectivity apply more specifically to affects already present in
psychoanalytic theory, but they were stated in a different spirit. They
have been introduced by psychoanalysts (Lacan, Mahler, Winnicott,
Kohut and others) who eventually referred to the infant most of the
time out of any experimental setting. The main influence of this type of
setting was to change the psychoanalytical parameters, which are difficult to fit to the procedure of science, into more submissive and
manageable parameters of a psychological nature. Dealing with such a
complex matter as affects this procedure can only have the effect of
changing a topic which has puzzled minds like Plato, Descartes,
Spinoza, Hume, and Kierkegaard into a skeletal model in which affect
is seen only from its observable features or with the help of a schema
modelled on the pattern of input and output. An axis is then privileged
between affect and action in a direct line. It is used to construct retrospectively a causality for affects which have to obey the basic linearity of
the latent link between affect and action. From this perspective it is not
denied that affects are mainly internalized structures, but the dominant
assumed relationship between affect and action overemphasizes the
externalized aspects of affective manifestations and builds retrospectively *ad hoc* schematic behaviourally understandable so called 'causal
factors' of affects.[4] The externalization of affective features can then
include the partner of a relationship (interrelations) to compensate for
the lack of an analysis of the inner aspects of affects. This will lead to a
more comprehensive model (affect attunement, Stern). Still one remains
in the behavioural sphere[5] and it is difficult to understand how one can

---

4   'Caregivers and infants mutually create the chains and sequences of reciprocal behaviours
that make up social dialogue' (Stern, 1985, p. 139).
5   'What is being matched is not the other person's per se but rather some aspect of the
behaviour that reflects the person's feeling state. The ultimate reference for the match
appears to be the feeling state (inferred or directly apprehended) not the external behaviour event. Thus the match appears between the expressions of inner state . . . We appear
to be dealing with behaviour as expressions rather than as signs or symbol and the vehicles
of transfer are metaphor and analogue' (Stern, 1985, p. 142). Finally here the direct link
is between behaviour and expression. Needless to say if behaviour can be singled out

draw from the findings of observational proceedings evidence for arguing that many basic principles of psychoanalytic theory have to disappear and should be replaced by others. It is generally unnoticed that these suggestions are based on the authority of 'science' and therefore are not questionable, at least before they prove to be false. It spares the researcher the elaboration of the most difficult and most speculative part of affects problematics: the relationship between the complex nature of affects and how they relate to the other components of psychic life, and how the transformation proceeds within the affective sphere and between the affects and the rest of psychic activity. Most of all, the major problem for psychoanalysts, that is, the connections between affects and the unconscious, is left out.

For instance, instead of connecting affects to drive, affects are referred to so-called 'vitality' in some cases. They are supposed to correspond to 'momentary changes in feeling states involved in the organic process of being alive' (Stern 1985, p. 156). In the end a reversal of perspectives takes place. If aspects of behaviour were the reflection of the 'single recognizable internal state' by which affect is defined, in the end the amodal affects, i.e. the basic structures which do not depend on the channels by which they express themselves, concern 'how the behaviour, any behaviour, all behaviour, is performed, not *what* behaviour is performed' (Stern 1985, p. 157). The danger of building a mechanistic model is escaped at the last moment by bringing into play the concept of virtuality which any rigorous analysis of affective phenomena would place at its start, in the context of a double perspective, intrapsychic and intersubjective.[6]

Finally, I assume that Daniel Stern's conclusions can be interpreted as coming to provide some psychological (psychoanalytically tainted) theory with a concept of replacement for what stands in them but also for some of the later developments about the extrapolations of the manifest context of the theory.

---

easily, expression has such a wide range of meanings pertaining closely to affect just as to communication from language to non-verbal devices that it is also difficult to understand how it can be seen as 'a single recognizable internal state'.

6　It is worth noticing that Stern borrows the idea of virtuality from Langer who defends the idea that in art the organization of perceptual elements induces feelings through a quality which is called 'virtual'. Stern adopts his idea by drawing a comparison with his own work: 'In spontaneous behaviour the counterpart to artistic style is the domain of vitality affects' (p. 159). He begs the question assuming an acceptable correspondence between the device of style in art and the amodal qualities of vitality affects. 'As we have seen these concern the manner in which conventionalized affect displays such as smiling and other highly fixed motor programs such as walking are performed' (ibid.). The comparison is only limited by contingencies (emphasis is mine).

Some theoretical considerations born from clinical experience

The influence of psychology on the theory of affects is far from being limited to the researchers who specialize in infant studies. I shall not repeat here the review published in previous works (Green 1973), I will just remind of some major contributions (Sandler 1987).[7]

'It would follow,' says Sandler, 'that the prime motivations *from the point of view of the mental apparatus* are changes in feeling states. While drives, needs, emotional forces arising from within the body are highly important in determining behaviour from the point of view of psychological functioning they exert their effect *through changes in feelings*. The same is true for stimuli arising from the external world. This approach removes feelings from their conceptual tie to the instinctual drive alone and gives them a central position in psychoanalytic psychology.'[8] It should be noted that Sandler's view, close to some extent to Rapaport's, copes with the difficult concept of unconscious affects though he is in fact talking of preconscious affects also.

With the exception of Lacan no modern theoretical contribution in psychoanalysis underestimates the importance of affect, struggling nevertheless with the difficulty of giving a convincing and articulated theory. The general inspiration has been to turn to situations where affects are met with major disturbances beyond the usual problems related to anxiety and depression. Peter Sifneos has proposed the concept of alexithymia which has been widely accepted though with certain modifications or reservations.[9] I want to emphasize that Sifneos is not only talking of a lack of verbal communication whether intrapsychic or intersubjective, but also of an incapacity for linking emotions with thoughts, ideas and phantasies. He extends his findings to other categories than people suffering from somatic diseases: alcoholics, drug addicts, psychopaths, etc. Finally, Sifneos considers that the determinism of the syndrome is in the central nervous system, combining a hyperactivity of some brain structures associated with other peripheral disturbances. Sifneos admits the possibility of secondary alexithymia caused by psychic traumas, but in the end he denies the existence of intrapsychic conflicts in them. It is to this particular topic of trauma that Krystal has addressed himself with rather disappointing results, which in most of Krystal's cases were also associated with traumas of tremendously significant and exceptional intensity (Krystal 1978). It is only with Joyce McDougall's work that we come back to the field of a purely psychoanalytic approach to affects. She has described 'disaffected' patients who, as a mode of survival,

---

7   See Sandler, chapter 19: 'The role of affects in psychoanalytic theory'.
8   Ibid., p. 296.
9   For a recent statement see Sifneos (1990).

evacuate eventually any representation related to past experiences in connection with drives or object relationships from their consciousness. They make a breach between their emotions and the mental representations to which they are linked. They extend their ignorance of feelings to the feelings of others. Another way of dealing with an analogous situation is the fragmentation and the scattering of the emotions, a defence which ends in a resomatization of affect and/or addictive behaviour. These addictions are not limited to the taking of drugs but extend also to sexual acting out. Otherwise these patients seem quite normal – McDougall calls them 'normopaths' – lacking psychic symptoms (McDougall 1989, ch. 7). Guttieres-Green has described a syndrome of *painful amnesia* in which the unusually extensive forgetting of memory is superseded by an intolerable, unexplainable pain for which no reason can be given (Guttieres-Green 1990). In these last works affects are not considered apart from representations. The emphasis is less on the descriptive features of the affects than on their connections, their moves in the different areas of the mind and fateful consciousness.

One has to return to distinctions that are classical in French psychoanalysis between Freud's differentiations distinguishing the concept of repression (*Verdrängung*), disavowal or denial (*Verleügnung*), rejection or foreclosure (*Verwerfung*) and negation (*Verneinung*) with their correspondences in other psychoanalytical sub-theories (Klein's 'denial', Bion's 'evacuation', etc.) It was thanks to Lacan that these differences have clarified the realm of what I have called primary defences in the service of *the work of the negative*. Incidentally Lacan himself had intentionally '*Verwerft*' (foreclosed) affect from his revision of Freud's theory, asserting that there was no room for it. It is not the appropriate time and place to discuss this at length. It has not been long since Michael Borch-Jacobsen, a philosopher, has shown how Lacan has completely missed the point in bypassing the role of affect in the mechanism of identification, which is central in Freud's conceptual body of knowledge (Borch-Jacobsen 1991).[10]

Some remarks about a psychoanalytic theory of affects

Assuming now that one returns to psychoanalytic experience, one must realize that a modern theory of affect will have to meet with some questions which await an answer.

Affects are psychic phenomena which display their links with the biological organism in a powerfully suggestive way. Assuming that there is a

---

10 Other philosophers such as Michel Henry have emphasized the role of affects as the core of subjectivity, totally neglecting the views of psychoanalysis.

large number of psychoanalysts who are otherwise convinced that any psychic phenomenon has its correspondence in physiology regardless of what can be demonstrated in this sense, what does such an observation amount to?

Why does one not invoke the same relationship when one speaks of representation? Is one implying that representations have no connection to brain structures? I do not suppose so. What is involved is that though affects are undoubtedly psychic structures in their own right, one part of them or some parts of them are accompanied by testifiable organic reactions which can be shown not only in the brain but also in other parts of the body outside the brain, whereas similar reactions with other processes that have brain correspondence do not manifest peripheral reactions so blatantly. This suggests as I have noticed before (Green 1977) that if association is the type of connection which assembles representations, most of the time discontinuously (as with language), the mode of action of affects is diffusion within the individual or between two or more individuals. This implies different sorts of consequence related with their damming up.

There is a possible source of confusion in our description. The word affect is used carelessly, sometimes for feelings, other times for emotion and sometimes for other states. I propose to reserve the term affect for the concept of a category of psychic phenomena including different expressions which can be subsumed in the following.

1   *Tonality* which refers to a connotation of any manifestation of psychic life. One is frequently unaware of it because it accompanies our psychic life, sometimes unnoticed behind our thoughts and representations. From time to time it makes itself known as moods, or, in different circumstances, when its usual manifestation is lost, as mild depression. It can be ordinarily perceived also through body dynamics or even more through the voice (Fonagy 1983).
2   *Feelings* happen when in the stream of tonality some experiences manifest themselves in which we are subjectively moved and involved.
3   *Emotions* add turbulence to the preceding, with the impression that the control over what is happening is lessened. They are most of the time transitory and intense experiences which shake us.
4   *Passions* are emotional states which are necessarily about or directed towards an object individualized as such. Passion invades the whole field of consciousness. Its significance overshadows the usually important matters of life. Unlike emotions it is long lasting.

These are the four main expressions of affect, which is the generic term for all of them. Needless to say there is a possibility of shifting from one state to another.

Now comes the crucial point: how can one imagine unconscious affects? But also, what conceptions of the unconscious should one rely on, in these times of disregard of Freud's metapsychology? Suspicion (if not more) grows towards his ideas. There is a reluctance to use them, especially in the case of some embarrassing concepts. It is not well thought of nowadays to mention the id. The present fashion is directed towards the object relationships theory which has some basis as it is obvious that Freud seems to have under-valued the role of the object. There is also a tendency to get rid of the psychical apparatus lightheartedly. It is noteworthy that the strongest evi-dence of the existence of the unconscious, i.e. the dream, is by nature mostly characterized by representations, in the context of inhibition of affects. Moreover, when affect takes the upper hand it is not long before the dreamer awakes. That happens with great intensity in nightmares which today we do not consider any more as a variety of dream but as failures of the dream-work.

An ever present but not always explicitly stated concern about affect is shown in the wavering opinions on the validity of the pleasure–unpleasure principle. Moreover, the relationship of affects to the body, to the self and the object, to fantasy, action and language are unanswered questions. But the most poignant and enigmatic problem is the way affects are bound to the experience of time. They are simultaneously the stronger indicators of the actualization of our involvement in the moment one is subjected to them (which I have called passivation) and, on the other hand, without any rec-ognizable landmarks they make us notice suddenly the passage of time or provide us with an insight of the tense in which they unfold their living dis-course – as if their timelessness can change into a sudden awareness of their belonging to definitely remote epochs of our lives, which are only called to instant resurrection before dissolving themselves in the unknown (Green 1984).

Affects: indirect approach and deduction

Among the many attempts to delineate affect, an interesting one is to address oneself not to the core of the phenomenon too obscure to be grasped in its essence directly, but to, if I may say, its surroundings and its expansions, the domains with which affects seem to share some border which acts not only as a limitation to affective phenomena but also eventually as a receptacle in which affects will pour, in special circumstances, changing their nature and being transformed into some other form. Such transformation occurs overtly with somatization as has been noticed also by Joyce McDougall. Another type of transformation is even more obvious: action – not to speak of acting out – is a way by which affects are, as we say, 'lived out'. As early as 1970 I grouped these two apparently opposite transformations of affect in a common chapter drawing parallels between somatization as a sort of acting in towards the body and acting out as a form of psychic blindness which could be compared to the escape from psychic awareness (Green 1970, pp. 885-1169).[11]

Besides, the attempt of language to absorb and convey affect by nomination is usual in everyday life. But one is amazed how many of the deaf dialogues are about the non-perception of the most common affects either in oneself or in the other. Fortunately there is some evidence that the case is not hopeless, as it is the major aim of poetry. We enjoy it but maybe we are not enough surprised that this achievement is possible. In doing so the emphasis is less on discharge than on communication through the channels of sublimation. Allow me to quote my favourite model of transcription of mother–infant observation.

> blest the Babe,
> Nursed in his Mother's arms: the babe who sleeps
> Upon his Mother's breast; who, when his soul
> Claims manifest kindred with an earthy soul,
> Doth gather passion from his Mother's eye!
> Such feelings pass into his torpid life
> Like an awakening breeze, and hence his mind
> Even in the first trial of its powers
> Is prompt and watchful, eager to combine
> In one appearance, all the elements
> And parts of the same object, else detached And loth of coalesce.
> Thus, day by day
> Subjected to the discipline of love,
> His organs and recipient faculties
> Are quickened, are more vigorous, his mind spreads,
> Tenacious of the forms which it receives.
> In one beloved presence, nay and more,
> In that most apprehensive habitude
> And those sensations which have been derived
> From his beloved presence, there exists
> A virtue which irradiates and exalts
> All objects through all in intercourse of sense.
>
> William Wordsworth, *The Prelude*, (1805 version)
> (Book II, 11, pp. 238-80)

11 First version of what was meant to become *Le Discours vivant* in 1973.

One comes now to the last point: the relationship of affects to phantasy. From the oldest times the relationship of affects to imagination has been permanently stressed. There one has a double directed relationship: imagination enhances affect, and affects are the strongest stimulation to imagination. At the bottom affects legitimate through faith (of any kind) the conduct of an existence. I wish to add that this very general function, which extends to the whole being, can also displace the affects of faith rooted in our fundamental attachment to any of the different issues that have been named: body, action, language, phantasy which can also serve as areas which welcome affects and help in their transformation in order, for instance, to serve ideology. Affects can be rationalized, and most of the time are. Moreover it is not without consideration that manic-depressive states were traditionally labelled as affective psychoses. It was a considerable achievement of psychoanalysis to point out that the loss of an object could lead to the replacement of the object by a part of the ego through primary identification and, as a possible consequence of this replacement, to an aggression against the self which results in the suppression of its own existence; faith turning into its opposite, with the same radical and uncompromising exigencies.

In trying to surround the mysterious domain of affective phenomena with the expectation that one could arrive at some apprehension of what would be our representations of unconscious affect, one has not succeeded in any way in getting a picture of what one is looking for. If one gives up this quest of finding this mythical shape considering the variety, multiplicity and manifold means of expression of affects, instead of focusing our attempt on building the missing link, why not acknowledge the fact that the reason for our ignorance is precisely what one is trying to discover. In other words, *the essence of affect is its dynamic attribute*, its capacity to seep into other domains and inhabit them and finally to transform both itself and the products of the area of the mind which it has occupied. Cathexis, which is closely associated with affect, means originally 'occupation of territory' which brought secondarily the meaning of investment. The oldest meaning of the verb 'to invest' is to clothe a person with qualities, insignias of office, rank, or to grant someone a power (the military meaning synonym, 'to attack', is related to besieging). There is a close relationship between invest and affect, as 'to affect' is of course to pretend, thus turning the garment that granted a distinction into a disguise. One also finds a common meaning to invest and to affect, both meaning to attack (OED), an extreme form of moving, touching, producing effect. But affect reaches a greater degree of generality in the community of meanings that it shares with invest, in that it refers to the action of practising, of attributing. All these meanings are not associated with the subsequent connotation of something that has to go through something else, which will impose itself later when the word will move towards its modern usage for feelings and emotion. From the primitive meaning one exception will individualize itself to facilitate a distinction with a simple action, which was already underlined with the military application of invest. This is the idea of 'force', which is essential to affect and finds its conceptual embodiment in the reference to conation. This last qualification accounts for the potentially disorganizing power of affect whether it appears suddenly, unnoticed, or, as it spreads, accumulates, pervades, and eventually takes hold of vast areas of the mind. One can see that the idea of quantity or of intensity is quite insufficient. It is necessary to consider its correlation to a transformational process which will influence evidently the psychic activities that will be submitted to the influence of affect, but in turn will influence the affects themselves. So one has arrived at a crossroads, considering alternately the mental relationships that can be inferred from the study of the transformations of affect and arguing also in favour of an independent line for affect organization, making the assumption that the transformational processes are essential to the inner structure of affects.

One has reached, if I may hope, the core of all affective phenomena: this reference to a force – which is not always noticeable as such but can always potentially manifest itself, movable by essence, capable of invading any or all parts of an individual, crossing even the borders of individuality to reach other entities, for instance groups; bearing an impressive capacity for unpredictable change, either being influenced by the structures it inhabits or transforming them, shifting from an inside polarity to an outside one and also consequently fixing itself either on the subject or being directed towards objects, forming the basis of the awareness of existence. This force, which is less susceptible to control than any other source of information, will have to meet two other psychical events which will shape its fate: first a basic principle of structuralization, second the effects of a counter-force as a consequence of that same basic principle.

One is familiar with the basic principle even if it is less present in our mind than in earlier times of the history of psychoanalysis. I am speaking of the pleasure–unpleasure principle. It can already be found in Plato's Phaedo. It is essential to think of it as referring not to affects as feeling states but rather as categorizing basically all experiences of the kind with the double predicate that one cannot avoid being submitted to. In contrast, considered alone, it cannot be a guideline in life. I assume the pleasure–unpleasure principle to be the ground for *primary symbolization*, i.e. it plays the role of a postulate that has the functions of establishing the first categorization of psychic events, not only in separating two types of experiences but also in linking, by inference, each type to its opposite. It is this basic distinction which accounts also for its momentous consequence in enabling us to superimpose on it another significant opposition between inside and outside, these terms having to be carefully handled in a way that I have not had the opportunity to discuss because of time limitations. Anyway, what the primary symbolization has succeeded in achieving is that the dividing principle which qualifies experience has led to an operation of separating the field of experience into two spaces. And finally this starting of differentiation gives rise to the transformation of the initial categories into a second system of classification in terms of good and bad which applies all the same to the former experience, now thus qualified, and to what the space divisions have enabled to be born: the objects.

Objects

When it has been said in the history of psychoanalysis that pleasure seeking activity should be restated rather as object seeking (Fairbairn), the idea struck many a colleague. Its success was based on a real problem drawn from Freud's work. I shall mention it briefly. The features of affect had in the beginning to deal with the structure of symptoms. The *Studies on Hysteria* discovered the strangulated affects as determining the clinical picture of the disease. It then proceeded to the consideration of anxiety which, from its very beginnings, had to take account of its multiple expressions. As such it is the main source which gave justification to the pleasure–unpleasure principle. But the more the examination of affects deepened, the more another type of affect had to be considered, because it could not be included among the different varieties of anxiety: mourning and its relationship to depression. This is less a discovery than a renewal of interest because it is easy to show that Freud never lost sight of its importance and specificity from the very beginning. In mourning it is not only a matter of the reversal of pleasure into unpleasure because of prohibited wishes or impulses, but also an impossibility, because of the loss of the object, to hope for any kind of gratification. The emphasis shifted towards the object, whereas in the beginning it was placed on the drives.

One should also consider that the threat of the loss of the object, beyond the dangers which belong to conscious awareness, implies a radical abduction of all gratifications depending on drive satisfactions, i.e. of all affects of pleasure. It is the confrontations to such extremes that force the replacement of the lost object by an important part of the ego, thus playing, without any hint of this transformation, the role of a surrogate at the cost of sacrificing its integrity. Instead of engaging oneself in a dead end discussion to decide whether the object or the drive is of greater importance, one should notice that a specific transformation of affect is identification whose roots have been elaborated by Freud *apropos* the relationship between mourning and melancholia. Now can be seen one of the fruitful contradictions of affects: not

287

only do they form the basis of categorizing experiences and take part in the differentiations of spaces and objects without having to locate themselves exclusively in any of them; because of their pervasive properties, they can also allow for a substitution between ego and object through identification. The object (of the drive) was first seen as highly substitutable and now appears as irreplaceable.

It follows from the hypotheses of the transformations of states of pleasure–unpleasure into good and bad experiences or objects, that some counter-force must come into play, known in the beginning by the name of repression. It is important to notice that if Freud had some doubts about the application of repression to affects (he considered that suppression was a more appropriate notion), he nevertheless thought that the task of repression could not end before unpleasurable affects were silenced. Later on he had to decide in his paper on fetishism that repression applied mainly to affects, as disavowal lent itself to perceptions. On the whole if modern psychoanalysis has emphasized the role of the object, as infant observations have extensively shown, one can ask oneself if the previous understatement was only motivated by a neglect of Freud's thought. In fact it is much easier to observe and describe interactional procedures. The so-called observed facts act as a palpable material overshadowing the interpretative network of the researchers. The conjectures of psychoanalytic uncertainties which are related to the unobservable remain for us provisional basic assumptions which better account for the complexity of the mechanisms such as those witnessed in the cure, for which no present method of replacement satisfies our need for the establishment of a convincing relationship between what is treated empirically, how it is dealt with, and what conclusions can be drawn from it.

For instance, if one shifts from the point of view of the drives towards a more extensive one considering other sources of affect, I do not know of any sound articulations relating the two aspects (drive or non-drive related) except in recourse to a psychology which stands far from psychoanalysis. If one also shifts towards the polarity of the object in relationship to affect, the concept of object is so confused a notion, mixing up psychological assumptions as remnants of academic psychology (with a recent reinforcement from cognitive sciences) and observational data, that the notion of affect looks as if it were just sprinkled with some psychoanalytic powder in such a way that one does not know what one is talking about; and, though being in a psychoanalytic environment, one finds oneself in front of a Tower of Babel (see the discussion during symposium of the FEP in Vienna in 1989. Green *et al.* 1990). I finally adopt the view that the pleasure–unpleasure principle is a better tool for the appreciation of affects than any other. It appears to me more revealing of the state of mind which guides all human beings, whether in analysis or not, especially if it is not so much a problem about the optimization of pleasure, but rather about the maximization of avoiding unpleasure even at a very high cost. And I am not convinced at all by the idea that affective states evolve around a state of equilibrium as most of the time I am rather struck by the irresistible temptation of an imbalance in favour of a gain of pleasure or of escaping unpleasure. It seems to be the rule in spite, as I said earlier, of a concomitant but ineffective awareness that the pleasure–unpleasure principle alone cannot be a practicable guideline for living.

The movement between the opposite polarities of self (I must confess I would have preferred to use the term ego) and object, inclines me to speak of oscillating alternatives to and fro between self and object. I am in no way alluding to attunement but to basic expressions which, for example, would be close to what is described in terms of projective and introjective identi-fication. The four expressions of affect – tonality, feelings, emotions, passions – distribute themselves along these two poles which I am less will-ing to qualify as self and object representations but as self and object cathexes through binding and unbinding processes.

Until now one has tried to consider affects with minimal references to representations. Considering their relationships cannot be avoided any longer. One of Freud's major findings about the vicissitudes of affects in neurotic states was the separate destiny of affect and representation (conver-sion in hysteria, displacement in obsessional neurosis, projection in phobia, etc.). Epistemologically speaking this dissociation was important because it showed that the symptoms were not only of an irrational nature but that they were, so to speak, breaking the 'natural' reactions of human beings. The change in psychoanalytical practice led to other organizations of symp-toms, where this occurrence was blurred and replaced by other concerns about the treatment of affect which have already been mentioned above. As the ordinary symptoms of these clinical pictures are well known I shall not linger on them, except to consider the frequency of negative therapeutic reactions and the part played in them by the unconscious sense of guilt which served Freud as the most typical example of unconscious affect.

Unconscious affects

I shall not dwell on this complex problem but will use its example to raise some questions. What is unconscious in such an occurrence? Is it the memory traces which take the form of representations to which one has to add a quota of affect? What would such a quota look like, considering that a particular characteristic of this feature is the absence of awareness and the denial on the part of the patient, who is otherwise by no means alexithymic.

If one admits that representations and affects when unconscious take different aspects, implying there are different ways of being unconscious, then affects which are strongly marked by quality – just as perceptions but obviously more intensely and with a wider spectrum – do not only obey repression when they have to be discarded but also have to be ignored when it happens that they have succeeded in crossing the censorship. They are then subjected to negative hallucinations just as perception undergoes the same treatment, and even thought processes also when they are expressed through language. But if it happens that they have made themselves known (after the intervention of different defence mechanisms), one can accept that they will take in the unconscious the status of processes devoid of qualities. Nevertheless, in contrast to unconscious ideas or thoughts they cannot achieve what representations are allowed to perform: to split in parts, to displace from one another, to condense, to combine in a more or less articulated way. Either they can attach themselves to representations favouring or opposing the new links, or they can express themselves in alternates of tension of release according to the surrogates which have been born from unconscious work. But one should not forget here our previous statements: the aspect of force, its dynamism in moving, its cathecting capacity and its pervasiveness, all of which attempt to alleviate tensions whether by diffusion and/or dilution, failing to prevent accumulation. If the role of the object is important in the final destination of affect, it is far from succeeding every time. The final result will happen according to the combination of intrapsychic and intersubjective relationships.

One has now to look at the connections of affects with representations. Classically all representations are born from perceptions or derive from them. Even if affects can accompany representations it is quite clear that they are not connected as representations. There is a dual system of opposition between representations and affects. First there is the fundamental connection between perceptions and representations; second, one has to consider the existence of a double system of representations relating these mental organizations either to things or to words. Unconscious representations are the products of these transformations which affect the materiality of these psychic manifestations. Moreover in Freud's mind the passage of conscious representations to unconscious ones does not involve a major change in the complexion or the texture of the representation. His discussion of a double inscription or of a change of cathexis in his paper on the 'Unconscious' does not indicate any idea of a different nature separating unconscious and conscious representations. The case is quite different with affect. It has already been noted that affects can take different forms of expression, but they do not essentially go through a transformational system which would convert one species of affect to another, equivalent to the translation of thing-representation to word-representation. Affect is detectable in language through the voice but they are the same affects as those that are expressed with the help of language but not necessarily present in it. I shall remind the reader here that for Freud the passage of affects through the preconscious was not relevant as to the nature of affects; this occurrence could explain the attempt to inhibit or to master affects but did not participate in any change in their structure.

It has already been seen that the change of register (somatic or acting, etc.) was in fact an issue which was no longer in the realm of affects.

It is by some natural inclination that one ordinarily considers affects as an accompanying phenomenon. Affects are used to define, to give quality, to connote a mental state because one thinks that affect gives its colour and tone to a representation. Why not, in some instances, reverse the statement and assume that affects could be a movement in expectation of some form? Tustin's work with autistic children seems to lead us in the same direction (Green 1985).

History

I am quite aware that many a reader will be puzzled by this approach, keeping is as a structural one, not bothering about the genetic concomitant or the developmental influences. My deliberate choice is based on a belief that we lack the means of being in touch with intrapsychic structures, with a developmental approach, on the one hand, and that we lack also the intellectual tools to form an adequate conception of temporality and historical development as far as our object is psychic activity and its relationship to the unconscious. But this so-called structural approach is stuffed with historical undertones. No one will deny that affects undergo a long and complicated history but it is not easy to find in them the evidence of what it tells. In fact, in the psychoanalytic situation a dual historical play goes on session after session and during the time of one session. I am not alluding here to what is explicitly designed as the history of the past nor to the fact of reconstruction. I am speaking of the unfolding of temporality in the way that psychic structures respond to each other and interlock together. One channel follows the way representations are delivered, retailed, yield in small change – *menue monnaie*, to use the French expression which expresses the idea of dividing into minute pieces. The other channel through affects is condensed, vaguely outlined, dense and compact or ungraspable where different layers belonging to diverse epochs press themselves with their load, sometimes invigorating sometimes threatening, in which the past has disappeared as a distinct category melted with the present. It is not only a matter of opposing, for instance, reminiscence and revival, but all the same the idea that if memories evoke the past, as far as affects are concerned, it is in the quality of their presence that Freud's idea of timelessness as characteristic of the unconscious takes form; although affects cannot bind together in the cookery sense, they can gather in a construction which cannot be easily dissected directly without the help of representations but which can give an irreplaceable flavour to things which are supposed to have gone forever.

At last I make the hypothesis that affect is not, as it seems, out of the representational field. As it is inevitably loaded with previous experiences it cannot but be an affect–representative which parallels the ideational representative. Affect would be the representative of the history of the subject-ego: a signifier of flesh. The ego would not only be the seat of anxiety but also the battlefield between the binding attempts at transformation (intrapsychic and intersubjective) and the unbinding turmoil which threatens its achievements in a disruptive flow, trying to create some inner intermediate structure between the body and the world.

There are as many reasons to think of a cooperation between the two systems, affective and representational (in the classical sense) as to think of an antagonism. If I may quote myself I shall remind the reader of the following: the psychic apparatus registers the traces of affective experiences before it is prepared to establish mnemic traces of perceptions; the whole aim of psychic work is to separate out the representations from the contradictory affective infiltrations, which are otherwise badly needed because they keep the apparatus in motion in search of new experiences of a promising quality, and the psyche finds itself threatened by diffusion which overwhelms from time to time the representations which seek articulation. This source of antagonism is due to the constitutional clumsiness and essential maladjustment of the human being.

Pregnancy and prominence

The statement I have just reminded the reader of was written in 1977. At that time I hardly knew René Thom except by reputation and my first contacts with catastrophe theory were incidental. But in 1987 – ten years later – we were both taking part in a symposium on the unconscious and science. Thom presented a paper entitled 'Saillance et prégnance' ('Prominence and pregnancy') which was introductory to a forthcoming book *Esquisse d'une sémiophysique* (*Draft on semiphysic*). The concept of *prominence* was to characterize any shape of sensibility of a qualitative discontinuity of a sensation or a perception. The different senses have different attributes as is shown for audition, vision, etc. It is the other category, *pregnancy*, which is of most interest for us. Thom thinks it should apply especially to superior mammals and considers it as biologically meaningful. He opposes *alternative pregnancies* and *repulsion pregnancies*. He borrows the theme from the German gestaltists. In his book published soon after he gives the following definition: 'One may regard pregnancy as an invasive fluid which propagates in the field of the perceived prominent forms, the prominent forms playing the role of a breach in the real from where the invading fluid of pregnancy percolates'.[12] He then adds 'emotional experience (affectivity), under the form of pleasure or pain, is the motor of the propagation of pregnancies'.[13] He emphasizes the influence of pregnancy on subjectivity. He makes the following statement that, although in living organisms excitations (or stimuli)[14] serve as biological regulators, '*affectivity can be seen as an agent which distorts (deforms) the structure of regulation*'. His development leads him to use the concept of cathexis (potential or actualized). He concludes his remarks: 'when a prominent form captures a pregnancy, it is cathected by this pregnancy; as a consequence it undergoes a transformation of its internal state which can produce external manifestation in its form: these are *the figurative effects.*[15]

It is noteworthy for those who are concerned with the scientificity of psychoanalysis that Thom considers language as a remarkably useful tool for the description of the world at human scale and even more useful than mathematical theorization. Moreover he does not think that the theory of prominence and pregnancy could be predictive but on the other hand extends its field even to language. He dares to uphold the idea that concepts are manifestations of pregnancies.[16]

In the French edition of *Le discours vivant* over twenty years ago, I came to the conclusion that the specificity of psychoanalytic theory was that it succeeded in bringing together the concepts of force and meaning in an integrated way which had not been achieved before Freud. This integration endows our conception of psychic activity with differently organized structures influencing each other. The wealth of the psychical world lies in the diverse heterogeneity of its constituents which acquires, by the necessity to elaborate the contradictions due to its diversity, its heterogeneity in the relationship between the internal and the external world which is responsible for the varieties of its productions.

I reminded the reader earlier that we were terribly dependent on the pleasure–unpleasure principle which could never be overcome entirely. I also remarked that one had to accept that it could not work by itself. I

---

12 These lines were written before the conference on Psychoanalysis and Literature, held in London, 6–7 November 1993, where Ronald Britton presented a paper on 'The prelude'. Our meeting at that point is not surprising even if our interpretations differ.
13 René Thom, *Esquisse d'une sémiophysique*, Inter Editions, 1988.
14 Ibid., p. 21.
15 Ibid., p. 29
16 Ibid., p. 31.

mentioned of course the reality principle. Not ignoring the fact that this is the subject of another work, I would like to suggest that today in psychoanalysis the reality principle has become a principle of uncertainty. In the course of science there has been a progressive awareness about the capacity of mankind to know. This achievement was not only based on a faithful description of reality. It was no longer possible to underestimate that other dimension, the constant creativity in the act of knowing, with all the risks of drifting away. This contradiction could not be overcome because it is part of the structure of our psychic endowment. But it was not until psychoanalysis was created that one could realize all its implications.[17]

17 This section was part of an earlier version of this paper. It does not appear in the paper written for Professor Sandler's Festschrift.

Postscript 3: On discriminating and not discriminating between affect and representation*

Prepublished paper for the 41st International Congress of Psychoanalysis, Santiago 1998

> It is the instincts, the feelings, that constitute the substance of the soul. Cognition is only its surface, its point of contact with what is outside itself.
>
> C.S. Peirce, *Reasoning and the Logic of Things*, 1898

> It is here in this highly specialized psycho-therapy situation rather than by direct observation of infants that the state of affair that is normal at the theoretical start in infancy can be studied.
>
> D.W. Winnicott, *Human Nature*, 1988

I Discriminating and not discriminating between affect and representation: questions

Listening in analysis

At the beginning of an analytic session, what frame of mind must I be in if I am to respond to what I think the situation requires of me? I place myself in the analyst's position, when, having forced myself to maintain as much as possible freely floating attention – as will be seen, this is no easy matter and sometimes encounters serious difficulties – I hear the analysand's communication from two points of view at once. That is to say, on the one hand, I try to perceive the internal conflicts that inhabit it and, on the other, I consider it from the point of view of something addressed, implicitly or explicitly, to me. The conflicts to which I refer do not concern the particular dynamic conflicts that would emerge in interpretation, but rather the way in which

---

*This postscript also appears in the *International Journal of Psychoanalysis*, 80, pp. 277–316.

the discourse in turn approaches and moves away from a kernel of meaning, or a group of such kernels of meaning, which are trying to break through to the conscious. One does not have to have a very precise idea of what activates or, on the contrary, impedes or diverts communication to perceive the movement that sometimes carries communication towards the most explicit or most precise expression, sometimes distances it from the verbal fulfilment of what is striving to be communicated. One may, therefore, perceive these variations intuitively without knowing the exact nature of the focus around which they gravitate and which will often appear more or less suddenly, sometimes perfectly clearly, sometimes in a more accidental way, in the course of the dialogue. It is in this second case that one's floating attention turns into investigatory acuteness; this occurs in an instant of reorganization in the analyst's mind of what has slipped under the fluidity of the reception of discourse of the patient's more or less free associative discourse in a state of suspended searching. What is being described here is not only the naming of resistance, as this appears at certain moments – especially defined at the approach of activated moments of transference – but also the underlying state over which the movements of the discourse appear before they are heard, or the basic oscillation of any resumption of speech by the analysand, unsure how acceptable it will be to the consciousness of both speaker and listener. A movement of convergence – but one that is far from being synchronic – allows the analyst's thinking to evolve from its identification of the analysand's transferential position at that moment towards a more general image of his or her overall conflicts in so far as they can be apprehended in the flow of discourse, or, again, towards what, at a particular moment, reveals the activation of a particular conflict and the way in which that conflict stands out in an overall configuration. Thus are put into perspective the general conditions of its emergence shared between what is seeking satisfaction through its expression and what expresses a feeling of danger in doing so without impediment. In other words, one is faced with a double relation: a particular local conflict referring to a more general conflictual state in the analysand – appreciable in terms of the relations maintained between the various parts of the discourse among themselves and the way in which the analyst's presence encourages or inhibits the form they take – and, on the part of the analyst, an examination of what is being communicated at the present moment, judged in terms of the general conflictual nature of the psychical life in so far as it is expressed in the analytic relationship caught between the ideal of communication free of all censorship and the vicissitudes of a wish to speak thwarted by imaginary fear and its consequences, which leads one to think that what is said here has narrowed the gap between it and action.

When, changing the vertex, I hear what is said as being addressed to me, I regard what I have heard from an angle in which the internal conflicts encounter, in their attempts to become externalized in speech, a reflexive return on to the subject who is speaking, a transformation produced by that publication of thought that, being addressed to another, engenders retroactively an echo of what he has said on to the person who said it, in accordance with an effect enhanced by the setting. The strange otherness of the analytic relation also produces symmetrically the idea that the causality that governs what has been said by the speaker alters the status of the addressee of the message. This addressee, regarded as witness or object of a demand, is changed in the internal world and becomes, unknown to the analysand, the *cause* of the movement that animates his or her speech. This is certainly what lies at the basis of any transference. The addressee – invisible in the analytic situation – is so to speak reduced to the movement of speech, merges into it and is now interpreted in terms of a double register. Although the analyst was, originally, consciously defined as the person to whom the discourse is addressed – indeed whose peculiar mode he or she has created – in an attempt to approach the patient's private world, unconsciously this condition of receiver of the message is changed into that of its inductor. The analyst becomes its provoker simply by the presence of the internal movements that spring both from what is addressed to him or her and from what animated the analysand to say such things. The separation between the subject's internal – affective – movements and their objectification by the discourse addressed to a third party collapses for the unconscious. One is now in a position in which the two are only one, the object to whom this discourse is addressed – that is to say – what is expressed by the patient's demand, expectation, hope about some other person – and its unconscious, subjective, in short instinctual, source become, unknown to the person who is speaking, more or less interchangeable. At this level, the addressee of the internal movements put into words is separated only by a thread from the tendency to see him or her as the causal agent of those movements. Certain consequences are expected from that cause, the discourse striving to arouse a response from the person to whom the discourse is addressed. It is no doubt tacitly hoped that this response will satisfy the demand addressed to him or her – a demand inherent in the very act of undertaking analysis – but peculiarly in that, by arousing it, it reveals to the addressee a desire that corresponds to the quest of which it is the object.

I am well aware that Melanie Klein's concept of the internal object tried to bring together these two aspects under a single heading, but I find it more interesting to separate them in order to understand better the way in which they relate to one another in a more or less contradictory way. These two aspects refer to what I have described as *double transference*: the transference on to speech and the transference on to the object (Green 1984). These seem to present themselves in a single form, but I believe that there is some advantage to be gained in distinguishing between them, if we are to understand more clearly the relations between the intrapsychical and the intersubjective. The mutual relations between vectorization by speech and the retroactive loops of the address to the object bring out certain features peculiar to analytic communication. The void that analytic speech addressed to an invisible – and therefore in some sense concealed – addressee must cross confers on that speech, in addition to renouncing the mastery required by the fundamental rule, the possibility of making it turn back to its source as soon as it is emitted.

> This void then ceases to be a mere medium transmitting the message and gives rise to a double effect; on the one hand, it produces a reflection of the enigma of polysemia that it has engendered in the addressee on to the emitter and, on the other hand, this void is reproduced in the speaker, an expression of the gap between the enigmatic source of speech and its finished product.
>
> (Green 1973).

From such a point of view – which is that of ordinary analytic situations – the evaluation of the interpretability of the discourse does not entail separating affect from other aspects of discourse; it would be artificial to do so, since it would isolate one element of communication that is intelligible only in its link with the others.

Perhaps it should be said in passing that when one turns to Freud's writings on affect, one notes that all the initial theorization springs essentially from differences in its relation to representation, on the basis of categorizations internal to the field of transference neuropsychoses. Although reflection on affect only continues when Freud has distanced himself from that starting point, what it gains in complexity and subtlety entails replacing the earlier differential view with representation by the various neuroses. Nor is it tenable to suppose that the modifications brought to the theory of anxiety may in themselves correspond to all the problems posed by the conception of affect. Indeed, does not *Inhibitions, Symptoms and Anxiety* explicitly admit as much in the addendum entitled 'Anxiety, pain and mourning'? When, in *Constructions in Analysis*,[1]

---

1 'It is familiar ground that the work of analysis aims at inducing the patient to give up the repressions (using the word in the widest sense) belonging to his early development and to replace them by reactions of a sort that would correspond to a psychically mature condition. With this purpose in view he must be brought to recollect certain experiences and the affective impulses called up by them which he has for the time being forgotten. We know that his present symptoms and inhibitions are the consequences of these things that he has forgotten. What sort of material does he put at our disposal which we can make use of to put him on the way to recovering the lost memories? All kinds of things. He gives us fragments of these memories in his dreams, invaluable in themselves but seriously distorted as a rule by all the factors concerned in the formation of dreams. Again, he produces ideas, if he gives himself up to "free association", in which we can

Freud later described the analytic work, this integration of affect is relativized by its insertion in the whole, including the various constituent elements of communication (memories, dreams, ideas arising in free association, allusions to events internal and external to the analysis, etc.). But it is also implicitly situated in a privileged position (by the repetition that marks its return into the text). That affect occupies the place of a privileged mediation between the past – not necessarily identified as such, explicitly, that is to say, limited to remembering – and the present actualized in the relation to the analyst, between what is explicitly felt and the actualization of psychical manifestations belonging to the past, not recognized by the consciousness. The description of the various forms of psychical events, of the memory made possible in the more or less untimely return of repressed motions, refers to what I have called the *heterogeneity of the signifier*, which term is to be understood here as the equivalent of the element of signification, the latter being expressed in a not univocal way through various channels, each according to its own mode. One can see, therefore, that what returns to the surface of analytic communication is extended over a spectre that mixes in various proportions an element whose content is usually appreciated in ideational terms and another that cannot be encompassed by the previous one, recognized as expressing 'motions', that is to say, movements in which affect is to be found, as a dynamic phenomenon, and the drive, as a concept theoretically accounting for it.

The affect–representation distinction

This distinction is reminiscent of Freud's earliest intuitions, by which psychical activity was divided into neurones, which might be compared with

---

discover allusions to the repressed experiences and derivatives of the suppressed affective impulses as well as of the reactions against them. And, finally, there are hints of repetitions of the affects belonging to the repressed material to be found in actions performed by the patient, some fairly important, some trivial, inside and outside the analytic situation. Our experience has shown that the relation of transference, which becomes established towards the analyst, is particularly calculated to favour the return of these emotional connections. It is out of such raw material – if we may so describe it – that we have to put together what we are in search of (Freud, *Constructions in Analysis*, 1937). These lines may be compared with similar observations from Winnicott: 'In terms of free association this means that the patient on the couch or the child patient among the toys on the floor must be allowed to communicate a succession of ideas, thoughts, impulses, sensations that are not linked except in some way that is neurological or physiological and perhaps beyond detection. That is to say: it is where there is purpose or where there is anxiety or where there is lack of trust based on the need for defence that the analyst will be able to recognize and to point out the connection (or several connections) between the various components of free association material' (Winnicott 1971a).

those units of ideational representations – attached to one another by facilitations – and moving quantities, the precursor of the future quota of affect. Of course, beyond the stage of the *Draft*, what remained was the idea that the psyche finds this conjunction in the intuition of its most intimate nature and, conversely, that certain forms disclosed by the neuroses may reveal a relative dismantling of these two types of closely linked manifestations, but which, in certain cases, may go their own way. It should be added that the encounter between the search for a regime of thought (free association) privileging the communication of psychical mobility combined with the suspension of censorship and prohibiting all active expression, a propensity that would be consecutive on that dynamism, induced and reinforced in relation to the ordinary conditions of verbal exchange, stresses the imbalance between these two elements. For the tendency to movement proper to the affect, one of whose orientations may be converted into act, when that act has invested the body, placing it in tension and forcing it to find an outlet for that orientation, sees its usual possibility of being attenuated, by its inclusion in a set of links, reduced. As for the representations, they possess the capacity to displace the particular charge of each in the investment of the network that makes it possible to hold their developed forms together. The relation of the thoughts established by the representative links is relaxed by the setting up of the regime of free association. Better still, one might say that the utterance itself proceeds to new forms of links, reshaping the old links that are trying to be re-established under the aegis of a signifying whole, placing them this time at the service of defence (rationalization), whereas elsewhere the utterance, from the point of view of the affect, has the opposite effect, namely, that it unleashes even more that part of itself that was associated with the representations. These conditions increase the internal contradictions of the transferential discourse.

In recent years, the decline of interest in those clinical tables that are not elucidated by analysis, in terms of the affect–representation division, has produced a break in continuity with classical theory. They call out for our attention. For either Freud's work has ignored them – despite a few dispersed comments, with no particular development from the point of view of affect (I am thinking of the analysis of the Wolf Man) – or the post-Freudian literature, apart from a few exceptions, has made progress in our knowledge of them only by adopting a point of view that has abandoned a concern for a differential approach in favour of a totalizing approach: that of the object relation.

Two remarks should be made here: first, the usefulness of maintaining a distinction that takes into consideration the specificity of affect appears when we examine certain disciplines. Without dwelling on neurobiology, which at present is showing new interest in the problem of affect, long neglected by researchers who are more concerned with fields of investigation in which information theories might be used to advantage, certain areas of clinical medicine are constantly referring to it. The problem of anxiety remains more than ever at the centre of analysis. I shall do no more than mention the category of so-called affective psychoses, in which the manic-depressive psychosis predominates. Although analysts rarely have an opportunity to confront them, we must not forget that depression remains a major pole of elaboration in psychoanalytic practice. More specifically, psychosomatic practice, in which elucidation on the basis of the concept of mental functioning has been decisive, attributes to the affective economy a crucial role in the intelligibility of the psychosomatic syndromes and sometimes in their genesis. The concept of alexithymy (Sifneos 1975) has been accepted in pathology. It combines a disturbance in the recognition and verbalization of affects, with, in certain patients, the intervention of a form of denial that has been compared to the foreclosure or radical rejection observed in psychotics.

Comparable disturbances have been observed among victims of traumas brought on by the holocaust (Krystal 1978). Unlike the situations referred to earlier, two factors must undeniably be taken into consideration here: although overwhelming, objectively recognized as such and rightly related to their postponed manifestations, the traumas do not yield the secret of how precisely they act on the psyche and inhibit the functions that might help some understanding of them to be gained. Remembering acts here like a repetition, scarcely less painful and sometimes more so than the trauma itself, time seeming to do nothing to attenuate the psychical pain. It is undeniable that there is a new source of reflection here that is, for me, the equivalent of the part played by war neuroses in Freud's revaluation of his theory, except that here it is not the shortage of representations that is lacking, but the unspeakable, affectively intolerable character of the situations evoked by them.

Second, the attempt to go beyond the affect–representation separation in the interests of a theory of object relations has no doubt made it possible to bring answers to questions that arise in analytic practice. However, the new paradigm surreptitiously brings out the problems that it wished to bury. Thus Melanie Klein warns against too literal an interpretation of her precise thought that the various mechanisms that she describes refer to *memories in feelings*. The monumental theoretical construction of Bion sets out from the *primary emotional experience*, the foundation on which the interventions of the psychical processes of differentiation, elaboration and transformation will be exerted. In a similar way and with different axioms, Winnicott was also to set out from *primary emotional development* whose relation to the body forms the basis for his own conception of the construction of the psyche. Any clinical picture that may be interpreted as a sign of bad psychical health is always related to a disturbance in emotional development. From the point of view of development, says Winnicott, the intellect itself cannot be ill (unless the brain is deformed or affected by physical disease) in the sense that the psyche may be ill in itself. Thus, although the affect was no longer specifically mentioned in the new theories, this was because it was regarded as a basic reference at the beginning of development.

Principal modalities of the affective life

One sets out from the situation in which listening to the analysand did not necessitate breaking down what was said into affect and representation. That is to say, the material did not make this distinction either indispensable or necessary. This was the case for the feeling present in all discourse and for moods. On the other hand, this distinction may arise of its own accord. In such a case, the affect ceases to be merged in the communication, but clearly dominates it in such a way that one cannot avoid the impression that what is being expressed claims to mobilize the essence of what the analysand is trying to communicate at that moment – or his or her reaction to it. The analyst can no longer relativize this part of the material by placing it in relation to all the data that have emerged together on this occasion. It is here that the analyst, thinking of the 'transport', to use an old French word, clearly sees the vital character for the analysand of what at present occupies his or her mind, at the same time as the analyst guesses the function of the defensive shield assumed by the solidification of psychical communication of this type. There is nothing surprising about such a duality between the conscious positive meaning expressed and the intuition of its defensive value when one remembers that, unlike the richness of possibilities of drift in the representations that open on to complicated semantic networks whose repression allows access to the preconscious only in a filtered way, while preserving in the unconscious what cannot be admitted into the consciousness, the fate of the affects whose emergence is blocked in this instance undergoes only a small number of transformations.

On this matter, one must stress the importance of the fact that, to remain within its most limited conception, the representation is marked by its reduplication in thing-presentation and word-presentation, a situation much richer in possible meanings than that which knows no other division but that between unconscious affect and conscious affect. In the latter case, it is rather impoverishment that characterizes its situation in the unconscious, by loss of the qualities of conscious affect. On the other hand, the quotas of affect may serve the purposes of the movements of representations. In the case in which it is presented in the form of its invasion, one may observe that not only does the affect appear to have as its aim to obstruct the exposure of subjacent representations, but that it ensures – or usurps? – a function of representation; that is to say, it compromises the process of linking the ways used by signification (concatenation linking the various forms of sig-nifier) by condensing around it, as if to prevent their full deployment, essential conflictual nodes, while anticipating their intelligibility by the object to which they are addressed.

> The affect appears to be taking the place of representation. The process of linkage is a linkage of cathexes in which the affect has an ambiguous structure. Insofar as it appears as an element of discourse, it is subjected to that chain, includes itself in it as it attaches itself to the other elements of discourse. But insofar as it breaks with representations, it is the element of discourse that refuses to let itself be linked by representation and takes its place. A certain quantity of attacked cathexis is accompanied by a quali-tative mutation; the affect may then snap the chain of discourse, which then sinks into non-discursivity, the unsayable. The affect is then identi-fied with the torrential cathexis that breaks down the dikes of repression, submerges the abilities of linkage and self-control. It becomes a deaf and blind passion, but ruinous for the psychical organization. The affect of pure violence acts out this violence by reducing the ego to hopelessness, forcing it to cede to its force, subjugating it by the fascination of its power. The affect is caught between its linkage in discourse and the breaking of the chain, which gives back to the id its original power.
>
> (Green 1973b)

This situation corresponds to the description, in French terminology, of emotion. It may be encountered conjuncturally at particularly highly charged stages of the transference in any analysand, or characterize a basic transferential style in certain patients. Bouvet noted this feature of the object relation in pregenital structures (Bouvet 1956–67). These descriptions take up from what used to be emphasized in the treatment of hysterics, but here, when this modality constitutes the background or constant basis of the transference, it is well beyond the frontiers of hysteria that this situation is encountered. What it expresses evokes rather an excessively painful reacti-vation of an ego threatened in the image that it would like to have of itself and an attempt to intimidate any approach from an object thought to threaten its integrity, to compromise its equilibrium (Green, 1986–90).

This brings me to another profile in which the aspect of crisis, more or less permanently maintained, is less to the fore than that of a passionate rela-tionship, sometimes ill-defined, in which the erotic aspect is not recognized by the person experiencing it. Indeed quite often what the analyst identifies as the disguising of an unconscious passion is expressed rather as a nostalgia detectable for no apparent reason or a constant sense of loneliness that allows amorous phantasies, which are usually arrested in their development when they admit their nature too openly, to appear only fleetingly. Passion is detected here only through the trace of disappointment, the vain expectation of a miracle, which by its very nature as a magical mode of hoped for satisfaction, relieves the subject of the task of formulating a desire whose historical origins he or she tries to blur and whose inscriptions, surviving even in his or her body, the subject refuses to recognize. One is often led to hypothesize, long before any more precise clues or signs corroborate the state of endless mourning that encloses the subject, unknown to himself or herself, in the maintenance of narcissistic suffering (Green 1983–91). In other cases, it will take the form of chronic sado-masochistic relations, displaced on to objects of secondary importance, that the complex intrapsychical conflicts will find material for their expression. But it is not unusual for one to meet links of the same nature, links more or less solidified in the course of time, renewed day after day, occupying the unmoveable centre of the existence of a subject in thrall to a demand for love addressed to a parental object. This demand alternates – in perfect symmetry – with the hold maintained over the child, who, for his or her part, clings to the hope of a final conquest, moreover enjoying unconsciously the secret knowledge that the exasperation or rejection that they will provoke are the surest means of strengthening the node of unsupersedable symbiosis. These cases are interesting because they provide, through the externalization of object relations, a clearer idea of the internal world of certain patients, or a comparable relationship – whose transference gives only an attenuated idea – is built up in the mind of the analyst in a manner that is often more constructed than experienced, beyond the concrete dramatizations evoked in the situation that I have just described. In any case, the problem is the same: how can interpretation succeed in linking phantasy scenarios – projected or acted upon – with a mental functioning whose communication would help the analysand to go beyond the unconscious satisfactions that he or she draws from them and which considerably limit a psychical life doomed to sterile repetitions and to open up a situation of enclosure within conflict?

I have described three affective modalities that correspond to the traditional divisions that language has established, namely feelings, emotions and passions. In the first, that of an overall, undifferentiated apprehension of the act of listening, the affect occupies the place of a tonality that is never absent from any discourse; feelings may be understood in this mode of communication. Even if they are detected for their own value, they remain subordinate to the intention of signifying verbally, which may indeed have recourse to other psychical means. The second modality, which is characterized above all by a predominance of the motional element, fragmenting, irruptive, disturbing the internal cohesion of the messages received or transmitted, establishes a more or less sudden change in which subjects find themselves in a false position both in relation to how they experience the situation in which they find themselves and in relation to what they see as their object in living, aggravating the gap that separates them. Lastly, the third relation, that of passion, is based on a durable situation and relates to an object conceived as unique and irreplaceable. Although, in life, it may happen that passions suddenly come to an end, what is being described here is the quasi-permanent style of certain transferences of mourning extending over the duration of that mourning. Of course, the hope of putting an end to the sometimes painful character of this way of being accompanies the psychoanalytic process, but one is only too often struck by the difficulty in mobilizing the modes of object relations organized so firmly and so rigidly that strive to maintain themselves despite what analysis may bring in terms of understanding their function and origins.

Epistomological difficulties

The difficulty in clarifying the states that I have just described stems not only from the obstacles that are encountered when proposing a satisfactory conception of the relations between affect and unconscious, the specific task of psychoanalysis. Affect, even considered from the point of view of the consciousness, remains a troubling enigma that goes beyond psychoanalysis, to philosophy or psychology, where it is met by no greater unanimity – in fact rather less. As for any hope of finding a solution in biology, because of the evident, well known links between affect and its bodily manifestations, despite the remarkable progress of studies in this area, it cannot be said that the question has been simplified, on the contrary – and one finds here the same limitations in finding an overall vision in which one might disentangle the tight imbrication of the affective manifestations with the other psychical activities examined in the light of cerebral explorations. One will therefore treat with a certain indulgence – but also with a positive appreciation of the modesty that they display – the following lines from Freud: 'we would readily express our gratitude to any philosophical or psychological theory which was able to inform us of the meaning of the feelings of pleasure and unpleasure which act so imperatively upon us. But on this point we are, alas, offered nothing to our purpose' (Freud 1920a). For it should be noted again that the categorization of the affective life according to states of pleasure or unpleasure – even when they are given different names (Spinoza's joy and sadness, Plato's pleasure and pain, etc.) – is, in the final analysis, the one that seems to be most generally accepted. However, the position taken by Freud radicalizes this distinction by attaching it to the instinctual life, which does not raise any difficulty for the relation between pleasure and sexuality, but leaves open the interpretation of unpleasure, since it cannot be linked to a drive and since one has a choice of various mechanisms to explain it (the failure of repression, anxiety as warning of an upsurge of instinctual demand, collapse of countercathexes, the breaking down of the excitement barrier by excessive quantities of excitations; the loss or threat of object loss, the precariousness of the ego's boundaries, the disapproval of the superego, etc.). This development of Freud's thought considerably complicates the problem by maintaining the notion of a beyond the pleasure principle (Freud 1920). We know how hesitant Freud was in his attempts to account for the psychical foundations of these states of pleasure and unpleasure in terms of relaxation and tension – attempts that came to no final conclusion.

It should not be thought that the distinctions that I have made amount to no more than a concern to differentiate affects according to their intensity, as Marjorie Brierley wished to do. If this aspect is present, it remains nevertheless dependent on the place of the affect in psychical communication, at the heart of the relations maintained between its various elements. The only psychoanalytic reality from which one is obliged to start is that of the discourse that encompasses the various forms of communication from self to self and from self to other, the aim of the latter being transmission, that is to say, transference. What is sought above all in the transmission is *participation* and that the other to whom the message is transmitted should come to occupy the place that is reserved in advance for him or her, unknown to the person who addresses him or her. To introduce meaning at this level may be premature, except to retain that acceptation that describes the effects of what is signified as giving rise to other representations or other signs linked by unconscious relations to that which is directly transmitted. And it will be less a question of meaning as it may be no more than a reverberation based on analogical evocations before leading, at best, to a new contact with oneself. Meaning will emerge there only retrospectively for what precedes cannot be assimilated to an unconscious meaning, only to the avenues that lead to it and which introduce it to it, that is to say, to the equivalent of that process of movement towards and away from meaningful focus of meaning that is revealed only as it approaches it. The paradox created by the existence of the unconscious is that what comes from that source manages to produce such effects without the relations between the unknown initial message and the evocations provoked by its form on arrival being perceived. The problem that faces the analyst is that of the way in which he or she can conceive of the forms supposedly present in the unconscious and their relation with what analysis teaches him or her of conscious phenomena.

The affect: conscious and unconscious

Freud proposes to consider the difference between function and tendency. The pleasure–unpleasure principle is a tendency of the psychical apparatus whose function seems to be the maintenance of excitement at the lowest possible level or, failing that, at a constant level (Freud 1920). Since Freud always maintained that a person's most fundamental aspiration, even if it regularly meets with failure, is the search for happiness, one may infer that such an ideal combines the absence of potential imbalance with an experience of happiness. The case of pleasure is more difficult to define, since its function of unquestionably pleasant relaxation is even more obviously so when that function has followed a state of sought tension. Furthermore, cumulative tension – even a pleasant one at an early stage – that is not followed up by relaxation would have little chance of being experienced as pleasant. Since the ego is recognized as the seat of the affects, it would be tempting to consider that the relation of the tensions provoked, inside or outside, to the agency that receives them ought to provide the key to the problem. One will then run the risk of giving too much importance to the regulatory control of the ego without answering the question as to the origins of the affect, for there is little doubt that if the ego is the locus in which the affect is expressed, a psychoanalytic point of view cannot stop short at this observation, except to deny the unconscious the power of generating affects. Certain analysts, embarrassed by the question, have tried to do just this, avoiding it by proposing to consider the content of the unconscious only as shaped by representations of things or forging an ad hoc concept of *'représentations-choses'* ('thing-representations', Laplanche 1984), the term ill concealing the wish to give the lion's share to representations because they are more accessible to thought. In fact, the aim of the *'représentation-chose'* hybrid is to get rid of the concept of drive and replace it in the unconscious with the object–thing graft. It is clear that the somatic base, in which Freud places the roots of the drive, fundamentally linked to affect, disappears from this terminological game, as does affect *qua* mental category. It is now easier to understand that the evacuation of affect from the unconscious has as its aim to weaken the 'motional' pole of the unconscious, closely linked as it is to the principal characteristic of the drive. Two further remarks have to be made. First, one wonders what relations affects maintain with the unconscious ego. Second, it should be noted that any affect that attains a certain degree of development is manifested insofar as it is experienced as movement emerging in the functioning of the ego, which cannot be accounted for by anything in the specificity of the organization that characterizes it, since it is on the contrary formed by cathexes at a relatively constant level, as is implied by the logic of the relation of the agencies and since one of its functions is to control excessive excitement.

These difficult questions have led to endless discussions as to the basic function of affect. Generally speaking, three main interpretations have emerged, involving in turn discharge, tension and signal. This last, semantic, conception of affect has often been presented as an alternative to the excessive place given by Freud to biology. It is difficult to see why, since the function of the signal is part of his conception of anxiety and presupposes no less a reference to biology. However, he was certainly not alone in taking into account the links between the emotions and the body, since it can also be observed in philosophy and psychology. I do not intend to spend any more time on these debates. On the other hand, I propose to make a possible clarification of the confusions on which they rest.

The attempt to define affect is based on the vague use of a term that refers sometimes to a dynamic process whose development in a temporo-spatial sequence is the fundamental characteristic 'affecting' the body beyond the ego at one of those stages, sometimes to the state itself at a time or stage of this development, by whose quality it may be perceived by the ego. Whenever dynamic movement is addressed, one is confronted by the need to bring together the relations that one presupposes between unconscious sources – stemming from the id – and the evidence of conscious manifestations experienced by and communicated by the subject, whereas when one concentrates on a particular affect one is inevitably led to take account only of the affective quality that belongs exclusively in the conscious affects.

Thus referred back to the relations between affect and unconscious, while admitting that it would not be logical to recognize the quality that they manifest in the conscious, I find it difficult to accept that they might be conceived of in the form of their tensions alone, because I do not see how on the basis of such states without quality the subject might succeed in availing himself or herself of the affective richness that can be observed in conscious life. The most complete, most precise definition that Freud gives of affect is to be found in the *Introduction to Psychoanalysis*, where he adopts a dynamic point of view. Analysing these 'highly composite' phenomena, he distinguishes between two kinds: on the one hand, certain innervations or discharges and, on the other, 'perception of the motor actions that have occurred and the direct feelings of pleasure and unpleasure which, as they say, give the affect its keynote' (Freud 1917). In my opinion, such a definition brings together different levels: the somatic (innervation–discharge), and the conscious (direct sensations and pleasure–unpleasure). I propose to consider the intermediary element, 'perception of the motor actions that have occurred', which Freud is careful to distinguish from direct sensations, since these relate to the unconscious level of the phenomenon; it is to be reduced neither to its somatic expression, nor to its conscious experience, but might be conceived as a perception of the unconscious ego traversed by internal movements devoid of quality. This indication may be transposable to clinical practice, the affect being perceived by the analyst according to the tensions of the discourse, even when the qualities are lacking in the conscious communication.

One must no doubt admit that, in the psyche, there are different ways of being unconscious. For the representations, it is conceivable that a set of ideas may be preserved in the form of memory traces, which, dissociated from their conscious context, are not only repressed, but recombined, having been subjected to the attraction of the pre-existing repressed. In this way they undergo a new subjection through the links that they contract under the influence of the reshapings of the unconscious and of the ego, undergoing the attraction of the pre-existing repressed. The blocks thus formed may be detached in whole or in part from the kernels of meaning that formed part of them and on which will bear the effects of the primary processes (condensation, displacement). These will circumvent the barrier of the preconscious only by means of disguises that will enable them to escape censorship. Nothing comparable is conceivable in the case of the affect. The result of its repression is first a suppression and although the psychical work does not stop in the unconscious in this case either, the forms of linkings and unlinkings that transform representations do not seem to be applicable to affects. Indeed the affect does not break up as representations can do. Consequently, there is not so much recombination as adjunction – 'constructions' of affect as Freud said (Freud 1915). Seeking equivalents for representative modifications, one would be struck by the much more limited character of the possible operations: turning back into its opposite or against itself, formations of symmetrical affects, opposed or complementary, experienced or projected, and, in cases of the most radical defence, inhibition or suppression (affective freezing). But here one comes up against a difficulty that cannot be underestimated. Although these operations are certainly those that clinical practice suggests, where the affect is concerned, it is more difficult to form any idea of the state of things than in the case of representation, where it is a matter of imagining its unconscious form. How is one to conceive of these various affective destinies when depriving them of their conscious quality? Their unconscious state in no way affects the essential status of representations, despite a double inscription, being content to transform their contents, whereas the unconscious affect brings about the disappearance of the quality that constitutes the essence of that by which it may be recognized even before the question of its meaning is posed. Its transition to the unconscious state that would subject it to operations in which what gives it its psychical value would be missing ought then to bear on quantitative tensions achieving their transformations, beginning with movements without qualities, while still having the capacity to turn back on themselves, to produce their opposite, to constitute themselves symmetrically, in complementarity or in opposition, perhaps in terms of models borrowed from bodily organizations. But it is certainly clear that the so-called operations cannot be assimilated to what may be observed at the level of the transformations of representations. I am well aware of the obscurities that remain beyond the answers that I have tried to give.

A final paradox may help us to see more clearly. One often finds – it is a common enough experience – that, when trying to communicate affects, even the simplest ones, one has a sense of failure, however well endowed one may be with verbal fluency and linguistic skill. And yet, literature in general, and poetry in particular – that relation to words that is confined to the printed marks on the page – arouses intense emotions in us. There is, therefore, in the relations between words themselves, independently of any physical support, simply in the interlinkings of their evocations, a possible affective genesis. The observation is valuable, on condition that one does not forget that the aesthetic emotion is not the emotion that one experiences in life. In the example chosen, the absence of the body was replaced by the body of words. This body of words must not be confused with the body itself, but one must recognize its ability to draw on the matter in which it originates and transform it into another form by the very combination of words and so achieve their vibration on another body.

The analytic situation is comparable neither to that of ordinary life, in which emotions are exchanged, provoke one another, complement one another, respond to one another, in human exchanges, nor to that of the emotions aroused by poetic language, to confine ourselves to verbal communication. This form of communication refers to an experience in which words, beneath the flux of excitement, are tempted to go beyond the limits of verbalized thought, seeking its exhaustion in action spurred on by phantasy. Nor is it distributed in the synchronic polyphony of the poem, because the movement that displaces it into the discourse of the analytic session, 'unframes' it from its present moment and captures it in the network of its past, homological resonances, striving to rediscover past pleasures, trying to create those that have never seen the light of day, reopening the trace of wounds still open from their non-event or renewing, sometimes cruelly, the anxieties of loneliness and distress.

This may be why there is some point in returning to the question of the naming of affects. We know how important it is in the relations of adult to child. Bion showed its role in the meeting between verbal apprenticeship and the depressive position. No doubt analytic speech – which, I have said, '*désendeuille*' language ('takes language out of mourning') (Green 1984) – gives, thanks to the detour of interpretation, an opportunity of rediscovering ways that have extended the resonances of words as far as the unconscious, but also an opportunity of anchoring them by the interposition of affect to their bodily sources. But when there truly is a recognition beyond naming, that naming is produced only because, when the word said is 'let out', its non-verbal associations follow a transport of thought free from attachments, free from the control that language exerts upon itself. Above all we must not conceive of this destiny in terms of translation, because what is important in it is not what is fixed in another expression, conceived, after all, on the model of language, but on the contrary what, bearing it, has taken it through spaces ever more distant from itself; just as a dream recounted after an interpretation given in the previous session makes it felt, witnessing what the incitement of speech has provoked in terms of psychical invention, which came about only through the detachment that it achieved outside the work of words in the 'magnetic field' (André Breton) of the unconscious.

Issues of affect

In the discussion on the function of discharge of affect, it should be remembered above all that Freud is trying to stress the difference from representation. Representation directly involves no manifestation that is expressed by a change in the state of the body. When the body undergoes transformations by regression, in the form of hallucination, for example, the experience of the body remains outside this process, except when the hallucination entails coenaesthesia. This is because, in fact, hallucination would be rather the locus of an interlocking between the regressions of thought and the reincorporation of certain psychical experiences. And although Freud concludes that there is no essential difference between dream material and the material of hallucination, it must be observed that in the dream he stresses the inhibition of affects. On the other hand, when I address forms of dream-life outside the framework of the dream itself, as in nightmares, night terrors or stage IV dreams, here on the contrary the affects invade the expressions of psychical life and in this general context two features absent from dreams make their appearance: first, the unblocking of motor inhibition, which sets in train reactions of flight or terror and, second, the resomatization of anxiety (Garma 1997). There is, therefore, a coherent constellation of psychical events that suggest that what is important is *the internal orientation of the process towards the periphery*, touching on layers of the psyche that relate to the corporal, even to the somatic. These levels of psychical activity come to the fore when the development of the affect is neither impeded, nor involved with representations taking place in the framework of ego processes that try to retain those manifestations in the psychical sphere. This direction taken by the affective cathexes occurs primordially towards the body, which manifests its change by emerging from its silent functioning to testify to a disorder that prefigures either a much hoped for pleasure, or a danger that mobilizes defensive solutions of flight or attack. In the latter cases, the ego calls up resources of motility, in the last resort, for the triggering off of the action. But this second stage, a consequence of the affective process, does not strictly speaking belong to it. It expresses, by a short circuit between psychical activity and motility, the extension to the behavioural sphere of the warning perceived in certain forms of the sleeper's psychical life, when the function of the dream no longer plays its role. That is why, in the analytic situation, the motor solution being excluded, all excitement will bear on the bodily reactions and the intensification of aggressiveness. Lastly, it should be added that such a breakdown in equilibrium may be the result of a situation encountered in the outside world as well as belonging to an internal conflictual activation concerning the instinctual life, since the representations associated with it have not succeeded in pursuing their task of elaboration and failed to include the affect in the unconscious organization.

Let us go further and, in an attempt to move one step further into what so far eludes our understanding, risk a hypothesis. When one brings together all the observations that give affect its particular character – internal orientation of the cathexes, extension to the sphere of the body, intensity of emotional experience, etc. – one may imagine the affective process as *the anticipation of a meeting between the subject's body and another body* (imaginary or present), a contact that would result either in the analogue of a sexual and amorous interpenetration or, on the contrary but in a comparable mode, the analogue of mutilating aggression, both threatening – for better or for worse – the subject's integrity. The affect would seem to resemble both a preparation for such an eventuality and the effect of foreseeing it in an accelerated way. Its precipitation in both senses of the term has above all the function of manifesting to the subject experiencing it the *absolute interiority* of the phenomenon, whatever its origins may be. This direction taken by the psychical processes seems to have the function of a forced sending back, forcing the obliging person to question his or her nature as subject. However rich and complex the meanings that occupy the psychical universe may be, whatever integrating capacity that universe may have, one constantly experiences the limits of its power. This power shows us that it is capable only to a very limited degree of melting the affect in the totality of the manifestations that constitute it. The loss of control that the ego risks renders suspect by this very fact the affective variations, however expected, that may surprise it.

From this dependence on the body, the psyche draws the lesson of its limits, both inner and outer. As I said once before, *the psyche is the relation between two bodies one of which is absent*. Let us now go back to the clinical aspects that are explicitly manifested in the torrential outburst of the affect: more or less partial disorganization of the ego (anxiety, panic, depersonalization), instinctual violence acted out in antisocial behaviour, decompensatory somatizations of psychical conflicts represent so many extreme polarities indicating the ways taken by a confiscated affective economy. For me, they are at once valuable clues at the frontiers of the affective life and lay down a limit to the knowledge that one can have of it. However, recent years have seen some remarkable advances into regions in which little light had previously penetrated, for example, psychosomatics and delinquency.

Psychical representative of the drive and instinctual impulse

These situations are scarcely ever encountered in analysis. Nevertheless, did Freud bring the descriptions that I have just given close to those with which he was to illustrate the new theory of the drives, just prior to revising the conception of the psychical apparatus and introducing the new concept of the id? The transformations that govern the transition from unconscious to id are changeable. By eliminating any allusion to representation in any of the descriptions that he was to give of the id from that time on – descriptions of a highly speculative kind – and its replacement by the idea of instinctual impulses, even more specifically of drives, Freud wished to stress, to remain within the area of clinical practice without necessarily following him in his speculations, three aspects in relation to the preceding descriptions: the somatic rooting (more directly inferred than with the unconscious of the earlier topography), the dynamic force crossing the frontiers between its agencies, and the repetition compulsion, which testifies to the ego's weak control over the drives. Even leaving to one side the difficult problem of the death drive, the changes that Freud made in the direction of what he believed to be the truth are of a nature to undermine analysts' morale. How is one to get to the bottom of those powers so resistant to all domestication by the most developed parts of the psyche when they are specifically stated to be the 'ultimate cause of all activity' (Freud 1938–40) and, furthermore, profoundly conservative? What is left for us to sell to our patients?

Many prejudices must be abandoned if one is to understand that what drives subjects to analysis, in every case, is not so much a desire to be cured as a compulsive need to rewrite their history in order to get on with their lives. The subjects do not know this history and do not even know how, in recreating it, they want it to be different or how this is to be done other than by making up themselves the fiction that they wish to see realized. This does not mean however that cure cannot be part of this project, but it is not bound up in an essential way with the unconscious desire of being analysed. When one thinks of all the colleagues who have been led by analysis to a scepticism that drives them to seek every pretext to hand to encourage modes of thought that are alien to it, one wonders whether cure has been the aim of their own analytic enterprise, for if this were the case, they would scarcely need to go looking for it elsewhere.

Freud certainly understood this when he made judgements that have been regarded as disillusioned, drawing attention to the weak plasticity of the elements of the id, their 'ultimate' determining value in the evaluation of our activities and the limited influence of our practice, more open to considerations originally less constricting. This is why he preferred the definition of the base of the psyche in terms of id, overcoming his earlier hesitation between instinctual impulses and representations. For both co-exist in the *Papers on Metapsychology* (Freud 1915), whereas only the first would be mentioned in the final model of the psychical apparatus (Freud 1923).

It is in the article on 'Repression' that we find the clearest expression of the idea of a *psychical representative* (*psychische Repräsentanz* or *psychischer Repräsentant*) made up of two elements, one ideational (the *Vorstellung Repräsentanz*), the other affective, defined quantitatively (quota of affect) (Freud 1915).[2]

The chapter on 'The unconscious' maintains an ambiguity, since in it Freud defines the primary processes by referring to instinctual impulses or wish impulses. However, at the time, he conceived of the unconscious only

---

2   It should be noted that the German term *psychische Repräsentanz* is not mentioned in the entry under 'Représantant psychique' in Vocabulaire de la psychanalyse (1967)by Laplanche and Pontalis. The omission is corrected in the English edition, *The Language of Psycho-Analysis* (1973), where we read that 'instinctual representative' 'psychical representative' and 'ideational representative' are used interchangeably by Freud, which is clearly not the case. In their translation of the article 'Repression' in the *Papers on Metapsychology*, Laplanche and Pontalis write: 'To designate this other element of the psychical representation, the name of quantum of affect is admitted'. (Strachey has: 'For this other element of the psychical representative, the name of quantum of affect has been generally adopted'.) It is clear, therefore, that the psychical representative includes one representational element (the 'Vorstellungsrepräsentantz') or ideational representative and another element: the quota of affect. In the French translation of the passage quoted above (vol. XIII, p. 197, in Freud, *Oeuvres complètes*, done under Laplanche's general direction), the difference between psychical and ideational is blurred: 'For this other element of *psychical representation* [my italics] (*représentance psychique*)'. The overall term 'representation' erases the specificity of 'psychical representative'. This distinction is clearly present in Freud himself. (See the article 'Représentation-représentant psychique', in Delrieu, *Sigmund Freud. Index thématique*, Anthropos, 1997 pp. 1159–62.) One may also note the absence of this same *psychische Repräsentanz* in the glossary of *Traduire Freud*, by A. Bourguignon, P. Cotet, J. Laplanche and F. Robert. *Repräsentantz* is sometimes translated as *incarnation*. One is far removed here from the concept at the frontier of the mental and the somatic, which expresses a move in the opposite direction from body to soul. When Freud writes the 'ideational content of the instinctual representative' (*S.E.* XIV, p. 156), he stresses the distinction – 'ideational' and 'instinctual' are not redundant terms, any more than psychical' is.

    To sum up, instinctual representative and psychical representative are synonymous and include the ideational representative and the quota of affect. The terminology is less easy to homogenize between object presentation and thing presentation. It is impossible, therefore, to assert that there is merely a verbal difference between psychical representative and ideational representative.

as made up of representations, an opinion that he was to abandon in *The Ego and the Id* (Freud 1923), without, however, formulating very clearly the status of the unconscious affect, except that is deprived of quality. However, he specifies that the sensations springing from internal perceptions derive from various strata of the psychical apparatus and that they are 'more primordial, more elementary, than perceptions arising externally', therefore from sources of unconscious representations. However, he never fails to stress the perceptive sharpness of the id in the dynamic oscillations of the instinctual states that inhabit it.

To sum up:

- it is on the subject of the repressed that Freud draws a clear distinction between representation and affect, when postulating a state in which they cannot remain distinct: the instinctual or psychical representative;
- as for the unconscious, in 1915, it is exclusively made up of representations, in the sense either of representation-representative, or of thing- or object-presentation. Repressed affects are reduced to the state of crude elements that may never the less come together in 'constructions'. However, the description of the primary processes refers to instinctual impulses or wish-impulses, in other words, representatives of the drive (from which will derive the various types of object-, then word-presentations.

This state of the theory foreshadows the foreseeable return in Freud's thought of the distinction between representation and affect. What was defined as the psychical representative of the drive will look very like the instinctual impulses that the psychical apparatus of 1923 were to present as the raw material of the id, *all allusion to the notion of representation (thing- or object- presentation, still less representation-representative) now disappears.*

So the theoretical movement drives Freud to push the foundation of the psychical organization towards a 'raw material such that there can be no division in it between affect and representation' (Green, 1973). Why, then, did the *Papers on Metapsychology* of 1915, while referring to the notion of psychical representative, not find it necessary to comment on it and why did Freud return to it later? For two reasons: first, because the reflections of 1915 concern the transference neuropsychoses and because the representations that they reveal remain under the domination of the pleasure principle; second, because clinical work concerning the unconscious and largely based on representations was often to end in failure, especially as Freud was discovering a 'beyond' the pleasure principle.

Already the *Papers on Metapsychology* suggested a need to take into account something other than representations. The article on 'The unconscious' stresses the value of object-cathexis. Until then (in particular in the article on 'Repression'), cathexis concerned only the quantitative charge borne by the representations, their strength added to it, so to speak. Now, object-cathexis concerns a process that is not be reduced to the cathexis of representations in the unconscious. Object-cathexis denotes something other than representations: a link maintained, at the very heart of the system, that knows only psychical reality, to referent-objects from outside the reality: 'object cathexis in general is retained with great energy, and more detailed examination of the process of repression has obliged us to assume that object cathexis persists in the *Ucs.* in spite of – or rather in consequence of – repression' (Freud 1915) in neurosis, unlike in psychosis. 'The system *Ucs.* contains the thing-cathexes of the objects, the first and true object cathexes'. In *Mourning and Melancholia*, the metapsychological elaboration will distinguish between the processes bearing on the cathexes, to those concerning us here and those relating to all the representations that, in the latter case, play a much less important role.

In fact, Freud's concern with representation reaches its limits towards the end of the *Papers on Metapsychology*: that of its co-existence and competition with affect, that of its relation to hallucination (which would be the form taken by psychical discharge as far as representation is concerned), that of its relation to object-cathexis. These are among the many signs foreshadowing its future decline – not to mention what Freud calls 'corporal innervation', which concerns hysterical conversion as well as psychomotor, hypocondriacal, sometimes delirious manifestations.

The conceptions of affect had to be modified insofar as affect was generally reduced to the role of accompanist to the singer of representation. What is suggested by Freud's later descriptions of the id is that one would be dealing, at best, with a state that falls short of the distinction between affect and presentation and, at worst, with the unrepresentable. What must be added is that they are 'critical affects' ever ready to invade psychical formations furthest removed from representation. In the final analysis, I will say that *the instinctual impulse is what will give birth to affect, once the meeting with the object-presentation has occurred*. To say of affect that it is the secondary product of a 'movement in search of form' (Green 1985) is to conclude with Freud that this psychical representative of the impulse seeking satisfaction will mobilize the traces of object-presentations left by earlier experiences of satisfaction. From this meeting between excitements deriving from the peripherical body and the dynamized memory of objects that brought satisfaction will be born the differentiation between the representation-representative and affect, the result of psychical elaboration. *The representation-representative is the object-presentation cathected by the share of the psychical instinctual representative coming from the body, soliciting what is external to itself in order that the change may occur in the psyche at least, whereas affect is the dynamic pursuit of that which, leaving the body, returns to it, having brought, in an immediate way, expectations, hopes and fears from the desired meeting with the object.*

When choosing the term instinctual impulse, Freud wished to stress the movement that is inseparable here from the idea of a transformation of state, the initial stage of communicating meaning. This is what he makes clear when he says that 'on its path from its source to its aim the instinct becomes operative psychically' (Freud 1933). Winnicott makes a formulation similar in spirit when he suggests the image of the *journey* of the subjective object to the object objectively perceived, the child creating the object close to his or her meeting with it, before that meeting actually takes place. Such a model assumes its value from the fact that in the absence of a meeting with the real object, it will be the capture of the movement by the primary processes that will be offered as a temporary substitute, which will not bring the wished for satisfaction, but will enrich the complexity of the psychical apparatus by ensuring the possibility of almost unlimited developments through the connections set up between unconscious, preconscious and unconscious. However, what radically alters the descriptions of 1923 in relation to the earlier ones is that the impulses will also bring with them a destructiveness that can no longer be attached to a type of satisfaction and which threaten to undo the complexity of which I have spoken. Such is the opening up that is made possible by the instinctual impulse that falls short of representation.

One meets in certain analysts a great deal of resistance to conceiving of psychical states in which affects and representations are simultaneously present in the unconscious (Kernberg 1976, 1982; Widlöcher 1992). However, this is what is implied by the content given to the id agency. Whether one accepts or rejects it, the question remains the same: *does one recognize the existence of psychical phenomena that do not belong to the consciousness and which cannot be accounted for by describing them in terms of unconscious representations?* If the answer is yes, how is it to be given a theoretical validity that will allow it to be recognized in clinical experience and how is one to conceive of the organization that brings them together?

Post-Freudian theorizations have thought to find a heuristic advantage in getting around the problem, refusing to allow themselves to be trapped in the impasses of relations between representation and affect. They have proposed alternative ways of regarding object-relations, exchanges between self and object, even transfero-countertransferential interactions, with no other concern but to define their functioning. Although these changes of vertex have undoubtedly opened up new horizons, *it is also undeniable that none of the alternative solutions has answered the questions posed by Freud: those of the relations between the somatic and the psychical, the relations at the heart of the psyche between the derivatives of corporal needs resulting from prematurity and of those born from contact with external objects possessing the ability to respond to them, the specific work and modes of transition between representations of the world of things and the world of words, the articulation between external objects and their forms in the internal world, differences between representations and cathexes, the opposition between psychical reality and external reality, ways of going beyond object-losses, etc.* This list does no more than state the problems without embarking on the answers that Freud gave them. Can it be said, then, that they are false questions? We have seen how clinical practice continues to refer back to them, either in the form of a failure in the representative activity (non–neurotic structures), or more radically still by the paralysis of the capacity to analyse and by the grip of the unrepresentable, already glimpsed from the time of Ferenczi and widely taken up in the recognition of extreme forms of anxiety (fear of annihilation, Melanie Klein; nameless agonies, Bion; torturing anxieties, Winnicott; essential depression, Pierre Marty; reduction of the double boundary, André Green, etc.). It is remarkable that authors as different as Bion and Piera Aulagnier, the first trained in the thought of Melanie Klein, the second in that of Jacques Lacan, should have tried to identify the psychical material covering a field less limited than that of representation. This led to such notions as *ideographs* (Bion 1963) and *pictograms* (Aulagnier 1975), which are similar in many ways to the indissociable mixture of representation and affect (Green 1970, 1973), all, in my opinion, being implicitly linked first to the Freudian concepts of instinctual representative, psychical (drive) representative, then to Freud's instinctual impulses – the creation of the second model of the psychical apparatus having contributed much to elucidating the question. All these new terms cannot be understood by seeing them as deriving solely from the concept of unconscious affect. They seem to be more elucidated by their relationship to the concept of instinctual impulse.

II The singularity of the states of affect–representation non–discrimination

Observations

How is one to give a description that is at once general enough and yet precise enough when the observations that come to mind seem to be so singularly bound up with the idiosyncrasy of each patient? Furthermore, is one to take what follows as a horizon – a very limited one, certainly – for no analyst can encounter the whole gamut of possible manifestations from which each individual will be able to draw certain aspects, of which the whole, even when incomplete, is meaningful.

1 General characteristics

The clinical treatment of borderline states and, in a more general way, of non-neurotic states has given rise to descriptions in which it is very difficult to analyse the material of these patients by stressing what is attachable to representations and what would relate to affects. Among the reasons that explain this state of affairs, the indiscernibility of affects perceived directly by the patient or aroused by the analyst's counter-transference is particularly striking. This situation goes hand in hand with a confusion of affects very marked by the ambivalence in which the internal conflicts attain no solution of temporary compromise, other than the production of symptoms, but give the impression of an open wound affecting the psyche, beyond symptomatology. The transference is as feared as it is demanding, negative reactions emanating as much from its direct manifestations as from the defences raised against its development. The situation is aggravated by the conjunction between the negative manifestation of hate, envy, hopelessness and inaccessibility to interpretations. Taking up Freud's formula that the object is known in hate, one might be tempted to complement it by affirming that here, moreover, hate is the way by which the subject achieves self-knowledge. Furthermore, especially when the transference is activated, the patient oscillates between a state of paralysis of thought and inability to communicate what he or she feels, not only because the affects are no longer expressible in words, but also because they become unidentifiable by him or her, while subjecting the patient to them, for their existence is not denied here. Rather than of a construction of affects one should speak of a confusion of affects that refer no longer to representations, but to unrepresentability. At these moments, analysts share deep within themselves the complexity of the unformulable, for they themselves, as soon as they emerge from a general appreciation of the subjacent anxiety, find themselves caught up in murky emotional states that are linked only to a very partial representation of the situation at that time, one that is particularly poor in content, from which they hope to see emerge some perceptible figuration, or to shape the phantasy of an imaginary figurability that would escape repression and of which they would acquire some understanding, thanks to a certain empathy (C. and S. Botella). It is not unusual at this moment for theoretical memories to come to mind, not in the form of ideas, but in a formal configuration both abstract in its content and poignant in its affective charge, without being able however to attach them precisely to an understanding of what is happening. There is a form of specific feeling in the analytic situation here; I do not know whether it can be encountered elsewhere, except perhaps in artistic creation, though artistic creation occurs in a solitary experience and is partially resolved in the work that springs from it.

The motive of this situation may be guessed in a permanent mobilization against an object from which everything is expected, but from which nothing can be obtained. When the conflict remains in the intrapsychical it cannot be said that it unfolds in relation to the unconscious representations that have constituted defences against anxiety, but that there is a massive mobilization of psychical activity that seems – whatever appearances may be to the contrary – to be on a war footing, opposing the analyst's interpretations with answers that range from insensitivity to the most radical rejection. All the descriptions that have come to my knowledge – some from eminent analysts, others from colleagues less well known who have shared their observations with me, knowing my interest in these problems – agree. Such analytic situations provoke in the analyst feelings of hopelessness, an impression that one is out of contact with the unconscious aspects of the patient or of his or her history: when analysts communicate their understanding of a patient's affects, they obtain no response. Analysts are not far here from a loss of confidence in their competence, which may go as far as to doubt the efficacity of analysis itself. This point of view is expressed more or less identically in the contemporary psychoanalytic literature (Winnicott 1971; Milner 1969; Searles 1965; Bollas 1992; Kohon, in press, among others). It is striking to observe that identical reactions are encountered as much in analysts experienced in the technique of object-relations as in those who conduct their analyses along more classical lines.

What is striking about these analyses is the absence in them of what I call *intermediary formations*, that is, stages that form links between psychical activity named as instinctual, archaic, primitive, etc., according to preference, and that of conscious communication. It is as if free association, by the relaxation of controls over thoughts, phantasies and affects, represented for the patient too great a risk of leading either to considerable disorganization, or to a state of hopeless dependency.

If one accepts the idea that affect is primarily a process that tends to diffusion and extension outside the frontiers of the psyche, it goes without saying that its major threat to the organization of the ego in which it resides is a loss of control over excitations. How, then, does the psyche react when confronted by affects that it cannot accept because they are disapproved of by the superego, or because of the threat of disorganization that their unimpeded development would entail? Various procedures are at its disposal.

(a) The defences

The *suppression* of affects is no doubt the commonest and most generally applied, all the more so in that it follows the course of the mastery of affects demanded by education and social life, except at times when a certain letting go is permitted (e.g. the football World Cup). Among the neurotics, defence may be confined to isolation. Does suppression mean, therefore, disappearance, even in the unconscious? One might think so if certain particularly significant examples did not argue in favour of the opposite: this is the case with the unconscious feeling of guilt, which is less explicable by a reconstitution of affects at the conscious level, in each circumstance in which it is solicited, than by the impression of an unconscious psychical matrix present in a permanent state and urging to expression self-punitive affects and behaviour as soon as the subject allows himself or herself to open up. The mechanisms of disguise that are more particularly suggestive of affect are centred around a *double return* (reversal into its opposite and turning upon the subject's own self), which, according to Freud, are supposed to act before the intervention of repression. One might add to them the production of affects symmetrical with those of the object or complementary to its own, even opposed, as if echoing, those that are transmitted in intersubjective contact. No doubt, too, the mechanisms of introjection and projection are not conceived outside a predominant affective base, but one might also argue that they go beyond them.

It might be considered that all the defence mechanisms ought to be cited here, on the grounds that they are supposed to warn of anxiety. But I have chosen those that bear particularly on affects that would trigger them off. If projection allows a 'placing' of affects outside self, which presupposes a certain externalization, this defensive procedure remains in the psychical sphere, even if transported into the other, that is to say, that it is susceptible to reshaping, even of recognition, thanks to the analysis of this very fact. Quite different is the case of two other destinies of affect: that of its *expulsion by the act*, which is supposed to reduce the intrapsychical tension that it engenders, or more radically still *somatization*.

(b) Formations of the unconscious
Turning now to the principal polarities of psychical activity as observed in psychoanalysis, one will find some remarkable peculiarities. The psychical productions that come to the aid of analytic work in order to approach, as far as possible, the unconscious, have ceased to function. I am speaking of *dreams*. They are not entirely absent, of course, but they are seldom mentioned, even when patients are aware of having had some; usually they are struck by amnesia. And when they do remember them, they recount them some time after having them (thus limiting the associative work) or even pass over them in silence. For a long time, they will be feared and, rather than serving the work of elaboration, they will, with their rather crude character, be little more than a psychical eruption. Their messages will return to the unconscious state without leaving any trace, despite their upsurge in the consciousness and their entrance on to the stage of the transferential processes. Later, when they are tolerated as a possible object of investigation, they will usually have a relieving function, as if they were understood as attempts to reduce tension rather than as a way of revealing unconscious

meaning, even though such a meaning exists. Concurrently, *phantasy activity* in the sessions is rare, poor, quickly stopped, or assumes a character that suggests that the gap with reality has been diminished, for it is less a matter of exposing a mode of thought that has become separated from consciousness and is distinguished from it only in that it provides an imaginary version regarded as the equivalent of the perceptions of consciousness and is difficult to analyse as the expression of conscious desire.

(c) On the real and the hallucinatory
Of course, a considerable part of the session is devoted to *recounting the events of the patient's life*. This represents a way of clinging to the real that allows the subject a certain objectification, sufficient reason to explain what he or she feels. This recourse to reality is evidence of vigilance with regard to the temptation that might arise of letting himself or herself go along with an associative function, which is felt as an invitation to indulge in 'crazy talk'. Such rigidity is to be found in what may be grasped of the patient's relations with external objects. These are always used to justify painful affects caused by misunderstanding, indifference, others' malevolence. The character of the relations with past experiences is entirely misunderstood.

One is surprised by certain forms of solidification in the relation to *internal objects*. Winnicott already indicated that in these cases the analyst does not *represent* the mother, but *is* the mother. I would add to this that, in the end, the analyst senses the mother's hallucinatory presence in the session between the analysand and himself or herself. This presence is evidence of incompatibility between the analytic work that is taking place in the analysis and the perpetually maintained internal fixation on the primary object. When subjects try to free themselves of this fixation, they seem to want to believe and to make others believe in the intrusion of the primary object, in order to defend their position of command over psychical activity. Indeed the term fixation is too approximate here, for in fact it is a matter of clinging, which, as I have shown elsewhere, is the opposite of a link, insofar as it expresses a position of immobility, whereas the link opens up the prospect of its transformation into other forms that, while maintaining a relation between different elements, can convey their themes by channels of communication, thus making it possible to envisage the initial relation from different angles and in wider contexts. Here the *repetition compulsion* is at work with impressive constancy. It concerns not only the acts of everyday life, relations to objects (internal and external), transferential affects, but also the impossibility in treatment of getting the patient to agree to refer to what took place in earlier relations. The technique of the here and now, in spite of appearances to the contrary, does not improve the situation; the place then assumed by denial will bear on the internal nature of analysed phenomena, or the relation that they maintain between themselves.

(d) The transference

The lever of psychoanalytic action is the *transference*, its essential given, which involves – beyond the affect–representation division – the incitement to movement of a psychical activity that cathects an unconscious object and allows contact between the traces left by objects from the past and the new object of the analytic situation, in a new and original formulation. Transference encourages the activation of psychical elements more particularly in relation to the dynamic aspect of the processes, namely affects. Their form, so difficult to communicate, is an impediment to analysis and to the discovery that they might convey some other meaning. This is why a subject's access to the recognition of unconscious affects arouses very strong resistance, especially in the analysis of those states of unconscious pleasure that are expressed, under the affect of repression, by conscious unpleasure. Similar resistance occurs when one tries to unveil the satisfactions behind certain forms of behaviour that may be associated with moral masochism. In fact, if a mediation were found to assist the awareness of this state of things, it would be through *identification*, which is no doubt the privileged form of affective recognition. However, identification may thus encourage confusion between the conscious aspects of the material. It ought always to be related to hypotheses concerning unconscious communication – especially as primary identification with the object is to be found in the primitive forms of narcissism. The paradox then is that the most intimate expression of subjectivity needs to find an echo in another in order to receive its meaning. Hence the importance of sharing affects in the analytic situation (Parat 1995).

There necessarily follows from this *a limitation in the ability to represent*. This may be observed session after session and often justifies a face-to-face position, since the usual position of the analyst, hidden from view, introduces in the analysand a feeling of emptiness that no phantasy production can fill and which takes the form of an absolute need of perceptual contact, since the activity of representation must maintain its support on an external foundation. The absence of the analyst produces the anxiety that one is not able, on one's own, to provide oneself with any representation of oneself – which is not far removed from an experience of death; it calls for the assistance provided by information, which I have often had to give, there and then, when the analysis is interrupted. This anxiety, bound up with the inability to represent, is no doubt based on the return of a state of psychical distress and the wish to avoid a feeling of invading frustration, which leads to anger, envy, hopelessness. Loneliness remains the dominant affect. It is the result of a narcissistic confinement brought about by a sense of one's inability to gain recognition for the legitimate character of anxieties or for the complexity of emotional reactions, sometimes accompanied by a desire not to allow the intensity of one's disarray to be perceived.

(e) Acting out and somatization

These transferences are marked by successive and sometimes more or less uninterrupted actings out. They express not so much a wish for instinctual satisfaction as behaviour involving flight and evasion. Often these seem motivated by a need for dissimulation that one eventually attributes to the desire to mask from others what one feels to be one's 'private madness' (Green 1990). But this is only one superficial aspect of it. Most of these questing attitudes are the result of unconscious prohibitions from the super-ego, preventing any apprenticeship through experience; any contact that would lead to anything other than disappointment; any activity that might lead to the development of one's abilities. Where do the unconscious non-instinctual satisfactions go? Into the satisfaction of an unconscious masochism whose role is the alienation to an internal object from which it is impossible to be separated. The reason for this state of affairs is related to very powerful destructive affects – of which the death-wish is a very developed expression, but which here as it happens never attains the status of a mere wish. It is a painful presence that would seem to be the double bottom of all psychical work. The peculiarity of this destructiveness is to address oneself to an object on which one is internally totally dependent. Dependence on the love of the object, but a love whose primitive forms ('ruthless love', Winnicott calls it), attest to what is inseparable from the most vital narcissism that makes up the subject's ego. The subject has introjected – this is the least visible aspect of dependence – the object's most paradoxical ways of thinking, which ultimately forbid any overall view of it. Strictly speaking, no image can be formed in this respect – again an effect of the limitation of the function of representation. The exposition of the object's affective incoherences has, as it is remembered or rediscovered through its displacements on to present objects, does not succeed in endowing it with a complex personal image, but attests to a prohibition to identify it by thought. And since thought can never give up that task, egged on by the wish to see the ego exercise a certain control as much over the object as over the manifestations that it provokes, its functioning becomes the occasion of a ceaseless struggle with no outcome. Power must remain with the object, to which sacrifice is due, in proportion to the many attempts to kill off representations that have drained the psyche of its dynamic and transformative potentialities. Nothing is more striking than the phenomenon of the negative hallucination of thought (its preconscious aspects linked with words), in which the manifestations of active negativism, suspending psychical activity ('I can't hear a thing you're saying'), or passive negativism ('From a certain point on, I stopped listening to you'), immobilize the progress of the analytic work.

If various degrees and various expressions are possible here – from dysfunctions, which are merely local regressions, to the most chronic forms, some, such as hypochondria (often attached to psychosis), which are diffi-cult to interpret – they may go as far as psychosomatic states in the strict sense, in which the abolition of affects may be accompanied by alexithymia, which prevents the recognition and verbalization of those affects that have succeeded in crossing the threshold of consciousness.

Sometimes this takes on strange aspects. Although, generally speaking, it expresses the consequence of psychical experiences in which it is laid down that there is nothing that can be thought about them – whereas the psy-chotic tries to think the unthinkable – this sometimes takes the form of a sequestering and mutilating capture. A patient who happened at a certain period to be living in the same district as me, and sometimes passed me in the street, said to me one day: 'I am alternatively fascinated by your red scarf and by a phantasy that my girlfriend says to me that she would like to go out with me naked under her coat' (this phantasy was expressed with the very clear purpose of distracting my patient from the importance that I had for him). A few days later, he was suffering from a severe blepheroconjunctivi-tis that required careful attention. Generally speaking, *corporal impregnation* is an eventuality that is always present and strongly rejected. Thus a patient felt obliged to give up his *eau de toilette* because he realized that it was the same one that I used: 'You and I, the same one, it would be horrible'. Then, a moment later, he added: 'When I came into this room, it smelt just like a room in which one has made love'. One is on the verge of hallucination here. Hallucination is potentially present in the relationship: it is ready at any moment to swamp the relation to reality. It is at this point that one becomes aware that, although what one is dealing with here is the erogenous zones, what characterizes the process is their diffusion to the whole of the ego. One sees, then, that thought must be always on tenterhooks to observe not only what is taking place in the psychical sphere, but also what may at any moment swamp it.

2 Particular clinical characteristics

The sense of being *swamped* is the most characteristic term used of these states. This is, of course, the case when it is a matter of anxiety, but it is not limited to that effect. Anxiety may be lacking in the picture in which other affects are involved: depression, hopelessness, rage, envy, etc. Generally speaking, it is the impossibility of struggling against this invasion that causes most pain. It is understandable that the means of defence employed by the most organized egos should be total insensitivity to the point of feeling nothing (McDougall 1989). But more striking still is the patient's attempt at the most acute moments to block any affective process by bringing into play a radical defence: psychical immobility – in fact, apparent death – since all vitality runs the risk of triggering off destructive or self-destructive affects. Signs of depersonalization often occur in this context. They may not take the classical form of the crisis of depersonalization and may express the patient's sense of strangeness and doubling, accompanied by pseudo-hallucinatory impressions (one patient saw God in the sky, another 'heard' his mother, who lived far away, calling him in the street as he was coming to his session). Many patients say that they are living in a permanent fog and remember a period in their past when this state was constant. Such states are verging on the indescribable: the fear of having a face-to-face relationship with a man (it happened to a woman in a context unconnected to neurosis) triggered off the impression that she was surrounded on all sides by a great shadow and felt obliged to withdraw into herself, as if threatened with annihilation. In the end, this withdrawal reduced her to an almost minimal psychical existence, so that she came to realize her internal emptiness. Her intense stare, usually expressing hostility, tried to hypnotize me. In fact, it diverted the search for what was taking place inside her towards – or rather against – me. She was later to admit that at such moments, contrary to appearances, she was in the grip of a negative hallucination in which she no longer saw me. As she approached my office, everything became unimportant, futile, indifferent: 'I have two great black holes in place of eyes, I see and I don't see'. And when she stared at me, she later admitted: 'In fact, I can't see you'.

It is the *body* that seems to absent itself at the approach of an encounter, the body that disinhabits the subject, driving it to ever more disembodiment. This continues in the sessions: 'When *I* speak, *you* move away. When *you* speak, you move closer to me and *I* move away . . . When I imagined speaking to you as you expected, freely associating, your body moved away from me'. This variation of distance from the object described by Bouvet (1956) leads in fact to a veritable disembodying: 'As you were talking to me, and I was trying to understand what you were saying, the more I tried, the less I understood, the words moved away, the sense of the words disappeared, the consonants moved off, only the vowels were left. All that made a huge cry'. The body sometimes expresses in its experience affective phenomena that are generally experienced on the psychical plane: 'I feel at once all-powerful and less than nothing; I feel that in my body'.

With innumerable manifestations of *splitting* co-exist states in which one witnesses the lifting of frontiers between the various sectors of the psyche, especially when pain breaks down the barriers. On the other hand, one is sometimes surprised by the absence of reaction to messages sent by the body: sometimes a porousness of the ego to excitations, both internal and external, sometimes segregation without communication. This kind of negative work bears on the most tenuous thread of communication. This defence is all the more urgent in that the encounter is phantasized in a chaotic and destructive way. Imagining us as in the fresco of the *Creation of the World*, God and Adam, index fingers almost touching, a patient told me that any reduction of the small gap was likely to trigger off an explosion in which she would disappear. Any phantasy of pleasure is experienced as a cataclysm, in which both parties disappear. And yet the distance maintained must not vary either, for if it is increased, not only would the subject lose the object, but she would also lose herself. Rather surprisingly, this may give rise to violent sadistic phantasies. In fact, it is a question not so much of sadism as such as of the expression of crude instinctual force, but one that has the peculiarity of never attaining an object in phantasy terms – it disappears as soon as it might be attained. Thus this body, invaded, submerged, inundated by the affect, oscillates between explosion and disappearance with, at its limit, the threat of object loss or of disintegration of the ego.

Whereas the *fusional phantasy* remains a predominant requirement, any imperfection in its fulfilment is felt as an intolerable narcissistic wound and brings into question the very mode of manifestation of the subject's presence: he or she feels panic at being 'with the whole of his or her body', as if susceptible to eliminating all psychical activity. An intense struggle is set up to restore narcissism by means of non-corporal modes of expression, in the forefront of which is intellectual work. This becomes the object of a persecution of thought because of the ever unsatisfactory character of the result, involving obsessional ruminations. The affect finds refuge in the erratic somatic sensations (a feeling that one's head is burning, contraction of the open jaw that might not be able to close again, bulimia) or sensations that belong more clearly to the psychosomatic syndromes. Sometimes psychosomatic short-circuits like symbolic actions, apparently in reaction to psychical separation, or when it is impossible to make contact with the object, are expressed by an exacerbation of a syndrome of physical pain. One cannot avoid the impression that pain expresses the struggle between a sequestered object and the unsuccessful attempt to detach oneself from its bonds in order to form new ones on the psychical mode. These traumatic moments mobilize great resistance to communication and to the reception of interpretations before their meanings of displacement are accepted by the subject.

Enactments of childhood situations organized into phantasy scenarios occur in sessions. It is not unusual for patients to turn up at their sessions with *a substitute transitional object*, a cushion, a piece of cloth serving as a blanket, rarely a typical childhood toy, such as a doll or teddy bear. One patient felt the need for many long years to hold her coat or mackintosh against her like a baby (she had never had one) and to stroke it. She was well aware that the article of clothing might be a representation of herself, an attempt to get back to a period when she was still an only child herself, an acted out phantasy in which she was both her mother and herself. This realistic explanation was contradicted by another, much more tragic one. After many years, she admitted to me: 'He's already dead, but he's still crying', an illustration of those tortures described by modern authors: 'When I'm well, he disappears and becomes part of me again'. This despair is inseparable from destructiveness, since any positive relation must necessarily be expressed in terms of disappointment, frustration. The rule then becomes to expect nothing and so lose nothing, but in fact the pleasure principle is thus inverted, the subject playing the one who loses wins. One is sure of losing; winning is uncertain and a matter of chance. As I have already suggested: to say no to the object is more important than to say yes to oneself. This is because negative affects are felt with extreme violence: the anger that would like to kill the object must itself be killed (that is to say, entail a mutilation of the ego), in order that the subject is not killed by it. The patient is aware of this internal destructiveness. The movement of a turning back on to oneself comes into play almost automatically whenever the turning back of hate into attachment is impossible. Hence aggressive desires towards the maternal object: 'When I hurt myself, I hurt her'.

The status of object never achieves an acceptable form: 'For me, the analyst is nobody and, although I know this, I imagine that he is everything for me'. An imaginary activity is set up, however, but it can practically never be presented at sessions: 'There's no connection between the woman I am when I'm not here and the women I am when I'm here'. Such patients are permanently struggling against a danger of loss: loss of the object, loss of representations of the object, loss of cathexis of the object and, in extreme circumstances, loss of cathexis of the ego itself, succumbing after all its defensive efforts, divided between the wish to master the object and the wish to destroy it.

When one is faced by situations closer to psychosis – while remaining within the framework of the borderline states – one sees the appearance in its early stage of transitory ideas, close to delusion: the world must be saved from destruction – a projection of the wish to safeguard the ego, which runs the risk of being dragged down into destructive wishes towards the object. At paroxystic moments, the most ordinary people, those one might meet in the street, look as if they are dying. It is as if life had to be under permanent surveillance. 'You just have to be on the lookout. You don't think', one patient said to me. And yet the boundaries that separate these states from evident psychosis are never crossed. A great obstacle to the alleviation of pain is the fear of being free. Hence the paradox of the analytic session, which must remain under a control that limits considerably the benefit that may be derived from it, because at the end of the session the subject is in pieces once more, without the means of putting himself or herself together again, to confront the demands of reality. To hear someone say 'You're free' is really the most fearsome thing, tantamount to being abandoned by the object, to a lifting of all control, the field left free to excess without limit and with no conceivable limit in view. Separation is always experienced not as access to autonomy, but as expressing the object's desire to be rid of the subject. The subject sees himself or herself as imprisoned in a world of the labyrinthine, incomprehensible enclosure, for whatever is alive is to be feared.

Communication is set up under strange auspices: 'Isn't it mysterious that you should tell me incomprehensible things and that I should reply with words I don't understand?' Phenomena of *negative hallucination* that might relate to external perceptions, or to thought, are disconcerting: 'I've tried to picture you in my mind. It's as if, looking into a mirror, I saw a black hole there'. This is actually what happened when this subject was in front of the mirror, being able to see her own features only if the first reflection was, in turn, reflected by another. 'There's nobody there or rather I know you're there, but I can't see you . . . All I can see is a mirror with a frame. It's completely black. When I do see something at last, it's a theatrical setting. But what I'd like to see there, in order to see me, is you!'

These remarks, which certainly give food for thought on the question of the *unrepresentable*, testify to the capture of the function of representation by instinctual derivatives. Representation cannot free itself from the external object and needs to surround it in imagination, which takes its place without being satisfied with its representation. It is an attempt doomed to painful failure. For this object is inalienable and could never fulfil the patient's wishes. You can neither abandon it, nor accept that it can abandon you. Sometimes these patients cannot go out of their homes: having planned to go out, either they cannot cross the threshold or, arriving at the bottom of the building, go back up again for no apparent reason: 'It's as if there's a rope holding me back and I panic if I try to go any further. A voice says to me: "No, you mustn't"'. It is not so much an injunction of the superego as a maintenance of absolute dependence, at the cost of sacrificing oneself: 'It's as if I might be drowned there, too, invaded, at the thought of doing as I like'. At its extreme, during a session, the direction of speech is delegated to the mother: in a session, it is she who decides what is present or absent, what is to be said or what is not to be said. This is not a representation of the mother: the mother is there 'in' the room. These phantasies, in which separation and devouring are associated, are projected on to the maternal object: 'She stops me living. She captures my vital forces for her own use, she tries to take my words, my dreams, my imaginings, my associations, my ideas, and I let her, because that's the price I have to pay to stay with her'. In life, this patient avoided contact with her mother, rejected opportunities of meeting her, but in thought she never left her. In words, too, she had nothing but hate for her, but in thought everything expressed the importance of behaving in a conciliatory way with a view to keeping her, though she continued to be distrustful of her. Sometimes the relation to the mother

329

can assume an almost hallucinatory form. One patient will be convinced, when he is in bed with his wife, that it is his mother who is in the bed. He displays tragic loneliness. 'I've no one to talk to, except you', he says, yet all too often what he says is pointless. Being unable to bear the frustrations of absence, in the grip of uncontrollable psychical destructiveness when this is pointed out to him, he will say quite rightly: 'It's paradoxical to wish to kill someone when one so wants him to be there'. This loneliness is accompanied by states of emptiness, non-existence, or as if the void were the only thing on which he could feed himself. The destructive propensity becomes familiar to the subject who is powerless to divert its course. It may be that his ultimate aim is to feed his need for self-punishment. In reality, strict control aims at shaping others to his requirements, in the intention of warding off threatening catastrophes, which his behaviour tends to lead to.

Denial of affects may reach extreme forms: 'I don't know what you mean by wishes. I can see that others may have them (to buy a car or a country house, to go away, to meet someone), but they mean nothing to me'.

Discussion

I have preferred to give a general view of the world in which these patients live, since each of them is very different from the others, with histories that vary considerably from case to case and whose seriousness cannot be defined in terms of a hierarchical grid. I am only concerned here with the subject of this work, namely, those clinical aspects in which affect and representation are caught up in the same psychical texture and are, in fact, indissociable. One is in the opposite situation here to the one in which such a distinction is possible: examining these two fundamental aspects of psychical life does not arise here, because they are merged in a single unity, even when one considers the repressed or unconscious part. At the beginning of this work, forms of discourse were encountered in which there was no call for the separation of affect and representation. For the whole that they formed would have been impoverished by such a distinction, although it was possible in theory. Here the lack of distinction seems to express an unsupersedable pain and to be placed at the service of a potential disorganization. It is pointless to say that although this world experienced by patients is close to nightmare, the analyst's counter-transference is particularly painful, oscillating between incomprehensibility and the feeling of finding oneself a prisoner in a situation without a solution. It is the symmetry of the counter-transference, reflecting the transference.

I shall now give my opinion on the theoretical elements needed in understanding these situations. I shall do so without referring to child development, because I do not believe that what is known of the subject

330

can really elucidate what is learned from these transferences in treatment.

These states result from the conjunction of several factors.

Although it is true that one sometimes encounters severe traumas from early childhood (illness, separation from the mother, being placed outside the family, excessive proximity), the most difficult thing in fact is to succeed in making a link between the consequences of these accidental circumstances and the clinical pictures observed, in which these traumas are sometimes absent, but in which the dysfunctionings are no less disturbing. Or rather, although the psyche has suffered in these cases in a similar way, this ought to be attributed, it would seem, to relations between the child and his or her parental imagos. One is confronted here with the difficult evaluation of relations with a maternal object that may be in turn phobic of the subject's instinctual activity, unrelenting in the imposition of beliefs, uncritical of one's own eccentricities, blind and deaf to the demands of the child's affective life and his or her personal psychical creations. Lastly, the case is almost constant, the maternal object quietly and permanently struggles so that the father occupies only an insignificant place in the subject's psyche, which does not exclude from the mother's mind, far from it, the idea that she has been an excellent mother, having lavished her deep love on the child. This at least is what the analysand's discourse leads one to believe. Although it would be both naive and erroneous to accept it uncritically, it would be just as much a denial to regard what he or she says as mere projection. In any case, as with Freud's theory of the trauma, all that interests me here is the patient's psychical reality. It sometimes happens that one is able to reveal a buried intergenerational transmission of conflicts masked by everyday life and which never the less have a certain elucidatory value. Not the least interesting thing about this comparison is the observation that in the final analysis the consequences of the traumas are similar to those in which traumas seem not to exist, both occurrences referring to maddening, uncontrollable, unpredictable, objects revealing positions that give us a glimpse of the fear of the child's vitality together with the extremely precocious projection of its future sexuality, often of unconscious anxieties. A permanent state of dissatisfaction or depression on the mother's part puts on to the child the burden of having to cure her of it, so that the individual who is expected to save the mother – the child – is at the same time the one who is shown that any attempt to do so is doomed to failure, because it can only aggravate the causes of his or her misfortune.

Hypotheses

Examining the clinical tables, it seems to me that their very diversity confirms Freud's final theory of the drives. My intention here is not to open up the dossier of controversies surrounding the Freudian theory of drives. However, with a view to clarifying my thinking, I shall say a few words about which of Freud's positions I am referring to. In the article 'Psychoanalysis', written for the *Encyclopaedia Britannica*, Freud sums up his thought in a way that seem to me to be both valuable and accurate. He explains how, from the dynamic point of view, psychoanalysis 'derives all mental processes (apart from the reception of external stimuli) from the interplay of forces, which assist or inhibit one another, combine with one another, enter into compromises with one another, etc. All of these forces are originally in the nature of *instincts*; thus they have an organic origin. They are characterized by possessing an immense (somatic) store of power ("*the compulsion to repeat*"); and they are represented mentally as images or ideas with an affective charge' (Freud 1926a). This seems to me to be sufficient to explain what I am referring to. For my part, I can see no other conception of the psychical topography that accounts for it more clearly. Furthermore, one has a strong impression that it is indeed the concept of instinctual impulse that enables us to get closer to the supposed theoretical condition of these states. It is a question here of impulses that have always to be suspended, slowed down, stifled, stopped in their dangerous potentiality and yet always likely to overflow their territory, to spread over the whole of psychical life without undergoing the organizing transformation of the different levels. Whether it is a matter of a discharge or not is in itself of little interest; what on the other hand seems very important is the internal orientation of the cathexes and the struggle against the possibility that they might achieve significant fulfilment. These patients often say: 'I don't know, I don't know . . . I don't understand'. But once one of them said: 'I don't know whether you are aware of how destructive that "I don't know" can be. It kills off all representation'. Destructiveness, however important it may be, cannot be separated from the erotic libido. The Eros of the life drives infiltrates the agencies of the ego in a brutal form and seems degraded by the no less brutal reactions that it entails (instinctualization of the defences; Green 1993). It is as if the sexual cathexes, rather than allowing the body to enjoy experiences of pleasure, while encouraging it to accept inevitable frustrations, took on a wild, obstinate character, threatening the subject's identity and, in the final analysis, making it unable to sustain an amorous relationship with a distinct object. In this case, the object can only be the source of profound distrust and permanent potential danger, involving a need to master it, to control it, making it assume tasks in reality whose ultimate explanation is to be found in warding off the projection of the subject's anxieties. It certainly seems to me that Freud's last theory of the drives is particularly brilliant here, especially insofar as the emergence of destructiveness, even when it undergoes certain vicissitudes in which it is borne towards the subject's cathexes in the outside world, remains very largely fixated at the level of the ego's functioning, forcing it into repetitive, often acted out behaviour, and into many, varied and extensive forms of evasion, protecting very badly from extreme narcissistic vulnerability to the most ordinary incidents of everyday life. One cannot but feel that, far from exercising the slightest mastery over overflowing and disorganizing affects, it becomes imperative to put the greatest possible distance between oneself and representations, the furthest removed as well as the closest, thus making them inaccessible – in other words, reducing the possibilities of drives and objects being linked by meaning. There remains, however, the question of how much account is to be taken of the unrepresentable, which is often the most important element.

At worst, this acute conflict may lead to impossible contradictions that can only lead to panic when confronted with chaos, whose effect would be destruction and paralysis. This may express insurmountable avidity, which demands, in spite of masochistic behaviour, the rejection of all compromise, even though the existence of patients seems intended to satisfy a cruel god. There is little point in speaking of ambivalence, for ambivalence seems to me to be crowned by a sort of *negative omnipotence* that, while rejecting everything, also appropriates everything, while annihilating it, in other words, to no purpose. It is pointless to say how difficult analysts find it, in cases such as these, to situate themselves as objects of transference, so much do the confusion and interpenetration of registers place them in an impossible situation: 'You would like me to choose, and I don't want to choose. You would like me to choose between life – that is to say, between life and death – and nothing. But I want them both: I want nothing and the rest. Between being there and not being there. And I want them both, at once, not to be there when I am there and to be there all the same. I don't want contradiction. I want neither of them, and sometimes that isn't enough, and I want them both'. I find here old descriptions in which I have stressed the negative rejection of choice. Not only 'not this and that', but 'neither this nor that' (Green 1990).

Generally speaking, the correction to be made to Freudian theory is to attach this instinctual functioning to the object. What contemporary clinical analysis has taught us is indeed the capacity of the object to encourage the intrication of erotic and destructive drives by recognizing them, accepting them, bringing to them a psychical response that allows their elaboration, while preserving their future. This psychical response must not be regarded as secondary to the instinctual cathexes directed towards the object. One must consider the internal work that alters the cathexis towards the object, placing it in relation with its imaginary response. This response intervenes therefore before the one that is actually given by it. An introjection takes place on the cathexis–internal and external response dyad, which becomes an indissociable totality. No doubt certain aspects of the response will be able to remain outside this introjection, but the impact on the psyche will depend on the reinternalization of the whole formed by the cathexis and the echo that it has provoked (Green 1997). The child has installed his mother in himself, in the demand that he has addressed to her, but now he will have to include her in his unconscious psyche, link her to the traces of earlier experiences, transforming her and giving her an individual, personal form, while leaving her open to future vicissitudes. In the absence of this situation, there will be set up the most destructive forms of what I have called the work of the negative (Green 1993). Repression will play only a limited role in it, whereas denial, splitting or disavowal will be constantly at work. Through them, the important thing, for the subject, is to achieve a non-recognition of self. The knowledge of these operational modes is of particular interest for the non-neurotic structures, sometimes, too, extending to psychosomatic structures. It is no doubt expected of me to speak of the structure of the ego. I think, however, that it is not necessary to embark on this subject, for, generally speaking, theorization does not go beyond the descriptive plane, whereas the conjunction between instinctual functioning, the role assumed by the object's responses and the work of the negative seems to me to account for them indirectly.

In situations in which the analysis is able to remain within the framework, I have described a *central phobic position* (Green 1998). This description concerns the function of association in the session. It is not intended as an analysis of phobogenic situations in the outside world, nor even those of the internal phobias, that is, those unrelated to projection outside. Nor is it to be situated in relation to the depth psyche, but in relation to the way in which the analytic situation, mobilizing and overthrowing relations between the agencies, as well as those between past and present, by mediation with the object, entails, on the part of the analysand, a phobic position that drives him to break off his associative function, thus expressing a state of intense fear of recognizing his unconscious anxieties. Here the mechanisms of anticipation play at least as strong a role as threats of resurgences from the past, regressions, or even the triggering off of anxieties, since the signal function of these seems to have been put out of action by a hypersensitive prescience. It is as if the analysand foresaw before the analyst where his associations might lead him, that is to say, to a point at which he would have to recognize a very painful reality. One of my patients evoked, by memories of a time when he was put out with a wet nurse, which he had begun to talk about many times, but not in this dramatic way, how he would anxiously await his parents' Sunday visit. Now, his father visited him regularly, but his mother never appeared: 'I saw my face looking towards the door, with an expression so full of anxiety, so tense, so desperate, that I said to myself: "It's not possible, it can't be me"'. It is not without interest to note that this 'memory' appeared more than ten years after the beginning of his analysis.

From then on it was possible to uncover this mode of defence in interpreting his behaviour in many activities and conflictual situations into which he seemed to plunge, totally subjecting himself to the unpleasantness of these situations, while giving himself the possibility 'of being elsewhere'.

I am making the hypothesis that the activity of cathexis is centred here around one aim: to bear on the surveillance of the psychical processes more than on their individualized contents, while making every effort to prevent the work of transformation and elaboration, starting from the instinctual impulses or perceptions, attempting to take form in the direction of phantasy, or to help the unconscious to reach preconscious functioning, for at this level the link between the representations would take place. Such a link ought to allow the support of object-cathexes, affects and thing-presentations, which would then undergo the mutation made possible by their link with word-presentations. The apparent diversion of attention from contents proceeds from a refusal to recognize their transgressive relation – in terms not only of prohibition, but also of the impossibility of being satisfied with the potentiality inherent in their representative condition. The transition to word-presentation produces a double virtuality to this acquisition: that of a new significant endowment and that of a return to the sources of object-representations. It is probably not within the reach of the conscious to grasp all its implications: what is important is to allow the movements of language to rest on the parallel, corresponding, analogous movement that animates the internal dynamic of conscious and unconscious thing-presentations. This is why it is the impulse, which Freud sometimes identified with thought, that is to be placed at the foundation of the psyche.

Verbalization will be able to link the extreme sophistication of the word-presentation system with a connection, not with the contents – which remain outside consciousness – but with the processes that govern the unconscious. These would be expressed after short-circuiting the preconscious, making it unsuitable for a mode of transmission between unconscious and conscious, by the non-recognition of their relations. In short, a first stake has presided over the transformations of the instinctual impulses in productions of the unconscious, but the conjunction with the sphere of representation has been rejected because its development at the preconscious level would have forced thought to take account of all its implications. These involve alterations of affect not only through its link to representation, but through its entry into the system of relays between thing-presentation and word-presentation. However, instead of sustained repression and the work of elaboration that stems from it, the messages reached from the deepest layers of the psychical apparatus infiltrate verbal communication and make it very obscure. This is the result of a number of convergent actions: the transformation of instinctual impulses into unconscious representations manages to retain only a small part of their cathectic energy. The role that should be played by the object in this transformation leaves most of the instinctual impulses in a crude form, escaping transformation into meaning and the symbolic organization of the unconscious. Those impulses unlinked by representation will prevent the second transformation – that of unconscious thing-presentations aspiring to become conscious through the mutation occurring with the development of the thought processes, in embryo in the unconscious but driven by a desire for greater fulfilment in the preconscious (thanks to language), without however the link with unconscious representations ceasing to be established through the filter of repression. What remains unelaborated at the level of the instinctual impulses prevents the development of binding processes through the mediation of the linguistic form provided by word-presentations. Affect, which ensures the continuity of cathexes and qualitatively modulates representative expressions, while preserving contact with the object-cathexes, sees the process of differentiation prevented by the persistence of the crudest forms of the oldest links to objects, cathected by the destructive impulses most intolerant of what is opposed to the direct expression of the drives and to the frustrations and disappointments that they have to undergo.

I am expecting someone to ask me if so much effort is worth the trouble, in the case of these patients. I will not deny that the result obtained in these structures is disproportionate to what can be done with a well constituted neurosis. However, it should be stressed that modifications to the functioning of the ego – a greater tolerance to receiving messages from the unconscious; to recognizing their source in the drives; to relaxing the links of dependence on the primal objects; to investing new fields of interest – do take place in the long term. It should be added that one scarcely has the feeling that any other method apart from, if not psychoanalysis as such, at least a continuing relationship with a psychoanalyst, is capable of bringing about such changes. Neither chemotherapy nor the so-called cognitive therapies provide better solutions. Only a measured, gradual, patient elucidation of the emergent aspects of the intrapsychical conflicts involving the ego and the object can link the activity of the drives, by saving it from the most sterilizing solutions of the work of the negative. Lastly, it is worth saying that only these long, often unrewarding analyses really allow us to understand the nature of the intrapsychical changes that take place under the intersubjective action of psychoanalytic work. What one has here is an irreplaceable access to knowledge of the psychical levels furthest removed from consciousness – which one cannot claim to account for solely by reference to pregenitality, since the erogenous fixations of this type undergo the assault of destructiveness, the combination of the erotic and destructive drives affecting relations between ego and objects.

336

Speculations

From *The Interpretation of Dreams*, Freud laid down with great precision what is at stake in the problem between processes and qualities. Setting out from the consciousness as 'a sense organ for the apprehension of psychical qualities', he distinguishes between peripherical excitations that reach the psyche through perception and, on the other hand, excitations of pleasure and unpleasure that he conceives as 'almost the only psychical quality attaching to transpositions of energy in the inside of the apparatus'. This is the modality by which the psychical systems, unconscious and partly preconscious, deprived of psychical qualities, appear to consciousness only on this condition: 'We are thus driven to conclude that *these releases of pleasure and unpleasure automatically regulate the course of cathectic processes*' (Freud 1900, S.E., V, p. 574). However, the need for more differentiated psychical operations requires that this first system is replaced by another, more independent of the signs of unpleasure. He then specifies that the activity of the preconscious, through its link with the traces of the signs of language, acquires the qualitative capacity proper to this second system: 'By means of the qualities of that system, consciousness, which had hitherto been the sense organ of perceptions alone, also became a sense organ for a portion of our thought-processes. Now, therefore, there are, as it were, *two* sensory surfaces, one directed towards perception and the other towards the preconscious thought-processes' (Freud 1900). This position of principle remains constant throughout Freud's work. It poses a problem only from two points of view: on the one hand, the search for the nature of the internal processes of transformation, from which result the states of pleasure–unpleasure; and, on the other, that of the upheaval brought by the belated awareness of the existence of states that would express something beyond the pleasure principle, as reflecting a failure of that principle. We must not recoil from the notion of psychical surfaces (to which Freud was to have recourse in defining the ego) on account of its pictorial character. It expresses the notion of a working surface and of the limits that allow us to situate what lies in front of them and what beyond them.

Perception, including the perception of the sensations of pleasure and unpleasure, form the boundary of one field: that of the external peripherical excitations and that of the internal affective qualias. Another 'front' of perception is that provided by the 'qualities' attached to language. One may then situate, short of the states of pleasure–unpleasure, the instinctual impulses and unconscious affects; between the sense-perceptions and the processes of thought, the unconscious or conscious representations, the word-presentations. The last form the second perceptual front, thought itself being, like the unconscious, devoid of quality, but acquiring qualities through its link with language.

337

As far as the first surface is concerned, receiving internal excitations from the consciousness, Freud never ceased to hesitate about the precise conditions of this transformation. Although it is true that he did not arrive at definite conclusions concerning the relaxation–tension relations to characterize pleasure and unpleasure, another aspect has been all too little noticed in the observations that he left us. Indeed, he was always concerned to specify that the translation of the states of pleasure–unpleasure into terms of psychical processes depended not so much on the absolute size of the cathexis as on *the modification of the quantity of cathexis or the oscillations of that quantity in the unit of time.* This observation, repeated in different forms, seems to be aimed only at an initial, rhythmic period – at the foundation of the experience of time – that will be characterized later by discontinuity. In another, very similar formulation, Freud speaks of a rate of diminution or increase in a given period. There may be matter for reflection here.

Furthermore, I must stress once again the internal orientation of the cathexes. By internal, I mean more specifically – since the representations are no less so – those that will move towards the physiological functions of the peripherical body. To understand this better, it should be remembered that, according to Freud in *The Interpretation of Dreams*, in relation to the organ of the senses that is consciousness, the psychical apparatus appears to it as external. Several times, Freud stressed this dimension of what I dare to call 'internal externality', just as he later described the id as external for the ego. One can understand these reflections only if one relates them to Freud's concern to give a description of psychical functioning that cannot be content with characterizing it as an internal world in relation to the external world. The setting up of an 'externality' inside the psyche itself is probably the result of the relations between the agencies, since consciousness can experience all that is outside itself only in terms of a relation of strangeness. It is what accounts for this paradoxical position. More radically still, it is beyond even the frontiers of the psyche that cathexes are driven, either because they cannot be elaborated by the structures that take pleasure in hand, or because their intensity threatens the ego's organization. But, this being the case, these excitations seem to link up with one of the two great polarities of psychical life, either those that depend on the perceptions, which would lead to action, or those that are rejected to that other original source that is the body.

These considerations are fully explained in the *Papers on Metapsychology*, in the chapter on the 'Unconscious', where Freud writes in a note: 'Affectivity manifests itself essentially in that motor (secretory and vaso-motor) discharge resulting in an [internal] alteration of the subject's own body, without reference to the external world; motility, in actions designed to effect changes in the external world' (Freud 1915a). Affirmations of the same kind are repeated on a number of occasions – Freud using the term corporal innervations to denote this destination of excitations in particular – concerning conversion, which, however, in this case, liquidate the affect.

What is essential is the idea that for these cathexes what has left the body returns to the body. This does not mean that they come back to their source, but they diffuse towards the functions that are to manifest themselves at its periphery. One also has to consider the ideo–motor 'corporal innervations' that intervene in the expression of emotions, complementing the information that subjects receive from their inner feelings with those that they allow others to perceive. Finally, when a certain threshold is crossed, these corporal innervations engage the motility of the life of relation. This looped circuit is characterized by its immutability, its diffusion and the undifferentiated character of the reactions that it arouses.

The so-called opposition between the conception of discharge and the semantic conception of affect is resolved in fact if one is willing to understand that, in its attempt to modify the state of the body, such a change necessarily entails a mode of auto-information given to the psyche that must never the less be distinguished from information transmitted by the double system of representations. The data that originate in the external world and which undergo the long detour of representative work, *insofar as they are addressed to the consciousness*, have as their aim in short the modification of the external world that results from the layered and linked representational systems. However, the motor actions involved by the affects mobilize elementary reactions (*acts*), whereas those relating to the representational systems would appear to be based on intentionality (*actions*). There is no point in short-circuiting this distinction in a single system (schemes of action). By linking them to representations, neurobiologists have forged the concept of 'representactions', which is of limited interest. In the final analysis, as I have suggested, it is through the elaborations of what governs at the outset the conjunction of psychical representatives of the drive and traces left by object-representations that a true internal psychical world is constructed, one doubling the external world. The initial aim of an immediate response is transmitted through the loops of transformation that have given rise to the internal elaboration of a world more acceptable to the subject, because the subject would include the means of not submitting too much to the consequences of trials caused by frustration and disappointment.

It is this overall conception that will be harmed by the observation of states beyond the pleasure principle. On the one hand, Freud observed that 'another occasion of the release of unpleasure, which occurs with no less regularity, is to be found in the conflicts and dissensions that take place in the mental apparatus while the ego is passing through its development into more highly composite organizations' (Freud 1920b). One cannot be content then with an opposition between a system governed by the pleasure–unpleasure principle, the second affect being produced under the effect of repression, and a system related to the reality principle, which would be capable of freeing itself from the influence of the first.

The most radical change discovered by Freud concerns the discovery that the once-termed 'automatic' regulation of the cathexes, according to the pleasure–unpleasure states, no longer holds. 'We thus reach what is at bottom no very simple conclusion, namely that at the beginning of mental life the struggle for pleasure was more intense than later but not so unrestricted: it had to submit to frequent interruptions' (Freud 1920c). It is here that Freud makes a crucial discovery, yet does not dare to propose the obvious solution, namely to relate this failure with the encounter between the instinctual impulse and its object. Yet he says with great clarity: 'The binding is a preparatory act which introduces and assures the dominance of the pleasure principle' (Freud 1920d). It is as if Freud were afraid to introduce the object too early in the establishment of the foundations of the psyche, as if he feared that the attention given to what he regarded as essential, namely, the activity of the drives, might be diverted in favour of a mode of structuring that would be dependent on the external and therefore more subjected to variations that would prevent the establishment of a theory that had general value. We know that he had to alter this point of view to some extent in *Inhibitions, Symptoms and Anxiety*, but all the later works testify to his return to the earlier view, which continues to place instinctual activity in the role that he had always given it, that of constituting the base on which psychical life is built.

But let us return to the more particular problem of affect. It seems to me, that, despite their very partial character, Freud's observations may serve to guide us in our reflection. What my clinical exposition has abundantly shown is what I have called the absence or the functionally inoperant character of *the intermediary formations, that is to say, of psychical productions organized by primary processes involving a relative work of differentiation between affect and representation.* Furthermore, as all the authors indicate, one cannot but be struck by these clinical pictures, which express rather undiscriminating modes of psychical functioning and, in various ways, in a more or less directly perceptible manner, states of non-separation between subject and object, of clinging to the object, in a destructive, masochistic mode of relation, imbued with imperious, undifferentiated sexuality, subjected to constant disappointment precisely in relation to persecution that would find its source in the primary object. I propose to clarify this point and this can only be done by introducing the object into speculations concerning the genesis of these mechanisms.

If one is willing to consider that the said intermediary formations organized by the primary processes may be regarded as concomitant with the establishment of the auto-eroticisms, the criterion of separation cannot be sufficiently apprehended simply by the existence or non-existence of an anxiety that would be related to the situation, an altogether too descriptive notion and one lacking explanatory foundation. Let us consider the possibility that the child would have to resort to those modes of organization in which the two great psychical axes defined by Freud, the state of pleasure–unpleasure and thought processes, may be related by dream and phantasy activities, to which should be added the category of play, whose importance Winnicott has demonstrated. These are the principal expressions, but not the only ones, of the functioning of these intermediary formations. *In short, the separation with the primary object can be affected only insofar as the child is able to fall back on his own psychical productions insofar as they keep him in contact with both the derivatives of his deepest instinctual needs and the limitations of reality.* I note the trace of the good functioning of this organization in analytic treatment, in what I have called the tertiary processes.

I am postulating that these mediations by the primary processes constitute an internal 'intermediary area'. From this centre will develop relations that are most susceptible to being worked on by the psychical apparatus between ego, objects, desires and the work of the negative. But what are the conditions required by the installation of this primary psychical organization whose existence is necessary to the development, richness and complexification of the intrapsychical and intersubjective relations? Here two tendencies come into opposition, that of Freud, who does not wish to take into account the affective relations between the child and his or her primary objects and, on the other hand, one that seeks explanation exclusively in observation of the perceptible manifestations of these exchanges. For my part, I adopt neither of these attitudes.

However rich the perceptual exchanges in the mother–child relationship may be, they cannot provide the key to those aspects of the construction of the internal world that I have just described. I recall the importance of the mother's role as 'psychical cover', as I have called it; namely, that function of the mother that makes possible the establishment of processes internal in their relationship to the unconscious – intermediary formations. I shall not go into the detail of my descriptions concerning the framing structure that follows the negative hallucination of the mother. On the other hand, I shall say that the possibility that these intermediary formations may be anchored in the psyche depends on the continuing maintenance of the maternal cathexis, which survives all the ups and downs of the relationship, even those aspects of it that may involve considerable destructive charges. Various authors, including Winnicott and Bion, each in his own way, have said as much. When Freud speaks of the variations of cathexis at a particular stage or over a period of time (reduction–increase), I shall interpret this remark by proposing the idea that it must involve for the child *the possibility of being recognized, by the maternal cathexis, at various stages of these variations in a given period, enabling him to link simultaneously, in himself and in his relation to the*

341

object, the kernel that allows him to reunify the various internal states and preserve them through the interest that he continues to arouse in the mother. It is this, in the final analysis, that makes possible the constitution of a psychical kernel, which Freud calls the pleasure-purified ego. Furthermore, this maternal cathexis is highly paradoxical, since it is subjected to the internal contradictions of being profoundly and massively mobilized towards the child and in the fullest possible way, at the same time as it must already involve, in embryo, an anticipation of the state in which the primary object will have to accept the detachment produced by the child's future access to autonomy. Such is the necessarily agonizing nature of the maternal link. This potential detachment, sketched out from the beginning, is precisely what will be able to prepare the ground for other objects and for the blossoming of the Oedipus complex, present from the child's origins, in the form of the mother's recognition of her link to the father and the contradiction that she may have to live through, created by the double corporal relation that she has with the child and with the father, without forgetting their differences. Perhaps it is now clearer why such a conception may account for what has been outlined above of the affect as cathexis of expectation, in the form of an anticipatory preparation for the encounter with an object that, when this encounter does not resonate with the reflected cathexis of the object, may be transformed into a desire for evacuation. This, I believe, is the true condition of the separation with the primary object. This separation occurs when, the cathexis of that object having been maintained through all its variations, the child 'lets go' of the object, because he can depend on the relays of his own psychical formations, which have partially been substituted for satisfactions with the primary object and make possible the persistence of the link with it under the primacy of a 'private reserve' that enables desires, satisfied or not, to be reappropriated by the child.

An essential contribution to our understanding of analytic treatment was made by Winnicott when he introduced the model of play to account for what occurs in clinical practice and in the transference. Beyond the Freudian intuitions, this shows that what appeared in treatment was a matter neither of mere repetition, nor, as Melanie Klein suggests, of being entirely dependent on a projective activity. The model of play accounted for an activity that returns, through its past cathexes, towards the object of the present situation, creating that object in anticipation of the subject's meeting with it. The completed view of the process, thanks to a phenomenon that Edelmann was to call 're-entry', is the reintrojection of the circuit, discovery and creation, shaping both the internal psychical organization and relations with the external world. At the end of a long session in which the analyst was the witness and object of movements of insight and destruction, at a stage when the time seemed to have come to authenticate the patient's quest of herself, he happened to say to her: 'All sorts of things happen and they wither. This is the myriad deaths you have died. But if someone is there, someone who can give you back what has happened, then the details dealt with in this way become a part of you, and do not die' (Winnicott 1971).

These speculations are the ones that have helped me most to give shape to the experiences felt, represented, thought about in the course of my relations with those patients presenting non-neurotic structures, that seem to me to put into question the discrimination between affect and representation, and attempt to find a solution in relations between instinctual impulse, object and work of the negative. It should now be clearer why I have expressed doubts as to the ability of empirical and so-called scientific observational approaches to account for the complexity of the facts presented by the analytic situation. However, I am quite ready to be convinced to the contrary, if I see the possibility that these studies respond to the problems that I have expounded. It is strange that the search for convergences, if not correspondences, sometimes comes from sciences furthest removed from those that one might suppose to be in close proximity to the psyche. Thus, it is in the mathematician René Thom that one finds a model of affectivity based on the concept of pregnancy (*prégnance*) (as opposed to that of prominence) (*saillance*) to account for continuity in certain psychical structures (Thom 1988). Thom's theory of catastrophies has been used in an attempt to produce a psychoanalytic model of affect that leaves a great deal to be desired (Sashin and Callaghan 1990). My attitude to neurobiology is less critical. Although I must admit that most of the work bearing specifically on the affect that has come my way has not elucidated the question for me very much, I do think that discussion with neurobiologists is dependent on the conceptions that they try to articulate in an overall view that respects the specificity of the facts relating to our discipline. I must acknowledge my debt here to the work of Gerald Edelmann, who has provided the only convincing view of the relations between the level of neuronal activity and the level of psychical activity, without the second ever being reducible to the first. Thanks to him, I arrived at the conclusion that when confronted by the many interactions between systems, interactions responsible for the phenomenological complexity that takes the form of an overall apprehension of functioning, 'below' the consideration of systems of re-entry into the cerebral organization, one arrives at the distinction between two great subsystems, neurobiologically distinct in their origins and tasks. On the one hand, there is the system of self, which brings together relations between the 'hedonistic system', to which, I believe, the drives and affects belong, and the cortical system. To the first system is opposed the (thalamocortical) system of relations with the external world, of the non-self whose connections are massively re-entering. It is solely cortical. Of course, the connections between the two systems, the limbic system and the thalamocortical, are many and complicated, but what it is essential to understand is the categorization of the values, whose most basic level is modified by epigenesis, experience and experience alone having the power to reorganize 'conceptual' categorizations, established under the influence of the first selections that have operated without instructions.

Reviewing the hypotheses subjacent to the proposed theories of consciousness, Edelmann numbers three: the physical hypothesis, the evolutionist hypothesis and the hypothesis of feelings and sensations (qualia). Coming close here to the ideas of Peirce, Edelmann affirms the irreducibility of the last, which appeals to the subjective experiences, feelings and impressions that accompany the state of things. It should be noted then that the whole study of consciousness cannot eliminate this order of factors, which, unlike those of physics, cannot be entirely shared with others. 'But no *scientific* theory of whatever kind can be presented without already assuming that observers have sensations as well as perceptions' (Edelmann 1992). One arrives then at the idea that for the study of consciousness – and *a fortiori* that of the unconscious – the best referent is other human beings, because their feelings form the indispensable basis on which we can correlate all their experiences.

The theoretical whole presented by Freud seems to be the only one that does not contradict this main schema, strongly insisting as it does on the internal orientation of affects, the tendency to diffuse into the body and forming through the affects of pleasure–unpleasure the primordial psychical kernel. This amounts to saying that the psychical transformations that give rise to the categorization of the states of pleasure and unpleasure are first and foremost messages intended to inform the subject as to what is happening inside him or her and to operate their selection according to this categorization of values permanently reshaped by experience. Setting out from the instinctual sources and returning to the body, affect seems to proceed to a closure of the subject on himself or herself. One must also take into account the detour that, through the expressions of emotion and others' response to them, makes it possible to connect the second circuit with the first, thus contributing to an increase in its richness. But this second circuit is installed only to return once again to himself or herself, not out of narcissism, but to take the measure of the vicissitudes of his or her relations to others.

However, these are merely speculations, the last word must remain with clinical experience. As one patient, whose existence was particularly affected by the economic disturbances of her affective life and who was finally able to overcome the misunderstandings of which that life was the object, once said to me: 'Only the truth works and brings relief – for a time'.

Conclusion

Despite the unquestionable progress made in our knowledge of affect, one is still waiting for a theory that would be unanimously accepted. One might well ask whether there will ever be such a theory. No doubt the obscurities surrounding the problem have something to do with this, but the nature of the phenomenon itself plays an even greater role. Whereas psychical phenomena relating to the intellect have aroused strong convictions that their solution was in sight, by resort to models inspired by cybernetics, artificial intelligence or computer science, rejecting outside the area of scientific investigation everything in the activity of the mind that did not satisfy the criteria that made it possible to approach it from this point of view – affectivity, in fact – until very recently one could not find equivalent theories that would take affectivity as their main focus and give rise to a general theory of psychic activity whose extension would be seen from this point of view. If at best there is a strong inclination to the idea of eliminating affective phenomena from the map of valid knowledge, there is even greater reticence to place affects in a dominant vertex from which the other concepts relating to psychical life would be ordered around it. Is this not because the very existence of affect and its supremacy over the whole psychical life would have something very wounding about it for our idea of mankind?

Even if one remains on the limited plane of the psychical aspects of affective life, the task is scarcely made any simpler. It is here that questions of method arise. It was hoped that salvation would come through greater attention being paid to the study of development and to the observation of babies, either alone or in relation to their mothers. But attention has not been paid to the fact that the advantage of a longitudinal systematics, spread out over time, entailed a concentration on external, behavioural aspects, which ran the risk of distorting our view of a phenomenon the first analysis of which revealed its essentially *internal* character. Furthermore, although

345

the dimension of lability proper to affect could be recognized as having a share in relational situations – of which, in any case, one would only know its externalizable aspects – it would depend above all on psychical transformations much more discreet than events taking place outside. For nobody, I believe, would dare to maintain that that part of the affective phenomenon that is externalizable is enough to give an idea of the internal processes that accompany it, nor that everything that takes place on the level of internal experience finds its externalization accessible to others' senses.

The very idea of the unconscious is opposed to it. The idea becomes even more complicated when one wishes to approach the problem of the unconscious respective to affective phenomena. And although for some, of whom I am one, the unconscious affect is a reality, for others this is far from being the case. For the first group, the affective unconscious cannot be superimposed on the description of the unconscious as conceived in relation to representation. I do not think that these problems are to be overcome by effacing such distinctions and considering only a single overall problematic in terms of internal objects that in any case cannot suppress the need to investigate different modes of functioning. If one is rather resistant to admitting this, it should be enough to recall what can be learned from psychosomatic pathology, in which the major role played by the affective economy has recently been recognized.

Although tied to the body, affective experience is none the less a subjective experience, that is to say, intentional and relational. But this still raises other questions whose answers elude our understanding. Who does not adhere to Pascal's celebrated proposition that the heart has its reasons that reason knows not of? Again, although the reference to intentionality must be recalled, in view of all the attacks from reductionism, it confronts us with the double task of defining, on the one hand, the intentional mode with regard to affect and, on the other, the way in which affect is articulated with other aspects of the psyche that are not saturated with affectivity, an articulation from which the overall conception of intentionality ought to emerge altered. As for the relational dimension, one is reminded of it as soon as one thinks of psychoanalysis, since the whole experience of the transference and counter-transference brings us back to it. But here I should like to take up a position that will seem to go against the current. It is not because everything that a psychoanalyst may know of the affective life passes through the prism of transferential experience and its counter-transferential connotations that the relational aspect must purely and simply be confused with the intentional aspect. Even when referring to internalized aspects of object relations, it is not self-evident to me that nothing escapes the relational perspective. Like Freud, I remain convinced that there are non-objectal and, consequently, non-relational aspects respective to the affective life. My interest in narcissism goes in the same direction, even if one thinks that narcissism may also be considered from a relational, non-objectal angle, as a relation of self to self. In short, I remain convinced that Freud's instinctual hypothesis has not yet had its day and that it corresponds to a structural reality that has not been exhausted by theories of the object relation, not that this implies that one must reject such theories. Above all, one should proceed to a differential distribution of the effects of both.

It is probably no accident if my conclusions bring me back to the concept of the drive. In the 1950s, there were many attempts to relate affects and drives. Everyone remembers the title of a famous book, *Drives, Affects, Behavior,*[1] which represented post-Freudian views on the question. It would be wrong to conclude that I favour a return to the ways of thought current in the period in which this work was written. In a word, I believe that the reference to behaviour is without foundation here and that the relations between drive and affect are far from simple. For me, affect – conscious as well as unconscious – is one of the phenomenal expressions of a concept: the one that Freud tried to define by the drive. It is the concept that throws light on the phenomenon, not the reverse. This does not mean that we ought to preserve intact Freud's theory of the drives, on the contrary. But the concept of the affect as the expression of one of the effects of the drive is one that I continue to hold, despite the many attacks that have been made on it.

For me, this implies two corollaries with which I shall end, indicating ways for future research. I say again, since it has to be repeated, so difficult is it to be heard, that it is illusory to seek the key to the mysteries of the affect by going back as far as possible into childhood, using whatever means are available to this effect. Such means can only short-circuit the essence of affective life, whose central phenomenon is internalization. On the other hand, in order to reach the deepest kernel of affects, it is necessary to refer to the fully developed forms of the affective life, which can only be experienced by the adult. This does not imply that observations of children are invalid, but only that one must give up regarding the study of childhood as an explanatory model. On the contrary, it must be recognized that such observations must refer to a mature affectivity, which, after the event, throws light on its earlier forms. I would add to this that the greatest danger facing psychoanalytic research in this last area is to slide into phenomenology, which can only lead to a surreptitious return to the psychology of consciousness. The second corollary is that one must give up a prematurely unitary view of psychical life. Everything leads us to believe that the psyche is heterogeneous, its fragile unity being in my opinion the consequence of this heterogeneity, which is also a guarantee of the infinite diversity of

1 *Drives, Affects, Behavior*, New York: International Universities Press, 1953.

347

human experience, production and creation. Once this is accepted, it is a vital task to define more clearly the relations between the affective aspects of the psyche and the other elements of psychical life.

One might be fearful, then, of seeing an exploded conception of psychical life prevail. Such a fear is without foundation, for the objective of psychoanalysis can only obey the complexity of the psychical object that Freud was to recognize in 'Constructions in analysis'. And, at the present time, the analysis of this complexity cannot avoid recognizing the peculiarities of the various functionings that operate in it. Indeed how can a unitary preoccupation be invoked when every psychoanalyst supports the basic hypothesis of the centrality of conflict in psychical life and in the unconscious?

It remains, of course, to understand more clearly the nature of the conflict, its aims and the terms that one can recognize in its constitution. This, I believe, is what analysis is.

Bibliography

Abraham, K. (1907–1925) *Œuvres complètes*, 2 vol. Paris: Payot, 1965–1966.

Abraham, K. (1942) *Selected Papers of Karl Abraham, M.D.*, trans. Douglas Bryan and Alix Strachey. London: Hogarth Press and the Institute of Psycho-Analysis.

Abraham, K. (1955) *Clinical Papers and Essays on Psycho-Analysis*, trans. Hilda Abraham and D.R. Ellison with the assistance of Hilda Maas and Anna Hackel. London: Hogarth Press and the Institute of Psycho-Analysis.

Ajuriaguerra, J. de and Hecaen, H. (1952) *Méconnaissances et hallucinations corporelles*. Paris: Masson., 1952.

Ajuriaguerra, J. de, Diatkine, R. and Badaracco, J. Garcia (1956) Psychanalyse et neurobiologie, *La psychanalyse d'aujourd'hui*, Paris: Presses Universitaires de France, vol. II.

Alvim, F. (1962) Trouble de l'identification et image corporelle, *Revue française de Psychanalyse*, 26, p. 5.

Angelergues, R. (1964) Le corps et ses images, *Evolution psychiatrique*, 2.

Apfelbaum, B. (1965) Ego psychology psychic energy and the hazards of quantitative explanation in psychoanalytic theory, *Int. J. of Psychoanalysis*, 46, pp. 168–83.

Apfelbaum, B. (1966) On ego psychology: a critique of the structural approach to the psychoanalytic theory, *Int. J. of Psychoanalysis*, 47, pp. 451–75.

Arlow, J. and Brenner, Ch. (1964) *Psychoanalytical concepts and the structural theory*, New York: International Universities Presses, 1 vol.

Arlow, J. and Brenner, Ch. (1969) The psychopathology of the psychoses; a pro posed revision, *Int. J. of Psychoanalysis*, 50, p. 5.

Aulagnier-Spairani (1967) La perversion comme structure, *L'inconscient*, 2, pp. 11–42.

Balint, M. (1957) The three areas of the mind: theoretical considerations, *Int. J. of Psychoanalysis*, 39, pp. 328–40.

Balint, M. (1960) The regressed patient and his analyst, *Psychiatry: Journal for the Study of Interpersonal Processes*, 23, pp. 231–3.

Balint, M. (1969) Trauma and object relationship, *Int. J. of Psychoanalysis*, 50, p. 429.

349

Bally, C. (1932) *Linguistique générale et linguistique française*. Paris: Francke.

Barande, I. (1968) Le vu et l'entendu dans la cure, *Revue française de Psychanalyse*, 32.

Barande, R. (1963) Essai métapsychologique sur le silence, *Revue française de Psychanalyse*, 27.

Begoin, J. (1969) *Le fantasme chez Melanie Klein*, document ronéotypé de l'Institut de Psychanalyse.

Benassy, M. (1953) Théorie des instincts, *Revue française de Psychanalyse*, 17, nos 1 and 2, pp. 1–76.

Benassy, M. (1965) La théorie du narcissisme de Federn, *Revue française de Psychanalyse*, 29, pp. 533–59.

Benassy, M. (1969) Le Moi et ses mécanismes de défense, in *La théorie psychanalytique*. Paris: Presses Universitaires de France, 1 vol., pp. 285–348.

Benassy, M. and Daitkine, R. (1964) Ontogenèse du fantasme, *Revue française de Psychanalyse*, 28.

Benveniste, E. (1966) *Problémes de linguistique générale*. Paris: Gallimard.

Beres, D. (1965) Structure and function in psychoanalysis, *Int. J. of Psychoanalysis*, 46.

Bigras, J. (1968) Esquisse d'une théorie de l'adolescence centrée sur le point de vue économique freudien, *L'inconscient*, 6, pp. 89–104.

Bion, W. (1950–1967) *Second thoughts*. London: Heinemann, 1967.

Bion, W. (1963) *Elements of psychoanalysis*. London: Heinemann.

Bion, W. (1969) *Learning from experience*. London Heinemann.

Bion, W.R. (1963) *Elements of Psycho-Analysis*. London: Heinemann Medical Books, Ltd.

Blau, A. (1955) A unitary hypothesis of emotion, anxiety, emotions of displeasure and affective disorders, *Psychoanalytic Quarterly*, 24, pp. 75–103.

Bollas, C. (1992) *Being a Character, Psychoanalysis & Self Experience*. New York: Hill and Wang, division of Farrar, Strauss and Giroux.

Boons, M.C. (1968) Le meurtre du père chez Freud, *L'inconscient*, 5, pp. 101–30.

Borch-Jacobsen, M. (1991) *Le lien affectif*. Paris: Aubier.

Borje-Lofgren, L. (1964) Excitation. Anxiety. Affect, *Int. J. of Psychoanalysis*, 45, pp. 280–5.

Borje-Lofgren, L. (1968) Psychoanalytic theory of affects. Panel report. Meeting of the American Psychoanalytic Association (1967), *Journal of American Psychoanalytic Association*, 16, pp. 638–50.

Botella, C. and Botella, S. (1992) 'Le statut métapsychologique de la perception et de l'irrepresentable', *Revue française de Psychanalyse*, 56, pp. 23–42.

Bourguignon, A., Cotet, P., Laplanche, J. and Robert, F. (1989) *Traduire Freud*, Paris: Presses Universitaires de France.

Bouvet, M. (1948–1960) *Œuvres psychanalytiques (1948–1960)*, vol. I: *La relation d'objet*; vol. II: *Résistances et transfert*. Paris: Payot, 1967–1968.

Bouvet, M. (1956) 'La clinique psychanalytique. La relation d'objet', in *Oeuvres psychanalytiques, I, La relation d'objet*, Paris: Payot, 1967.

Bouvet, M. (1960) 'Dépersonnalisation et relations d'objet', in *Oeuvres psychanalytiques, I, La relation d'objet*, Paris: Payot, 1967.

Bowlby, J. (1960) Grief and mourning in infancy and early childhood, *Psychoanalytic study of the child*, XI. New York: Intern. Univers. Press.

Brierley, M. (1937) Affects theory and practice, *Int. J. of Psychoanalysis*, XVIII; republished in *Trends in Psychoanalysis*. London: Hogarth Press, 1949.

Brunswick, R.M. (1940) The pre dipal phase of the libido development, *Psychoanal. Quart.*, 9, pp. 293–319.

Bychowski, G. (1956) The ego and the introjects, *Psychoanal. Quarterly*, 25, pp. 11–36.

Bychowski, G. (1956) The release of internal images, *Int. J. of Psychoanalysis*, 37, pp. 331–8.

Bychowski, G. (1958) The struggle against the introjects, *Int. J. of Psychoanalysis*, 38, pp. 182–7.

Bychowski, G. (1967) The archaic object and alienation, *Int. J. of Psychoanalysis*, 48, p. 384.

Canguilhem, G. (1968) *Etude d'histoire et de philosophie des sciences*. Paris: Vrin.

Castoriadis-Aulagnier, P. (1975) *La violence de l'interprétation, du pictogramme à l'énoncé*. Paris: Presses Universitaires de France.

Chasseguet-Smirgel, J. (1962) L'analité et les composantes anales du vécu corporel, *Canadian Psychiatric Assoc. Journal*, 7, p. 16.

Chasseguet-Smirgel, J. (1963) *Corps vécu et corps imaginaire dans les premiers travaux psychanalytiques*, Canadian Psychiatric Assoc. Journal, 27, p. 255.

Chomsky, N. (1957) *Syntactic Structures*, trans S. Gravenhoge. Holland: Mouton.

Chomsky, N. (1968) *Language and Mind*. New York: Harcourt Brace Jovanovich, 1972.

Cournut, J. (1991) *L'ordinaire de la passion*. Paris: Presses Universitaires de France.

Daitkine, R. (1966) Agressivité et fantasmes d'agression, *Revue française de Psychanalyse*, 30, p. 15.

David, C. (1966) Réflexions métapsychologiques concernant l'état amoureux, *Revue française de Psychanalyse*, 30, p. 115.

David, C. (1966) *Représentation, affect, fantasmes*. Enseignement de l'Institut de Psychanalyse, document ronéotypé.

David, C. (1967) De la valeur mutative des remaniements post-œdipiens, *Revue française de Psychanalyse*, 31, p. 813.

David, C. (1967a) Investissement et contre-investissement, *Revue française de Psychanalyse*, 31, p. 231.

David, C. (1967b) L'hétérogénéité de l'inconscient et les continuités psychiques, *L'inconscient*, 4. pp. 3–33.

David, C. (1967c) Etat amoureux et travail du deuil, *Interprétation*, I, pp. 45–70.

David, C. (1969) Quelqu'un manque, *Etudes freudiennes*, 1–2, pp. 39–54.

David, C. (1972) La perversion affective, dans *La sexualité perverse*. Paris: Payot.

Deleuze, G. (1969) *Logique du sens*, Ed. Minuit, 1 vol., p. 392.

Delrieu, A. (1997) *Sigmund Freud, Index thématique*. Paris: Anthropos (Diffusion Economica).

Derrida, J. (1967) *De la grammatologie*. Paris: Minuit.

Derrida, J. (1967) *L'écriture et la différence*. Paris: Seuil.

Derrida, J. (1967) *La voix et le phénoméne*. Paris: Presses Universitaires de France.

Diatkine, R. (1966) Agressivité et fantasmes d'agression, *Revue française de Psychanalyse*, 30, p. 15.

Diatkine, R. and Favreau, J.A. (1956) Le caractére névrotique, *Revue française de Psychanalyse*, 20, p. 151.

Donnet, A. (1997) *Sigmund Freud, Index thématique*. Paris: Anthropos (Diffusion Economica).

Donnet, J.-L. (1995) *La Divan bien tempéré*. Paris: Presses Universitaires de France.

Donnet, J.-L. (1967) L'antinomie de la résistance, *L'inconscient*, 1, pp. 55–82.

Donnet, J.-L. and Pinel, J.-P. (1968) Le problème de l'identification chez Freud, *L'inconscient*, 7, pp. 5–22.

Edelmann, G. (1992) *Bright Air, Brilliant Fire, On the Matter of the Mind*. New York: Basic Books.

Eissler, K.R. (1969) Irreverent remarks about the present and future of psychoanalysis, *Int. J. of Psychoanalysis*, 50, pp. 461–72.

Engel, G. (1962) Anxiety and depression withdrawal: the primary affects of unpleasure, *Int. J. of Psychoanalysis*, 43, pp. 89–97.

Ey, Henri (1960–1966) *L'inconscient*, VIᵉ Colloque de Bonneval (1960), avec la collaboration de Diatkine, R., Green, A., Laplanche, J., Lebovici, S., Leclaire, S., Perrier, F., Stein, C. and Lacan, J. *et al.* Paris: Desclée de Brouwer, 1966.

Fain, M. (1966) Régression et psychosomatique, *Revue française de Psychanalyse*, 30, p. 451.

Fain, M. (1969) Ebauche d'une recherche concernant l'existence d'activités mentales pouvant être considérées comme prototypiques du processus psychanalytique, *Revue française de Psychanalyse*, 33, p. 929.

Fain, M. and Marty, P. (1964) Perspectives psychosomatiques sur la fonction des fantasmes, *Revue française de Psychanalyse*, 28, pp. 609–22.

Fain, M. (1965) A propos du narcissisme et de sa genèse, *Revue française de Psychanalyse*, 29, p. 561.

Fain, M. (1966) Intervention au rapport de E. et J. Kestemberg, *Revue française de Psychanalyse*, 30, p. 720.

Fain, M. (1969) Réflexions sur la structure allergique, *Revue française de Psychanalyse*, 33, p. 243.

Favez-Boutonier, J. (1961) Ce qui n'est pas verbal dans la cure, *La psychanalyse*, 6, pp. 237–9.

Federn, P. (1953) *Ego psychology and the psychoses*. New York: Basic Books.

Fenichel, O. (1941) The Ego and the affects, *Psychoanalytic Review*, 28, pp. 47–60, also in: *Collected Papers*, vol. II. New York: Norton.

Fenichel, O. (1953) *La théorie psychanalytique des névroses*, Presses Universitaires de France, 2 vol.

Ferenczi, S. (1924) Thalassa: A theory of genitality, *The Psychoanalytic Quarterly*, 2, pp. 361–403, 1933.

Ferenczi, S (1932) Confusion de langues entre l'adulte et l'enfant, trad. de l'allemand par V. Granoff, *La psychanalyse*, 6, pp. 241–54.

Fine, B.D. and Moore, B.E. (1967) *A glossary of psychoanalytic terms and concepts*, The American Psychoanalytic Association.

Fonagy, I. (1983) *La vive voix*. Paris: Payot.

Freud, A. (1936) *Le Moi et les mécanismes de défense*, trad. A. Berman, Presses Universitaires de France, 1949, 1 vol., p. 162.

Freud, A. (1965) Diagnostic skills and their growth in psychoanalysis, *Intern. J. of Psychoanalysis*, 46, p. 31.

Freud, S. (1886–1939) *The Complete Psychological Works of Sigmund Freud, Standard Edition*. London: Hogarth Press, 23 vol.

Freud, S. (1900) *The Interpretation of Dreams, S.E.*, V.

Freud, S. (1915) *Papers on Metapsychology, S.E.*, XIV, pp. 152, 156.

Freud, S. (1915a) *Papers on Metapsychology, S.E.*, XIV, p. 179.

Freud, S. (1917) *Introduction to Psychoanalysis, S.E.*, XVI, p. 395.

Freud, S. (1920a) *Beyond the Pleasure Principle, S.E.*, XVIII, p. 7.

Freud, S. (1920b) *S.E.*, XVIII, p. 10.

Freud, S. (1920c) *S.E.*, XVIII, p. 63.

Freud, S. (1920d), *S.E.*, XVIII, p. 63.

Freud, S. (1923) *The Ego and the Id, S.E.*, XIX, p. 22.

Freud, S. (1926a) 'Psycho-Analysis', *S.E.*, XX, p. 265.

Freud, S. (1926b) *Ihibition, Symptôme et Angoisse*, trad. J. Laplanche et al., Presses Universitaires de France, 1973.

Freud, S. (1933) *New Introductory Lectures on Psychoanalysis, S.E.*, XXII, p. 96.

Freud, S. (1937) 'Constructions in analysis', *S.E.*, XXIII, p. 257.

Freud, S. (1940) *An Outline of Psycho-analysis, S.E.*, XXIII, p. 148.

Garma, L. (1997) 'Approches critiques de la clinique de rêve et du sommeil', in *Confrontations psychiatriques*, no. 38, pp. 115–40, 'Psychiatrie et sommeil 20 ans après'.

Geahchan, D.J. (1968) Deuil et nostalgie, *Revue française de Psychanalyse*, 32, p. 39.

Gill, M.H. and Klein, G.S. (1964) The structuring of drive and reality, *Int. J. of Psychoanalysis*, 45, p. 483.

Gillibert, J. (1968) La réminiscence et la cure, *Revue française de Psychanalyse*, 32, p. 385–418.

Gillibert, J.(1969a) Le meurtre de l'imago et le processus d'individuation, *Revue française de Psychanalyse*, 33, p. 375.

Gillibert, J. (1969b) La pensée du clivage chez Freud, *Etudes freudiennes*, 1–2, pp. 227-48.

Giovacchini, P. (1967) The frozen introject, *Int. J. of Psychoanalysis*, 49, p. 61.

Glover, E. (1939) The psychoanalysis of affects, *Int. J. of Psychoanalysis*, XX, pp. 299–307.

Glover, E. (1945) The Kleinian System of Child Psychology, in *Psychoanalytic study of the child*, I, New York: Int. Univ. Press.

Glover, E. (1947) Basic mental concepts, their clinical and theoretical value, *Psychoan. Quarterly*, 16, pp. 382–406.

Glover, E. (1956) *The Early Development of the Mind*. London: Imago.

Green, A. (1960) L'œuvre de Maurice Bouvet, in *Revue française de Psychanalyse*, 24, pp. 685–702.

Green, A. (1960–1966b) Les portes de l'inconscient, in *L'inconscient*, VIᵉ Colloque de Bonneval. Paris: Desclée de Brouwer, pp. 17–44.

Green, A. (1960–1966c) L'inconscient et la psychopathologie, in *L'inconscient*, VIᵉ Colloque de Bonneval. Paris: Desclée de Brouwer, pp. 331–5.

Green, A. (1962–1968a) Sur la mère phallique. Exposé lu à la Société psychanalytique de Paris (15 mai 1962), in *Revue française de Psychanalyse*, 32, 1968, no. 1, pp. 1–38.

Green, A. (1962a) L'inconscient freudien et la psychanalyse française contemporaine, in *Les temps modernes*, 195, pp. 365–79.

Green, A. (1962b) Note sur le corps imaginaire, *Revue française de Psychanalyse*, 26, numéro spécial, pp. 67–83.

Green, A. (1962c) *Pour une nosographie psychanalytique freudienne*. Texte ronéotypé pour une introduction à la discussion sur la nosographie psychanalytique devant la Société psychanalytique de Paris (déc. 1962 – janvier–février 1963).

Green, A. (1963a) La psychanalyse devant l'opposition de l'histoire et de la structure, *Critique*, 194, p. 649.

Green, A. (1963b) Une variante de la position phallique narcissique considérée plus particulièrement sous l'angle du jeu et des fonctions de la sublimation et de l'idéal du Moi, *Revue française de Psychanalyse*, 27, 1963, pp. 117–84.

Green, A. (1964a) Du comportement à la chair. Intinéraire de Merleau-Ponty, in *Critique*, 211, pp. 1017–46.

Green, A. (1964b) Névrose obsessionnelle et hystérie. Leurs relations chez Freud et depuis, in *Revue française de Psychanalyse*, 38, nos 5–6, pp. 679–716.

Green, A. (1966a) L'objet (a) de J. Lacan, sa logique et la théorie freudienne, *Cahiers pour l'analyse*, 3, pp. 15–37.

Green, A. (1967a) Métapsychologie de la névrose obsessionnelle, in *Revue française de Psychanalyse*, 31, no. 4, pp. 629–646.

Green, A. (1967b) La diachronie dans le freudisme, *Critique*, 238, p. 359.

Green, A. (1967c) Le narcissisme primaire: structure ou état, in I. *L'inconscient,* 1, pp. 127–57; II, *L'inconscient*, 2, pp. 89–116.

Green, A. (1967d) Les fondements différenciateurs des images parentales. L'hallucination négative de la mère et l'identification primordiale au père, in *Revue française de Psychanalyse*, 5–6, pp. 869–906.

Green, A. (1968b) Intervention au rapport de O. Flournoy et J. Rouart sur *l'acting out: l'acting (in/out)* et le processus analytique, XXVIIIᵉ Congrès des Psychanalystes de Langues romanes (Paris, 29, 30, 31 octobre et 1er novembre 1967), in *Revue française de Psychanalyse*, 32, nos 5–6, pp. 1071–76.

Green, A. (1969a) *Un oeuil en trop. Le complexe d' Œdipe dans la tragédie.* Paris: Minuit. *The Tragic Effect*, trans. Alan Sheridan. Cambridge: Cambridge University Press, 1979.

Green, A. (1969b) Le narcissisme moral, *Revue française de Psychanalyse*, XXXIII, pp. 341–74.

Green, A. (1969c) Sexualité et idéologie chez Freud et Marx, *Etudes freudiennes*, 1–2, pp. 188–217.

Green, A. (1969d) La nosographie psychanalytique des psychoses, in C. Laurin and P. Doucet (eds) *Problematique de la Psychose*, Excerpta Medica Foundation, 1 vol.

Green, A. (1970) 'L'affect', *Revue français de psychanalyse*, vol. XXXIV. Paris: Presses Universitaires de France.

Green, A. (1970) 'L'affect', *Revue française de psychanalyse*, vol. XXIV. Paris: Presses Universitaires de France.

Green, A. (1970) Répétition, différence, réplication, *Revue française de Psychanalyse*, 34, pp. 461–501.

Green, A. (1971) La projection: de l'identification projective au projet, *Revue française de Psychanalyse*, 35, pp. 939–60.

Green, A. (1972) De l''Esquisse' à 'L'interprétation des rêves', *Nouvelle Revue de Psychanalyse*, no. 5, pp. 155–80.

Green, A. (1973) Cannibalisme: réalité ou fantasme agi, *Nouvelle Revue de Psychanalyse*, 6, 27–52.

Green, A. (1973) *Le discours vivant.* Paris: Presses Universitaires de France.

Green, A. (1973) *Le discours vivant. La conception psychanalytique de l'affect.* Paris: P.U.F.

Green, A. (1977) 'Conceptions of affect', *Int. J. of Psycho-anal.*, 58, 129–57.

Green, A. (1983) 'Le langage dans la psychanalyse', in *Langages.* Paris: Les Belles lettres.

Green, A. (1983) *Narcissisme de vie, narcissisme de mort.* Paris: Minuit.

Green, A. (1984) 'Le langage dans la psychanalyse', in *Langages*, Les Belles Lettres.

Green, A. (1985) 'Réflexions libres sue la représentation de l'affect', *Rev. fran. de Psychanalyse*, 49, 773–88.

Green, A. (1985) *Propédeutique, La métapsychologie revisitée*, 'Réflexions libres sur la représentation de l'affect'. Éditions Champvallon, 1995.

Green, A. (1986) *On Private Madness*, chapter 9, 'Passions and their vicissitudes'. London: Hogarth and Institute of Psycho-Analysis.

Green, A. (1993) *Le travail du négatif.* Paris: Minuit.

Green, A. (1997) *Les chaînes d'Eros.* Paris: Odile Jacob.

Green, A. (1998) 'La position phobique centrale', Conférence à la Société Psychanalytique de Paris, 7 January 1998.

Green, A. en collaboration avec Schmitz, B. (1958) Le deuil maniaque (à propos d'un cas), in *Evolution psychiatrique*, 1, pp. 105–21.

Green, A. *La folie privée*, chapter 4, 'Passions et destins des passions'. Paris: Gallimard, 1990.

Green, A. Innes-Smith, J., Sandler, J. and Segal, H. (1990) Papers given at the symposium of the European Federation of Psychoanalysis in 1989, *Psychoanalysis in Europe Bulletin*, 35.

Green, A. (1969d) La nosographie psychanalytique des psychoses, dans *Problématique de la psychose*, ed. C. Laurin and P. Doucet, Excerpta Medica Foundation, 1 vol.

Greenson, R. (1961) L'empathie et ses phases diverses, *Revue française de Psychanalyse*, 25, p. 807.

Greenson, R. (1969) The origin and fate of new ideas in psychoanalysis, *Int. J. of Psychoanalysis*, 50, pp. 503–16.

Greenson, R.R. and Wexler, M. The non transference relationship in the psychoanalytic situation, *Int. J. of Psychoanalysis*, 50, p. 27.

Greimas, A.J. (1966) *Sémantique structurale*. Paris: Larousse.

Greimas, A.J. (1966) Structure et histoire, *Les temps modernes*, 22, no. 246, pp. 814–27.

Grinberg, L. (1986) 'Pulsions et affects: des modèles plutôt que des théories', *Psychoanalysis in Europe Bulletin* 26–7.

Groddeck, G. (1909–1953) *The Meaning of Illness*. London: Hogarth, 1979.

Grunberger, B. (1957) Essai sur la situation analytique et le processus de guérison, *Revue française de Psychanalyse*, XXI, no. 3.

Grunberger, B (1968) Le suicide du mélancolique, *Revue française de Psychanalyse*, 32, p. 574.

Guttieres-Green, L. (1990) 'Problèmatique du transfert douloureux', *Revue française de psychanalyse*, LIV, pp. 407–420.

Guttman, S.A. (1965) Some aspects of scientific theories construction and psychoanalysis, *Intern. J. of Psychoanalysis*, 46, p. 129.

Hanly, C. (1978) 'Instincts and hostile affects', in *Int. J. of Psychoanalysis.*, 59, pp. 149–56.

Hanly, C. (1982) 'Affect et pulsion', in *Psychothérapies*, no. 4, pp. 147–54.

Hartmann, H, (1939–1959) *Essays on Ego Psychology*. Lodnon: Hogarth and Institute of Psychoanalysis, 1964.

Hartmann, H., Kris, E. and Lœwenstein, R.M. (1947) Comments on the formation of the psychic structure, *Psychoanalytic Study of the Child*. New York: Int. Univ. Press, vol. II, pp. 11–38.

Hartmann, H., and Kris, E. (1945) The genetic approach in psychoanalysis, *Psychoanalytic Study of the Child*, vol. I.

Hartocollis, P. (1997) 'Affects in Borderline disorders', *Borderline Personality Disorders*. New York: International Universities Press, pp. 495–507.

Holt, R.R. (1965) Ego autonomy reevaluated, *Int. J. of Psychoanalysis*, 46, p. 151.

Isaacs, S. (1952) The nature and function of phantasy, in M. Klein, P. Heimann, S. Isaacs and J. Rivière, *Developments in Psycho-Analysis*, edited by Joan Rivière. London: Hogarth Press and the Institute of Psycho-Analysis, pp. 67–121.

Jacobson, E. (1953) The affects and their pleasure-unpleasure qualities in relation to the psychic discharge processes in *Drive. Affects. Behavior*. New York: Intern. Universities Press, pp. 38–66.

Jacobson, E. (1964) *The self and the object world*. New York: Int. Univ. Press.

Jacobson, E. (1971) *Depression*. New York: International Universities Press.

Jakobson, R. (1949–1963) *Essais de linguistique générale*, trad. N. Ruwet, Ed. Minuit, 1 vol., p. 260.

Joffe, W. G. and Sandler, I. (1968) Comments on the psychoanalytic psychology of adaptation with special reference to the role of affects and the representational world, *Int. J. of Psychoanalysis*, 49, p. 445.

Jones, E. (1929) Fear, Guilt and Hate, *Int. J. of Psychoanalysis*, 10, pp. 383–97.

Kaywin, L. (1960) An epigenetic approach to the psychoanalytic theory of instincts and affects, *J. of the American Psychoanalytic Assoc.*, 8, pp. 613–58.

Kernberg, O. (1969) A contribution to the ego psychological critique of the Kleinian school, *Int. J. of Psychoanalysis*, 50, p. 317.

Kernberg, O. (1976) *Object Relations Theory and Clinical Psychoanalysis*. New York: Jason Aronson.

Kernberg, O. (1982) 'Self, ego, affects and drives', in *Journal of the American Psychoanalytic Association*, vol. 30, no. 4, pp. 893–917.

Kestemberg, E. and Kestemberg, J. (1966) Contribution à la perspective génétique en psychanalyse, *Revue française de Psychanalyse*, 30, pp. 580–713.

Khan Masud, M. (1969) Les vicissitudes de l'être, du connaître and de l'éprouver dans la situation analytique, *Bull. Assoc. psychanal. de France*, 5, pp. 1–13.

Khan, M.M. (1964) Ego distortion, cumulative trauma and the role of reconstruction in the analytic situation, *Int. J. of Psychoanalysis*, 45, p. 272.

Khan, M.M. (1969) The role of the collated internal object in perversion formation, *Int. J. of Psychoanalysis*, 50, pp. 555–66.

Klauber, J. (1968) On the dual use of historical and scientific method in psychoanalysis, *Int. J. of Psychoanalysis*, 49, p. 80.

Klein, M. (1921–1945) *Essais de psychanalyse*, trad. M. Derrida, introduction N. Abraham and M. Torok, Payot édit., 1967, 1 vol., p. 452.

Klein, M. (1930) L'importance de la formation du symbole dans la formation du Moi, trad. par M. Spira, *La psychanalyse*, 2, 1956, pp. 269–88.

Klein, M. (1932) *La psychanalyse des enfants*, trad. J.-B. Boulanger, Presses Universitaires de France, 1959, 1 vol., p. 317.

Klein, M. (1957) *Envy and Gratitude*. London: Tavistock.

Klein, M. (1968) *Contributions to Psycho-Analysis, 1921–1945*. London: Hogarth Press and the Institute of Psycho-Analysis.

Klein, M. and Riviére, J. (1967) *Love, Hate and Reparation*. London: Hogarth Press.

Klein, M., Heimann, P., Isaacs S., and Riviére, J. (1952) *Development in psychoanalysis*. London: Hogarth Press.

Kohon, G. (in press) *No Lost Certainties to be Recovered*, (Sexuality, Creativity, Knowledge).

Kris, A. (1956) The recovery of childhood memories in psychoanalysis, *Psychoanalytic Study of the Child*, 11, pp. 54–88.

Krystal, H. (1978) 'Self-representation and the capacity for self-care', in *Annals of Psychoanalysis*, 6. New York: International Universities Press.

Krystal, H. (1978) 'Trauma and affects', *The Psychoanalytic Study of the Child*, 36, pp. 81–116.

Lab, P. and Lebovici, S. (1969) Théorie psychanalytique du fantasme, in *La théorie psychanalytique*. Paris: Presses Universitaires de France.

Lacan, J. (1936–1966) *Ecrits*. Paris: Seuil, 1966; *Ecrits: A Selection*, trans. Alan Sheridan. London and New York: Routledge, 1977.

Lacan, J. (1968a) La méprise du sujet supposé savoir, *Scilicet*, 1, pp. 31–41.

Lacan, J. (1968b) De Rome à 53 Rome 67: la psychanalyse. Raison d'un échec, *Scilicet*, 1, pp. 42–50.

Lacan, J. (1968c) De la psychanalyse dans ses rapports avec la réalité, *Scilicet*, 1, pp. 51–9.

Lacan, J. (1968d) Propositions du 9–10–1967 sur le psychanalyste de l'école, *Scilicet*, 1, pp. 14–30.

Lagache, D. (1957a) Vues psychanalytiques sur les émotions, *Bulletin de Psychologie*, t. XI, 3, p. 140.

Lagache, D. (1957b) Fascination de la conscience par le Moi, *La psychanalyse*, 3, pp. 33–46.

Lagache, D. (1961) La psychanalyse and la structure de la personnalité, *La psychanalyse*, 6, pp. 5–54.

Lagache, D. (1964) Fantaisie, réalité, vérité, *La psychanalyse*, 8, pp. 1–10.

Lagache, D. (1966) Le point de vue diachronique en métapsychologie, *Revue française de Psychanalyse*, 30, p. 811.

Lalande, A. (1968) *Vocabulaire technique and critique de la philosophie*. Paris: Presses Universitaires de France.

Landauer, K. (1938) Affects, Passions and Temperament, *Int. J. of Psychoanalysis*, XIX, pp. 388–415.

Laplanche, J. (1967) La défense and l'interdit, *La Nef*, 31, pp. 43–56.

Laplanche, J. (1968) La position originaire du masochisme dans le champ de la pulsion sexuelle, *Bulletin de l'Association psychanalytique de France*, 4, pp. 35–53.

Laplanche, J. (1969) Les principes du fonctionnement psychique, *Revue française de Psychanalyse*, 33, pp. 185–200.

Laplanche, J. (1970) *Vie et mort en psychanalyse*. Paris: Flammarion.

Laplanche, J. (1984) *Nouveaux fondements pour la psychanalyse*. Paris: Presses Universitaires de France.

Laplanche, J. and Pontalis, J.-B. (1964) Fantasme originaire, fantasmes des origines, origine du fantasme, *Les temps modernes*, 215, pp. 1833–68.

Laplanche, J. and Pontalis, J.B. (1973) *The Language of Psychoanalysis*. London: Hogarth Press (original publication in French, 1967).

Lebovici, S. (1968) *Psychanalyser*. Paris: Seuil, 1 vol., p. 189.

Lebovici, S. (1969) Les mots du psychotique, dans *Problématique de la psychose*, ed. C. Laurin and P. Doucet, Excerpta Medica Foundation, pp. 35–43.

Lebovici, S. and Diatkine, R. (1954) Etude des fantasmes chez l'enfant, *Revue française de Psychanalyse*, 18, pp. 108–55.

Lebovici, S. and Diatkine, R.(1961) La relation objectale chez l'enfant, *La psychiatrie de l'enfant*, III. Paris: Presses Universitaires de France, fasc. 1.

Lebovici, S., Diatkine, R. and Ajuriaguerra, J. de (1968) A propos de l'observation chez le jeune enfant, *La psychiatrie de l'enfant*, vol. I, fasc. 2, pp. 437–74.

Leclaire, S. (1965) Le point de vue économique en psychanalyse, *L'évolution psychiatrique*, pp. 189–219.

Lewin, B. (1963) Reflections on affect, in *Drives. Affects. Behaviour*, éd. R. Loewenstein. New York: International Universities Press.

Lichtenstein, H. (1965) Towards a metapsychological definition of the concept of self, *Int. J. of Psychoanalysis*, 46, p. 117.

Little, M. (1961) Sur l'unité de base, *Revue française de Psychanalyse*, 25, p. 749.

Little, M. (1966) Transference in borderline states, *Int. J. of Psychoanalysis*, 47, p. 476.

Loewenstein, R. (1963) Some considerations on free association, *J. of the American Psychoanalytic Association*, X, pp. 451–73.

Lœwenstein, R. (1966) La psychologie psychanalytique de Hartmann, Kris, Lœwenstein, *Revue française de Psychanalyse*, 30, p. 775.

Lœwenstein, R. (1967) Defensive organisation and autonomous ego functions, *J. of Amer. Psychoanalysis Assoc.*, XV, pp. 795–809.

Luquet, P. (1957) A partir des facteurs de guérison non verbalisables de la cure analytique, *Revue française de Psychanalyse*, 21, pp. 182–209.

Luquet, P (1962) Les identifications précoces dans la structuration et la déstructuration du Moi, *Revue française de Psychanalyse*, 26, pp. 117–309.

Luquet, P (1969) Genése du Moi, in *La théorie psychanalytique*, Presses Universitaires de France, 1 vol., pp. 237–70.

Luquet-Parat, C.J. (1962) Les identifications de l'analyste, *Revue française de Psychanalyse*, 26, p. 289.

Luquet-Parat, C.J (1967) L'organisation œdipienne du stade génital, *Revue française de Psychanalyse*, 31, p. 743.

Lustman, S.L. (1969) The use of the economic point of view in clinical psychoanalysis, *Int. J. of Psychoanalysis*, 50, p. 95.

Luzes, P. (1969) Les troubles de la pensée en clinique psychanalytique, *Revue française de Psychanalyse*, 33, p. 727.

Lyotard, J.F. (1968) Le travail du rêve ne pense pas, *Revue d'esthétique*, pp. 26–61.

M'Uzan, M. de (1967a) Contribution à la discussion sur l'investissement and le contre-investissement, *Revue française de Psychanalyse*, 31, p. 238.

M'Uzan, M. de (1967b) Expérience de l'inconscient, *L'inconscient*, 4, pp. 35–54.

M'Uzan, M. de (1968) Acting out 'direct' and acting out 'indirect', *Revue française de Psychanalyse*, 32, p. 995.

M'Uzan, M. de and David, C. (1960) Préliminaires critiques à la recherche psychosomatique, *Revue française de Psychanalyse*, 24, p. 19.

M'Uzan, M. de (1968) Transferts et névrose de transfert, *Revue française de Psychanalyse*, 32, p. 235.

Mahler, M.S. (1969) Perturbances of symbiosis and individuation in the development of the psychotic ego, in *Problématique de la psychanalyse*, ed. C. Laurin, and P. Doucet, Excerpta Medica Foundation, pp. 188–97.

Major, R. (1969) L'économie de la représentation, *Revue française de Psychanalyse*, 33, p. 79.

Male, P. (1964) *Psychopathologie de l'adolescent*. Paris: Presses Universitaires de France.

Male, P. and Favreau, J.A. (1959) Aspects actuels de la clinique and de la thérapeutique des troubles affectifs de l'enfant, *La psychiatrie de l'enfant*, II, fasc. 1, pp. 148–96.

Mallet, J. (1956) Contribution à l'étude des phobies, *Revue française de Psychanalyse*, 20, I–II, pp. 237–93.

Mallet, J. (1966) Une théorie de la paranoïa, *Revue française de Psychanalyse*, 30, p. 63.

Mallet, J. (1969) Formation et devenir des affects, dans *La théorie psychanalytique*. Paris:Presses Universitaires de France.

Martinet, A. (1965) *La linguistique synchronique*. Paris: Presses Universitaires de France.

Marty, P. (1958) La relation objectale allergique, *Revue française de Psychanalyse*, 22, pp. 5–35.

Marty, P and Fain, M. (1955) Importance du rôle de la motricité dans la relation d'objet, *Revue française de Psychanalyse*, 19, pp. 205–84.

Marty, P. and M'Uzan, M. de (1963) La pensée opératoire, *Revue française de Psychanalyse*, 27, p. 345.

Marty, P, M'Uzan, M. de and David, C. (1963) *L'investigation psychosomatique*. Paris: Presses Universitaires de France.

McDougall, J. (1972) L'anti-analysant en analyse, *Revue française de Psychanalyse*, 36, p. 167.

McDougall, J. (1972) Primal scene and sexual perversion, *Int. J. of Psychoanalysis*, 53, pp. 371–84.

McDougall, J. (1989) *Théâtre du Je*, Gallimard.

McDougall, J. (1989) *Theaters of the Body*. New York: Norton.

McDougall, J. (1982) *Theaters of the Mind: Illusion and Truth on the Psychoanalytic Stage*. New York: Basic Books (1985) (revised edition, New York: Brunner/Mazel, 1990).

Merleau-Ponty, M. (1964) *Le visible et l'invisible*. Paris: Gallimard.

Miller, J.A. (1966a) La suture, *Cahiers pour l'analyse*, 1, pp. 39–51.

Miller, J.A. (1966b) Table commentée des représentations graphiques des 'Ecrits' de Lacan, *Cahiers pour l'analyse*, 1, p. 171.

Miller, J.A. (1968) Action de la structure, *Cahiers pour l'analyse*, 9, pp. 93–105.

Milner, M. (1969) *The Hands of the Living God, an Account of Psycho-Analytic Treatment*. London: Hogarth.

Mises, R. (1964) L'intégration du père dans les conflits précoces, *Revue française de Psychanalyse*, 28, p. 371.

Mises, R. (1966) Introduction à la discussion des aspects cliniques de la régression dans les formes psychopathologiques de l'adulte, *Revue française de Psychanalyse*, 30, p. 431.

Moddell, A.H. (1971) The origin of certain forms of pre-œdipal guilt and the implications for a psychoanalytic theory of affects, *Int. J. of Psychoanalysis*, 52, pp. 337–42.

Moddell, A.H. (1984) *Psychoanalysis in a New Context*. New York: International Universities Press.

Monchaux, C. de (1962) Thinking and negative hallucination, *Int. J. of Psychoanalysis*, 43, p. 311.

Moore, B.E. Some genetic and developmental considerations in regard to affects, see Borje-Lofgren (1968).

Moser, U., Zeppelin, I.V. and Schneider, W. (1969) Computer simulation of a model of neurotic defence processes, *Int. J. of Psychoanalysis*, 50, p. 53.

Myerson, P.G. (1969) The hysteric's experience in psychoanalysis, *Int. J. of Psychoanalysis*, 50, p. 373.

Nacht, S. (1958) Causes and mécanismes des déformations névrotiques du Moi, *Revue française de Psychanalyse*, 22, pp. 197–203.

Nacht, S. and Viderman, S. (1961) Du monde préobjectal dans la relation transférentielle, *Revue française de Psychanalyse*, 23, p. 555.

Nacht, S. and Recamier, P.-C. (1958) La théorie psychanalytique du délire, *Revue française de Psychanalyse*, 22, p. 417.

Nacht, S. and Recamier, P.-C. (19XX) Les états dépressifs: étude psychanalytique, *Revue française de Psychanalyse*, 23, p. 567.

Nelson, M.C. (1967) On the therapeutic redirections of energy and affects, *Int. J. of Psychoanalysis*, 48, p. 1.

Neyraut, M. (1967) De la nostalgie, *L'inconscient*, 1, pp. 57–70.

Neyraut, M. (1968) A propos de l'inhibition intellectuelle, *Revue française de Psychanalyse*, 32, p. 761.

Novey, S. (1959) A clinical view of affect theory in psychoanalysis, *Int. J. of Psychoanalysis*, 40, pp. 94–104.

Novey, S. (1961) Further considerations on affect theory in psychoanalysis, *Int. J. of Psychoanalysis*, 42, pp. 21–31.

Ogden, T. (1994) *Subjects of Analysis*, Northvale, New Jersey and London: Jason Aronson.

Parat, C. (1995) *L'affect partagé*. Paris: Presses Universitaires de France.

Pasche, F. (1953–1968) L'angoisse et la théorie des instincts (1953); Autour de quelques propositions freudiennes contestées (1956); Régression, perversion, névrose (1956); Réactions pathologiques à la réalité (1958); Le symbole personnel (1960); L'antinarcissisme (1964); Notes sur l'investissement (1965); Une énergie psychique non instinctuelle (1967); Quelques péripéties d'un retour à Freud (1968), in *A partir de Freud*. Paris: Payot.

Pasche, F. and Renard, M. (1956) Réalité de l'objet et point de vue économique, *Revue française de Psychanalyse*, 20, pp. 517–23.

Peirce, C.S. (1898) *Reasoning and the Logic of Things, The Cambridge Conferences, Lectures of 1898*, K. Laine Ketner editor, Cambridge, MA, Harvard University Press, The President and Fellows of Harvard College, 1992.

Peto, A. (1967) On affect control, *Psycho. Study of the Child*, 22.

Pouillon, J. (1966) Présentation: un essai de définition, dans Problèmes du structuralisme, *Les temps modernes*, 246, pp. 769–90.

Pulver, S.E. (1971) Can affects be unconscious, *Int. J. of Psychoanalysis*, 52, pp. 347–55.

Racamier, P.-C. (1966) Esquisse d'une clinique psychanalytique de la paranoïa, *Revue française de Psychanalyse*, 30, p. 145.

Rangell, L. (1953) A further attempt to resolve the problem of anxiety, *J. of Amer. Psychoanalytic Association*, 16, pp. 371–404.

Rangell, L. (1967) Psychoanalysis, affects and the human core: on the relationships of psychoanalysis to behavioral sciences, *Psychoanal. Quarterly*, p. 36.

Rangell, L. (1969) The intrapsychic process and its analysis – a recent line of thought and its current implication, *Int. J. of Psychoanalysis*, 50, p. 65.

Rangell, L. (1990) The psychoanalytic theory of affects, in *The Human Core, The Intrapsychic Base of Behaviour*. New York: International Universities Press, vol. I, pp. 307–24.

Rank, O. (1924) *The Trauma of Birth*. New York: Harcourt Brace.

Rapaport, D. (1950) *Emotions and memory*. New York: International Universities Press.

Rapaport, D. (1953) On the psychoanalytic theory of affects, *Int. J. of Psychoanalysis*, 34, pp. 177–98.

Rapaport, D. (19XX) The structure of psychoanalytic theory, *Psychological Issues*. New York: International Universities Press, vol. II, no. 2, Mon. 6.

Renard, M. (1955) La conception freudienne de névrose narcissique, *Revue française de Psychanalyse*, 19, p. 415.

Renard, M. (1969) Le narcissisme, dans *La théorie psychanalytique*. Paris: Presses Universitaires de France, 1 vol., pp. 180–214.

Renik, O. (1990) 'Comments on the clinical analysis of anxiety and depressive affect, in *Psychoanalytic Quarterly*, LIX, no. 2, pp. 226–48.

Ricœur, P. (1965) *De l'interprétation*. Paris: Seuil.

Ricœur, P. (1965) *Freud and Philosophy: An Essay on Interpretation*, trans. D. Savage. New Haven, CT: Yale University Press.

Rosen, V.M. (1969a) Introduction to panel on language and psychoanalysis, *Int. J. of Psychoanalysis*, 50, p. 113.

Rosen, V.M (1969b) Sign phenomena and their relationship to unconscious meaning, *Int. J. of Psychoanalysis*, 50, p. 197.

Rosenfeld, H. (1947–1964) *Psychotic states*. London: Hogarth.

Rosenfeld, H. (1969) Contribution to the psychopathology of psychotic states: the importance of projective identification in the ego structure and the object relations of the psychotic patient, in *Problématique de la psychose*, ed. C. Laurin and P. Doucet. Excerpta Medica Foundation, pp. 115–27.

Rosolato, G. (1959–1969) *Essais sur le symbolique*. Paris: Gallimard, 1969.

Rosolato, G (1962) L'hystérie, structures cliniques, *L'évolution psychiatrique*, XXVII, p. 225.

Rosolato, G (1967) Etude des perversions sexuelles à partir du fétichisme, in *Le désir et la perversion*. Paris: Seuil.

Rosolato, G (1969) Signification de l'Œdipe et des fixations prégénitales pour la compréhension de la psychose, in *Problématique de la psychose*, ed. C. Laurin and P. Doucet. Excerpta Medica Foundation, pp. 153–67.

Rouart, J. (1967) Les notions d'investissement et de contreinvestissement à travers l'évolution des idées freudiennes, *Revue française de Psychanalyse*, 31, p. 193.

Rouart, J (1968) Agir et processus psychanalytique, *Revue française de Psychanalyse*, 32, p. 891.

Rycroft. C. (1968) *A Critical Dictionary of Psychoanalysis*. London: Nelson.

Sachs, O. (1967) Distinctions between fantasy and reality elements in memory and reconstruction, *Int. J. of Psychoanalysis*, 48, p. 416.

Sandler, J. (1987) *From Safety to Superego*. London: Karnac Books.

Sandler, J. and Sandler A.-M. (1978) On the development of object relationships and affects, *Int. J. of Psycho-Anal*, 59, pp. 285–96.

Sandler, J. and Sandler, A.-M. (1998) *Internal Objects Revisited*, Chapter 4, 'On Object Relations and Affects'. London, Karnac Books.

Sandler, J. and Joffe, W.G. (1969) Towards a basic psychoanalytic model, *Int. J. of Psychoanalysis*, 50. p. 79.

Sandler, J. and Nagera, H. (1964) Aspects de la métapsychologie du fantasme, *Revue française de Psychanalyse*, 28, p. 473.

Sartre, J.-P. (1940) *L'imaginaire*. Paris: Gallimard.

Sashin, J. (1985) Affect tolerance: a model of affect response using catastrophe theory, *J. Social Biol. Structure*. 8, 175–202.

Sashin, J.I. and Callaghan, J. (1990) A model of affect using dynamic systems, in *The Annuals of Psychoanalysis*, vol. 18, pp. 213–31.

Sauguet, H. (1969) Introduction à une discussion sur le processus psychanalytique, *Revue française de Psychanalyse*, 33, p. 913.

Saussure, F. (1974) *Course in General Linguistics*. London: Fontana Collins.

Schafer, R. (1962) The clinical analysis of affects, *J. of the Amer. Psych. Association*, 12, p. 275.

Schilder, P. (1950) *L'image du corps*, trans. F. Gantherbet, P. Truffert. Paris: Gallimard, 1968.

Schmale, A.M. (1964) A genetic view of affects with special reference to the genesis of helplessness and hopelessness, *Psychoanalytic Study of the Child*, XIX, p. 287.

Schmitz, B. (1967) Les états limites: introduction pour une discussion, *Revue française de Psychanalyse*, 31, p. 245.

Schur, M. (1960) Phylogenesis and ontogenesis of affect and structure-formation and the phenomenon of repetition compulsion, *Int. J. of Psychoanalysis*, 41, pp. 275–87.

Schur, M. (1967) *The Id and the Regulatory Principles of Mental Functioning* London Hogarth and Institute of Psychoanalysis.

Schur, M. (1968) Comments on unconscious affects and the signal function, see Borje-Lofgren.

Schur, M. (1969) Affects and cognition, *Int. J. of Psychoanalysis*, 50, pp. 647–54.

Scott, W.C.M. (1962) A reclassification of psychopathological states, *Int. J. of Psychoanalysis*, 43, p. 344.

Scott, W.C.M. (1964) Mania and mourning, *Int. J. of Psychoanalysis*, 45, p. 373.

Searles, H. (1965) *Collected Papers on Schizophrenia and Related Subjects*. London: Hogarth.

Searles, H. (1979) *Countertransference and Related Subjects, Selected Papers*. New York: International University Press.

Segal, H. (1964) *Introduction to the work of Melanie Klein*. London: Heinemann.

Sempé, J.-C. (1966) Projection and paranoia, *Revue française de Psychanalyse*, 30, p. 69.

Seton, P.H. (1965) Use of affect observed in a histrionic patient, *Int. J. of Psychoanalysis*, 46, p. 226.

Shapiro, T. and Stern, D. (1980) Psychoanalytic perspectives on the first year of life. The establishment of the object in the affective field, in *The Course of Life: Psychoanalytic Contributions Toward Understanding Personality Development*, Vol. I *Infancy and Early Childhood*, ed. S.I. Greenspan and G.H. Pollock, NIMH.

Shentoub, S.A. (1963) Remarques sur la conception du Moi et ses références au concept de l'image corporelle, *Revue française de Psychanalyse*, p. 271.

Shevrin, H. (1978) Semblances of feeling: the imagery of affect in empathy, dreams, and unconscious processes: a revision of Freud's several affect theories, in *The Human Mind Revisited, Essays in Honor of K. Menninger*, ed. S. Smith, pp. 263–94.

Sifneos, P. (1975) Problems of psychotherapy in patients with alexithymic characteristics and psychical disease, in *Psychotherapy and Psychosomatics*, 26, pp. 65–70.

Sifneos, P. (1990) *La Psychosomatique aux Etats-Unis. Le concept d'alexithymie*, Laboratoire Delagrange.

Spiegel, L. (1966) Affects in relation to self and object, *Psychoanalytic study of the child*, 21, pp. 69–92.

Spitz, R. (1954) *La première année de l'enfant*. Paris: Presses Universitaires de France, 1958.

Spitz, R. (1959) La cavité primitive, *Revue française de Psychanalyse*, 23, pp. 205–34.

Spitz, R. (1964) Quelques prototypes de défenses précoces du moi, *Revue française de Psychanalyse*, 28, p. 165.

Stein, C. (1962) L'identification primaire, *Revue française de Psychanalyse*, 26, p. 257.

Stein, C. (1964) La situation analytique, *Revue française de Psychanalyse*, 28, p. 235.

Stein, C. (1966) Transfert et contre-transfert ou le masochisme dans l'économie de la situation analytique, *Revue française de Psychanalyse*, 20, p. 177.

Stein, C. (1968) Le père mortel et le père immortel, *L'inconscient*, 3, pp. 59–100.

Stern, A.L. (1967) L'enfant significatif de l'Œdipe, *L'inconscient*, 3, pp. 131–56.

Stern, D. (1985) *The Interpersonal World of the Infant*. New York: Basic Books.

Stern, D. (1991) Affect in the context of the infant's lived experience: some considerations, *Int. J. of Psychoanalysis*, 69, pp. 233–8.

Stewart, W. (1967) chap. 6: 'Affects', dans *Psychoanalysis: the first ten years 1888–1898*. New York: Macmillan, 1967, p. 154 sqq.

Tausk, V. (1919) On the origin of the 'influencing machine' in schizophrenia, trans. Dorian Flegenbaum, *The Psychoanalytic Quarterly*, 2, pp. 519–56.

Thiel, J.H. (1966) Psychoanalysis and nosology, *Intern. J. of Psychoanalysis*, 47, p. 416.

Thom, R. (1988) 'Saillance and pregnance' dans *L'Inconscient and la Science*, ed. R. Dorey,. Paris: Dunod, pp. 64–82.

Thom, R. (1988) *Esquisse d'une sémiophysique*. Paris: Inter Editions.

Torok, M. (1968) Maladie du deuil et fantasme du cadavre exquis, *Revue française de Psychanalyse*, 32, p. 715.

Ullmann, S. (1952) *Précis de sémantique française*. Paris: Francke.

Valabrega, J.P. (1969) La psychanalyse savante, *L'inconscient*, 8, pp. 7–26.

Vallenstein, A. *Affects, reviviscence des émotions et prise de conscience au cours du processus psychanalytique* (Communication au Congrès de Psychanalyse d'Edimbourg, 1961), *Revue française de Psychanalyse*, 28, p. 93.

Vendryes, J. (1923) *Le langage*. Paris: Albin Michel.

Viderman, S. (1961) De l'instinct de mort, *Revue française de Psychanalyse*, 25, p. 89.

Viderman, S. (1967) Remarques sur la castration et la revendication phallique, *L'inconscient*, 3, pp. 59–90.

Viderman, S. (1968) Genése du transfert et structure du champ analytique, *Revue française de Psychanalyse*, 32, p. 1011.

Viderman, S. (1968) Le rapport sujet-objet et la problématique du désir, *Revue française de Psychanalyse*, 32, p. 735.

Viderman, S. (1968) Narcissisme and relations d'objet, *Revue française de Psychanalyse*, 32, p. 97.

Viderman, S. (1970) *La construction de l'espace analytique*. Paris: Denoël.

Vincent, J.-D. (1986) *Biologie des passions*. Paris: Odile Jacob.

Weinshel, E. (1968) Some psychoanalytic considerations on Moods, see Borje-Lofgren (1968).

Widlocher, D. (1964) Le principe de réalité, *La psychanalyse*, 8, pp. 165–92.

Widlocher, D (1969) Traits psychotiques et organisation du Moi, in *Problématique de la psychose*, ed. C. Laurin and P. Doucet. Excerpta Medica Foundation, pp. 179–87.

Widlocher, D (1992) De l'émotion primaire á l'affect différencié, in *Emotions et affects chez le bébé et ses partenaires*. Paris: ESHEL.

Winnicott, D.W. (1935–1963) *De la pédiatrie à la psychanalyse*. Paris: Payot, 1969.

Winnicott, D.W. (1957–1963) *The maturational processes and the facilitating environment.* London: Hogarth, 1 vol. p. 295.

Winnicott, D.W. (1965) A clinical study of the effect of a failure of the average expectable environment of a child's mental functioning, *Int. J. of Psychoanalysis*, 46, p. 81.

Winnicott, D.W. (1966) Psychosomatic illness in its positive and negative aspects, *Int. J. of Psychoanalysis*, 50, p. 209.

Winnicott, D.W. (1971) *Playing and Reality.* London: Tavistock.

Winnicott, D.W. (1977) *Through Paediatrics to Psychoanalysis*, with an Introduction by M. Maseed R. Khan. London: Hogarth Press and the Institute of Psycho-Analysis.

Winnicott, D.W. (1988) *Human Nature.* London: Free Association Books.

Wollheim, R. (1969) The Mind and the mind's image of itself, *Int. J. of Psychoanalysis*, 50, p. 209.

Zetzel, E. (1965) The theory of therapy in relation to a developmental model of the psychic apparatus, *Int. J. of Psychoanalysis*, 46, p. 39.

Index

NOTE: Page numbers followed by *n* indicate information is to be found only in a note.